AMERICAN AUTOPIA

Midcentury: Architecture, Landscape, Urbanism, and Design
Richard Longstreth, Editor

AMERICAN AUTOPIA

An Intellectual History of the
American Roadside at Midcentury

GABRIELLE ESPERDY

University of Virginia Press
CHARLOTTESVILLE AND LONDON

Everything good is on the highway.
—Ralph Waldo Emerson, "Experience" (1844)

University of Virginia Press
© 2019 by the Rector and Visitors of the University of Virginia
All rights reserved
Printed in the United States of America on acid-free paper

First published 2019

9 8 7 6 5 4 3 2 1

Library of Congress Cataloging-in-Publication Data
Names: Esperdy, Gabrielle M., author.
Title: American autopia : an intellectual history of the American roadside at midcentury / Gabrielle Esperdy.
Description: Charlottesville : University of Virginia Press, 2019. | Series: Midcentury : architecture, landscape, urbanism, and design | Includes bibliographical references and index.
Identifiers: LCCN 2019014784| ISBN 9780813942957 (cloth : alk. paper) | ISBN 9780813943107 (ebook)
Subjects: LCSH: Automobiles—Environmental aspects—United States—History—20th century. | Automobiles—Social aspects—United States—History—20th century. | Cultural landscapes—United States.
Classification: LCC HE5623 .E87 2019 | DDC 306.4/8190973—dc23
LC record available at https://lccn.loc.gov/2019014784

Cover photograph: Signs on Las Vegas Boulevard, near Sahara Avenue, in 1966. (Photograph by Denise Scott Brown; The Architectural Archives, University of Pennsylvania by the gift of Robert Venturi and Denise Scott Brown)

CONTENTS

List of Illustrations   vii
Acknowledgments   xiii

Introduction   1
1. The Car and What Came of It   15
2. Roadside Metropolis   71
3. Autopia and Its Discontents   123
4. Learning from Autopia   175
5. The Twilight of Autopia   265

Notes   317
Index   343

ILLUSTRATIONS

Black-and-White Figures

1. Reyner Banham in Los Angeles in 1972, with the billboard designed by Deborah Sussman   xvi
2. Automobile Club of America, West 54th Street, New York, as it appeared in 1948   17
3. Gulf station, Baum Boulevard and St. Clair Street, Pittsburgh   22
4. Ford Motor Company Sales and Service Building, Woodward Avenue, Highland Park, Michigan   25
5. Neon sign manufactured by Walker & Co. of Detroit   33
6. Knud Lönberg-Holm, diagrams related to service station layout and operations   40
7. Knud Lönberg-Holm, drawings for an aluminum and glass gas station prototype   40
8. Knud Lönberg-Holm and Seiichi Washizuka, design for a stadium with provision for parked spectators   45

9. Frank Lloyd Wright, Gordon Strong Automobile Objective project, 1924–25   46

10. Park and Shop, Connecticut Avenue, NW, Washington, D.C.   50

11. Parking Garage for Marshall Field, Evanston, Illinois, 1937   57

12. Albert Frey, photograph of motor camp at Kingman, Arizona, individual cabin and carport, 1933   58

13. Albert Frey, photograph of motor camp at Kingman, Arizona, site and cabins, 1933   59

14. [Albert Frey], aerial perspective of motor camp at Kingman, Arizona, 1933   60

15. The "pretzel" in Queens and an autocamp in Florida, 1938   65

16. "Avarice, ill-focussed [sic] energy, sheer stupidity," drawing, 1941   68

17. U.S. 1 in the vicinity of Gum Springs, Virginia, 1930   88

18. Map depicting route of U.S. 1, 1938   90

19. Ilya Ilf, photograph of highway gas station at unidentified location (probably U.S. 30 near Camden, New Jersey), 1937   92

20. Marion Post Wolcott, photograph of view from Pulaski Skyway in Jersey City looking east toward American Can Company factory and Manhattan skyline   95

21. Hutchinson River Parkway, Saxon Woods, New York   97

22. U.S. 1 in New Jersey   98

23. Dorothea Lange, photograph of New Mexico Desert, Highway Number 70, 1938   99

24. Arthur Rothstein, photograph of Lincoln Highway approaching Paradise, Pennsylvania, 1941   100

25. "And Here Is New England, the Seaboard, the South," General Drafting Company map   102

26. Erwin Raisz, landform maps   114

27. U.S. 40 in Funkstown, Maryland   116

28. "On the Eastern seaboard of the U.S. . . . the urban centers along the old highway U.S. 1 are growing together," drawing   120

29. Margaret Bourke-White, photograph of segregated tea room in Elkridge, Maryland, 1938   126

30. Margaret Bourke-White, photograph of Esso Refinery in Linden, New Jersey, 1938   127

31 Edward Clark, photograph of "Clog up on U.S. 1 in Maryland [College Park]," 1955   135

32. Christopher Tunnard, diagrams of three stages of urban development, 1950   138

33. Street and signage in New London, Connecticut, 1950   139

34. Hoot Owl Café, Los Angeles   148

35. Andreas Feininger, photograph of Route 66 in Seligman, Arizona, 1949   151

36. Baltimore Beltway under construction, 1955   159

37. Alan Dunn, cartoon for Lewis Mumford's "The Highway and the City," 1958   163

38. Admiral Wilson Boulevard, Camden, New Jersey, 1952   168

39. Canal Street, New Orleans   169

40. Marion Post Wolcott, photograph of children feeding ducks at Greenbelt, Maryland, 1938   171

41. Alt-U.S. 90 around Houston   172

42. Connecticut General Life Insurance Company Headquarters, Bloomfield, Connecticut   179

43. Eliot Elisofon, photograph of New Jersey Turnpike in Hackensack Meadows   187

44. Paul Rudolph, rendering of Temple Street Garage, New Haven, Connecticut, 1959–63   189

45. Julius Shulman, photograph of Milliron's Department Store, Los Angeles, front ramp to rooftop shops and parking   192

46. Julius Shulman, photograph of Milliron's Department Store, Los Angeles, rear ramps from parking lot   193

47. Northland Shopping Center, near Detroit, Michigan   194

48. Southdale Shopping Mall, near Minneapolis, Minnesota   196

49. J. B. Jackson, drawing depicting aerial view of highway at night   204

50. "The entrance to a city cluttered up with billboards... a suggestion for improvement," drawing   211

51. Ernie's Hamburger Heaven, on U.S. 66 west of Saint Louis, Missouri, and the Boardwalk in Marin County, California   213

52. Typical strip, median strip on limited-access road, and service loop development, drawing   215

53. Conoco Glass House on I-44 in Vinita, Oklahoma   217

54. Freeway diagram with Max Bill's *Tripartite Unity* (1948–49)   218

55. Interstate 80 at Carquinez Strait in California with U.S. 40 at right   219

56. Freeway approach to San Francisco   221

57. Embarcadero Freeway as seen from the street, with the Ferry Building in background   222

58. MOTATION (in photographs) applied to the description of a trip on the Embarcadero Freeway   226

59. MOTATION (in diagrams) applied to the description of a trip on the Embarcadero Freeway   227

60. "Abstraction notation of motion and space," drawing   230

61. Quick perspective sketch with overpass   232

62. Quick perspective sketch with vertical sign   232

63. Night diagram of Central Artery in Boston   233

64. Ed Ruscha, *Twentysix Gasoline Stations: Standard, Amarillo, Texas,* 1962   241

65. Ed Ruscha, *Twentysix Gasoline Stations: Standard, Figueroa Street, Los Angeles,* 1962   242

66. Union 76 gas station, Beverly Hills, California   245

67. TWA Flight Center, Idlewild Airport, New York City   253

68. Johnie's Coffee Shop, Wilshire Boulevard, Los Angeles   254

69. Connecticut Post Center, U.S. 1, Milford, Connecticut   258–59

70. "Chaos in Echo Park"   261

71. "Commercial Non Plan on Sepulveda Boulevard"   262

72. Mels Drive-In, from *American Graffiti,* 1972   264

73. Day and Night Diner, Palmer, Massachusetts   290

74. White Tower New York #10, West 168th Street and Broadway, New York   294

75. Warren Lee, "Design for a Refreshment Building," 1934   305

Color Plates (following page 168)

1. Disneyland's "Autopia" ride shortly after the theme park's opening, July 1955
2. Robert Venturi and Denise Scott Brown driving south on Las Vegas Boulevard, near Sahara Avenue, 1968
3. John Steuart Curry, painting of "gimcracks" on the highway, 1934
4. John Steuart Curry, painting of gas pumps and highway signs, 1934
5. John Margolies, photograph of Tail o' the Pup Hot Dog Stand, Los Angeles, 1981
6. John Margolies, photograph of the Big Duck, roadside building on Long Island, 1967
7. Typical commercial strip (probably U.S. 1 in Woodbridge, Virginia), circa 1970
8. Speedway Boulevard in Tucson, Arizona, 1970
9. Allan D'Arcangelo, *U.S. Highway 1, No. 3,* 1962
10. West End of Glitter Gulch (Fremont Street), Las Vegas at night, circa 1953
11. Melvin Zeitvogel, sign for Buick dealership at El Cajon Boulevard and 34th Street, San Diego, 1959
12. Motorists line up at a Texaco gas station on New York's Long Island, summer 1973
13. Installation view of *Signs of Life: Symbols and the American City,* Renwick Gallery, 1976
14. John Margolies, photograph of Tascosa Drive-In Theater, Amarillo, Texas, 1977
15. Shell Service Station, Winston-Salem, North Carolina, 2005
16. Signs on Las Vegas Boulevard, near Sahara Avenue, 1966

ACKNOWLEDGMENTS

In 1992, in my first professional gig as an architectural historian, I spent the summer documenting Connecticut's Merritt Parkway for the Historic American Buildings Survey. While my colleagues worked on measured drawings of the roadway, the structures, and the plantings, it fell to me to explain why it all mattered. The Merritt's importance as a design was obvious enough, and much of my research was concerned with the Art Deco bridges, the naturalistic landscape, and the rustic guardrails and signage. But the more I dug into the Merritt's history, the more I understood that the parkway's significance as a scenic corridor and commuter route for metropolitan New York had as much to do with what was intentionally missing: grade crossings, billboards, and wayside commerce. In the 1940s, the Merritt's most notable feature might well have been its lack of resemblance to the cluttered roadsides of U.S. 1 in southern New England. Though I didn't realize it that summer, in writing the history of the Merritt Parkway and the parallel stretch of the Boston Post Road, I was laying the foundation for *American Autopia*.

Two years later, I was in the audience of a session on "The Modern Roadscape and Postmodern Consciousness" at the 47th annual meeting of the Society of Architectural Historians in Philadelphia. Sadly, I don't remember what David Gebhard had to say about the evolution of the traditional highway strip after 1970, but Steven Izenour's paper on "the good the bad and the ugly," illustrated with glass lantern slides of roadside buildings, made a lasting impression. Having studied art history at Smith College, I thought I knew from lantern slides: they were black-and-white and featured canonical works like the Parthenon and the East Front of the Louvre. But Izenour's were full of saturated color and decidedly noncanonical buildings, and they were as unforgettable as David Lynch's *Blue Velvet:* vivid, intense, and surreally American.

In between those two events, in classes on modern and contemporary architecture at the CUNY Graduate Center, Rosemarie Haag Bletter introduced me to the view from the parking lot, not only as a theoretical proposition, but also as a way of comprehending the spatial and programmatic logic of buildings designed by architects ranging from Frank Lloyd Wright to Venturi Scott Brown. She also taught me the value of considering the broadest possible range of modernist and architectural objects as appropriate subjects of scholarly inquiry, intellectual prodding that led me to modernized storefronts of the 1930s as the subject of my dissertation and first book. In *Modernizing Main Street,* the automobile was a key, but supporting player, as I charted changes to traditional commercial centers during the interwar decades. In *American Autopia* the car takes center stage, but this book is not a sequel, even as it considers the continued and outward growth of cities and suburbs in the postwar decades. That's because *American Autopia* is more precisely an intellectual roadmap to the automobile's circuitous journey through midcentury architectural and urban discourse.

For a few years, I thought about calling this book "Architecture's American Road Trip," not because it especially explained the subject, but because it seemed to reflect my own meandering route toward what the book finally became, full of dead-ends, detours, and the like. I didn't really need to *drive* from New York to Los Angeles to consult the Reyner Banham papers at the Getty Research Institute, or from L.A. to Albuquerque to use the J. B. Jackson papers at the University of New Mexico, but it was a lot more fun than flying. Along the way and across the country, this project benefited from the wisdom of numerous colleagues who, if we can bear a few more car-centric turns of phrase, went the extra mile, rode shotgun, looked under the hood, and offered extremely good directions. Special thanks to David Smiley, who first suggested that all this car stuff warranted a book-length investigation, and to Richard Longstreth and Simon Sadler, who supported the project from the beginning and gave it a jump start on several occasions when it nearly stalled.

I am also extremely grateful to those colleagues who invited me to present my research or to write about autopia while the project was still under construction. These include Marta Gutman, Kate Holliday, Medina Lasansky, Reinhold Martin, Joanna Merwood-Salisbury, Ford Peatross, David Salomon, Andy Shanken and Şevin Yildiz. Thanks as well to graduate students at Harvard, the University of Virginia, and especially the New Jersey Institute of Technology, for the opportunity to test-drive many of my ideas about the midcentury roadscape. I offer my deepest appreciation to Nancy Levinson of *Places,* who has been an invaluable editor, collaborator, and intellectual sounding board for the duration of this project. Jesús Escobar, Patricia Morton, and Anne Savarese have my gratitude for their ongoing advice and support, as does Catherine Boland Erkkila for her assistance in the last mile. For their good humor and boundless patience, I thank Boyd Zenner and Mark Mones of the University of Virginia Press.

American Autopia benefited indirectly and ineffably from the collective creativity of DesignInquiry, a tribe of thinkers and makers who occupy the happy liminal space between my professional and the personal spheres. Emily Luce encouraged me to start blogging about buildings and cars and highways. Anita Cooney gave me the quiet, skylit studio where most of this book was written. The late John Margolies, roadside photographer par excellence, deserves special mention: when it came to architecture on the highway, we disagreed about almost everything, but he was encouraging and generous to the last.

Finally, as always, this book would not have happened without Julie Hertzog, loving wife, loyal friend, and always steady copilot . . . over the Jersey state line, on the boardwalk way past dark, on a rattlesnake speedway in the Utah desert.

INTRODUCTION

When Disneyland opened in the summer of 1955, one of its most popular rides was a car-themed attraction in Tomorrowland. A full year before construction began on the Eisenhower Interstate System, visitors to the new park in Anaheim encountered what was billed as a miniaturized version of their highway future in an immersive amusement the Imagineers called "Autopia" (see color plate 1). Behind the wheel of the ride's sporty coupes, built at ⅝ scale and equipped with single-cylinder engines, Autopia's drivers cruised at speeds of up to 11 miles per hour on a mile-long ribbon of asphalt complete with straightaways, looping overpasses, and two lanes of traffic.[1] Though fitted out with a swoopy entrance pavilion and featuring sponsor billboards proclaiming Richfield Oil as "years ahead" of its competition, Autopia's prospective outlook was most obvious midway through the ride when its roadway paralleled the tracks of the Santa Fe & Disneyland Railroad that circled the park, chugging through the major theme areas. When the SF&D entered Tomorrowland, the steam engine and passenger coaches passed within inches of Autopia's roadsters. Given Walt Disney's twin obsessions with nostalgia and futurism, this moment of locomotive-automotive congruence can hardly have been accidental. But in 1955, most Disneyland visitors

Figure 1 (*facing page*). Reyner Banham in Los Angeles in 1972, with the billboard designed by Deborah Sussman for the documentary *Reyner Banham Loves Los Angeles*. (BBC Publicity Photo)

probably failed to grasp its meaning, because however much the SF&D sentimentally conjured an American past, Autopia barely suggested an American future.

It's not that the ride wasn't revved up with go-go optimism, but in the United States in 1955, as readers will discover in the pages that follow, "Autopia" was a place and an idea that already existed well beyond the boundaries of the theme park, even if the literal term had not yet been applied to it. Walt Disney inadvertently made this clear during a televised "progress report" that featured a helicopter ride from the Disney Studios in Burbank to the Disneyland construction site in Anaheim. Calling the journey to Disneyland by car "a pleasant 50-minute trip across town," Disney traces the 40-mile route in his voice-over narration, noting its most significant features as the camera captures them from the air: the Hollywood Freeway, with its four-level interchange downtown and deep cut through the Cahuenga Pass; the four surface lanes of Western Avenue, which Disney claims is the "longest, straightest city street in the world"; and the Santa Ana Freeway as it heads southeast and "straight on to the Disneyland turnoff." The camera pans lovingly over a perfectly formed cloverleaf while Disney ticks off "the super highways of America": parkways, turnpikes, and freeways, which he thoughtfully defines for the TV audience in those parts of the country still subjected to toll roads. Finally, as the helicopter approaches Anaheim, Disney notes that the park's location was chosen in consultation with "traffic experts" for its accessibility from the surrounding metropolitan region and its lack of space restraints—that is, the ability to accommodate 10,000 parked cars. What becomes clear during this flyover of the city Disney described as growing "outward instead of upward" is that even as Disneyland's Autopia was still under construction in Orange County, a Los Angeles Autopia already existed in fact, if not in name.[2]

And so did an American Autopia, a United States of the Automobile that emerged years before Disney started buying orange groves in Anaheim in the 1950s—as even Mickey Mouse could attest, autos and their affects being prominent in his earliest cartoons, including *The Barn Dance* (1929) and *Traffic Troubles* (1930).[3] As a place, American Autopia extended from coast to coast, in large cities and small towns and along the millions of miles of roads that connected them. As an idea, American Autopia loomed large in the national psyche, transforming the customs of the country in seemingly every conceivable way. As a book, *American Autopia* is about the invention of that place and the history of that idea as it took form in the United States in the middle decades of the twentieth century. Cutting a wide swath across the country on traffic-clogged arterials, wide-open federal highways, and postwar interstates, this book ranges from the birth of the auto industry in the 1910s to the aftermath of the oil embargo in the 1970s, and from the earliest appearance of car-oriented, gas-food-lodging buildings to their initial listing on the National Register of Historic Places. *American Autopia* is only indirectly about the social, economic, and architectural evolution of these car-centric environments, largely because this territory has received a great deal of serious scholarly attention since the 1980s, notably in groundbreaking documentary and interpretive work by Chester Liebs, Richard Longstreth, and others.[4] This book's trajectory is distinct because it examines familiar automotive habitats principally by peering through the windshield with architects, planners, geographers, critics, historians, and other cultural observers who scrutinized the car's impact on the American landscape at midcentury. As it crisscrosses these United States of the Automobile in the vastness of the country's physical and psycho-geographic extent, *American Autopia* is one part intellectual history and one part roadside genealogy. Offering Geertzian thick description of the autopian conditions that cultural observers found in places shaped by the car, which meant pretty much everywhere in the United States in the middle of the twentieth century, the book attempts to make sense of their attitudes and ideas, and the values and significance they attached to the architecture and urbanism that I am calling autopia. Before immersing ourselves in the details of autopia and in the details of their autopian observations, the word itself requires attention.

Disney Imagineers were not the first people to join "auto" and "utopia" to form a neologism that reflected American automotive impulses in the twentieth century. That honor may belong to Carl F. Schader, the Los Angeles real estate entrepreneur who opened the Autopia Motor Court in 1929 on a heavily traveled stretch of Van Buren Street in Phoenix, Arizona, where four east–west federal highways overlapped (U.S. 60, 70, 80, and 89). Though Schader claimed "autopia" as a registered trade name when promoting his roadside tourist complex in advertisements and marketing brochures during the 1930s, by 1949 the *Los Angeles Times* regarded it as a generic, if somewhat pretentious term for what was, by then, more commonly called a motel. Whether it was proprietary or commonplace, after the regional operator who leased Schader's Autopia that same year changed its name to the prosaic Continental Motor Lodge, it seemed clear that "autopia" had not yet entered the American vernacular, even if the United States was already far along in transforming itself into something many believed resembled an automobile utopia.[5] And when Disneyland opened six years later, though the "freeway ride," as it was labeled in the theme park's original renderings, got plenty of press, the term "Autopia" rarely described the auto-oriented cityscape beyond the Magic Kingdom. In fact, when "Autopia" initially appeared in print it was usually to compare the amusement ride and the urban reality, in tones ranging from bitterness to bemusement. One visitor observed the irony of fighting traffic on a freeway while driving *to* Disneyland, only to wait on line in order to drive on a freeway *in* Disneyland. Another noted wryly the aura of authenticity the ride possessed, as Autopia's congestion, accidents, and vehicular breakdowns managed to reproduce the woes of freeway driving as well as its joys.[6]

Within a decade of Disneyland's opening, however, a remarkable transposition of the term occurred. Though phrases like "L.A.'s very own Tomorrowland 'Autopia'" still appeared, on its editorial page, the *Los Angeles Times* also began referring to the City of Angels as an autopia, though without the capital letter, without quotation marks, and without the theme park. A 1960 editorial calling for increased investment in road building and improved highway technology in Southern California opened with a matter-of-fact acceptance of the status quo "in the autopia known as Los Angeles." A 1964 editorial on expanding freeway development was more circumspect as it probed the potential danger of autopia: if Los Angeles failed to invest in mass transit and to minimize residential displacement in freeway building, the city would become "an autopia where cars are more important than people."[7] When describing urbanism in Los Angeles, autopia had become shorthand for an urban place in which automobiles were an unassailable priority.

Shortly before this editorial appeared, concerned Angelenos formed a citizens group known as ABLE (Action for a Better Los Angeles Environment) to ensure that the urban balance between cars and people did not tip irrevocably to the former. When columnist Art Seidenbaum publicized ABLE's agenda in the *L.A. Times,* he suggested that the group—and the city—needed a champion, someone with taste and wit and showmanship who might rise above petty self-interest and local politicking in order to explain Los Angeles to itself. A year later, in December 1965, Seidenbaum was in the back seat as one of ABLE's founders gave an unlikely candidate for the job his first driving tour of Los Angeles. When L.A. architect Herbert Kahn invited British critic and historian Reyner Banham to join him in a "mobile seminar" through the city's "sprawlscape" of linear development and the "concrete intestines" of its surface roads and freeways, the Englishman expected "to be in agony the whole time" because, as he put it, "the horror of Los Angeles is a European legend."[8] As it turned out, Banham's reaction to Los Angeles was very nearly the opposite, as was clear in the title of his 1972 documentary *Reyner Banham Loves Los Angeles.* Banham, perhaps more than anyone else, became the booster-apologist-contrarian most responsible for making L.A. synonymous with *autopia* (see figure 1).

In his earliest work on Los Angeles, a series of BBC radio talks subsequently published in *The Listener* in 1968, Banham was fully committed to exploring the role of the automobile on the development of the city's expansive urbanism, though he did acknowledge the importance of the inter-urban streetcar system in establishing the pattern for a far-flung, but nonetheless unified metropolis. While Banham investigates the freeways and surface roads with respect to spatial transformation and racial segregation in "Roadscape with Rusting Nails," he seems most interested in the "culture of rampant automobilism" that characterized the city.[9] This culture remains Banham's intellectual preoccupation throughout his 1971 monograph *Los Angeles: The Architecture of Four Ecologies.* Indeed, from the book's first pages, Banham's analysis of the relationship of Angelenos and their environment—that is, the city's ecologies—is predicated on the physical and psychological impact of the car, and his language is suffused with the car's aura. The first chapter, "In the Rearview Mirror," lays out Banham's project to document architecture and urbanism in "Internal Combustion City," where "mobility outweighs monumentality" and where the freeways should have crowned Los

Angeles's "tutelary deity" in representations both civic and secular.[10] The car is so critical to his argument in virtually all of the succeeding chapters (even if it is most explicit in those dealing with transportation and the "fantastic" architecture of the roadside), that by the time Banham gets around his fourth and final Los Angeles ecology, identifying it as "Autopia" seems all but inevitable.

Significantly, Banham uses "Autopia" only once in the Ecology IV chapter of *Los Angeles* (in the title) and he never directly defines or explains the term. Nor does he mention Disneyland's Autopia, though he alludes to the ride earlier in the book, when describing the theme park as a transportation fantasy dedicated to "illicit pleasures of mobility."[11] Banham clearly assumed that the meaning of "Autopia" would be comprehensible to his readers, regardless of their familiarity with Disneyland or Los Angeles. Art critic Peter Plagens was familiar with both, but he thought Banham's usage was little more than "un-euphious slang" for what Plagens derided, in the pages of *Art Forum,* as the "car shtick" of Southern California.[12] Here, however, Plagens was closer than he probably realized in helping to clarify the term's meaning, since *shtick,* in the sense of habits, mannerisms, or idiosyncrasies, was precisely what Banham meant when he deployed Autopia as an ecology. As Banham's text implies, "Autopia" obviously consisted of the freeways themselves, as an infrastructure of asphalt, signage, off-ramps, and the "tributaries" of the surface roads, all of it amounting to "a single comprehensible place." But "Autopia" also embraced the norms and behaviors the freeways engendered. Thus, for Banham, "Autopia" is a physical place *and* "a complete way of life." Taken together, these produced "a coherent state of mind."[13] Banham's broadly ecological approach to the impact of the car in Los Angeles provides an important framework for *American Autopia*'s exploration of the same issue at national scale. Borrowing from Banham's *Los Angeles,* this book examines the interconnectedness of driving, as a distinctive human activity, with buildings and landscapes that defined a particular culture at a particular moment in time. And though this project is indebted to Banham's groundbreaking work, there is a key difference between *American Autopia* and *Los Angeles.*

Early in *Architecture of Four Ecologies,* Banham memorably claims that he learned to drive in order to "read Los Angeles in the original." *Los Angeles Times* architecture critic John Pastier called Banham's grasp of mobility as native tongue "a remarkable insight," but he took Banham to task for regarding driving in L.A. as a homogenous monoculture, and for thus failing to distinguish between what it meant to drive as a commuter (per most Angelenos) and as a tourist (per the visiting historian). This flattened the L.A. urban experience and distorted Banham's perception of the city because only by ignoring its mundane realities, Pastier believed, was Banham able to interpret Los Angeles as "a huge delicious fantasy." The historian would have done better, Pastier suggests, "to apply his considerable intelligence and talents to an appraisal of Los Angeles' public, everyday environment—not in a pop-touristy sort of way but with more seriousness."[14] Unwittingly, Banham confirmed the validity of Pastier's critique when he used that same pop-tourist approach in a contemporaneous assessment of another desert city spawned by the railroad and sprawled by the automobile.

Writing in *West,* the *Los Angeles Times* magazine, in 1970, Banham offered a paean to Las Vegas that is strikingly similar to what Pastier regarded as his blinkered view of Los Angeles. At night, Las Vegas was an embodiment of "American Fantasy," with the casinos and multistory signs that lined Las Vegas Boulevard offering visitors "one of the great works of collective art in the Western World." Stretched out along the Strip, these were best experienced by "leisurely automotive transport," preferably in a "rented Mustang or Cadillac." By day, however, the city beyond the Strip came into focus, and this, Banham complained, had little to offer anyone except members of the misfit classes he identified as "visual masochists, parking-lot freaks [and] connoisseurs of cracked asbestos sheeting and overloaded utility poles."[15] Where Las Vegas residents fit into this schema, he doesn't say. The only respite Banham-the-tourist could find in the Vegas daylight was, predictably, on the new freeway that paralleled the Strip. Regardless of his critical prowess, whether in Las Vegas or Los Angeles, Banham favors the starry-eyed reflections of someone vacationing in Disneyland rather than the hard-nosed observations of someone living and working in a mobilized metropolis. To put it another way, in both cities, Banham misreads autopia because he mistakes it for Autopia.

This semantic distinction between lower- and uppercase contains an important lesson for the project of *American Autopia*. As this book probes the relationship of the automobile to architecture and urbanism at midcentury, it attempts to give equal consideration to the ubiquity of autopia as an ordinary condition and to the singularity of Autopia as a conspicuous landmark, whether in the physical space of the roadside or the discursive space of the popular and professional literature through which the automobile utopia was imagined, celebrated, surveyed, and debated. Los Angeles and Las Vegas loom large on the roadside *and* in the literature: in many ways, they were *American Autopia*'s twin sparks, but this has less to do with their built landscapes per se than with the architectural discourse they inspired. In particular, two iconic texts in the Autopia-with-a-capital-A category prompted this project as conceptual points of departure, as methodological lodestars, and as stops on the intellectual itinerary this book ultimately became. *Los Angeles: The Architecture of Four Ecologies* is the first stop; *Learning from Las Vegas* by Robert Venturi, Denise Scott Brown, and Steven Izenour is the second, though the importance of the latter to *American Autopia* is best understood by returning to Reyner Banham and his 1970 comments about Las Vegas in the magazine *West*.

After the pop enthusiasms that characterized his assessment of the Strip at night, Banham turns more scholarly, considering Las Vegas through the lenses of art history and contemporary culture. His references run the gamut from the frescos of Michelangelo to the journalism of Tom Wolfe, whose early 1960s criticism of Las Vegas Banham deems pioneering. Banham also mentions the ongoing research of architect and planner Denise Scott Brown, who had first visited Las Vegas in 1965, by which time, according to Banham, it had become a "mandatory stop-over" for international architecture students touring North America. Scott Brown acknowledged being inspired partly by Wolfe and partly by her professors at the University of Pennsylvania, who, she later recalled, encouraged her to go to the American Southwest and find out for herself what was happening in "the emerging automobile cities."[16] By 1970, when Banham wrote about her in *West,* it was two years after the famous Las Vegas studio she taught with Robert Venturi at Yale, and two years before the publication of the now classic book that emerged from their efforts to document and theorize space, symbolism, and automotive scale in the American city and on the American highway (see color plate 2).

Toward the end of his *West* article, Banham calls out Scott Brown for failing to provide the historical context of urban development in her Las Vegas analysis, which he claimed to know from "her famous lecture," though he was surely also familiar with "A Significance for A&P Parking Lots or Learning from Las Vegas," the 1968 article she and Venturi published in *Architectural Forum.* (Banham wrote for the journal in the 1960s.) Specifically, he accuses Scott Brown of learning from Las Vegas when she should have been learning from Los Angeles: the lessons she was seeking on the Strip circa 1970, Banham argued, could and should have been gleaned from Wilshire Boulevard circa 1940. Las Vegas Boulevard may have been "the main drag of the universal supercity of the American dream," Banham conceded, but Wilshire, as "a linear stretched-out automotive downtown," was its "true ancestor."[17] Notwithstanding his mild *mansplaining* to the woman who'd been a founding faculty member of UCLA's urban design program, Banham had a valid point.

The Strip was so overwhelming as a place and dazzling as an experience that it projected an exaggerated sense of singularity. Ever the historian, Banham was making it clear that the Strip was not an autonomous architectural and urban form, but one with clear and direct typological precedents. Here, however, Banham's infatuation with Los Angeles again had interpretive consequences that are relevant to the subject of *American Autopia,* as he privileges the extraordinary Autopian monument while largely ignoring the everyday autopian condition. Though Banham rightly argued that Wilshire Boulevard represented "the kind of townmaking that was natural and native to the motor age," when he concluded that "Miracle Mile couldn't have happened anywhere else in 1927," he was overreaching.[18] Even in the 1920s and 1930s, as *American Autopia* will make clear, the car-oriented commercial impulses that produced Miracle Mile were already shaping developments across the United States. They may not have been as comprehensive in terms of design and land-use planning as A.W. Ross's vision for Wilshire Boulevard, but they represented, nonetheless, a physical and cultural reorientation toward the automobile. In the burgeoning autopia of the United States, Los Angeles may have been exceptional, but it was not an exception—and the same was true of Las Vegas, as Denise Scott Brown already understood.

Her analysis of Las Vegas was not as ahistorical as Banham implied. Rather, it was informed by sufficient consideration of "historical tradition," from the Italian piazza to Versailles, to convincingly argue for, of course, the significance of A&P parking lots. For Scott Brown and Venturi, the parking lot, and its relationship to the supermarket, was equally informed by more recent historical developments, namely the thirty-year evolution of commercial architecture from the pedestrian orientation of Main Street to the motorist orientation of the highway. Comprehending this shift is, for them, prerequisite to learning from Las Vegas, and it also indicates the degree to which they, unlike Banham, registered differences between autopia and Autopia. Throughout their analysis of architecture in/as space they distinguish between "the commercial strip" and "the Strip": the former is the landscape that encompasses "existing, commercial architecture at the scale of the highway," while the latter is its "example par excellence." While they sometimes deploy "the Commercial Strip" with capital letters to refer to the morphological category they are studying, they only use "the Strip" to refer to Las Vegas Boulevard. As for the rest of the built environment transformed by the automobile—that is, the entirety of autopia—they allow for that too, noting that the drive-in church and drive-in restaurant could be scrutinized (and understood) using the same analytical tools they were applying to the casinos since, as they put it, "this is a study of method not content."[19]

Venturi and Scott Brown revealed the basic principle of that method in the study's first sentence: "Learning from the existing landscape is a way of being revolutionary for the architect."[20] But because they applied this method to the existing landscape of a city that, in their terms, defined place exclusively through "intensified communication along the highway," the content—those gigantic signs and their commercial iconography, the ordered chaos and the complex built form—largely overshadowed the method. They had intended for the lessons of "A Significance for A&P Parking Lots" and *Learning from Las Vegas* (1972) to be applicable anywhere, and they demonstrated this repeatedly in both texts, in brief analyses and passing references to commercial strips along other highways (U.S. 1, U.S. 13, and U.S. 66, for example) that provided minor evidence in support of their major case study, that portion of U.S. 91 between downtown Las Vegas and McCarran Field. Nevertheless, in discussions of architecture and urbanism at the time, the

Strip dominated the conversation. And so did Venturi and Scott Brown. By so polemically and effectively "learning from the existing landscape," they became the embodiment of "being revolutionary for the architect." So iconoclastic did Venturi and Scott Brown appear when their Las Vegas work was new, and so influential did their ideas become, that the architects and their theories largely overshadowed a parallel body of work that emerged well before they first drove the Strip in 1965–66. Alternately popular, professional, applied, and speculative, and dating from before World War II and after, this work suggested how architects, planners, and others with a stake in the built environment might learn not only from Las Vegas, and Los Angeles, too, but from existing landscapes across the United States that had been similarly transformed by the automobile.

American Autopia revisits much of this work, but the book's goal is not to contextualize *Learning from Las Vegas* or *Los Angeles: The Architecture of Four Ecologies*. In recent years scholars like Deborah Fausch, Martino Stierli, Aron Vinegar, and Nigel Whitely have undertaken this important task, and have successfully illuminated the sources and influences that gave rise to the pivotal studies of Venturi, Scott Brown, and Banham.[21] But much of this excellent scholarship has tended toward a kind of all-roads-lead-to-Rome historiography, which is both understandable and perhaps unavoidable when navigating such monumental texts of architecture and urbanism. *American Autopia* takes an intentionally different route toward a different destination. In the chapters that follow, we traverse the American Autopia, visiting major landmarks and those off the beaten path, encountering prominent figures and those who are more obscure, and tracking autopia's existing landscapes and idealized roadsides to map the farthest reaches of its midcentury intellectual ferment. Inevitably, however, some people and projects have been left standing on the metaphorical roadside, but readers should not construe this as a judgment of their initial significance or subsequent influence. Like any itinerary, *American Autopia* is necessarily selective, since the sheer quantity of historical material could easily have overwhelmed the narrative (or produced a book of twice the length). Though *American Autopia* slows down for some attractions on the historiographic highway while speeding past others, the author intends the route to be as representative as possible of autopian ideas and attitudes, especially (though not exclusively) as they were understood from the vantage point of U.S. architecture and urbanism.

As a travelogue of the American Autopia, the book commences with the car itself, examining how architects beginning in the 1910s responded to its growing presence on streets and highways across the United States, in cities, suburbs, and the increasingly developed countryside. Using professional literature as a guide, the first chapter focuses mainly on car-centric building types, while also exploring how designers grappled with the meaning and significance of speed and mobility as these challenged conventional notions of architecture and planning. After dealing with the car in relation to the individual building, the book moves on to the car at metropolitan scale. Chapter 2 focuses more on geography and less on architecture as it deals with the emergence of the roadside as a literal and figurative place whose cultural consequences were understood as locally, regionally, and nationally important. By the 1950s, the United States had so thoroughly accommodated its buildings, neighborhoods, roadsides, and highways to the automobile that the decentralized metropolis became a recognizable urban morphology. Chapter 3 considers the way architects and urbanists responded negatively to this transformation of place by critiquing the autopian order as a physical form and challenging it as a cultural condition. Chapter 4 follows the emergence and thorough development of what could be considered a counter-critique by disparate and mostly unaffiliated architects, urban designers, theorists, and other intellectuals who accepted the urban order of the automobile on its own terms from the early 1950s to the early 1970s, believing there was something to be learned from autopia, for good or ill. The ideological quarrel over autopia's value and autopian values, in architecture, in urbanism, and in U.S. society as a whole, might have continued unabated had history not intervened in 1973 with the OPEC oil embargo. The book's final chapter examines the disruptive impact of the 1973 oil crisis on attitudes toward autopia as a way of life, paying particular attention to the roadside nostalgia that seeped into U.S. cultural discourse in the 1970s and 1980s. By way of conclusion, this chapter surveys efforts in those decades to historicize the buildings and landscapes of what was already understood as autopia's recent past. By then, the United

States had long since naturalized its car-centric reality, but the situation was vastly different at the twentieth century's start, when a pre-automotive innocence still hung in the air, when horseless carriages rumbled down Main Streets congested with trolleys and pedestrians, and when the road to autopia was barely a county two-lane, much less a highway to national destiny.

1

THE CAR AND WHAT CAME OF IT

If the automotive age commenced on October 7th, 1913, when Model Ts began rolling off the moving assembly line at Henry Ford's factory in Highland Park, Michigan, the precise moment of autopia's establishment as a place created by the car is harder to pin down. Chronologically, autopia's origins do parallel the rise of the Tin Lizzie, because in the years after its 1908 debut and especially after Fordist production methods lowered manufacturing time and retail cost, the Model T transformed the car from a luxury object into an affordable commodity. As car ownership expanded across the United States, from fewer than 200,000 registered motor vehicles before the Model T to more than 20 million in its last year of production in 1927, so, too, did an extraordinary range of automotive accommodations in the built environment, from asphalt paving to traffic signals, from garages to curbside pumps.[1] Whether welcome or intrusive, these changes were mostly modifications to systems and institutions that already existed: stables in which cars outnumbered horses; grocery and farm stores that sold gasoline along with food and feed. Increasingly, however, cars required—and their drivers desired—an infrastructure of their own: motor highways, standardized signage, and landmarks by which this brave new world might be navigated. This chapter

Facing page: detail of fig. 11, Parking Garage for Marshall Field

considers the emergence of car-centric spatial realms from the perspective of architects as they confronted the challenges, and imagined the possibilities, of the coming autopian order.

The earliest motor highways were already underway in 1907, when planning commenced for the Bronx River Parkway and the Long Island Motor Parkway.[2] Due to complications with funding and land acquisition, the 15.5-mile public road through the Bronx and Westchester wasn't completed until 1923. On Long Island, however, William K. Vanderbilt completed the world's first limited-access high-speed roadway purpose-built for automobiles in a little over a year. His 45-mile private road through Nassau and Suffolk counties welcomed its first drivers in October 1908. Charging a $2 toll that signaled motoring elitism, Vanderbilt's parkway also featured tollhouses designed by John Russell Pope. With pitched roofs, shingled dormers, and brick quoins, these rustic buildings were among the classical architect's earliest independent commissions. For motorists with the financial resources to drive the Long Island Motor Parkway, these were also some of autopia's earliest architectural landmarks.

When Vanderbilt's parkway opened in 1907, such landmarks existed on both coasts and points in between, in forms both workaday and monumental. In Seattle, south of downtown on the industrial waterfront of Elliot Bay, a sales manager for Standard Oil of California worked with a local engineer to open what some call the world's first gas station, on land opposite the company's main storage terminal. The unprepossessing station was off the street and consisted of only a holding tank, covered by an awning and fitted out with a measuring gauge, a valve, and a hose that dispensed a set amount of gas directly into the fuel tanks of waiting vehicles. This feature alone, which eliminated messy and dangerous intermediate containers, must have been sufficiently convenient to lure motorists to the station's remote location, far from Seattle's business center and residential neighborhoods.

If those off-the-street Standard Oil pumps were a tentative step toward an evolving typology, across the country in Manhattan, the Automobile Club of America (ACA) was a luxurious hybrid, offering a variety of enticements to select motorists in the opulent surroundings of its new headquarters on West 54th Street. Though in period photographs the ACA appears like an institutional intruder among low-rise brownstones, the midtown blocks west of Broadway were already the center of the city's "automobile district." As such, 54th Street near 8th Avenue was an appropriate location for an elite social club dedicated to promoting "automobilism" at local and national levels and counting Astors and Vanderbilts among its early members. This exclusivity is reflected in Ernest Flagg's Beaux-Arts scheme for what amounted to a palazzo with plenty of parking. With a two-hundred-foot street frontage and room for three hundred cars, the ACA housed what the *New York Times* claimed was the largest garage in the world in 1907. This went unmentioned in the architectural press, which focused on the building's stylistic embellishments. Flagg's eight-story loft building had a concrete structural frame enlivened with a glazed terra-cotta facade, most elaborately at the clubhouse level where rooms for meeting, dining, and lounging were located. Above were parking and service levels, illuminated by ample factory glazing and electric lights, and including lifts, turntables, and washing stations. The top floor contained a state-of-the-art skylit repair center staffed by professional mechanics, but available to members (or their chauffeurs) who wished to tinker with their own machines.[3] While this programmatic mixing of spaces for automobiles and socializing was novel for the time—the equally

Figure 2. Automobile Club of America (Ernest Flagg, 1907), West 54th Street, New York, as it appeared in 1948. (Photograph by Wurts Bros. [New York, N.Y.]/ Museum of the City of New York, X2010.7.1.13288)

THE CAR AND WHAT CAME OF IT

17

opulent Royal Automobile of London had no such facilities in its new Pall Mall headquarters—it was not all that different from an arts club with studio space or an actors club with a stage. Laying the cornerstone of the 54th Street clubhouse in March 1906, and sounding very much like a Gilded Age capitalist, the ACA's president declared that the building "should stand as a vital force of our modern civilization and illustrate at all times what is best and most serviceable in the future development of the motor industry."[4] Here was a lofty cultural goal to match the club's aesthetic and programmatic aspirations.

In the coming years, few car-oriented buildings would possess such grasping civic grandeur. They did not lack ambition, but their designers understood that what was *best* and *most serviceable* in the city center required a different expression in the automobile's expanding urban territories. Within a few decades, as sociologists Ernest Burgess and Robert Park recognized as early as 1925 in their classic study of urban growth, as the impact of the automobile spread beyond the central business districts through the transitional zones and the residential neighborhoods, out past the suburbs and the periphery and on into the countryside, it would challenge urban expectations and forge new definitions of urban form.[5] But as all that was happening there was also a disturbance of a smaller order as the nexus of car and building upended architectural conventions and confounded architectural proprieties.

Architect Meets Car

In Pittsburgh, by the 1910s, the railroad suburbs of the city's East End had become "the heart of motordom," especially the automobile row developing along Baum Boulevard. Lined with garages and dealerships, the boulevard's 1.5-mile length was a segment of the Lincoln Highway, the nation's first transcontinental auto route, a 1913 designation that intensified Baum's auto-orientation. The boulevard was also home to the Pittsburgh chapter of the Automobile Association of America and to Motor Square Garden, an exhibition venue that hosted the first Pittsburgh Auto Show in January 1914.[6] A month earlier and two blocks west, an equally notable motoring attraction appeared on the scene when the Gulf Oil Refining Company opened a drive-in service station "fully equipped with the latest and most modern appliances."[7] A far cry from Standard Oil's baldly pragmatic station in Seattle, this was a consumer-oriented retail outlet attuned to location, marketing, and design. The latter was entrusted to James H. Giesey, a man described in his obituary as "the personal architect for the Mellon family of Pittsburgh." Gulf was a Mellon company; the service station was built on Mellon-owned land; several Mellons lived nearby. Though family connections likely secured Giesey the job, his competent eclecticism — neoclassical at a university, neo-Tudor for an office building — probably didn't hurt.[8] But what style was appropriate for an automotive service station?

Writing in 1893, architect and theorist Henry Van Brunt accurately described the situation Giesey would confront twenty years later: "The architect, in the course of his career, is called upon to erect buildings for every conceivable purpose, most of them adapted to requirements which have never before arisen in history." After listing a bewildering assortment, including railway buildings, mercantile structures, casinos, and skating-rinks, all accommodating "the complicated conditions of modern society" — Van Brunt observed that in their "essential character" these buildings had "no precedent in architectural history."[9] Writing a year before Karl Benz introduced the world's first production automobile, Van Brunt does not mention of the motorcar, but had he lived a few years past 1903, he might have viewed it as one of modern society's more complicated conditions. Even before the turn of the century, the architecture profession had taken notice of the new machine, considering its cultural potential and observing its swift impact on the built environment. As early as 1898, *American Architect and Building News* — a journal that architectural historian Mary Woods has described as "the profession's voice" circa 1900 — began reporting on a range of car-related developments: how automobiles made European sketching trips more leisurely and affordable; how automobiles aided urban sanitation since cars were cleaner than horses from a street-cleaning perspective; how inevitable it was that within a few years institutions like museums and libraries would provide "storage-room and care" for patrons' motorcars. Architects, the magazine cautioned, needed to keep their "manners and practices" in step with increasingly auto-oriented times.[10]

To this end, after 1900, though wide-ranging motoring commentary continued in multiple architecture journals, in news items about the preservation of El Camino Real for auto-tourism or the widening of Fifth Avenue to deal with car congestion, the automotive notices were increasingly pragmatic.[11] Architects were counseled to include place names in building inscriptions as an aid to the "automobilist" whose daily "locomotion" meant he might reasonably have "a dozen towns on his itinerary." Similarly, they were reminded to consider "automobile loads" when designing stables and carriage houses since the presence of cars in these facilities was bound to increase. Indeed, such "automobile stables" and "garages" (after the French verb *to shelter*) were some of earliest car-oriented buildings featured in the plate sections of American architecture journals.[12] In 1910, when automobile ownership in the United States topped half a million, nearly every issue of the *Brickbuilder* featured at least one example, from small private garages attached to suburban houses to larger detached garages on country estates to urban mixed-use, or live-park, structures with studios and apartments above street-level car storage.[13] In their inoffensive historicism and competent space planning, these garages offered little in terms of stylistic or programmatic innovation, but their presence on the pages of a national design magazine augured the car's expanding presence as a subject and object of American architecture.

Three years later, just as James Giesey was confronting the problem of designing an automotive service station in Pittsburgh, the *Brickbuilder* published the results of its first automobile-centric competition in an issue devoted almost entirely to the car and its architectural requirements. There was nothing unusual about the call for submissions, the latest installment in the competitive prize for a terra-cotta building design the journal had issued annually since 1900. But careful readers of the competition announcement in the October 1912 issue would have noted that the program was an unmistakable product of the modern and automotive age. It called for a building labeled a "public garage" and including automotive sales and service. Its "Main Street" location was resolutely urban, occupying "the corner of a city block in the automobile district." Thus, the competition's organizers tacitly acknowledged that the car had already engendered distinct types and shaped new territories, like the auto rows that existed in New York and Pittsburgh. Whether it had produced a new architecture remained to be seen, and there was little in the brief to suggest that it might, though the organizers welcomed any "original devices" that might add "value" to a building of this "character." When the winning designs appeared in the spring of 1913, character—or lack thereof—was at the heart the jury report. While much of the jury's disappointment stemmed from unimaginative use of terra-cotta cladding, they were equally frustrated by the lack of designs that were "festive in character," something they agreed was requisite for a combination garage–auto-sales-and-service building.[14] So restrained were the prizewinning entries that a profusion of classical foliated archivolts, Gothic tracery, and Baroque swags barely lessened their sobriety. Even the signage was muted, as if, despite the brief explicitly stating their necessity, the designers felt that automobile-related advertising was somehow beneath their dignity. Only architect Valare de Mari's second-place design, with a Puginian corner tower and crowning parapet emblazoned with oversized lettering, acknowledged the realities of the commercial sphere, where high visibility and legible marketing were essential aspects of Main Street architecture.

Back in Pittsburgh, James Giesey confronted similar realities as he dealt with the unprecedented problem of designing an automotive service station located in a prominent commercial area at the edge of the city's automobile district, which was also surrounded by upscale residences. Balancing commercial character with domestic scale, Giesey produced a scheme both brash and modest. His Gulf station was the first building on its large triangular site, and Giesey placed it toward the eastern apex of Baum Boulevard and South St. Clair Street, connecting it to both via elegantly curved concrete drives. With a row of handsome houses as the station's nearest neighbors, Giesey gave the small building a dignified air, designing a lozenge-shaped pavilion with a brick base and tall windows flanked by pilaster-like jambs. These rose to a broad canopied roof that extended sufficiently to shelter

Figure 3. Gulf station (James H. Giesey, 1913), Baum Boulevard and South St. Clair Street, Pittsburgh, Pennsylvania. (Gulf Oil Corporation Records, Detre Library and Archives, Senator John Heinz History Center)

patrons, cars, pumps, and attendants. Inside was an office, storage space for motor oil, and a restroom opened to customers, free of charge. At a moment when motor (as opposed to horse-drawn) transportation was viewed as a municipal improvement, the station looked the very model of a City Beautiful urban amenity. At the same time, Giesey grasped the importance of what would later be called "curb appeal," meaning the station needed a degree of visual excitement to attract the attention of "scorching" motorists, travelling at speeds of up to 20 miles per hour. For Gulf, this meant transforming the canopy into a marquee with electric lights below and above. Underneath the canopy, they judiciously encircled the work area; atop the canopy, they spelled out "Good Gulf Gasoline" and "Supreme Auto Oil," loosening up the station's Beaux-Arts restraint with a touch of Great White Way pizazz.

Balancing commercial needs and civic ambitions, Geisey suggested a workable model for claiming the gas station as architecture, albeit of a minor variety, but the profession, at least in its published discourse, failed to notice. In fact, for the rest of the decade it paid scant attention to the new typology, but not because of the gas station's small scale, or with a shift in professional focus prompted by the United States' entry into World War I. Instead, it was as if architecture had adopted a wait-and-see attitude toward the automobile and was content, for the time being, to merely note the "rapidly extending use of the motor car." The architecture profession was not alone in adopting this stance: as reflected in *Engineering News-Record,* engineers were similarly cautious until after the First World War, even though they were already being called upon to adapt existing roads, highways, and bridges for automobile use.[15] For architects, this reticence was partially justified by the automobile's instability as a shaper of built form in this period, due mainly to its inherent dynamism in the years after assembly-line production shook up the industry. This is the point Frederick Fairbrother made in two articles that appeared in *Architectural Forum* in August and September of 1920. As a designer in the office of Albert Kahn, Fairbrother was well positioned to observe the automobile's impact on architecture, which he described as "a changeable problem." Tracing the industry's "meteoric" growth after 1913, Fairbrother noted the car's widening sphere of building activity, moving beyond manufacturing plants to distribution and administrative centers, sales- and showrooms, service and repair stations and, finally, to retail facilities for dispensing gasoline and charging batteries. For Fairbrother, each building type offered the opportunity for architectural innovation, whether dealing with programmatic challenges or defining an appropriate "character" for an expanded range of auto-related buildings. This was especially important because, as Fairbrother observed, these buildings were no longer confined to peripheral industrial zones, but occupied all manner of commercial districts, from "automobile rows" in the urban center to the attenuated spines of "Broadways and Michigan Avenues" across the country.[16]

A year later, one of Fairbrother's colleagues at Albert Kahn Associates offered a similar assessment of "architecture and the automobile industry." Though Wirt Rowland concurred that the car was a boon for building, he was more pointed about the question of character as manifest in the "architectural pretensions," both modest and grand, of buildings related to motorcars. While Rowland did not believe that the influence of the automobile yet compared with the cultural forces that gave rise to Greek temples and Gothic cathedrals, among contemporary "commercial forces" it had produced a "a distinctly modern type of architectural design." The problem was that architects had not yet come to terms with its proper architectural expression. Instead of spending their time vainly adapting historical precedents to the unprecedented commercial types the car had generated, architects needed to accept that automotive buildings had more in common with the automobiles themselves: both were standardized and practical. In drawing this parallel, anticipating Le Corbusier's pronouncements in *Vers une Architecture,* Rowland concluded that designing buildings for cars offered "the opportunity to perfect [them] by repetition and experiment." By way of illustration, he discussed a number of automobile buildings Kahn's office had completed. These were not the great factories for which Kahn was famous, but the smaller (though still large) buildings with which car makers and buyers would regularly interact, like the Ford Sales Building in New York, the Ford Motor Company Sales and Service Building in Highland Park, and the Cadillac and Packard Sales and Service Buildings, both in Detroit.

Like the factories, these were designed on a reinforced concrete modular system, but their public function as a site of interaction between the car companies and driving consumers necessitated a less utilitarian design. Though Rowland cautioned against "cleverness," ornamentation of surface to convey commercial character was unavoidable. At Highland Park, the Ford Sales and Service Building sits directly along Woodward Avenue where its reductive classicizing details—flattened bands suggestive of Doric capitals, blank discs distributed at intervals along what appears to be an architrave, and Pewabic tiles that read as metopes—served as a human-scale buffer for the massive manufacturing plant stretching behind it. In choosing this building as an exemplar of automotive building design, Rowland makes it clear that he is uninterested in "the idea of a new architectural style [that] obsessed" many of his contemporaries. But in addressing the question of style head

on, his article made an important contribution to what emerged as an abiding concern for designers of a wide range of car-related buildings.[17]

Toward a Minor Architecture

Stylistic issues were prevalent even as technical data about automobiles became prominent in U.S. architecture journals in the 1920s, reflecting not only increasing rates of car ownership, but the degree to which owners were demanding a built environment to accommodate their cars. As early as 1920, when there were 7.6 million vehicles on the nation's roads, *American Architect* began tracking the

Figure 4. Ford Motor Company Sales and Service Building (Albert Kahn Associates, 1905), Woodward Avenue, Highland Park, Michigan. (Image from the Collections of The Henry Ford)

number of registered automobiles in the United States, publishing data supplied by the *Automobile Trade Journal.* The significance of this information to architects became clear when *American Architect* reported that labor shortages, material scarcities, and high costs in the construction industry were directly connected to the "tremendous growth" of the automotive industry, which was absorbing workers and capital goods at a rate those in building and its allied trades and professions considered alarming. The car was even blamed for the acute housing shortage that followed the end of World War I. Because those not connected to the auto industry were unable to "fully appreciate" the extent of its growth in recent years, *American Architect* felt duty-bound keep its readers informed about its developments.[18]

Eventually, the opportunities the car seemed to present to architects outweighed such concerns. The "new problem" of the automobile was a subject "worthy of detailed discussions," which the journals fostered by providing all necessary "diagrammatic data" concerning the car. From turning radii to the lengths, widths, heights, and weights of typical Fords and Cadillacs (representing the low end and high end of the market), automobile specifications appeared in engineering and construction columns in architecture magazines throughout the 1920s.[19] In *Architectural Forum,* Tyler Stewart Rogers devoted an entire article to the design implications of automobile dimensions, illustrating it with a sample questionnaire that included scale renderings of a "typical" passenger car and truck with blank spaces to fill in precise measurements. Rogers sent his questionnaire to 172 manufacturers and received detailed information on nearly 80 vehicles. Rogers claimed his was the first attempt to compile such data for the use of the design professions, and there is no reason to doubt him. Trained in landscape design at Harvard, Rogers spent his career as a writer and consultant on the technical aspects of architecture. He championed the publication of reference data for architects and promoted the circulation of the specialized knowledge he believed architects needed to master practice in the twentieth century, whether related to developments in the building sciences or transportation. In his *Forum* article of 1920 Rogers noted that there was "surprisingly little written" about automobile dimensions. Indeed, reference manuals like *Architectural Graphic Standards* and *Time Saver Standards,* which would become the profession's go-to resources for such information, were still more than a decade away, and when the first edition of *Graphic Standards* finally appeared in 1932, its "motor vehicle data" was limited to a single page that included trucks and buses, along with cars.[20] Back in 1920, Rogers published an analysis of his collected automotive data to fill a void, confident that it represented a sample sufficient to keep architects abreast of current "tendencies in motor car design."[21] This was not for their edification as drivers—though car companies had been advertising in the architecture press for a number of years—but because, as Rogers observed, architects were regularly being called upon to design parking spaces, turnarounds, and overhead clearances for the multitude of buildings with which cars now came in regular contact.

Of these, buildings designed specifically, if not exclusively, for automobiles already constituted what *Architectural Forum* called an identifiable class of "minor architecture." They were *minor* by virtue of their "moderate cost"; they were *architecture* because they displayed a noticeable "improvement" in design and planning—to such an extent that for virtually every type of car-related building, both owners and occupants had come to appreciate that "good architecture" possessed an "advertising and sales value which must be reckoned with."[22] Having established auto-oriented buildings as properly within the realm of architecture, and having supplied technical data relating to their programming, the comprehensive building-type study was the next logical chapter in an automotive practicum for architects. One of the earliest to appear in a U.S. design magazine was Alexander C. Guth's "The Automobile Service Station," a twenty-three-page spread published in *Architectural Forum*'s July 1926 issue. Guth was a Milwaukee architect who had studied at Columbia under Charles McKim and Thomas Hastings. Since 1918, he had been in partnership with Herman Buemming, with a practice that ranged from tall office buildings to single-family residences to service stations, one of which Guth published in the *Forum* alongside seven other case studies that included plans, photographs, and specifications.

In a lengthy article that preceded the case studies, Guth offered an overview of the history and evolution of the service station type with a particular emphasis on programmatic variations, ranging from the merely utilitarian, with little more than sheltered pumps, to a highly developed community amenity complete with "powder puff" rooms for women. He dealt with these variations in great detail, highlighting the essential differences in a series of typical building and site plans with distinct configurations to accommodate traffic lanes, canopies, service bays, restrooms, offices, and so forth depending on the needs and ambitions of the proprietor. He discussed pumps, tanks, and draining pits as convincingly as landscaping, lighting, and signage, though he reserved his editorializing for the latter since these aspects of station design were the most contentious with respect to aesthetics and commercialism. Judicious planting of small lawns and flowerbeds would "add materially to the attractiveness of the entire place." Nighttime illumination, though its value was measured "mostly in terms of advertising," was nonetheless "a most interesting problem," since the manipulation of floods, standards, and ornamental fixtures offered architects apparently limitless opportunities for achieving "harmony and effectiveness." Signage, he acknowledged, was already the subject of much debate, but architects needed to accept "yes, more and larger signs!" as an unavoidable service station requirement. Still, he was confident that with architects' involvement, "ugly signs of yesterday" would give way to "dignified signboards" of irreproachable "decorative value." These same adjectives recur in his extended and opinionated discussion of style. While gleefully calling out stations as "bizarre" and "Wizard of Oz" (more than a decade before the 1939 film adaptation) or as satisfactorily legible at "less than 40 miles per hour," Guth's stylistic critique centers on what he calls "localism," an architectural approach for which he makes a cogent and consistent argument.[23]

For Guth, this term referred to the style and appearance of other service stations in the area and to the general character of the station's locale, whether it was a village, a small town, a city, or a region. He noted, for example, how stations throughout New England frequently had colonial features "to make the buildings more consistent architecturally with their environment." In the suburbs and the country, whether in Westchester or Wisconsin, "charm" and "quaintness," more than a particular style, would indicate that a building was "appropriate" for its setting. Guth encouraged architects to consider local building customs regarding form and materials, for a simple reason: in competitive gasoline retailing, "monkey sees, monkey does," causing station owners and operators to copy the same design features as the station down the road. And since the design of that station, Guth believed, was most likely derived, however diffusely, from "local architectural traditions," it was the architect's job, in fact his "duty," to reproduce those traditions as faithfully as possible, rather than giving in to what he derided as slavish, hasty imitation. For Guth, the proper expression of localism was the essential "problem" of gas station design, but it was also related to the gas station's status within architecture's hierarchies of practice and discourse. As a building type, he argued, the service station was related to other typologies shaped by "popular demand," notably the railroad station, and was deserving of the same legitimacy and respect as architecture.

At the same time, however, the gas station was "unique in the annals of building"—serving a new transportation technology that required a massive physical infrastructure and connected to a global economic network, yet having the appearance, in the mid-1920s, of a modest local enterprise. As a type of such a recent "invention," it was utterly devoid of architectural precedents and sentimental attachments: the gas station, Guth argued, was no "little red school house" and for this reason the type gave rise to stations in the form of "Chinese pagodas" and "Mohammedan mosques." Localism offered a corrective to such roadside follies, which Guth believed squandered the architectural opportunity the gas station truly represented, one that was as large "as almost any other problem that confronts the architect of today." But localism was really only a temporary solution since the type was still evolving and "its final and ultimate form has not yet been reached." Guth predicted that in ten years' time its appearance and use would be "far beyond anything that obtains today even in its most advanced form."[24] He wasn't wrong, and the reason is as clear as the difference between the well-known picturesque imagery typical of 1920s stations and, for example, the streamlined prototypes Walter Dorwin Teague designed for Texaco in 1936. These differences could be summarized in a single word: modernism.

The emergence of modernism in the United States in the 1920s and 1930s was cultivated to a great extent by the country's major architecture journals, namely *American Architect, Architectural Forum,* and *Architectural Record,* each of which made profound contributions to American architectural discourse in these decades. Indeed, as historians like Hyungmin Pai and Susanne Lichtenstein have argued, in large measure, these magazines *were* American architectural discourse with respect to their dominance in mainstream professional practice. This was particularly true in the years between the wars, as they expanded their content beyond printed portfolios of recent buildings to include topical articles and opinion pieces on subjects mandated by editorial policy. In the late 1920s, the direction of those policies took a decided turn toward modernism, a reorientation that the onset of the Great Depression, and the changes it brought to architectural practice, may have hastened. Leading the way was the architecture magazine with the largest U.S. circulation at the time: *Architectural Record*. Founded in 1891 as a genteel, artistically minded and literary sort of magazine, the *Record* emerged by 1930 — especially under the leadership of its managing editor, A. Lawrence Kocher — as a professional technical journal that provided an important forum for progressive thought and critical debates about architecture. Throughout the 1930s the *Record*'s contributors read like a who's who of American modernism, including practitioners, theorists, critics, and historians. Mardges Bacon usefully characterized the *Record* in this period as representing "two ideological camps within the avant-garde: the formalist concerned with style and the production-based concerned with functional design."[25] If, in each issue of the *Record,* these modernist partisans were frequently at odds over aesthetics, symbolism, technics, and mechanization, their attitudes unexpectedly aligned over the subject of the automobile.

Data-Driven Design

In 1928, after more than three decades in print, *Architectural Record* introduced a new and larger trim size, "a concession," editor in chief Michael Mikkelson declared, "to a universal demand for standardization." According to Mikkelson, this did not reflect a change in editorial policy, which remained committed to accurately reflecting architectural practice in the United States; rather, he claimed, it acknowledged that the magazine's format had finally caught up to its content.

Having recorded "the origins of modernism" evident in the work of Louis Sullivan, the magazine was now reflecting the latest "avenues of departure for evolutionary experiment," obvious in the work of Frank Lloyd Wright, but especially as "amplified abroad" and reintroduced stateside. He was certain developments in Europe would have a pronounced impact in the United States as "standardized shapes and machine-made surfaces will find their logical place in design." As modernism found a place on the pages of the *Record* in the coming years, the magazine transformed its form and content in order to keep pace.[26] Frederick Goudy, a modern designer of the Arts and Crafts variety, initiated the update with a cleaner layout and, especially, more and larger illustrations. By the early 1930s, however, certain sections of the magazine clearly stood apart, with graphics that were bolder, sparer, and clearly showed the influence of the Bauhaus and the New Typography. These were due largely to the guidance of Danish architect Knud Lönberg-Holm.

Lönberg-Holm moved in De Stijl and Constructivist circles in the late 1910s and early 1920s and was a founding member and longtime delegate of the Congrès International d'Architecture Moderne. He is perhaps best known for an antihistoricist and never-submitted entry to the 1922 Chicago Tribune competition that circulated widely in Europe, where it was praised by progressive architects like J. J. P. Oud, Walter Gropius, Erich Mendelsohn, and Le Corbusier. Lönberg-Holm immigrated to the United States in 1923 and the following year began teaching at the University of Michigan, offering a foundation course based on the Bauhaus model. During the mid-1920s he traveled the country, recording his impressions of New York, Detroit, and Chicago with a 35mm Leica, and bringing a European modernist sensibility to bear on his scrutiny of the country's rapid modernization and development. In his photographs from this period, sixteen of which Mendelsohn included in his polemical picture book *Amerika,* Lönberg-Holm uses tight crops and extreme foreshortening to frame what Mendelsohn called "the gigantic" of American skyscrapers and factories and "the grotesque" of extended streetscapes connecting them.[27] In all of these images, Lönberg-Holm exemplifies the "giddiness of perspective" that Mendelsohn ascribed to the European seeing the United States in the 1920s, as he captured the dynamism of the modern city evident in its buildings, billboards, neon signs, illuminated marquees, streetlights, electrical wires, traffic signals, and cars—both parked and moving. However much these pictures heralded photography's "new vision" in the 1920s, they also anticipated Lönberg-Holm's burgeoning interest in the technical and cultural processes that created the modern city and were embodied by infrastructure and superstructure, both commercial and automotive.

Recently, scholars have positioned Lönberg-Holm as a critical go-between in the interwar decades, feeding American culture to the European avant-garde while simultaneously distilling modernist objectivity for stateside consumption. If his contributions to *Amerika* and other avant-garde publications constituted the former, he achieved the latter principally through his work for the F.W. Dodge Corporation, which published *Architectural Record* and the *Sweet's Catalogue File*. Lönberg-Holm joined the *Record*'s editorial board in 1927, eventually assuming full responsibility for *Technical News and Research,* a new section that extended the magazine's redirection toward modernism, and what Hyungmin Pai has called its "cognitive project," by exploring the implications of new conditions of modern life, particularly the impact of mass production and institutional planning. Indeed, Pai goes so far as to state that *Technical News and Research* "initiated a fundamental break from traditional architectural discourse" and set the *Record* on an entirely new editorial course, one that Susanne Lichtenstein usefully characterizes as the journal's emergence as an "information brokerage."[28] That term underscores Lönberg-Holm's contributions: by the mid-1930s he had also been appointed research director of *Sweet's Catalogue,* which he not only redesigned, but entirely reconceptualized as a project of modern information design. In these U.S. periodicals and publications, Lönberg-Holm's rationalist approach borrowed heavily from Otto Neurath's Isotype, applying his method for universal pictographic communication to the presentation of technical data relating to architecture and building and shaped by modern conditions.[29]

The June 1930 issue of the *Record* was one of the earliest to reflect Lönberg-Holm's influence, in a building-type study on "The Gasoline Filling and Service Station." As envisioned by *Record* editor Kocher, the purpose of these studies was intentionally didactic, as they unabashedly sought to cultivate "an improved architecture." Though only four years removed from Alexander Guth's comparable study in *Architectural Forum,* Lönberg-Holm's work, both in form and content, looks like a clarion call from the future, or the outskirts of Dessau. The study's opening pages make Lönberg-Holm's ambitions patently clear: sparse asymmetrical layout, geometric sans-serif typeface (Rudolf Koch's 1927 *Kabel*), and bleed cut illustrations. A nighttime photograph of a neon sign is strategically cropped so the aluminum channels and glass tubes forming the letters G-A-S appear to hover in mid-air, like objects in a Moholy-Nagy photogram. Though he had photographed many similar signs in his travels across the United States, Lönberg-Holm obtained this image from Walker & Co. of Detroit, an outdoor advertising company that was an early adopter of neon, fluorescents, and other emerging illumination technologies of the period. In Lönberg-Holm's hands, a ubiquitous figure of the 1920s roadside becomes a modernist readymade deployed in the service of professional education.

The schooling continues on the following page where Lönberg-Holm, unlike Guth, who treated the gas station mainly as an isolated site of consumption, renders it unmistakably as the end point of a larger network of domestic refining and delivery. He does this less through didactic text than through three highly legible images that scale down, top to bottom on the page, from industry to long-haul and last-mile transport: an aerial view of a tank farm (probably Standard Oil's facility at Bayonne, New Jersey); Texaco tanker cars on a railroad siding and a heavy duty truck pulling double tanker trailers. Lönberg-Holm limits his explanation to a single terse sentence: "Tanks and stations are

Figure 5. Neon sign manufactured by Walker & Co. of Detroit, from "The Gasoline Filling and Service Station," *Architectural Record,* June 1930.

links in one chain." This established, he reveals a larger motive using the same images polemically to make an argument about gas station design. Tank, railcar, truck—these are "characteristic forms, easily read," each possessing "clear definition of function [and] economy of form and material."[30] Any lingering doubts about Lönberg-Holm's modernism are put to rest by the form and content of the main article.

While Alexander Guth's study included a "specification and data sheet" detailing materials, equipment, and costs per square foot, for Guth the *problem* of the gas station was almost entirely stylistic. For Lönberg-Holm, by contrast, it was entirely functional, even *sachlich,* and his study consistently reinforces this approach. He begins by outlining those functions: to fuel, maintain, and repair gasoline-powered "traffic instruments," by which he meant cars, ships, and planes. (It is a reflection of the building type's newness that in 1930 "gas station" could refer to filling up and servicing vehicles other than automobiles.) Restricting his study to "land traffic," Lönberg-Holm lists ten determinants that shape the gas station as a commercial enterprise, related to the station's "income-producing capacities" and to consumer and operator "demands," and as a design problem. He considers architecture and planning at two scales: the gas station should possess "maximum plastic unity of the basic units" and "maximum organic relation to the community," both considered in terms of programming and siting.[31] His basic units include not only spaces for access and exit, maintenance and repair, and gasoline sales and display; he also regards signage and illumination and toilets and restrooms as essential "units" requiring comprehensive design and integration. This applies equally to the gas station's position in its community, formally and socially, and Lönberg-Holm's consideration of these issues is far more incisive than Alexander Guth's declarations about localism.

Where Guth saw style, Lönberg-Holm sees the necessity of dealing with catchment area and demographics influencing "the class of trade desired," the gas station's proximity to such local features as "shopping centers, recreation centers [and] business centers," and special circumstances in which the gas station is planned as part of a larger complex, from hotels and campsites to transit terminals. Lönberg-Holm even considers the role of the gas station in planning "future community developments." Like Guth, he is attentive to existing context, but he has a narrower view of which local circumstances should influence gas station design, particularly because he sought to demonstrate how architects might mediate the "often conflicting interests of commerce and community." To Lönberg-Holm's obvious chagrin, these competing interests had dominated gas station design for far too long. Among the many examples he cites as evidence of commercial excess are the Richfield Beacons, a series of 125-foot towers located along U.S. 101 and U.S. 99, the major Pacific coast highways of the 1920s. Placed at fifty-mile intervals, the illuminated towers ostensibly contributed to air traffic safety, but their oil-derrick shape, gigantic neon letters, and the gas stations at their base revealed them to be as much a marketing gimmick as a civic gesture. As such, Lönberg-Holm condemned their "commercial spirit." He wasn't averse to illuminated signage; in fact, he analyzes it in detail according to daytime and nighttime visibility and legibility at varied driving speeds on different roadway types in disparate weather conditions. But as "tower advertising," the Richfield Beacons displayed "complete disregard for community rights." In reality, however, in many cases the communities in which Richfield Beacons were located consisted of little more than a crossroads and a name on a map. If Lönberg-Holm fails to acknowledge this, it is because he wants to make a larger argument about commercialism and community.

Repeatedly throughout the article, Lönberg-Holm notes how the pressures of competition and the necessity of advertising in the early 1920s had produced — here, he and Alexander Guth are in complete agreement — a surfeit of "Greek sheetmetal temples, Dutch windmills, Chinese pagodas" and other examples of roadside exuberance that "violated" community standards. While more recent stations may have heeded those standards, they pleased Lönberg-Holm no better because, in taking their design cues from "adjoining residential or ecclesiastical architecture," they were not allowed "to be what they are." Overtly demonstrating a functionalist credo, Lönberg-Holm argued that "architectural merit" was dependent upon the "perceived differentiation" of functions being "easily read." At the community level, then, "the home, the school, the city hall, the factory and the filling station should be clearly recognized."[32] Translating functional clarity into legible design was the underlying goal of Lönberg-Holm's analytical approach to this typology and all others the car would ultimately generate. As a modernist he was committed to the idea that a functional building should indicate its functional efficacy by avoiding eclectic form—never acknowledging, of course, that a gas station shaped like a pagoda might, in fact, have been as resolutely functional in terms of program as one that embodied modernist aesthetics.

Throughout the gas station study, Lönberg-Holm's analysis is unmistakably data-driven, and he is explicit about the fact that he consulted with numerous oil and auto industry experts, from Standard Oil engineers to Westinghouse researchers to retail specialists at Warren Platt's *National Petroleum News.* From the car manufacturers themselves Lönberg-Holm gathered complete car dimensions for 38 popular makes and models of 1930. While Tyler Stewart Rogers had written *about* automobile dimensions in 1920, a decade later, Knud Lönberg-Holm actually published automobile dimensions. In the intervening years, car ownership rates in the United States had more than doubled, from fewer than 87 vehicles per 1,000 people to more than 217 per thousand, with most of the increase occurring in middle-income households (due mainly to the loosening of credit in the years after World War I).[33] As the car became a fact of life for middle-class consumers, it also became a workday reality for American architects, and this undoubtedly influenced Lönberg-Holm's decision not to interpret the automobile data, but to present it for architects' use as objectively as possible, in an easy-to-read, nine-column table. This format was not a merely a graphic convenience—it was an integral part of part of Lönberg-Holm's methodology for aiding reader comprehension through efficiency-optimized layouts.

Keeping the text to a minimum, Lönberg-Holm translates his analysis into bullet points and numbered lists that appear on nearly every page of his study. These culminate in a full-page "Checking List" with 21 categories and 118 itemizations. These cover every conceivable aspect of the gas station as a building type, from location, layout, and lighting to pits, pumps, and plumbing, and ultimately to "form," the term he prefers to "style," undoubtedly for its precision and palatability from a modernist perspective. Though "style" does not appear anywhere on the Checking List, elsewhere in his 24-page study, Lönberg-Holm uses variants like *styled* and *styling* as terms of opprobrium, and he doesn't pull any punches in his critique of stylistic indulgences. He regards colonial and rustic stations as inappropriate for dense urban contexts because contrasts of height and materials are too severe, using a Cape Cod–cottage filling station dwarfed by multistory firewalls to make his point. These were tolerable only in the "natural setting" of a rural county or a leafy suburb, where, for example, the stations Gilmore Clarke and Penrose Stout designed for the Hutchinson River Parkway are said to resemble a tidy New England farm, notwithstanding their Westchester location. Less tolerable to Lönberg-Holm was tricking up the air compressors "without reason" to look like old-fashioned water pumps. Similarly, he had little patience for the overly picturesque details of Clarence Stein's gas station for Radburn, New Jersey, despite their seeming appropriateness in a town that was effectively a garden city, albeit one for the "the motor age." For Lönberg-Holm the steeply pitched roof, the thick canopy columns, and the station's overall symmetry were not justified by expense, operation, or customer use. These features amounted to little more than "unnecessary sacrifices to a false 'architectural styling.'" This was "stage setting," not the "impersonal" and "standardized design" to which he was fully committed.[34]

Well aware that even *styled* gas stations could be standardized, as oil companies repeated branded building elements across multiple retail units, Lönberg-Holm aligned his notion of standardization with modernist ideals of mass production, clearly shaped by the designers and theorists with whom he was in regular correspondence during this period: Oud, Theo van Doesburg, Gropius, even Buckminster Fuller. And though most readers of *Architectural Record* in 1930 probably failed to notice, Lönberg-Holm signaled his familiarity with their contributions to contemporary modernist discourse, such as Oud's "Architecture and Standardization in Mass Construction" (1918), Van Doesburg's "Towards a Plastic Architecture" (1924), and Gropius's "New Architecture and the Bauhaus" (1925). His discussion of gas station design is inflected with their concepts of regularity, uniformity, flexibility, and plasticity, as well as their more concrete aspirations for factory-finished materials and factory-built units. Lönberg-Holm thus recommends "elementary forms" and "elementary colors"; "visual unity" and "smooth surfaces"; "no ornaments or decorations" and "limited number of materials"; "corners rounded" and "minimum vertical supports." It's a form-making checklist that anticipates Henry-Russell Hitchcock and Philip Johnson's formulation of the International Style in their MoMA exhibition and book; but even if Lönberg-Holm deploys his phrases and catchwords with comparable polemical intent, he claims that these design decisions are not arbitrary aesthetic choices. Indeed, he takes pains to explain them functionally, noting they would "increase appeal to the driver" at the same time they enhanced operational and maintenance efficiencies.[35]

To support his explanations and clarify his meanings, Lönberg-Holm included two dozen diagrams, charts, and architectural drawings in the building-type study. As a body of work, these are early examples of the rationalist information design that would characterize his *Sweet's* collaborations with architect C. Theodore Larson and graphic designer Ladislav Sutnar in the 1940s and 1950s. When they appeared in *Architectural Record* in 1930, they illustrated his checklists with graphic simplicity. Layout diagrams of hypothetical service stations analyzed traffic flow for multiple site scenarios and program arrangements, from corner lots to extended pump islands. The bold arrows that indicated the direction of cars from highway to station and back are depicted intentionally as gentle curves to emphasize streamlined movement. Flows are also critical to the chart that depicts filling and service operations, both at the level of representation and the level of meaning. Utilizing what he would later describe as the "visual flow pattern" that was essential to the "mechanics" of readability and comprehension, Lönberg-Holm depicts the spatial and circulation relationships between fixed station equipment (tanks and pumps), customer and supply vehicles (cars and trucks), and service functions like lubrication, washing, and repair.[36] Using arrows, circles, and enumerations as visual shorthand, he creates a sophisticated adjacency diagram that renders captions almost unnecessary. Ably translating automotive data into architectural programming, Lönberg-Holm proves himself an information architect avant la lettre.

Modernism in the Service of the Automobile

In "The Gasoline Filling and Service Station," Lönberg-Holm proves himself a capable architect of buildings as well, including two of his own schemes among the dozen or so stations represented by scale drawings in the study. Given his dissatisfaction with the architectural *styling* of so many contemporary stations, ground plans rather than perspectives and elevations dominate the illustrations. This allowed him to avoid reproducing historicist details he found problematic and to emphasize instead the functionality of the station layouts irrespective of aesthetics, and he favored those standardized stations produced by big oil companies, like the Standard Oil spinoff SOHIO which, through a Philip Johnson connection, had commissioned Alfred Clauss and George Daub to design a series of glass and enameled steel stations that Johnson subsequently featured at the Museum of Modern Art. Lönberg-Holm illustrates his study's single European example with plan, section, two elevations, and a perspective, the only station he documented so thoroughly. In these drawings, Franz Nöcker's design for BP OLEX in Cologne appears efficient and simplified, with a butterfly roof that extends from a small, round-sided office to form a canopy for the pumps and car lanes while also serving as a base for freestanding sign letters paralleling the road. Throughout the study, the only stations that match the modernity of Nöcker's are those Lönberg-Holm designed himself, and he may well have included the German example to place his own work in an international architectural context. Certainly, with their line weights and axonometric renderings enhancing the effect, his gas station projects show how thoroughly Lönberg-Holm absorbed the lessons of De Stijl, the Bauhaus, and the Berlin Constructivists—and how effectively he translated these into forms legible for mass communication in pages of *Architectural Record* and, by extension, mass reproduction on the roadsides of America.

Lönberg-Holm produced a number of gas station design studies in the mid-1920s, and his sketches fall somewhere between Mendelsohn's dynamic buildings and Mies's brick and concrete villas, reimagined for the expanding urban territories of someplace like Woodward Avenue/MI-1 as it passed through uptown

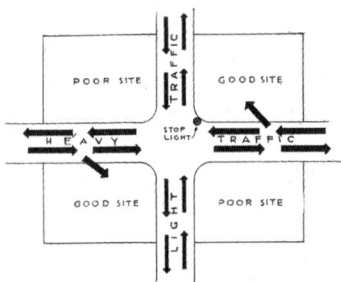

Diagram showing how the relative value of corner sites is determined by the traffic beacon. The station should be at the corner where the heavy traffic is stopped by the signal

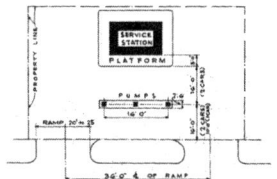

Layout showing minimum required dimensions

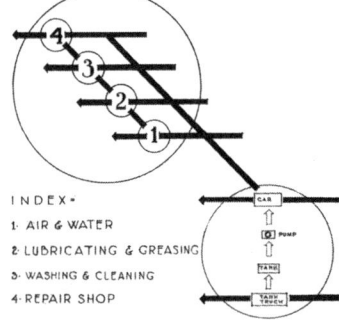

INDEX:
1. AIR & WATER
2. LUBRICATING & GREASING
3. WASHING & CLEANING
4. REPAIR SHOP

Operation Chart.
Filling and service operations should be clearly separated.

Figure 6. Knud Lönberg-Holm, diagrams related to service station layout and operations, from "The Gasoline Filling and Service Station" *Architectural Record,* June 1930. (Permission courtesy of Knud Lönberg-Holm Archive)

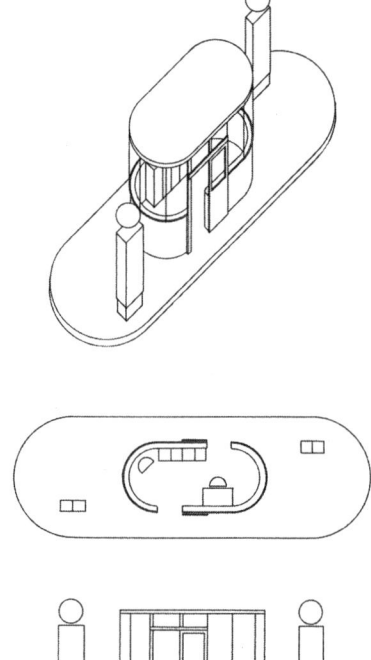

Figure 7. Knud Lönberg-Holm, drawings for an aluminum and glass gas station prototype, from "The Gasoline Filling and Service Station," *Architectural Record,* June 1930. (Permission courtesy of Knud Lönberg-Holm Archive)

Detroit, where Lönberg-Holm lived at the time. With their boldly asymmetrical compositions, expanses of plate glass, hyperextended cantilevers, super-graphic signage, and strategic use of color, these modernist gas stations were unlike anything to be found on U.S. highways or in U.S. architectural journals at that time. Unsurprisingly, given his polemical arguments about functionalism (and his downplaying of formal design concerns), when preparing these schemes for inclusion in his *Architectural Record* study, Lönberg-Holm reined in their exhibitionism and stressed their visual unity and logic of spatial organization—precisely the things he highlighted in the bulleted text that ran alongside. He also specified their easy-to-maintain materials—aluminum and glass—and their potential for prefabrication, describing his scheme for a combination pump island and salesroom as "factory-made units" that were "easily assembled in the field."[37] The reader must take his word for it—the drawings are either radically abstract or utterly schematic—and there is no evidence that he ever attempted to put such stations into production. For Lönberg-Holm, the ultimate objective of standardized design, at least on a conceptual level, was the mass-produced building, and as he offers a cogent explanation and step-by-step rationale for the factory-made gasoline service station, he comes very close to proclaiming an architectural manifesto for the age of the motorcar.

Lönberg-Holm was clearly frustrated that, despite the proliferation of service station chains with standard designs, as yet "little has been done to develop factory-built units"—at least as far as he knew. In fact, as the research and fieldwork of Chester Liebs and Richard Longstreth has revealed, prefabricated station buildings offered for sale via mail-order catalogues were already numerous by the mid-1920s.[38] Lönberg-Holm acknowledged the complications of prefabrication with respect to local building codes and transportation from factory to building site, but he believed advantages of "economy, comfort, and appearance" made them superior to typical on-site construction, where variables of job oversight, multiple contractors, worker skill, and building materials were always a factor in assuring quality and timely completion. Even more vexing to Lönberg-Holm was the fact that the manufactured buildings that *did* exist (i.e., of which he was aware) were mostly imitations of traditional materials like stone and wood. On this point he was intransigent: factory-built units should be "as 'impersonal' in form as the mechanical equipment. All 'architectural styling' should be avoided." Like a good modernist, Lönberg-Holm refused to concede that the *impersonal* was as conscious a design decision as the imitative. Instead, unsurprisingly, he insisted his motivation was purely practical—that is, simplicity of maintenance and universal adaptability to sites of any condition or character, be they urban, suburban, or rural. What he did concede was that impersonal form was appropriate regardless of whether a gas station was factory-produced or built on site. He lauded the standard design of Associated Oil stations of the late 1920s as "light, easily erected structures." The station in the accompanying photograph is a simple canopied pavilion with a metal frame and infill panels of glass and enameled steel. That Associated Oil stations of the same standard design were frequently infilled with brick veneer and faux stone, rendering them what Lönberg-Holm would have called "stage settings," was not something the author-architect acknowledged—at least not directly. Instead, he praises the illustrated example for its "rational use of materials." Here, and in all Associated Oil units that followed the specifications for the standard design, were buildings that did "not pretend to be anything other than filling stations." This was as frank a declaration of a functionalist aesthetic as Lönberg-Holm makes anywhere in his extended gas station study, which, overall, is more concerned with programmatic efficiency than with architectural form.[39]

This distinction is key to understanding the significance Lönberg-Holm's "Gasoline Service and Filling Station" study, as well as his subsequent contributions to the architectural discourse of the automobile into the 1930s. Whether he considered the car's impact on architecture from the perspective of typology, technology, or urbanization, modern form was, he would insist (protesting too much), the justifiable result of objective analysis and not an a priori goal. In the fall of 1929 when Lönberg-Holm was in the midst of his gas station research, he received a letter from Bauhaus director Hannes Meyer that captures the spirit of this approach in Meyer's description of his efforts to redirect the curriculum of the Bauhaus away from what he called "purely artistic training" toward a pedagogical model more appropriate for "today's more scientifically oriented cultural view." While

Lönberg-Holm's building-type studies and technical reviews hardly constituted a curriculum, it is not a stretch to see them as a form of professional development or continuing education, and his editorial work into the 1930s has strong parallels with Meyer's polemics of the same period. "Building is nothing but organization," Meyer wrote, "social, technical, economic, psychological organization."[40] This was the terse conclusion to an expansive statement on "bauen" that Meyer published in the Bauhaus annual in 1928, but it could just as easily have been something Lönberg-Holm published in *Architectural Record*—though he might have been tempted to add "automotive" as another key dimension of building organization.

That was certainly the motivation of Lönberg-Holm's next authored contribution to *Architectural Record,* a project that appeared in an article on stadium planning. With absolutely explicit intentions, this stadium explored design for the automobile while revealing the inherent tensions of functionalism as dogma. Lönberg-Holm developed his scheme in collaboration with Seiichi Washizuka, a 1927 graduate of the University of Michigan, and theirs was the only hypothetical project featured in "Stadium Planning and Design" in the *Record*'s February 1931 issue, which may suggest that Lönberg-Holm was responsible for its inclusion. The article's author, Myron Serby, was an architect then in the employ of the American Institute of Steel Construction, under whose aegis he had just published a treatise on stadiums that is still cited as a standard reference work. In that book and in his *Record* article, Serby acknowledged that providing parking for automobiles was a necessity in contemporary stadium design, though his recommended ratio of one acre of parking for every 3,000 seats (roughly one parking space for every 20–30 spectators) suggests an era not yet fully autopian, when sports fans were still more likely to arrive by subway than freeway.[41] Regardless of the numbers, Serby's assumption was that spectators' cars would be accommodated in surface parking set aside during initial site planning. Lönberg-Holm had other ideas.

His inventive hybrid combines the venue and the parking in a single structure that fuses the multilevel seating conditions of a typical stadium with the multilevel parking conditions of a typical garage. Made possible by technology that had been standard for car and truck garages for a decade, the stadium deploys four circular/helical auto ramps with entrances at the corners of the site providing access to five parking levels, plus the roof. In an alternate scheme, single-run ramps throughout the stadium replace the ramp towers, but the effect is the same: on levels one through five, drivers park their cars and walk forward toward ramps that take them to their seats one level above. On the uppermost level, they drive their cars to the edge of the cantilevered roof deck and watch the game from inside their parked vehicles. In 1931, using the roof for both parking and spectating was at once a grand gesture and a gimmick, one likely borrowed from the autodrome atop Mattè-Trucco's Fiat Lingotto in Turin (1916–23).

Lönberg-Holm surely knew the Fiat factory, where the rooftop test track was the culmination of the manufacturing process, since it had been an object of fascination for modernists from the moment of its completion. Of course, there's some artistic license in Lönberg-Holm's transposition from factory to stadium since, here, the cars on the roof are pointedly static. His "provision for parked spectators" is all the more notable because it appeared two years before auto-parts salesman Richard Hollingshead opened his patented, first-in-the-world, drive-in movie theater in Camden, New Jersey in June 1933. Reporting on this event in its August issue, *Architectural Record* made note of the outdoor sound system, but seemed more impressed that the sloped-up terracing of the wide semicircular rows allowed vehicles to enter and exit without "disturbing the audience"—meaning the people watching the movie from the comfort of their parked cars.[42] Though the section and perspective of Lönberg-Holm's stadium don't convey a similar level of construction detail, other aspects of the project are unmistakable: a potential for egress congestion and a suggestion of cultural import. In this project, Lönberg-Holm reimagines the stadium, a social institution and building typology with roots in the ancient world, for the automotive age, not through modest accommodation or gradual evolution, but through a conscious architectural act.

In this respect, Lönberg-Holm's stadium design has obvious parallels with Frank Lloyd Wright's Gordon Strong Automobile Objective of 1924–25, and these go well beyond a shared interest in monumentalizing the ramp. When he was working on the stadium for parked spectators, Lönberg-Holm was probably unfamiliar with Wright's unrealized project for a boldly spiraling, car-centric ziggurat—though he may have been aware of its existence through correspondence with

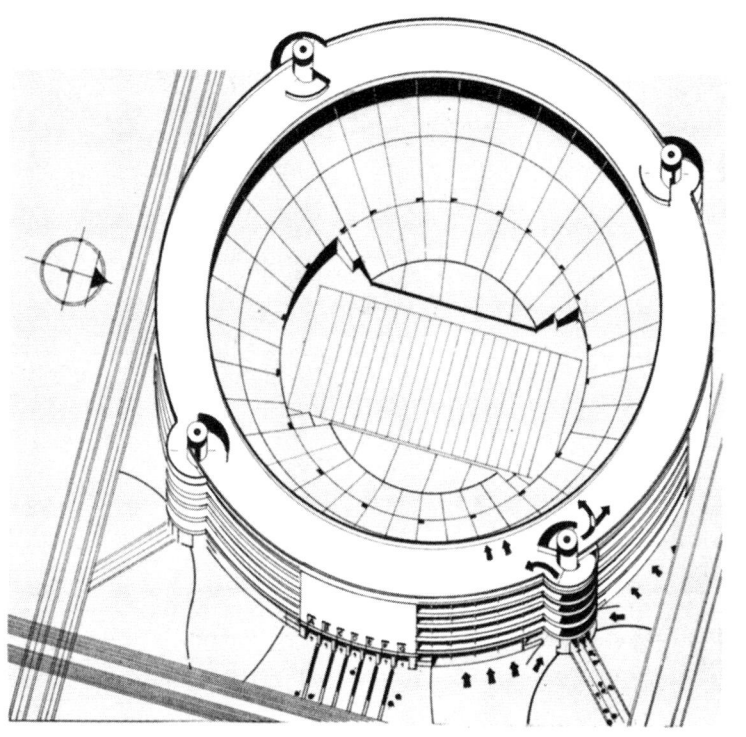

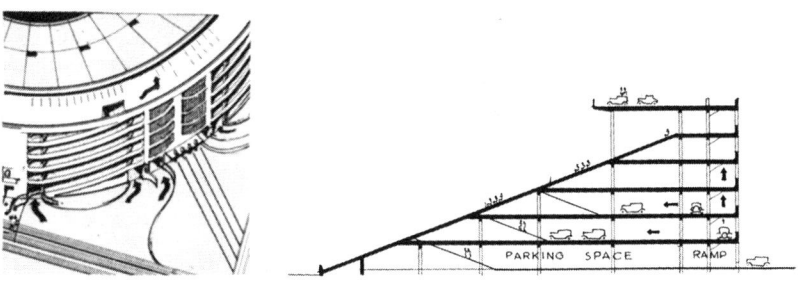

Figure 8. Knud Lönberg-Holm and Seiichi Washizuka, design for a stadium with provision for parked spectators, from "Stadium Design and Planning," *Architectural Record*, February 1931. (Permission courtesy of Knud Lönberg-Holm Archive)

Figure 9. Frank Lloyd Wright, Gordon Strong Automobile Objective project, 1924–25. (Copyright © 2019 Frank Lloyd Wright Foundation, Scottsdale, AZ; all rights reserved; The Frank Lloyd Wright Foundation Archives [The Museum of Modern Art | Avery Architectural & Fine Arts Library, Columbia University, New York])

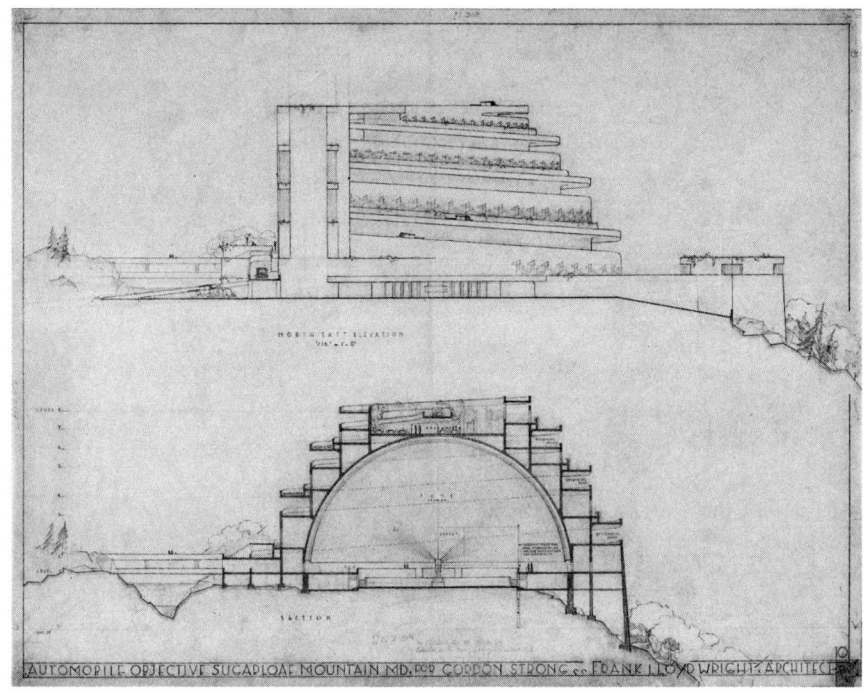

Erich Mendelsohn, who discussed the project while visiting Wright at Taliesin shortly after he'd seen Lönberg-Holm in Michigan. Wright's project began when businessman Gordon Strong commissioned him to design a resort-cum–tourist attraction on Sugarloaf in the Blue Ridge Mountains of Maryland, northwest of the District of Columbia. Both men used the term "automobile objective" literally to refer to a structure to be built at the mountain summit as a motoring destination. Beyond this, their semantic differences were profound. For Strong the mountain was the goal; the "objective," as a building, was a simply a twentieth-century version of a lookout, an observation tower with added recreational features, along with space for parked cars. Where Strong saw the automobile as the means to an end, Wright saw it as the means *and* the end: in other words, the automobile was literally the objective. Hence, cars dominate the final scheme with great ascending and descending auto ramps pushed to the building's exterior, wrapped tightly around a planetarium at the core. This was experiential architecture, like a scenic drive contained within a single building. "Sitting comfortably in their own cars," members of the motoring public would, Wright declared, find themselves "in a novel circumstance with the whole landscape revolving about them." It was, as historian Mark Reinberger succinctly put it, "an architecture for the automobile in motion."[43]

Wright's plan to foreground the moving car as "a novel entertainment" was not part of Gordon Strong's dream for Sugarloaf: he wanted a more conventional building in which visitors parked their cars and got out to enjoy the view. For Wright, this was a grave disservice to man and machine, the impact of which he expressed in portentous cultural terms. Forcing visitors out of their cars would mean "leaving the automobiles in which they both now really live and have their beings, still 'parked' aside,—betrayed and abandoned as usual." Though the irreconcilable differences of their competing visions for how cars and humans should commune with nature ultimately killed the project, Wright was not ready to abandon the Automobile Objective. Five years later, he redeployed it in his earliest vision for the new urban order of Broadacre City, revealed first in his Kahn lectures at Princeton in the spring of 1930 and then, a year later, when the lectures were published as *Modern Architecture* around the same time Lönberg-Holm's stadium appeared in the *Record*. As Wright repurposed his automobile objective for Broadacre City, he minimized its novelty, stressing instead its role as a social magnet, something that would "gratify what is natural and desirable in the get-together instinct of the community." While it remained monumental, even heroic, in scale, it became a part of Broadacre's everyday landscape, one of many new building typologies that responded to the changed conditions of U.S. life in the twentieth century, when, in Wright's terms, the automobile had become "a machine in normal use."[44]

Trends and Types

Circa 1930, what constituted the automobile's normal use in the United States was still in flux because its transformative potential was not yet fully grasped.

Well into the 1920s, the car still followed the social and spatial patterns that had developed with older means of conveyance, in tandem with the pedestrian, the carriage, and the railroad. As Lewis Mumford observed in *Technics and Civilization,* the car's early promoters and advocates "made no attempt to introduce appropriate utilities which would realize its potential benefits." By the early 1930s, this was beginning to change, as Lönberg-Holm attempted to demonstrate in another *Technical News and Research Study* in *Architectural Record.* In June 1931, a year after he introduced the car as a subject of sustained architectural inquiry, Lönberg-Holm turned his attention to "Planning the Retail Store." While on its face this subject was so all-encompassing it seemed to defy a single typological study, Lönberg-Holm reduced the store to its most basic function as "an outlet for the distribution of commodities," thus offering design strategies that could be augmented to meet the discreet needs of anything offered for sale, from drugs to groceries to clothing. To Lönberg-Holm, however, the automobile trumped and transcended those needs, becoming a catalyst for new forms across multiple retail categories. He begins by setting the car into a broader context of urban growth and consumer change, including settlement patterns that favored decentralization and consumption habits that favored larger stores and corporate chains. Standardization and mass production, shrinking family size and women working outside the home, new modes of transportation and the expansion of broadcast media—these are among the "trends" that Lönberg-Holm identifies as having "changed the scale of time and distance in retailing," thus shaping its business and spatial practices in the twentieth century.[45]

Lönberg-Holm was not alone in noting these phenomena: trade journals like *Chain Store Age,* sociological studies like Robert and Helen Lynd's *Middletown,* and popular chronicles like Frederick Lewis Allen's *Only Yesterday* all registered similar effects. Allen's best-selling informal history opens with a day in the life of Mr. and Mrs. Smith, white middle-class Americans whose quotidian car use was an essential dimension of the "return to normalcy" that characterized the 1920s. After breakfast, "Mr. Smith gets into his automobile to drive to the office . . . on the open road—a good deal more open than it will be a decade hence." At some point during the day, Mrs. Smith, who had stopped patronizing her neighborhood store, gets into *her* car to drive to a chain grocery in order to "save twenty-seven cents on her daily purchases." Less anecdotally and based on their research in Muncie, Indiana, the Lynds observed the "wide diffusion of the automobile culture" on Middletown's "equilibrium of habits," noting that by 1930, and across many socio-economic groups, using the car for shopping, leisure, and driving to work — in a 45-mile radius — had become the norm and not the exception.[46]

Lönberg-Holm highlighted the impact of the automobile as a starting point for recommending surveys of economic and demographic statistics informed by car use at the local level, from the "density and nature of the traffic" to the "shifting of retail trade areas." These went hand in hand with his suggested analysis of factors governing location and site conditions, including access to parking facilities, filling stations, and "legibility areas [and] lines of vision for pedestrians and motorists."[47] In recommending such surveys as the "research" necessary to precondition a successful store design, Lönberg-Holm anticipates by five years the collection of comparable retail data in the 1936 Real Property Inventories completed in twenty-three U.S. cities. As reported in *Architectural Record* that same year, these inventories revealed, for example, that in some suburbs of Cleveland there were more gas stations than food stores, and that they tended to occupy four times as much street frontage.[48] Without this level of detailed data at hand, Lönberg-Holm makes use of national statistics supplied by the U.S. Department of Commerce and domestic trade associations, quantifying and qualifying it into comprehensible principles, criteria, and checklists. He also offers suggestions for further reading, including his own *Record* gas station study and Frederick Kiesler's *Contemporary Art Applied to the Store and Its Display,* also from 1930 and dedicated, like Lönberg-Holm's work, to demonstrating the relevance of European modernism for stateside designers.

Kiesler came to the United States from Austria around the same time Lönberg-Holm arrived from Denmark and they traveled in the same émigré and avant-garde design circles. Circa 1930, they were collaborating with Buckminster Fuller on *Shelter,* the short-lived but influential journal that promoted radical functionalism over aestheticized formalism. Like Lönberg-Holm's gas station study, Kiesler's book on store display was easy-to-swallow didacticism that mixed practical advice with polemics.⁴⁹ Both of these studies used copious illustrations to highlight what the authors viewed as examples of good, bad, and promising design as informed by the programmatic issues described in the text. But Lönberg-Holm complicates the relationship between text and image—thus undermining his analysis of emerging retail forms—by offering modernist housing estates like the Hook of Holland (J. J. P. Oud, 1924) and Dessau-Törten (Walter Gropius, 1926–28) as exemplars of *retail* design. While he may be making an argument for mixed-use development, and while he may identify the shopping block of each estate, including Oud's iconic terminating pavilions with their rounded all-glass storefronts, the depicted views are utterly devoid of the very things Lönberg-Holm deals with in his study: the pragmatic essentials of merchandise, shoppers, signage, and cars.

The last two, at least, are visible in the only American project he includes in the retail study, the Park and Shop in the District of Columbia. This shopping plaza, a block of ten stores with parking for nearly four dozen cars, was still relatively new when it appeared in Lönberg-Holm's study, having opened in Northwest Washington late in 1930. Developer Shannon & Luchs, a prominent local real estate firm, and architect Arthur B. Heaton were well acquainted with just the sort of statistics and preconditions Lönberg-Holm recommended. Indeed, these were precisely the factors they brought to bear on the Park and Shop's final form, particularly in what, at the time, were its most notable features: it was set back from the principal motor route of Connecticut Avenue to provide a generous parking area and, at the corner of its L-shaped block, it grew to a double height (marked by pitched roof, dormers, and a cupola) to increase visibility

Figure 10. Park and Shop (Arthur B. Heaton, 1930), Connecticut Avenue, NW, Washington, D.C. (G. Eric and Edith Matson Photograph Collection, Library of Congress, Prints and Photographs Division, LC-DIG-matpc-11650)

and legibility to northbound traffic—the cars headed away from downtown toward outlying residential areas. But in "Planning the Retail Store," none of this is mentioned; in both the caption and the text, Lönberg-Holm is silent about the project's form and meaning. Was Lönberg-Holm's modernist distaste for the vaguely colonial styling of Heaton's architectural treatment of the Park and Shop clouding his assessment of the project? Or, despite his usually careful architectural analysis, had he simply failed to notice how innovative the Park and Shop really was in fulfilling his prime directive that "the shopping center should be readily accessible to automobile shoppers in large numbers"?[50]

Though Lönberg-Holm used the term "community shopping center" in the text, uncharacteristically, he didn't actually define it as a distinct architectural type; it may well be that he really didn't know what he was seeing in the photograph of the new shops on Connecticut Avenue. As Richard Longstreth has shown, in its accommodation to the car, the Park and Shop represented a clear break from existing patterns of the neighborhood shopping center. Though it retained the size and retail mix, it borrowed more directly from the drive-in markets that were commonplace by the 1920s, mostly on the West Coast. Consisting of individual but coordinated food stores occupying a block of contiguous units set back from the street, drive-in markets were, according to Longstreth, the first retail type that did not directly service the automobile, but was nonetheless "fundamentally reorganized for the motorists' convenience."[51] Lönberg-Holm's friend and CIAM associate Richard Neutra designed several of this type himself, including, by 1931, a few unrealized projects that had already been published in journals like *Chain Store Review, American Building,* and even in *Architectural Record,* where his "Proposed Drive-In Market, Los Angeles," a steel-framed, open-front, semicircular structure with a flat roof and an extended canopy, appeared in June 1929.[52] It is highly likely, then, that when Lönberg-Holm was preparing "Planning the Retail Store," he would have had passing familiarity with the distinctly car-centric type, even if he did not make a connection to D.C.'s Park and Shop.

A year later, when Neutra's Dixie drive-in market, a project for Lexington, Kentucky, appeared along with the Park and Shop in a feature on "Neighborhood Shopping Centers," the parallels were unavoidable.[53] Though this May 1932 article had no byline, it has the hallmarks of a Lönberg-Holm contribution, or at the very least, reflects his direct influence on editorial content in the *Record*. In this context, the Park and Shop, despite its revivalist detailing, is held up as a model of rational planning that stands in marked contrast to the "Coney Island Architecture" of the typical Main Street with which it is juxtaposed on the article's first page. While the caption notes the Park and Shop's architectural uniformity as a positive attribute of the design, this is highlighted only after an explanation that the parking "does not interfere with traffic of the main thoroughfare." Indeed, parking and traffic dominate the article in two pages of diagrams depicting various site plans that respond to distinct roadside conditions (curbside, mid-block, corner, narrow), retail programs (gas and store combinations), and community locations (i.e. "shopping center at entrance to suburban community" along a highway that serves as a conduit to and from the city and the country). In the data-heavy article, any mention of design-as-style is avoided until the very last sentence, which suggests focusing on a "feature" with an obvious car-oriented, programmatic rationale—like a clock or sign tower—rather than on an "'architectural' treatment." Given the *Record*'s predisposition toward modernist functional planning, the quotation marks around *architectural* were as effective as any exegesis of the text, whether they were placed there by Lönberg-Holm or a like-minded colleague sharing the magazine's masthead at the time.[54] Ultimately, for the *Record*'s editors, the question of style or its avoidance mattered only to the extent that it obscured or clarified more pressing issues when exploring the architectural consequences of the automobile. By the end of the decade, when "park and shop" was applied like a generic tag and the community shopping center had evolved into a full-fledge typology, "style" had dropped out of the discussion almost entirely.

In 1940, when the *Record* published an extensive study on the community shopping center it was concerned almost exclusively with planning—and that planning revolved almost exclusively around the car, as the *Record* announced with a simple declaration: "Today's housewife drives to her neighborhood shopping center." Included here were detailed time-saving standards and a checklist with "14 ways to better shopping-center design." Many of these dealt directly with auto-related concerns like traffic, parking, and circulation, but even items like site, topography, landscaping, and durability were premised on the requirements of the car: flat sites if winter driving conditions were an issue; plantings impervious to exhaust; building life expectancies that recognized the possibility of changing trading areas. In articulating the "planning principles" that should govern shopping center design, Cornelius Earl Morrow of the Regional Plan Association was unequivocal: "shopping centers have to be arranged for the convenience of the motor-car shopper," and this meant recognizing that it had to break from "obsolete patterns"—pedestrian-oriented street systems "not adapted to the use of the automobile."[55] That had been gospel since at least 1934 when theorists and designers Catherine Bauer and Clarence Stein published "Store Buildings and Neighborhood Shopping Centers" in the *Record*. Bauer and Stein were more evocative, but they came to the same conclusion that most commercial shopping streets—Main Streets—were "hang-overs from the past" that failed to recognize that the car had been a "dominating feature" of American life for over two decades. Not only did the typical Main Street lack adequate provisions for parking or a smooth flow of traffic, but the buildings themselves were wholly unsatisfactory in their strict frontality and flat displays. "Show windows," the authors noted dryly, "are of little use to people driving by in automobiles."[56]

Adaptation to the automobile was also Morris Ketchum's underlying theme in "Services for Sale" of 1941, which focused on the retail sector in which human labor, rather than manufactured goods, was the store's "living product." Here, Ketchum, an architect later responsible for some of the boldest store designs of the 1940s, paid particular attention to how laundries, florists, cobblers, and other stores in this oldest of retail categories were negotiating the realities of the auto age by coming to terms with the drive-in. Though he suggested this was already a well-developed retail sector, Ketchum still found it necessary to explain "the what and why of the drive-in business" to architect readers who might have otherwise failed to notice that "shopping distance is measured in minutes not miles." For Ketchum, the issue of distribution was key to understanding the drive-in because when customers arrived by car, the service retailer eliminated the costs of pick-up and delivery. As a building-type study, the thrust of the article was on design principles that changed to accommodate different types of service, but Ketchum was clearly attuned to how layout and appearance also changed depending on "whether customers are pedestrians or motorists." Ketchum intimated that stores serving the latter group were the most important, especially those drive-ins "on the city's fringe, strategically located between the business core and the outer layer of suburban homes." These, Ketchum predicted, "may foreshadow a city pattern of the future."[57]

The Automobile and Architecture's Expanded Field

That prediction gets at a crucial reason *Architectural Record*'s editors were preoccupied with the automobile—they understood that it foreshadowed the future of architecture and urbanism given what was happening in the present. In 1930s, the car's impact seemed to multiply at a dizzying rate, as presented not only in the *Record,* but increasingly in *American Architect* and *Architectural Forum* as well. News items, technical updates, portfolios, and case studies catalogued an astounding array of auto-related developments, from equipment (self-leveling elevators) to urban conditions (traffic congestion), all of which seemed intended, as Lönberg-Holm's like-minded productivist colleague Roger Sherman, then *Architectural Forum*'s managing editor, opined in the *Forum* in 1931, to force American architects out of their "cloistered culture" into a confrontation with "modern problems." Of course, such problems were not the exclusive domain of the automobile, but Sherman's concluding exhortation to counteract the architect's professional marginalization highlighted just how oil-soaked architectural discourse had become: "They who sit in an ivory tower cannot drive a motor car—and progress lies over the horizon."[58] In the 1930s, that horizon was inevitably filled with cars. Despite the Great Depression, after bottoming out in 1932, vehicular sales gradually increased, and by 1936 there were more than 23 million cars on U.S. roads. The field of architecture, the major professional journals implied, ignored those cars at its peril.[59]

Much of this coverage fostered the perception of the automobile as a promising domain for expanding professional practice and cultivating new forms of architectural expertise, especially given the contraction of large-scale and conventional building activity during the Depression. As a result of these economic realities, smaller projects like service stations, commercial strips, and other explicitly car-related types attracted extra professional attention, as did opportunities for architectural service in which the connection to the car was attenuated, but still essential. In 1933, for example, as the impact of the Depression continued to sink in, the *Record* surveyed architects who had taken leadership roles in aiding the profession's recovery, asking them to respond to the query, "How can architects develop business?" William Orr Ludlow, chairman of the AIA's Committee on Industrial Relations, offered a response that was predicated, ultimately, on the prominence of the automobile in American culture. In the contemporary United States, Ludlow argued, technological efficiencies would reduce working hours across all sectors (i.e., white-collar and blue-collar), and this would expand leisure hours. The increase in leisure would, in turn, accelerate the decentralization already underway in U.S. cities. According to this logic, Ludlow concluded that "the automobile has nearly revolutionized our manner of living, and it is going to be the means of making the greatest use of out-of-doors and the buildings to go with it."[60]

Even without the Depression as a backdrop, the car is evident in numerous architectural projects presented as news items, design ideas, and editorial provocations: a dramatically cantilevered traffic tower designed by Mies van der Rohe to heighten visibility while minimizing disruption of vehicular movement; skyscrapers built over parking garages proposed by Harvey Wiley Corbett to deal with car congestion in the urban core; recreational infrastructure planned by Gilmore Clarke, who also argued for transportation as "a wider sphere" and "an expanding field" for modern design, noting that as "motor traffic has crowded the highway," it created demand for "whole new categories of specialized types of buildings."[61] As reflected in the journals, even U.S. architecture schools were responding to the realities of an auto-centric nation—from the upstart Art Center in Los Angeles (founded 1930), where Kem Weber was offering a studio on roadside stands and drive-in restaurants, to the august School of Architecture at Princeton, where Henry Wright was supervising thesis work that continued his own research into town planning "for the motor age."[62]

Throughout the 1930s, and with a frequency that seemed to outstrip the annual model changes from Detroit, came a veritable parade of "special building types" keyed to the motor age. These went well beyond the service station and the drive-in market—though their permutations and iterations were impressive enough. By 1938, the *Record* reported that the drive-in market was so familiar as a type that it could be designed "in reverse" yet remain recognizable, as demonstrated by the "motorized market" Wilbur Henry Adams proposed for Detroit. On the street level, moveable food stands occupied the entire perimeter of an oblong structure with parking confined to the building's interior. The second floor provided additional retail space; the third floor contained a cafeteria and gave access to a large playground on the roof. Adams, who had worked for Raymond Hood on Rockefeller Center, had clearly absorbed Hood's "city under a single roof" ideal, even for a modestly scaled building in a city with a fraction of the density of New York.[63]

In Miami Beach, Igor Polevitzky and T. Triplett Russell combined a Gulf station serving cars and boats with a hotel, restaurant, and tackle shop. In Jersey City, Barney Gruzen refined a service station in relation to an adjacent Big Bear supermarket to create a cohesive "automobile shopping center." In Evanston, Graham, Anderson, Probst and White placed roof deck parking atop a multibay Firestone service station, thus maximizing the profits of a structure built as a taxpayer. In all three cases, whatever the merits of the individual buildings—and all are fine examples of commercial modernism of the mid-1930s (Gruzen cites Erich Mendelsohn and Willem Dudok as precedents)—it is how the journals positioned them within contemporary architecture and automotive culture that is noteworthy. The "good design" of Polevitzky and Russell's Gulf Station and Hotel stands apart from the "ubiquitous hot dog stand, which mars so many scenic highways." The "imposing" presence of its lighthouse tower is justified as a product of its location at the end of the County Causeway and by its function as actual marine beacon. Notes on Gruzen's Super Service Center refer to the established habits of "the motorized public," those car-driving consumers who left their cars for lubing, fueling, and washing while they shopped—even those who, in the midst of the Depression, were seeking out the thrifty deals offered at a discounter like Big Bear. In Evanston, the roof deck served the opposite end of the retail spectrum: customers of the adjacent Marshall Field department store, who by 1936 demanded convenient on-site parking as a perquisite of patronizing what was the retailer's

Figure 11. Parking Garage for Marshall Field (Graham, Anderson, Probst and White, 1936), Evanston, Illinois, from "Design Trends: Parking Garages," *Architectural Record*, May 1937.

second branch location (also designed by Graham, Anderson, in 1929).[64] Similar commentary accompanied the *Record*'s publication of C. W. Dickey's Waikiki Theater in Honolulu in 1938: the building's tropical moderne style rated barely a mention, but much was made of its accommodations to "autoists": ample parking, an illuminated pylon sign, and a motor boulevard location (on Kalakaua Avenue, Waikiki's main drag) four miles from downtown. Beyond these specific features, the building's very existence was offered as proof that even far away from the continental United States, "the auto is exerting the same pressure on building design."[65]

THE CAR AND WHAT CAME OF IT

If the *Record* used the Waikiki Theater to demonstrate the car's geographic reach, it used tourist cabins and camps to demonstrate the car's economic reach, especially as a barometer of building activity during the Depression decade, which it tracked over several years from the shifting perspectives of business, design, and criticism. In December 1933, in an article that was probably under Lönberg-Holm's purview, the *Record* identified the construction of roadside cabins as the only sector of the building industry that had experienced sustained growth and expanded activity after the onset of the Depression (this wasn't accurate, as building modernization also grew). There were 400,000 of these so-called *autoist shacks,* the article claimed, worth an investment of more $60 million, excluding land costs, almost all of it since 1929. There was no attempt to explain this growth as a social phenomenon—that is, one caused by the Depression, as unemployed and cost-conscious Americans took to the road and found themselves in need of cheap lodgings (a situation *Harper's Monthly* had just described).[66] Rather than seeking the cause, "Roadside Cabins for Tourists" analyzed the effect: after ticking off typical prices, conveniences, and special features, the article considered the broader consequences of auto camp growth: the redevelopment of fallow agricultural land in rural areas and waste landscapes on the urban periphery and new pressure on in-town hotels to accommodate cars and offer a greater range of rooms options.

Figure 12. Albert Frey, photograph of motor camp at Kingman, Arizona, showing individual cabin and carport, reproduced in "Roadside Cabins for Tourists," *Architectural Record,* December 1933. (Albert Frey Collection, Palm Springs Art Museum, 55-1999)

In terms of design and layout, there is a subtle endorsement of unstudied simplicity and efficiency: cabins are "practical and inoffensive" and possess a "sound architectural treatment without waste and unnecessary decorations." These descriptions accompany illustrations of motor camps at Kingman, Arizona, and Raton, New Mexico. The photographs are credited to the Swiss architect Albert Frey, then thirty years old and not yet settled in Palm Springs, but with a stint in Le Corbusier's office already under his belt. Frey had also co-designed the Aluminaire House, exhibited at MoMA, with *Record* editor Lawrence Kocher, who may have commissioned the photographs, which Frey took during a cross-country car trip in 1932. The published Kingman photograph shows the relationship between the individual cabins and carports. Unpublished photographs preserved in the Frey archives show that he thoroughly documented the motor camp site, capturing the relationship of the lightweight frame and clapboard buildings and Kingman's arid landscape, on U.S. 66 on the edge of the Mojave Desert. Frey was probably responsible for the uncredited drawings as well, since the plans and aerial perspectives have the nervous graphic energy and the *Charette* stencil lettering (the typeface was then uncommon in the United States) that Frey learned from Corbusier. Frey identifies the camp's programmatic elements, including the gas station and communal showers, along with the trees and shrubs carefully planted to attract motorists seeking respite from the dust and sun of the highway. In Frey's renderings, these motor camps, most likely planned by the owners of the gas stations around which they were built, become knowing sketches of a modernist vernacular, one Frey describes as both practical and inoffensive. When the tourist camps were architect-designed, like those published in a 1935 portfolio, the editorial thrust didn't change: it emphasized the prefabrication of the wall sections of Julian Whittlesey's wood-framed cabins in Wilton, Connecticut (designed when the architect was a Resettlement Administration consultant) and the off-the-shelf and shop-built elements of Earl von Storch's tourist village for an unspecified location.[67]

Figure 13. Albert Frey, photograph of motor camp at Kingman, Arizona, showing site and cabins, from Frey scrapbook labeled "Arizona Motel." (Albert Frey Collection, Palm Springs Art Museum, 55-1999)

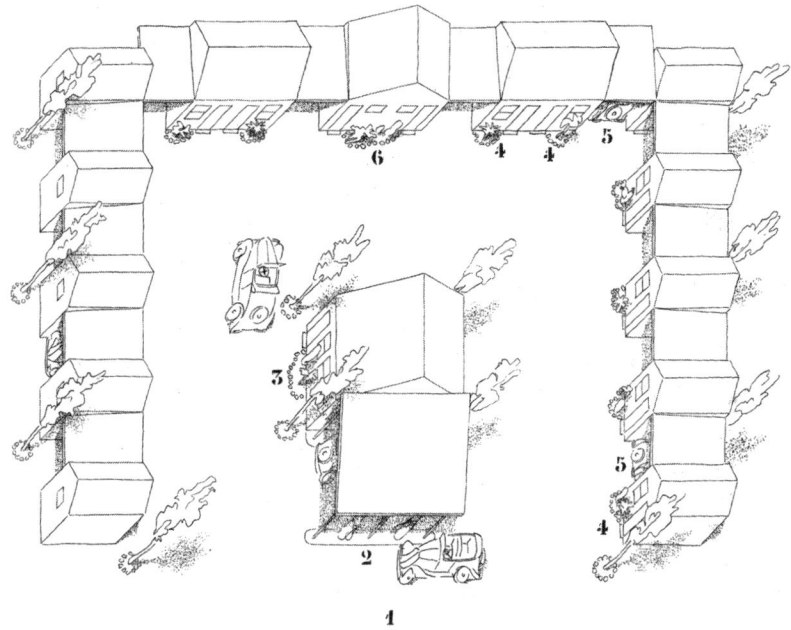

Figure 14. [Albert Frey], aerial perspective of motor camp at Kingman, Arizona, from "Roadside Cabins for Tourists," *Architectural Record*, December 1933.

Critic and erstwhile *Record* editor Douglas Haskell wrote unfavorably about the involvement of architects in auto camp design, claiming they spent more time on fake dormers than on rational planning. In assessing those camps he saw as "architecture in the vernacular," he was somewhat kinder, though he complained that auto camps outside Los Angeles and Denver were shabby enough to qualify as "roadslums." Still, Haskell's real interest in auto camps was to connect popular taste and elite theorizing, a rhetorical stance that would characterize his criticism in the 1950s (see chapters 3 and 4). While acknowledging the gap of imaginative creativity that separated Wright's Broadacre City and the typical auto camp, Haskell discerned important parallels. Though Wright projected a community in its entirety, while the auto camps were "embryonic communities" at best, Haskell recognized their common origin in "the nucleus of the gas station."[68] Haskell had clearly been paying close attention to Wright's argument that contemporary gas stations, tourist camps, and even roadside markets could be construed as "the future city in embryo"—and it is not insignificant that both men had logged many miles of cross-country driving and, as a result, were better acquainted with the American roadside than most of their architectural contemporaries. For Wright, the individual building, regardless of its architectural merit, but assuming it was propitiously located, might grow into "a neighborhood center" that could eventually generate an entire community.[69] In this Wright was not alone; Lönberg-Holm made similar arguments: auto-oriented retail forms should be planned as "nuclei for future community developments."[70] If techno-romantic Wright, techno-functionalist Lönberg-Holm, and techno-populist Haskell all found common ground in the urban potential of the quotidian typologies of the automobile, it was because each of them understood that the gas station and other car-related building types were the most visible symptoms of a condition of mobility that had emerged by the 1930s as an important dimension of modern American culture, and, ultimately, modern American urbanism, as we will see in chapter 2. The car didn't create this condition, but it most certainly drove mobility into the foreground of contemporary consciousness in the United States.

The Affects of Mobility

The synergy between mobility and the automobile is obvious, since the words denoting a capacity for movement and a vehicle propelled by an internal motor have the same French and Latin roots. In terms of cultural significance, the automobile's own mobility was at least on par with the mobility it bestowed upon its users. In *The Education of Henry Adams,* the eponymous American historian reflected on this duality while exploring the meaning of technology around 1900, prompted by the same visit to the Exposition Universelle in Paris that inspired his famous pairing of "the dynamo and the virgin." Initially, Adams is wary of the automobile's growing power, describing it in terms worthy of the *Inferno:* terrible, threatening, destructive, "a night-mare at a hundred kilometers an hour." Eventually, Adams comes to admire the motorcar's technological complexity, holding the automobile in the same high esteem as the dynamo. Adams purchased his first car in 1904 in order to tour the Île de France, claiming that only the automobile could unite his varied destinations "in a reasonable sequence," something the architecture press realized at about the same time. What he comes to appreciate about driving between the great Gothic cathedrals, in addition to the apparent convenience, is the way car travel reenacted the grand sweep of history, at a rate "of a century a minute."[71] His earlier anxiety is assuaged by an erudite take on the consequences of mobility.

Adams's attitude resonates with what may be the earliest car-centric neologism: *automobility* originated early in the twentieth century as a straightforward synonym for motor travel, but it quickly transcended this limited usage: by 1922 the *New York Times* declared that in the United States, "truly we are . . . an automobilic people," for whom cars had begun to mean more than transportation, and "automobility" appeared on the paper's editorial page again in 1931, when the *Times* noted with satisfaction, the theory that "civilization is measured by the degree of the people's mobility."[72] With incredible swiftness, in a few short decades, automobility came to encompass the broadest culture of the car: its material artifacts and its spatial domains, as well as the political and economic policies that supported their proliferation. Along the way, as Cotton Seiler demonstrates in *Republic of Drivers,* automobility was constructing American subjectivity and reifying the car's association with modernity and freedom of a distinctly U.S. variety.[73]

In the context of architecture and urbanism, Frank Lloyd Wright made this connection explicitly and emphatically not only in his 1930 Princeton lectures, but also in *The Disappearing City* of 1932, and in the statement that accompanied Broadacre City's debut at Rockefeller Center in April 1935. In each case he connected the car with the country's so-called core values of individuality, which he understood as choice and self-determination, along with geographic and social mobility. The motorcar was not merely a satisfactory manifestation of form following function. For Wright, it was also a symbol of lofty democratic principles. "The Machine," Wright opined, had become "a sword to cut old bonds and provide escape to Freedom," whose locus was somewhere far beyond the limits of the congested vertical city epitomized by the skyscraper.[74] Within *Architectural Record,* where Wright published his Broadacre statement simultaneously with the model's display in New York, mobility is an oft-repeated watchword, a synonym for a cultural predisposition whose spatial consequences were increasingly difficult to ignore. Stiles O. Clements may not have ascribed the same lofty ambitions to his firm's commercial work in in Los Angeles, but he used strikingly similar language to describe its motivations. When Coulter's Department Store eyed expansion to the growing commercial district of Wilshire Boulevard, company executives decided not to open a branch; instead, in 1937, they shuttered their downtown store and made Wilshire their flagship. Clements contrasted the old and new locations as urban morphology: the dense grid of downtown was "congested" and "centralized"; the linear strip of Wilshire was "spread out" and "open to views." It was, Clements explained, "the influence of increased human mobility" that caused this change in the city's fabric. Of necessity, this registered in the architecture as well. With 60 percent of patrons arriving by car, the rear entrance providing access from the parking area was given prominence in the design.[75]

Clements's testimony offered proof that mobility had become "a controlling factor in design," as the *Record* suggested a few months earlier, in a *Design Trends* feature that appeared in the August 1938 issue. This "Mobility" study, most likely a collaboration between Knud Lönberg-Holm and C. Theodore Larson, considered the impact of mobility in contemporary American life, from industrial productivity and distribution, to population migration and settlement, to information flows. In the 1930s, they argued, mobility touched every imaginable sort of human activity. To comprehend its cultural importance, mobility needed to be understood as both cause and effect. They teased this out in the text by explaining, for example, the significance of the assembly line as a manufacturing technique and a trope in use well beyond the factory. Their illustrations were far more tangible, showing vehicular evolution from the stagecoach to the airplane to demonstrate the impact of "increased speed and efficiency."[76] Speed as a technological fact is depicted in photographs from 10 miles per hour for a horse-drawn streetcar to 150 miles per hour for a Pan Am hydroplane. Speed's impact is depicted in an Isotype, reproduced from Hacker, Modley, and Taylor's *The United States: A Graphic History,* showing decreased travel time between Pittsburgh and Philadelphia from 6 days in 1857 to 2 hours in 1937. This "modern conquest of space," and the concomitant mobilization of the people had profound consequences, as described in

Graphic History, creating great metropolitan areas that ended social isolation, offered economic opportunity, and gave rise to new institutions.[77] By the mid-1930s these opportunities and institutions were already well known and had even been measured to some extent. In his groundbreaking 1925 urban sociological study *The City,* Ernest Burgess described mobility as an urban metabolic "pulse" that helped explain population movement and multiplying social contacts.[78] Burgess analyzed transit rides per capita and automobile registrations per locale to comprehend mobility and urban growth; the *Record*'s editors analyzed mobility and urban growth to enumerate design challenges: "Thus, the problem of building design becomes that of integrating constantly improving elements of design to meet the increasingly complex requirements of an increasingly mobile society."[79]

Addressing this problem required a clear expression of "a relationship between space ... and time," but this was not the aestheticized formulation of "space-time" that Lönberg-Holm's CIAM colleague, the Swiss historian Sigfried Giedion, would soon articulate in the 1938–39 Harvard lectures that became *Space, Time, and Architecture* (1941). Where Giedion looked to cubism and futurism as precedents for contemporary design, Lönberg-Holm and Larson offered quantifying data points: space calculated as "area, bulk, weight," and time measured as "speed, coordination, efficiency." How these factored into a building project depended on whether one was designing a structure that was mobile itself or a structure that promoted mobility—that is, "the movement of people and things"—even if the structure was static. So pervasive was mobility at this point in the twentieth century that, according to the *Record*'s editors, every imaginable type of built object fit into one of these categories. The paired images on the article's first page subtly reinforce this idea as applied to the nation's mobilized citizenry: above is an aerial view of a highway interchange in Queens; below is panoramic view of an auto camp in Florida. In the latter, the factory-built, auto-hitched dwellings in Sarasota clearly register as mobile structures, even when parked row upon row in a grassy field; in the former, the so-called "pretzel" that marked the intersection of the Grand Central and Interboro Parkways at Union Turnpike in Kew Gardens was a structure that explicitly promoted mobility. These parkways freed drivers from the congestion of surface streets and rendered the surrounding area valuable

Figure 15. The "pretzel" in Queens and an autocamp in Florida, from "Mobility," *Architectural Record,* August 1938; photos by Fairchild Aerial Surveys and Ewing Galloway.

for development now that it was accessible by car.[80] In 1938, despite their vastly different scales, both embodied the mobility, modernity, and urban possibility characteristic of the burgeoning automotive age.

These larger concepts, rather than any design specifics, were really the point of the *Record*'s mobility study, as extended quotations from the National Resources Committee make clear. Franklin Roosevelt established the NRC in 1935 to spur federal and state cooperation in public works, and until the United States entered World War II, it functioned as a clearinghouse for New Deal ideas concerning industrialization, transportation, and population redistribution. Mobility was a keynote of numerous NRC reports that examined, among other things, the planning implications of "a Nation on wheels." In borrowing this broadened outlook for "Mobility," the *Record* initiated a new direction in the architectural discourse of the automobile, evident in a desire to move beyond individual auto-oriented buildings toward a consideration of the car in the larger urban landscape and in the metropolitan region as a whole. But even as the conceptual depth of field expanded, mobility remained a critical frame, as one final study of the prewar period makes clear. On the occasion of its 50th anniversary, *Architectural Record* convened a group of MIT professors to consider the impact of a half-century of science and technology on the theory and practice of architecture. The group included two young academics who would become MIT administrators after the war, and the participation of future architecture dean Lawrence Anderson and future humanities dean John Burchard reflects the interdisciplinary cultural analysis the magazine sought. The *Record* published their findings in two parts early in 1941. Part I, in the January issue, examined changes brought about by new materials and methods, notably reinforced concrete and the steel frame. Part II, in the February issue, analyzed changing social attitudes toward building or "the demands society makes of architecture." Surveying the demands that were particular to the years since 1891, the MIT confab found it "amazing" how many were the direct result of "changes wrought by the internal combustion motor, changes which may be summarized by the word 'mobility.'"[81]

According to Anderson and his colleagues, the past fifty years had mobilized people, things, and ideas, first through the railroad and then through the automobile. Considering the key differences between these two transportation modes in terms of physical and social realities and transformations, their analysis is as cogent as it is anticipatory of postwar developments—although there is a degree of myopia where the car is concerned. They compare the expense of railway rolling stock and trackage not with the investment in highway infrastructure and auxiliary facilities the car ultimately required, but with the accessibility of inexpensive automobiles, thus underestimating the car's true cost. They compare track mileage in key years not with highway mileage for those years, but with the number of cars and trucks produced. Despite the apples-and-oranges quality of the comparison, their point is crystal clear: in 1941, the railway is in decline, and the automobile is ascendant. However important this conclusion was within the realm of transportation, its real significance transcended that narrow sphere: the railroad was a "concentrator" and a "centralizer," while the car was the opposite. Anderson and his coauthors are careful to acknowledge, however, that the automobile didn't create decentralization; rather, it intensified and accelerated decentralization by extending patterns established, in particular, by the streetcar systems already in place in the nineteenth century. When they fast-forward to 1941, they note that the "effects of dispersion" were not yet fully understood and the "potentialities in the motor car for the radial expanding community [had] been but feebly realized." What did exist was not pleasing to the authors: "avarice, ill-focussed [sic] energy, sheer stupidity" is the caption that accompanies one of the article's few illustrations, a cartoonlike drawing of a highway strip on the urban periphery. There's a sign identifying it as U.S. 5, but this is clearly meant to be anywhere USA circa 1941. The landmarks are instantly recognizable, as much from the pages of *Architectural Record* as from the American roadside: there are billboards, gas stations, auto junkyards, pylon signs attached to old houses, a building shaped like a windmill, another topped by a colonial cupola and set back from the road with parking in front. Anderson and his colleagues don't blame the automobile for creating this landscape, nor do they fault it for not yet realizing its potential as a shaper of buildings and settlement patterns. Instead, they place the roadside into a continuum of

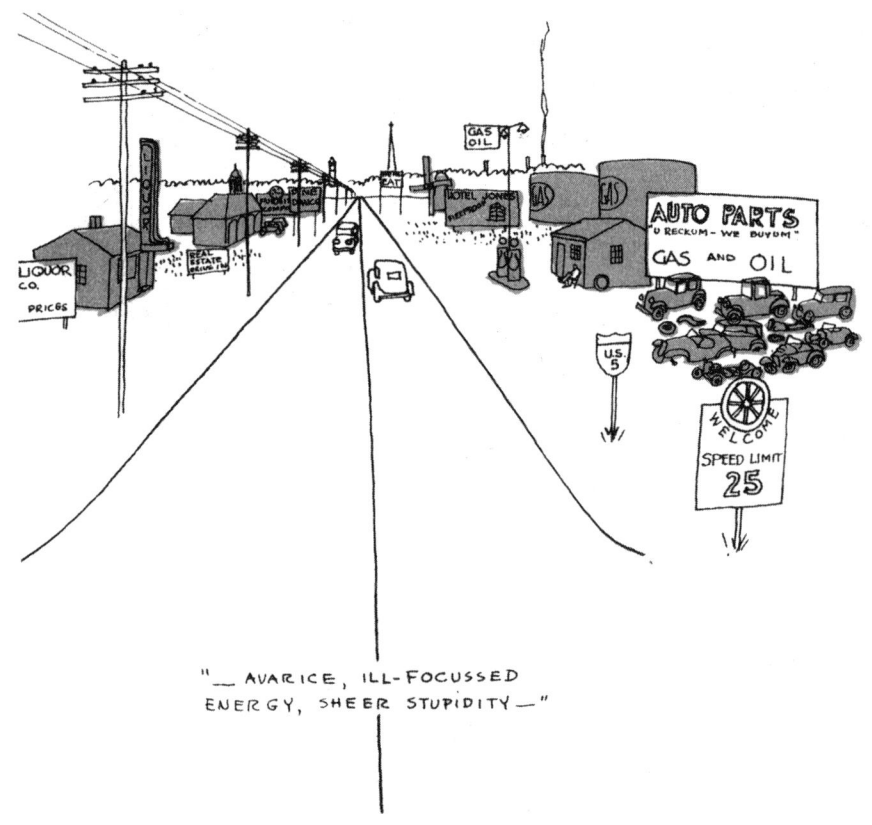

Figure 16. On the urban fringe: "avarice, ill-focussed [sic] energy, sheer stupidity," from "American Architecture 1841–1941," *Architectural Record*, February 1941; drawing by William H. Haible and S. Leonard Krause.

the automobile's cultural evolution. The rush to satisfy the demands of mobility in the first decades of the twentieth century created "undesirable conditions" that must be dismissed as "evidence of architecture's birth pangs." By the late 1930s, this first stage of the motor age was giving way to a "corrective and palliative" phase in which new and better prototypes for buildings, highways, and cities would gradually emerge. From this would come a period in which, finally, "human values are rediscovered."[82] There is optimism inherent in the suggestion that humanism would someday emerge from the culture of the motorcar and mobility—and in the United States in 1941 that optimism typified the midcentury American Autopia, not only in its faith in the car's architectural possibilities, some of which we have just considered, but in its acceptance of the car's power to remake the nation into a new kind of urbanized place, one whose expanding social and geographic boundaries we will explore in the next chapter.

2

ROADSIRE METROPOLIS

During the second half of the twentieth century, the interstates so thoroughly transformed our understanding of the highway that it is easy to forget that an earlier, impressively developed system already existed in the United States before Dwight Eisenhower signed the Defense Highway Act into law in 1956. Built piecemeal between the world wars by states and localities (frequently leveraging federal funds) and sometimes by ballyhoo promoters, the majority of these were two- and four-lane highways, which were not divided, grade-separated, or limited-access. They generally passed through cities and towns, rather than around them, though bypasses became more common as car traffic became more congested. Existing state and local routes were systematized through federal designations in 1925 and made recognizable through shield-shaped, numbered signage put in place across the country immediately thereafter. By the time the interstates superseded them in the years after 1956, these U.S. highways had cohered into a comprehensive national network and a mythologized cultural landscape whose breadth and length were mapped by road-tripping writers as diverse as John Steinbeck, Vladimir Nabokov, and Jack Kerouac, but also by interlocutors whose aspirations were less literary-minded.

Facing page: detail of fig. 24, Arthur Rothstein's photograph of the Lincoln Highway (U.S. 40) approaching Paradise, Pennsylvania

It was on these pre-interstate highways that the true urbanistic impact of autopia was first discerned, as the motor road begat the motor roadside to produce what art historian Ulrich Keller identified as "the American highway habitat" and geographer Karl Raitz called one of the country's "central transformational experiences."[1] It was also on these pre-interstate highways that midcentury urbanists, especially those designers, planners, geographers, and critics who made the metropolitan landscape the subject of their work, came to terms with automobility as a new way of experiencing the world from inside a car, as motion and space were subsumed into a continuous sequence perceived through the windshield. In recent years, diverse scholars have charted the experiential modes of automobility, from "auto-flâneurs" to "zoomscape" and "drive."[2] At midcentury these same modes inflected an emerging urban discourse, helping to theorize an expanding cityscape and to imagine a roadside metropolis. With mobilized perception came a shift in perceptual scale, as individual buildings gave way to the streetscape as a whole, moving from the successive blocks of the city center, with its dense and contiguous street walls, to miles of highway on the periphery, where jagged and perforated roadscapes dominated, and then, ultimately, to extended car-oriented corridors that crossed municipalities, counties, states, and even the country in its entirety. This amounted to a sort of SMLXL automotive urbanism, one that was recognized and analyzed much earlier than is generally understood, as this chapter will explore from a range of perspectives, both popular and professional, hypothetical and experiential.

Roadtown

One of the earliest visions of an American roadside metropolis had nothing to do with the automobile, even though, when Edgar Chambless's self-published *Roadtown* appeared in 1910, there were nearly half a million registered motor vehicles in the United States and they were being driven on more than 200,000 miles of "improved" or "surfaced" roads. These were mostly on the East Coast, which left two million miles of *unimproved* roads nationwide.[3] For Chambless, an autodidact and patent expert, this meant that the car had yet to produce an infrastructure substantial enough to serve as the foundation, however fancifully, for the linear urban utopia he proposed. Instead, his *Roadtown* was built literally upon the railroad: a continuous concrete building stretching out across the continent with mile after mile of stacked residential and commercial spaces connected by a rooftop promenade and serviced by "a railway in the basement"—like inter-urban and intra-urban train lines operating on different levels. Chambless did not completely ignore automobiles in *Roadtown:* he marveled at the speeds they achieved using rubber tires; he admired electric runabouts because they ran clean and without noise; and he valued the object lesson on collectivity that Americans supposedly grasped when driving on what he called "cooperative" (read public) roads. Nonetheless, Chambless did not view the automobile as portending the future of either transportation or the city. Yet, but for the literal continuity of its built form, *Roadtown* was predictive, even prophetic of the automotive urbanism that emerged in the middle of the twentieth century. "Horizontal transportation devices," from the railroad to the streetcar, Chambless argued, had already undermined the concentrating and congregating tendencies of traditional urban patterns exemplified by the centralized city. "A line of city through the country"—where no one lived "more than two or three minutes from the drug store"—was the logical next step.[4]

Two decades later, despite positive publicity and seemingly constant self-promotion, *Roadtown* was no closer to reality, and with the onset of the Great Depression, Chambless began promoting it anew. By 1933 he was stressing the potential for job creation implicit *Roadtown*'s construction and emphasizing what he saw as the disastrous consequences of twenty more years of expanding car ownership and auto-oriented road construction. Now, Chambless accurately discerned the car's urbanistic cause and effect: "The automobile expanded the urban radius still further and, because of the street space it occupies, added greatly to congestion." Only the "highly urbanized strip" of *Roadtown* could alleviate the urban conditions the car had exacerbated—ironically by occupying the same spaces the automobile was then in the midst of colonizing: "the suburban lands of existing cities" and "wholly new developments in territories now sparsely settled."[5] What Chambless failed to grasp was that a highly urbanized strip already existed, even if it was more the result of commercial opportunism than infrastructural utopianism. Either way, it was, de facto, roadtown, a portmanteau that had, by then, moved beyond Chambless's narrow, capital *R* definition and into the mainstream of urban discourse in the United States.

As early as 1921, in a plea for comprehensive city and regional planning, landscape architect Warren H. Manning described a "road town" extending north, south, east, and west from New York City. Here "a continuous ribbon of a town," growing apparently without organization or oversight as once open land, "between the villages" of Connecticut, Long Island, and New Jersey, was "rapidly . . . filling in." For Manning, roadtown was an inevitable development, if not byproduct, of the incremental historical evolution of the nation's still nascent highway network out of the "easy ways" of the Native American trails and portages that preceded European settlement. In Manning's day, this was most clearly illustrated by the Wickquasgeck Trail that gave way to Broadway, the Post Road, and what in 1921 he still called the Atlantic Highway (it would become U.S. 1 in 1925). From the seventeenth to the twentieth centuries, from New Amsterdam to Harlem to the Bronx and on through New England, a continuous string of villages lined the coastal route, portions of which were paved by the end of the nineteenth century, all of which was designated an auto trail by 1915, and stretches of which had been so transformed by widening, straightening, and commercial and residential development that a highway preservation association was formed a decade later. Manning historicized the "ribbon village" of the northeast roadtown in order to draw attention to its cultural value, but he also knew that because of the car, it was already spreading out beyond the historic network, following the pattern other communication technologies (e.g., telephone and radio) "with a radius that has no limit in our world or in its accessible atmosphere." Around this time, meatpacking magnate J. Ogden Armour made a similar observation about the country as a whole. The United States was "a nation knit together" by the car, Armour suggested, in an editorial that appeared originally in his company's house organ, *Armour Magazine,* and was subsequently reprinted in periodicals ranging from *American Motorist* to *American Architect.* "Once the city was the city and the country was the country," Armour declared. "Today they merge into one another." For Armour, the transformation of the village into what he called the "rural metropolis that one finds here and there, everywhere" was evidence of the "wondrous changes" wrought by the automobile.[6] Armour, a motoring enthusiast and founding member of the Automobile Club of Chicago, was more effusive in his automotive appraisals than Manning, whose measured tones reflected decades of design experience (*he* was a founding member of the American Society of Landscape Architects). Though Armour was promoting a populist good roads movement and Manning was advocating professional highway planning, both men understood that roadtown had aesthetic and economic consequences that extended far beyond the right-of-way.

Benton MacKaye, the pioneering forester and planner, understood this as well, though he analyzed roadtown (and even cited Chambless) mainly as a prelude to proposing its opposite, "the townless highway," a model motorway intended to control wayside development and ease traffic congestion through zoning, grade separations, bypasses, and access roads. In MacKaye's proposal, a critical counterpart to the townless highway was what might be called the highwayless town, a compact community type that, by his own description, was one part New England village and one part Radburn, New Jersey, with the clear pedestrian-to-motorist balance and separation that a reference to Stein and Wright's "town for a motor age" implied. By 1930, when MacKaye began discussing the townless highway and the highwayless town, he had already spent nearly a decade working to establish the Appalachian Trail, the Georgia-to-Maine footpath for which he is best known today. Though at first glance the Appalachian Trail would seem to have little in common with roadtown or its correctives, MacKaye did not promote the AT simply for recreation, but as a new type of regional community, an extended corridor "neither urban nor rural." There are parallels here with the way Manning and Armour had interpreted roadtown, which isn't surprising since, at its most basic, MacKaye conceptualized the AT as "a transportation project" that would, in effect, develop an infrastructure for hikers and walkers akin as to those developed for the railroad and the motorcar.[7]

MacKaye had been considering the expanding influence of the motorcar since at least 1916, when, according to his biographer, he was one of the first planners to grasp the significance of the Federal Aid Roads Act, which for the first time provided federal money for the construction and maintenance of state roads. From then on MacKaye kept a keen eye on the expansion of the nation's highway system, paying particular attention to its impact on land use and development. After he met Lewis Mumford in 1923, when the two men joined Clarence Stein to form the Regional Planning Association of America (not to be confused with the Regional Plan Association of New York), MacKaye began to consider land-use patterns in historical context. Under Mumford's influence, MacKaye situated roadtown as the denouement, though not yet the resolution, of the "fourth migration" in America history. For Mumford, and for MacKaye after him, these migrations were a way of conceptualizing not only distinct (and overlapping) periods in American history, but distinct (and overlapping) types of settlement that followed the initial colonial conquest of what became the United States. In an influential and much-cited 1925 article published in *The Survey,* a leading progressive journal, Mumford assigned distinct modes of transportation to each migration period, and MacKaye repeats these verbatim in his townless highway/highwayless town proposals.

In the first migration, land pioneers opened up the American West for agriculture in covered wagons; in the second, industrial pioneers established mill and factory towns via river and canal boats and the railroad. The third migration saw the concentration of financial and human capital in expanding urban centers that became modern metropolises, with railroad and streetcar lines terminating in congested downtowns typified, for Mumford, by "cities where buildings and profits leap upward in riotous pyramids." For Mumford these earlier periods set the stage for the fourth American migration, already evident in the 1920s and founded on "the technological revolution" of his own day, which had rendered the "the existing layout of cities and the existing distribution of population out of square with our new opportunities." The automobile, in other words, was enabling urban decentralization and deconcentration, not in the exclusively linear pattern of the railroads, but "areally," across previously unsettled but newly accessible territory.[8] In Mumford's then-optimistic view, if the rapid transportation promised, but not yet fully delivered, by the automobile was coupled with sound planning at the regional scale—treating existing centers and subcenters coextensively—then in the fourth migration the United States might find a way to correct the urban, suburban, and rural ills that had plagued the country for roughly a century. (After witnessing three more decades of continued auto-oriented development, Mumford became considerably more pessimistic; see chapter 3.)

By the mid-1920s, across a variety of disciplines and media outlets, analyses like Mumford's were appearing with greater frequency, as the car's pervasive influence became increasingly difficult to ignore. In 1924, the American Academy of Political and Social Science, one of the oldest learned societies in the United States, devoted an entire issue of its *Annals* to "The Automobile: Its Province and Its Problems." In his foreword to the issue, University of Pennsylvania political scientist Clyde L. King observed what was by then an accepted truth, that no aspect of American life was "untouched by the automobile." Even as sociologists and economists explored such diverse topics as the car's impact on the home and the church, farming and education, and literacy and public health, they viewed its dispersive effect on urban/suburban/rural settlement as the necessary starting point for virtually every analysis they undertook. Not only had the car "widened municipal boundaries," it had also extended "the territories over which civilized man holds dominion."[9] If this was the automobile's *province,* its *problems* stemmed from the same questions of planning—or lack thereof—that interested both Lewis Mumford and Benton MacKaye.

Even before he fully articulated the townless highway and the highwayless town, MacKaye was building on Mumford's historical framework with respect to the automobile. In his 1928 book *The New Exploration,* MacKaye echoed Mumford, citing the importance of sequential migration waves and arguing that during the third and fourth migration, the railroad and then the car brought about a "metropolitan invasion" of the country's "wilderness" (unsettled) and "indigenous" (colonial) lands. Here, following the lines of railway track and asphalt path was "a species of standardized excrescence"—in the form of billboards, gas stations, hot dog stands, chain stores, and even "in Main Street generally"—that was taking the place of the earliest cities and towns as surely as "the tentings of an incoming army." Though his language anticipates the critiques of urban/suburban sprawl that would characterize the second half of the twentieth century, MacKaye also naturalizes roadtown, giving it almost geological significance by comparing its relentless morphology to the fluvial valleys left behind when the ice sheets receded.[10]

It is this tone of inevitability and acceptance, rather than militaristic and consumerist pejoratives, that inflects the language MacKaye uses in "The Townless Highway" and "Townless Highways for the Motorist" in the *New Republic* and *Harper's* in 1930 and 1931 (the latter coauthored with Mumford). This is not to imply that MacKaye is above deploying contemporary roadside polemics, like those of the anti-billboard movement then gaining ground in the United States, but in this early autopian moment, he pointedly refrains from condemning the automobile. Instead, he blames the people.

For MacKaye, the car had been utterly misunderstood: Americans received the automobile as the vehicular successor to the "homely and companionable" horse-drawn buggy, rather than comprehending it as the disruptive transportation device it really was. As a result, the car, its infrastructure, and its broader culture were stuck in the "Kerensky stage," waiting for an "October revolution" that never seemed to come. Meanwhile, because of this "unthinking" and "backward" point of view—rather than anything intrinsically wrong with the automobile itself—the car's impact on the built environment had been deleterious. In their technological naiveté, MacKaye argued, Americans had given the "horseless carriage" unfettered access and uninterrupted frontage, and this, in turn, had produced "continuous haphazard wayside development." By the early 1930s, MacKaye saw this type of development advancing across the continent, propelled by the forces of "uncontrolled migration" of people and goods moving in cars and trucks along local roads and arterial highways. Though MacKaye believed the migratory "drift" was "automatic and unplanned," its results were substantial, evident in the endless ribbons of roadtowns and motor towns "congealing between cities" from one coast to the other.[11] Though neither of his townless highway articles was illustrated, his evocations of the roadside's past, present, and proposed future anticipate those that would circulate in engineering and planning circles throughout the decade. The New England Regional Planning Commission depicted "the problem of the roadside" as a trio of yesterday, today, tomorrow images in which a peaceful pre-automotive Main Street is contrasted with a contemporary corridor choked with vehicular traffic and continuous roadside development, and, finally, an idealized grade-separated, limited-access, fully landscaped, high-speed motorway that closely resembles MacKaye's townless highway ideal.[12] As an advocate of scenic beauty and the preservation of open space, MacKaye was principally interested in roadtown's environmental effects, but there were others in the 1930s for whom roadtown's social and economic consequences were at least as significant.

An American Institution

In 1934, *Fortune* magazine went so far as to proclaim the roadside "a great industry," predicated, as MacKaye and Mumford had similarly observed, on a supposedly national inclination toward mobility and migration. But in Henry Luce's pioneering business periodical, especially in the midst of the Great Depression, it was the $3 billion contribution "the Great American Roadside" supposedly made to the nation's financial bottom line that ultimately made it newsworthy. At least that's what *Fortune*'s editors touted in the headline. Referencing "The Great American Roadside" a half century after its publication, art historian Karal Ann Marling called the *Fortune* article "an investigative report," but this fails to capture the spirit of the piece, which had little in common with the exposés and muckraking journalism of the day.[13] Instead, James Agee, already a *Fortune* staff writer at the age of twenty-four, considered the balance sheets of roadside enterprises by dutifully offering statistics supplied by the American Automobile Association and local chambers of commerce about the number and profitability of businesses like tourist cabins, restaurants, and retail stands. Gas stations were missing from his accounting, though it is uncertain if this was because *Fortune* had dealt with them in a previous issue or, as is more likely, because Agee — notoriously reluctant to hand off his work to his editor — simply had not gotten around to writing about them before the article went to press.

The omission really did not matter because Agee was not interested in providing a comprehensive examination of the roadside as an industry, at least not as *Fortune* would have defined it. A closer parallel would be Theodor Adorno's and Max Horkheimer's culture industry trope. The Frankfurt School exiles, after all, developed their famous formulation about capitalism, mass consumption, and mass media while living and driving in Southern California in the early 1940s. Though they don't discuss the roadside directly in *Dialectic of Enlightenment* (1944), they briefly consider the automobile and its social effects, the commercial development of the urban periphery, and even the editorial content of *Fortune* magazine within their broader critique of cultural conformism and the reproduction of sameness as "mass-deception."[14] In "The Great American Roadside," Agee is far less skeptical than Adorno and Horkheimer would prove to be, and he would have likely disagreed with their contention that consumers were so victimized by capitalism that they had no capacity to resist the seductions of mass culture. Nonetheless—and this is where he anticipates their subsequent arguments—Agee absolutely understood how those seductions operated in the contemporary United States, especially within the regimes of automobility embodied by the roadside, which he had spent two months experiencing as research for the *Fortune* piece.

The roadside, as Agee described it, was an "organism" that could only be understood by comprehending its individual elements—the road, the establishments, the people, the cars—as "inseparable" parts of the "vital" whole. Each needed the other for the roadside organism to thrive. Gasoline, it was unnecessary for Agee to state, was the roadside's lifeblood. He may have avoided this particular rhetorical flourish, but that was only because he was depicting the evolution of the roadside as a national narrative of biblical import, to say nothing of environmental determinism: The continent was vast, "so God made the American restive. The American in turn and in due time got into the automobile and found it good." So good, in fact, that the car did not satisfy the American desire for movement, but instead only made it more acute, transforming it, in Agee's terms, into "the most compelling of American racial hungers." (Here, the *American* race is understood to be Caucasian.) He doesn't stop there: following Karl Marx and anticipating Edward R. Murrow, Agee declared that the automobile had become "the opium of the American people." Elsewhere, this lyrical bombast gives way to a consumerist patois of brand names and highway signs—the Beautyrest mattress, the Bar B-Q sandwich, the Mo-Tel—but "The Great American Roadside" is not satire, as Agee makes patently clear in the text (which includes a mild gibe at Sinclair Lewis).[15] It is, instead, ennobling of the everyday. Though less elegiac than Agee's *Let Us Now Praise Famous Men* (1941), "Great American Roadside" is akin to that better-known work, which also began as an assignment for *Fortune,* in that it probes the commonplace in order to search for deeper truths. Here, quite seriously, Agee explores the structures and practices of what we would now call the vernacular landscape of the automobile to reveal them as authentic embodiments of American folkways while simultaneously imbuing them with epochal significance.

The article's centerfold is a map of the United States highlighting, in addition to each state's post–Repeal Prohibition status, the federal highways that supported the "main streams [of] the U.S. Migrations," especially, but not exclusively, those that were seasonal and touristic. These included the major north–south coastal roads, U.S. 1 and Highway 101; those that followed historic overland routes west like the Santa Fe Trail (part of U.S. 66) and the Oregon Trail (U.S. 30N); and those cross-country routes originating in the automotive era, like the Lincoln Highway (U.S. 30) and the Broadway of America (U.S. 70). From Agee's perspective, so many people traveled so many miles so "casually" on 900,000 miles of "hard-fleshed highway" that all previous historical migrations looked like nothing more significant than "a smooth crossing on the Hoboken Ferry." And wherever on these highways this great wave of migrants paused "to trade"—be they vacationers, day trippers, day laborers, commuters, or shoppers—the Great American Roadside emerged as "the most hugely extensive market the human race has ever set up."[16] Agee describes both the order and chaos of the roadside marketplace in vivid terms, from the regional foodstuffs, crafts, and souvenirs available for purchase to the customs of negotiating for overnight lodging and sizing up an attraction before pulling off the highway.

John Steuart Curry's paintings, commissioned by *Fortune* and reproduced in full-color, complement Agee's observations with generalized rather than specific illustrations. Executed in the American Regionalist artist's easy pictorial style, and based on Curry's travels in the Midwest in the summer of 1934, the vignettes capture the typical roadside experience of the mid-1930s: travelers sit around an auto court campfire after they've stopped for the night; diners crowd the counter of a highway café during a mealtime rush. In another vignette, the signage of a tidy filling station competes with a fantastic menagerie, including elephants and a polka-dot zebra beckoning to passing motorists, though it is not clear if these "gimcracks" are lawn ornaments or children's toys (see color plate 3). One of the most surprising images hints at the roadside's surreal qualities. Running as a banner (or a billboard) above the article's title, is a *horror vacui* depiction of advertising and highway signs, gas pump globes, a hotdog, and a couple of beer bottles—all of them lit from within and floating freely in a hallucinatory haze, as they might appear in the dark after too many miles on the road (see color plate 4).

Most of the photographs that accompanied "The Great American Roadside" were less evocative. Mainly supplied by the Keystone and International News photo agencies, they are straightforward depictions of tourist cottages, wayside motels, and mimetic roadside stands, including Freda Farms, on the Berlin Turnpike in Connecticut, a building shaped like three cartons of ice cream that was subsequently the subject of a widely circulated Russell Lee/Farm Security Administration photograph from 1939. Walker Evans, in his first assignment for *Fortune* and his first pairing with Agee, supplied a view of a small cabin, his tight framing and deep depth of field giving a quiet dignity to the humble structure.[17] More suggestive were the sequential photographs captioned "Along the Great...American...Road." These were clearly intended to illustrate changing infrastructure and wayside development from urban to suburban to rural to unsettled, most strikingly in the contrasting images of a traffic-clogged commercial corridor typifying Main Street, USA and an unpaved double track somewhere in the western desert. Taken together, these images offer a subtle visual response to Agee's most meaningful analysis of the car and the highway.

Carefully woven into the narrative, in between anecdotes about roadside entrepreneurs and their car-driving patrons and calculations of daily expenditures on gas, food, and lodging, was Agee's assessment of the roadside's urbanistic significance. Describing the migratory flow, or more precisely its gravitational pull, along the nation's short-drive and long-haul highways, Agee observed that "the lodestones appear to be set about the periphery." At continental scale, this implied an inexorable movement toward the coasts and abhorrence of the "middle vacuum" of the Midwest; at local and regional scales it implied something very different. As the American automotive "hypnosis" had intensified in the 1920s and the 1930s, distinctions between town and not-town were slowly eroding, and, as Agee perceived, mobility was simultaneously the cause and effect. The result was already discernable as an urbanized form. The roadside, Agee declared, was "a new kind of town," and existing towns had "all but turned themselves into roadsides."[18] Significantly, Agee avoids even a hint of causality here. "The Great American Road" may have been one of his dramatis personae, but there is no mention of road paving, widening, or construction as contributing to the growth of the roadside, much less any consideration of what it meant to have unregulated and unfettered *private* (free market) development along the expanding network of *public* (federally financed) thoroughfares. But then, unlike Chambless or Mumford or MacKaye, Agee is neither critiquing automotive urbanism nor proposing an alternative. Rather, he is analyzing its emerging physical and cultural structures to understand its ongoing contributions to "the American scene"—and in this analysis, as literary critic Jeff Allred has keenly observed, Agee's interpretation moved the road beyond the instrumentalism of a transportation corridor into the territory of the profoundly cultural.[19]

"The Great American Roadside" may not represent "the formal discovery of American highway culture," as some historians have suggested, but Agee's *Fortune* article is significant as one of the earliest analyses to take the roadside on its own terms as "an American institution," with all of the fixity and importance this implied. The *Oxford English Dictionary* defines "institution" as pretty much anything (law, custom, social practice) that serves the needs of a community or "the general ends of civilization," even a civilization founded on the automobile. By midcentury in autopia, the Great American Roadside was, unequivocally, an institution, one whose values, significance, and meaning—to say nothing of form and function—were increasingly deemed worthy of scrutiny. Indeed, at the very end of his *Fortune* article, Agee goes so far as to suggest, with what may be mild facetiousness, that someone ought to write a trilogy "in full homage" to this distinctly American institution. Such a work was destined to become a classic, or at the very least remain relevant, Agee wryly assured his readers, as long as restlessness and mobility remained the American's animating spirits.[20] In fact, work on a trilogy only slightly removed from Agee's suggestion would shortly commence with the unlikely sponsorship of the U.S. government. The Feds, it turned out, did not only finance highway construction; they also financed highway culture.

Highway Routes

In 1935, the U.S. Congress authorized $6.2 million to support the newly created Federal Writers' Project (FWP) of the Works Progress Administration. Over the next eight years, more than four times that amount was spent to employ the 10,000 writers who contributed to the 400 books and pamphlets of the *American Guides,* a monumental New Deal publishing venture that included guides to states and regions, as well as counties, cities, and small towns. Like many of Roosevelt's initiatives, the project was intended to leverage public funds in order to stimulate the economy without impinging on free enterprise and/or the operations of the free market. In this case, the ostensible fiscal goal of the *American Guides,* in addition to getting writers off the dole, was to promote tourism as a way to loosen consumer spending. As was frequently the case with New Deal initiatives, the series' ideological goal was even more ambitious. In Lewis Mumford's view, the *American Guides* were "the first attempt, on a comprehensive scale, to make the country itself worthily known to Americans." In that simple statement Mumford grasped the essence of the series' documentary ambitions—for in making the United States legible and accessible to its citizens, the *American Guides* stood to make a profound contribution, not simply to "American patriotism," as Mumford asserted, but also to American self-representation.[21]

In her 1999 analysis of the series, Christine Bold suggests that the guides were nothing less than "arbiters of public culture," which mapped the nation's local, regional, racial, ethnic, gender, and class identities as compellingly as they mapped its buildings, landscapes, and historic sites. As Bold argues, that mapping amounted to an editorial agenda that conferred "cultural ownership of particular sites, spaces, and places" through the inclusions, exclusions, and hierarchies evident on the pages of every *American Guide,* which were, in turn, rendered authoritative through federal sponsorship of the series.[22] This granting of significance and meaning operated most obviously at the level of guidebook entries and essays, in *which* recognizable landmarks, events, and customs were featured. If, for example, *Idaho: A Guide in Word and Picture* (the first to be published, in January 1937) gave equal textual and photographic coverage to potatoes and craters, whether this resulted from the author's discretion or the mandate of Washington watchdogs, it effectively canonized the state's agriculture and its geology.[23]

In *Washington: City and Capital* (the second guide published, in April 1937), the cultural imprimatur the WPA guide bestowed was more complicated. In sharp contrast to the deliberate racial exclusions that characterized the majority of the *American Guides,* the Washington volume devoted one of its longest overview essays to the past and present of African Americans in the District of Columbia. It would seem that a volume dedicated to presenting "as complete a picture as possible" of the nation's capital could hardly ignore the community that then represented 27 percent of the city's population, which is precisely why Henry Alsberg, FWP's national director, approached poet and critic Sterling Brown, then serving as the FWP's national editor for negro affairs, to write "The Negro in Washington." Brown's essay was as unstinting in its celebration of African American achievements as it was stinging in its condemnation of contemporary injustices, from the squalor of alley dwellings to the indignities of being "jim-crowed" in a city in which "segregation seems an accepted fact." Elsewhere in the guide, selected (and select) black institutions were included in appropriate geographic or thematic sections. As straightforward tokenism this would be problematic enough, but this wasn't tokenism so much as a touristic packaging of African American culture that made places like the U Street Corridor's legendary Howard Theatre (made famous by Duke Ellington, and others) safe for consumption by white Americans.[24] This, after all, is what guidebooks as a literary form do: they package places for touristic consumption, revealing their intrinsic worth by endowing them with easily apprehended extrinsic meaning. In the pages of the *American Guides,* this was as true of Washington's Howard Theatre as it was of Idaho's Crater of the Moon—and it was equally effective in presenting the territories of the automobile as a new kind of modern landmark.

Cars make an appearance in both the Idaho and Washington volumes. In the Idaho guide, along with rock formations and waterfalls, seven highways are included as "major points of interest" because of their engineering. Most of these were state and federal routes cutting through mountainous terrain, like the Galena Summit pass of U.S. 93 in the Boulder Mountains, which today is part of the Sawtooth Scenic Byway.[25] Cars get an early, though negative, mention in the Washington guide when the editors grouse about traffic congestion, claiming the streets are as perilous as those of New York, London, and Paris, and lament that the nation's capital possesses one car for every three people, the highest number per capita in the United States. This "notable curse" was significant enough for the editors to give exact figures for 1935: the District's 210,000 registered cars were daily augmented by between 50,000–75,000 vehicles from Virginia and Maryland or owned by "transient motorists" from other states. In the architecture section, Roderick Seidenberg, FWP art and architecture editor and a friend of Lewis Mumford who shared his progressive ideals, complained bitterly that the city lacked parking facilities adequate to handle all of these cars. He went so far as to blame the McMillan Commission for its lack of foresight where the automobile was concerned (even though its report for the development of the District's monumental core and park system, issued in 1901 and implemented in 1902, was a document of the pre-automotive era). Seidenberg also takes the designers of the Federal Triangle to task for placing a desire for classical grandeur over the traffic realities produced by the "humble vehicles" of federal workers, which should have dictated a decentralized planning scheme. Instead, in what he calls "a pretty revenge," the new government buildings—all raised podiums, extended colonnades, and limestone facades—have become little more than a backdrop for "an encircling string of cars." A photograph of the Federal Triangle showing row after row of cars parked in front of the new post office building seems to underscore this point, but because it appears in the introductory essay, the image's editorial intention is unclear. Several hundred pages later, however, the Washington guide is unambiguous in its attitude toward the car when it provides motor tours along the Rock Creek and Potomac Parkway and the Mount Vernon Memorial Highway, both newly completed at the time of the book's release, with descriptions of each road's scenic features and historic highlights.[26]

Car travel was fundamental to the *American Guides,* both organizationally and conceptually, and nearly every volume in the series that dealt with more than a single locality (i.e., wasn't a city guide; the District of Columbia was an exception) included an extensive section of geographically arranged automobile tours with descriptive entries, precise directions, and mileage. The *American Guides* were hardly the first publications to promote auto-tourism, as oil company pamphlets from the 1920s make clear, but they were certainly among the most comprehensive. Reviewing the series in 1941, just after the publication of the final state volume, Frederick Gutheim described them as anti-Baedekers that were, instead, "guides for the motor age." What this meant as a practical matter was surely clear to Gutheim, an urban planner and American studies professor at Barnard College, who claimed he had driven 15,000 miles with the *American Guides* in hand.[27] This kind of car touring was only possible because of the degree to which the national highway system had filled out with signage and road markers — to say nothing of hardtop — since the first federal designations in 1925. Even in remote and rural Wyoming, the 1941 guide boasted that the "network of oiled highways" made it possible to travel the state's length and breadth in a single day. This meant more than easy touring since, according to the authors, it ended social isolation and introduced modern conveniences. So important was this road network to Wyoming's contemporary identity that the volume's subtitle is "a guide to its history, highways, and people."[28] This attitude was in sync with National Tours Editor Katherine Kellock, who viewed the automobile as a modernizing and unifying force and wanted this reflected in the guides. The emphasis on motor touring in the guides also reflected Kellock's basic assumption of a middle-class audience and basic premise that driving could be an edifying experience, a position mandated by the FWP's national director. When designing motor tours, Henry Alsberg declared, "every effort should be made to make the traveller feel when he is traveling this or that highway that he is covering historic ground."[29] For Alsberg, the road was a conduit, offering efficient passage through, and easy access to, a continuum of history.

There were also instances in the *American Guides* when the road, in effect, became history, usually *by design* in a literal sense. As featured in the Washington guide, the Rock Creek and Potomac Parkway was notable because it embodied the highest achievements of contemporary scenic road building as the technical and aesthetic coordination of engineering, landscaping, and architecture. The Mount Vernon Memorial Highway (MVMH), connecting the District of Columbia and George Washington's family estate in Fairfax County, Virginia, had similar formal

Figure 17. U.S. 1 in the vicinity of Gum Springs, Virginia, south of Alexandria and north of the Mount Vernon Memorial Highway (under construction), 1930. (Historic American Engineering Survey, Library of Congress, Prints and Photographs Division, HAER VA-69)

characteristics. Its real significance, however, lay in its intentional development as an alternative to U.S. 1 and a veritable pilgrimage route and between the nation's capital and the building sometimes described as "the Mecca of America." In the introduction to the Mount Vernon motor tour, *Washington: City and Capital* explicitly contrasted the two roads: with its "scientific" pitches and "cloverleaf" intersections, the MVMH was "the most modern of highways"; with its "blatant signs" and "ugly little buildings," U.S. 1 was "largely commercial and uninteresting."[30] Here, the goal was to explain the recommended route, and justify the avoidance of U.S. 1, at least for a twenty-mile stretch due south of Washington.

Elsewhere, the *American Guides* described U.S. 1 in a similar fashion: for long sections of the 2,300-mile length between Calais, Maine, and Key West, Florida, the road was "depressingly ugly," but U.S. 1 was also "the chief line of communication between centers of the Atlantic Seaboard States." As such, the highway was inextricably linked with "important events" in the history of the nation, from colonial settlement to modern industrialization. A series comprised of what WPA Administrator Harry Hopkins called "written descriptions to the most important sections of the United States" could hardly bypass the historic highway in the guides for the fourteen eastern states through which U.S. 1 passed.[31] But Tours Editor Kellock had something more radical in mind: in 1938, U.S. 1 became an *important section* of the country in its own right when the Federal Writers' Project published the first volume of what would become the *American Guide*'s "Highway Route" trilogy, the only interstate volumes in the entire FWP series.

"Never again, with this book in his car," the *New York Times* opined in its 1938 review of *U.S. One: Maine to Florida,* "will the travelling motorist have any excuse for regarding the road as merely the shortest distance between two points."[32] Katherine Kellock must have appreciated this sentiment since it so clearly summarized her intentions for the highway route books, which, in turn, echoed the position James Agee had articulated in *Fortune* a few years earlier. This reviewer grasped that the highway, as road and roadside, was much more than a transportation corridor: it was embodied history, economic opportunity, and a manifestation of American culture, even as it was a path leading from one place to another. Kellock had specified as much in her highway route editorial guidelines. Anticipating J. B. Jackson's study of *odology* (see chapter 4), she argued that the road should be understood as a narrative that unfolded geographically rather than chronologically, and that the social, cultural, economic, and political histories of towns along specific routes were related to "the history of the route itself and most points of interest are closely related to the main theme"—that is, the highway itself, which the book's cover map makes tangible, despite modest abstraction, as a thin red line cutting across the entirety of the eastern United States.[33]

Evidence in support of this geographic narrative was on every mile of U.S. 1 and every page of *U.S. One,* including sections bookending the guide: a twelve-month listing of annual events along the highway included everything from yacht races in Maine to dog races in Florida, from Yale's commencement to the sounding of the Liberty Bell on New Year's Eve.

Following the volume introduction was a nine-page listing of regional foods organized by state, presenting a literally movable feast from the Canadian border

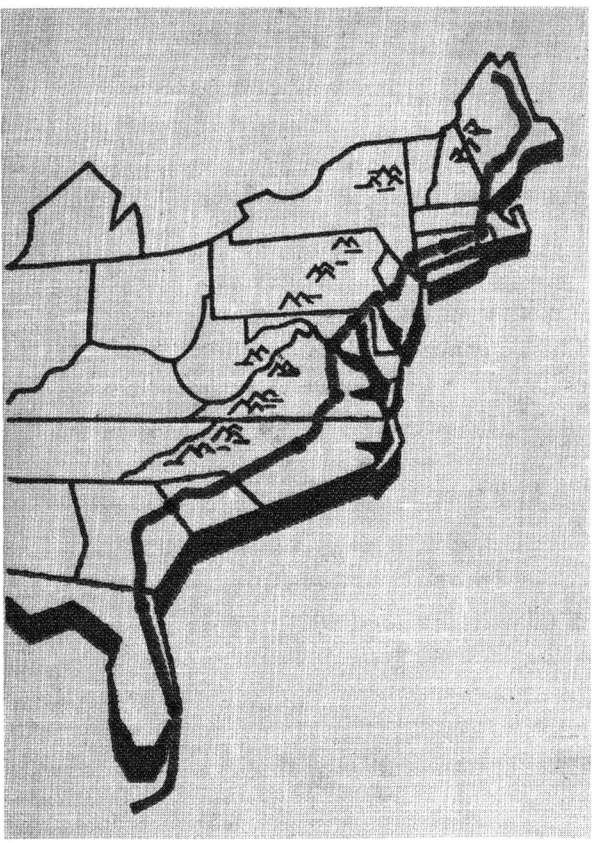

Figure 18. Map depicting route of U.S. 1 from Federal Writers' Project, *U.S. One: Maine to Florida*, 1938.

to the Keys: apple fritters in Maine, lobster rolls in New Hampshire, baked beans in Massachusetts, scrapple in Pennsylvania, soft-shell crabs in Maryland, and so on down the East Coast, ending with, among other state delicacies, boiled peanuts in Georgia and arroz con pollo in Florida. The motorist was encouraged to sample these dishes not merely as on-the-road sustenance, but as an act of cultural preservation, one that was unambiguous in the accompanying text. In an era when, according to the guide, modernization, urbanization, and even women working outside the home had led to the decline of "food standards" and the rise of "quick service" and meals prepared by "mass-production processes" (the first McDonald's would open in 1940), regional specialties were increasingly regarded as "relics of a more leisurely way of life." But since roadside food purveyors would inevitably respond to consumer demand, in seeking out these dishes, the driving/eating public would help spur their revival. In expressly encouraging motorists to cultivate what we would now call *slow food,* the "special foods" section of *U.S. One* reveals an ideology that permeates the entire guide, though rarely so explicitly. If, under Kellock's editorial leadership, the highway guide hoped to teach American motorists how to eat, it also intended to teach them how to see, amounting to a sort of covert manifesto for *slow driving* on a road that *U.S. One* characterized as one of the country's leading "express highway."[34]

Katherine Kellock was educated at Columbia University, where she was exposed to the progressive historiography of Charles Beard; she was employed as a social worker at the Henry Street Settlement, where she was exposed to the progressive reforms of Lillian Wald. Both experiences informed her work as national tours editor for the *American Guides.* In an oft-quoted memo to FWP Director Henry Alsberg, Kellock suggested that Charles and Mary Beard's *The Rise of American Civilization* (1927) be required reading for every writer on the project because it provided "a perspective on what is important and unimportant," and she quoted the Beards' famous opening sentence: "The history of civilization, if intelligently conceived, may be an instrument of civilization." Thus, for Kellock, the Beards offered a rationale for approaching the guidebooks as operative history that would present a usable past to the American public. The guides' "real purpose," she argued, was "to educate Americans to an evaluation of their own civilization."[35] In *U.S. One* that evaluation began the moment those Americans got behind the wheel with the guidebook in hand, and the significance of this point of view in 1938 should not be underestimated. There is a parallel here in the work of Soviet humorists Ilya Ilf and Yevgeny Petrov, who took a series of American road trips in 1935: "America is located on a large automobile highway," they declared in their travelogue's first English edition (1937), in a chapter describing the role of the car in the physical and cultural geography of the United States.[36] They do not foreground the car in the book, but the car was essential to how they framed the country. Katherine Kellock

Figure 19. Ilya Ilf, photograph of highway gas station at unidentified location (probably U.S 30 near Camden, New Jersey) from *Little Golden America*, 1937. (Photograph courtesy of Roma Liberov)

may well have known Ilf and Petrov, as her husband Harold worked in public relations for the Soviet Embassy in Washington during the time of their trip. Even if she didn't, Kellock would have appreciated their nonhierarchical approach to the country. When looking back on their four months touring the United States, Ilf and Petrov claimed that what they remembered most clearly was not Washington's memorials, New York's skyscrapers, or the mountains and canyons of the American West. It was something far less monumental and far more ubiquitous: a highway intersection with "two roads and a gas station against a backdrop of wires and advertising billboards." The scene described here was captured in an Ilya Ilf photograph the authors provided with an ur-Autopia caption: "This right here is America!"[37] That same expansiveness of content is what set the highway route books apart from others in the *American Guide* series.

Throughout the highway route books, major monuments and well-known historic sites are highlighted—the Old North Church, half a dozen state capitols,

battlefields from the Revolutionary and Civil Wars—along with notable locales whose significance was of a decidedly more recent vintage, like the naval submarine base at Groton in Connecticut, the amusement park at Rye Playland in New York, the Resettlement Administration community at Greenbelt in Maryland, and the hard-packed sand speedway at Daytona Beach in Florida. Far more numerous in the guide's mile-by-mile descriptions were the attractions and points of interest in between: a bathing pavilion in Narragansett, Rhode Island; a dance hall outside Baltimore, Maryland; tobacco warehouses in South Hill, Virginia; a mule market near Columbia, Tennessee. While these highlights might be conventionally characterized as minor or everyday, as buildings and places to be noted only in passing, in a three-hundred-page guide to a two-thousand-mile highway, one could reasonably assume that *everything* was to be noted only in passing, glimpsed from a moving car heading north or south on U.S. 1. It is the depth of field that is critical in *U.S. One:* regardless of how fast the motorist might actually travel the highway, at the perceptual level of the guidebook the speed was slow enough to focus on seemingly every element of the roadscape, from the curbside to the horizon. As Frederick Gutheim observed in 1941, the guides were neither "take-you-by-the-hand expeditions" nor "pensive descriptions of the picturesque." Rather, embracing "the brisk, steady fifty mile an hour pace of the modern highway," they presented the breadth of the United States in "short, meaty sentences and tenths of miles."[38]

Nowhere is this pace and perceptual focal length more apparent than in the New Jersey section of *U.S. One.* It begins, ironically, by counseling drivers who "prefer scenery to speed" to take an alternate route (NJ-27) since the 68-mile stretch of U.S. 1 through the Garden State is designed mainly to move "the heavy traffic" flowing between New York and Philadelphia. Despite this admonition, there is plenty of *scenery* described in the eleven pages that follow, but much of it is not the type that would have been considered conventionally scenic in 1930s guidebook terms—the kind Katherine Kellock dismissed as "quaint." Instead, the descriptions of this intensely urbanized stretch of U.S. 1 reflect Kellock's mandate that the *American Guides* include both the "attractive and unattractive" in the American landscape, as well as her expansive parameters of what constituted historical and contemporary significance, particularly her belief, following Charles and Mary Beard, that technological and industrial development was evidence of progress in a modern civilization.[39] Thus, though geological *monuments* are duly noted, including the cliffs of the Palisades along the Hudson and the rock intrusion of Snake Hill in Secaucus (which inspired the Prudential Insurance logo), they fail to inspire *U.S. One*'s authors the way human-altered landscapes do.

When describing the Newark and Hackensack Meadows, although an occasional alighting heron is mentioned, it is the transformation and degradation of the wetlands the guidebook describes in detail, pointing out the trash heaps, coke mounds, incinerator chimneys, and railroad drawbridges as the defining features of the meadowlands "own skyline." The description reads like an industrial pastoral, and becomes positively rhapsodic as U.S. 1 reaches the Pulaski Skyway, the 3.5-mile viaduct (completed in 1932) that rises above the marshy confluence of the Hackensack and Passaic Rivers. The highest point of the elevated roadbed offers panoramic views of the metropolis, some of which are captured in a contemporary view of the Skyway by photographer Marion Post Wolcott. Down below are "great garbage dumps" and hundreds of cars parked "in neat formation" in a factory lot; in the middle ground are the towers of midtown and downtown Manhattan; in the distance, are the headlands of New York harbor—the visual effects of the entire scene intensified by smoky haze and glinting sun. Only one sour note intrudes: the Skyway's parking prohibition makes "use of field glasses impracticable." Drivers would have to continue a few miles south to find respite. There, at Newark Airport, acclaimed as a triumph of land reclamation and financial investment, the guidebook provided directions to a public parking area where "the motorist may watch take-offs and landings at the busiest airport of the Nation." Motorists wishing to enjoy the spectacle at night, when the field was floodlit, were counseled to arrive by 8:30 PM. Nighttime effects were also notable as U.S. 1 passed through Elizabeth, because after dark, the storage tanks of Standard Oil's Bayway Refinery were illuminated with colored lights. Also visible from U.S. 1 in Elizabeth were the Bayonne and Goethals Bridges, which were called out not only as "distinguished engineering," but as works of design comparable "with outstanding architectural monuments"—an attitude almost modernist in its cultural outlook.[40]

However impressive the guide's celebration of New Jersey's industrial landscape,

Figure 20. Marion Post Wolcott, photograph of view from Pulaski Skyway in Jersey City looking east toward American Can Company factory and Manhattan skyline. (Farm Security Administration—Office of War Information Photograph Collection, Library of Congress, Prints and Photographs Division, LC-USF33-031247-M4)

the most significant demonstration of Kellock's faith-in-progress ideology was her conceptualization of the highway as site and content, using U.S. 1 to convey national achievement, past and present. Nearly every page of the New Jersey section offers superlatives about the condition of the road. From the New York state line to the Pennsylvania border, U.S. 1 was a "superhighway . . . paved almost entirely with concrete." After crossing the George Washington Bridge, the highway "twists through a breath-taking series of underpasses and overpasses." On the Pulaski Skyway it becomes a "pioneer achievement" of concrete and steel, one that solved (for a time) the problem of moving 35,000 cars daily through "one of the most congested traffic areas in the world." Farther south in New Jersey, at Woodbridge, it crossed N.J. 4 (today N.J. 35) in a cloverleaf-shaped grade separation the guide notes as the country's "first highway intersection of this type." All this heraldry of modern infrastructure does not mean that road/roadside development was always admired. In the description of the highway just north of the cloverleaf, where U.S. 1 passed through what was still largely farmland, the guide noted that although red barns and dairy cows could still be glimpsed from the road, "the construction of the speed highway" meant they would eventually be crowded out by the "attendant lunch rooms and filling stations" that already lined much of U.S. 1 in the state.[41] This mild critique did nothing to undermine the significance accorded the highway throughout *U.S. One*. Even when there was "little in the landscape to divert the driver's attention," there was always "the long straight path of concrete lying ahead," which the driver might contemplate and evaluate as part of the American civilization.

This is surely what is depicted in "US 1, Stretch of New Jersey," one of thirty photographs Katherine Kellock selected to illustrate *U.S. One*. Most of the book's illustrations are recognizable as touristic attractions on or near the highway, whether they are scenically, historically, architecturally, or technologically significant: the Okefenokee Swamp, Philadelphia City Hall, and Greenbelt, Maryland, for example. There are also views of the Bayonne and George Washington Bridges, as well as another roadway, the Hutchinson River Parkway in Westchester County, New York. This photograph shows the parkway not where it crosses over U.S. 1, but farther inland where the right-of-way passes through a county park. The image frames the gently curving road with the lushness of the Hutchinson's Gilmore

Figure 21. Hutchinson River Parkway, Saxon Woods, New York, from Federal Writers' Project, *U.S. One: Maine to Florida,* 1938.

Clarke–designed landscape: flowering trees in the foreground, a thick canopy of trees in the background, light opposing traffic in the middle distance.

"US 1, Stretch of New Jersey" is of another order entirely. Four lanes of hardtop stretch to the horizon, two on each side of a painted median, punctuated by telephone poles, a few signs (advertising tourist cabins), and indistinguishable roadside buildings in the distance. The vantage point is neither elevated (from an overpass) nor oblique (from the right-of-way); rather, it is an uninterrupted, almost wide-angle view of U.S. 1 framed by a windshield from inside what is presumably a moving automobile. Photographs shot inside-to-outside using the car windshield as a framing device appear frequently in the 1950s and 1960s (see color plate 2), but they were unusual in the 1930s, even though one of Roy Stryker's "shooting scripts" for photographers employed by the Farm Security Administration included a call for "pictures taken through wind-shield 'from the place the driver sees the road.'"[42]

Figure 22. U.S. 1 in New Jersey, from Federal Writers' Project, *U.S. One: Maine to Florida*, 1938.

That is precisely what is depicted in "US 1, Stretch of New Jersey." Though the driver's torso is cropped from the frame, the driver's right hand prominently grips the steering wheel, not only directing us toward the highway, but aligning us explicitly with the visual perspective of the motorist.

The significance of this perspective is clear when the New Jersey picture is compared with more typical New Deal highway photographs, such as those produced under the auspices of Roy Stryker's Farm Security Administration (FSA), which Rexford Tugwell famously charged with introducing "Americans to America" in a pictorial equivalent to the *American Guides*. Dorothea Lange's view of U.S. 70 in New Mexico and Arthur Rothstein's view of U.S. 40 in Nevada are two examples. Without the frame of the windshield and the car interior, without any automotive reference beyond the blacktop itself, big sky dominates scenes that evoke continental vastness more than human occupation. Some of this emptiness stems from

Figure 23. Dorothea Lange, photograph of New Mexico Desert, Highway Number 70 (U.S. 70), 1938. (Farm Security Administration—Office of War Information Photograph Collection, Library of Congress, Prints and Photographs Division, LC-USF34-018272-C)

Figure 24. Arthur Rothstein, photograph of Lincoln Highway (U.S. 40) approaching Paradise, Pennsylvania, 1941. (Farm Security Administration—Office of War Information Photograph Collection, Library of Congress, Prints and Photographs Division, LC-USF34-024502-D)

the lonely American West landscapes being depicted, an effect heightened by the middle-of-the-road vantage point. But even in photographs of highways running through more settled and populous regions of the country, like Rothstein's view of the Lincoln Highway in eastern Pennsylvania, shot from the shoulder of the road, there is no attempt to privilege the car or the motorist, as occurs in the New Jersey picture.[43]

Though Rothstein, along with his FSA colleague Lincoln Highton, contributed several photographs to *U.S. One,* "US 1, Stretch of New Jersey" is uncredited. Regardless of the photographer's identity, he or she produced one of the most distinctive illustrations to appear in the highway route books or *American Guide* series as a whole. "Stretch of New Jersey" makes it clear that U.S. 1, the highway, was the locus, subject, and object of *U.S. One,* the guidebook, and it reinforced a critical aspect of the highway route volumes in particular and the *American Guides* in general: driving had become a way of knowing, and the highway had become a habitat. The former implied the array of visual and even haptic perceptions that autopian Americans might activate; the latter embraced the continental dispersion of the species' natural range.

America is Big

A *Life* magazine feature that appeared in July 1938, a few months after the publication of the *American Guide*'s first highway route volume, when more than a dozen state and city books were already in print, gave credence to these positions. At first glance "America: Millions of People Set Out to See Their Country" appears as little more than a celebratory photo essay promoting summer tourism with color photographs of man-made and natural landmarks like the Taos Pueblo, Mount Rushmore, the Catalina Casino, and the Grand Canyon. But these pictures are accompanied by five distinctive maps that offer a more complex view of the country, one clearly in sync with the mandates of Katherine Kellock and the Federal Writers' Project. This may be obvious in retrospect, but it was unstated at the time: given that Henry Luce, *Life*'s publisher, famously disliked the New Deal and distrusted its programs, he was not likely to promote New Deal guidebooks in his magazine. But their influence is unmistakable on the maps. The first depicts the United States in topographic relief with arrow-cum–dotted lines indicating the flow of summer travel along what would be the major federal highways if these were shown on the map. The other four maps are regional—Far West, Rockies and the Plains, Midwest, East Coast (plus Ohio)—suggesting "what to see in America." These suggestions are provided graphically and textually, and in both cases seem to borrow heavily from the *American Guides* when recommending regional foods; noting flora, fauna, and celebrity; and highlighting monuments both major, minor, and oddball. Highways are invisible in these regional maps as well, with the representations of the monuments floating freely in the blank field inscribed within state lines. What the maps suppressed for graphic legibility, the text rendered explicit when explaining the nation's ritualistic summertime wandering: "With his roads and automobiles the modern American is the world's most mobile man."[44]

Figure 25. "And Here Is New England, the Seaboard, the South," from *Life*, 27 June 1938. (General Drafting Company map copyright © Kappa Map Group LLC, [800] 829-6277; used with permission)

Here, *Life*'s editors could easily have been quoting Frank Lloyd Wright, who had trumpeted mobility as a core American value since at least 1930 and had embraced it as a key motivation of his "new community plan" for Broadacre City. Wright proclaimed that the "gift" of the motorcar had already brought about the "general mobilization of the human being." When coupled with telecommunications (i.e., the radio and the telephone), the result was unmistakable: "The horizon of the individual has immeasurably widened." Translated into Broadacre City, Wright created an urban morphology defined by its horizontality and its expanse: "The horizontal line of the machine age indefinitely extended as the greatest architectural highway . . . the flat plane of the machine age expanded into the free acreage . . . of the free democracy."[45] By the 1930s, such horizontality and expanse were increasingly legible in the American landscape. Wright's Broadacre City was built, as a literal model and a conceptual framework, upon the national grid established by Jefferson's Land Ordinance of 1785, implemented in subsequent years through the six-square-mile townships, platted using the Public Land Survey System, which were discernable on any map of the territory west of Pennsylvania. At the same time, however, he had clearly absorbed the new sense of scale brought about by the new experiential modes that accompanied the mid-twentieth-century normalization of accelerated transcontinental travel by air and highway. Wright would probably have agreed with *Life*'s observation, in that same July 1938 travel guide, that air travel was teaching Americans to understand "another sort of geography—the cosmic kind."[46] By plane, at 200 miles per hour, you could grasp the entirety of the continental expanse, all 2 billion acres, especially in the checkerboard townships of what was already becoming fly-over America. By car, at 40 or 50 miles per hour (what you'd expect from a 4- or 5-cylinder car in the 1930s), you could experience the country's extensiveness at local and national scales: on one- and two-lane farm-to-market roads; on rural and arterial highways that followed the survey lines in a way the railroad never did; on 4-lane trunk-lines and through-routes that formed the federal coast-to-coast network featured in the *American Guides* series and in *Life*'s own summer itineraries.

If, for Wright, the highways were not yet "great architecture," three million miles of American roads clearly added up to something: these "facilities for lateral movement"—of which, he claimed, Americans were rightly proud—offered the possibility of "a new freedom for living in America" in which "democratic values" in society and aesthetic values or "quality" in buildings, landscapes, and infrastructure were the rule and not the exception.[47] While what existed was far from perfect—with its telephone poles, billboards, gas stations, strips, and miscellaneous effluvia—its promise, for Wright, lay in the basic reality that brought the autopia into being: there were twenty-three million cars in the United States, and one in five Americans already had "machine in hand." As such, the citizen-in-car became, in Wright's view, a unified vehicle for producing profound urban transformation: "After all he himself is the city. The city is going where he goes and as he goes." Through this "ubiquitous mobilization," in which the mile-by-car had replaced the block-by-foot as a new measure of urban space and time, the city was spreading out "far away and thin" with an astonishing result: "the city is nowhere or it is everywhere." Wright was insistent in stating his preference for what amounted to a roadside metropolis at continental scale, an urbanized landscape characterized by "integration over the whole surface of the nation."[48] His claim that this ideal was also practical was tenable only because of the sheer physical size of the United States, a fact *Life*'s editors stated with a simplicity that generally eluded Wright: "America: It Is Big."[49]

Though he pointedly avoided mentioning it in his 1947 assessment of the state of the nation, the country's bigness was not lost on American journalist John Gunther when he returned to the United States in 1943 after many years as a foreign and war correspondent. By then, Gunther was already the best-selling author of *Inside Europe* (1936) and its two successors, *Inside Asia* (1939) and *Inside Latin America* (1941), books that profiled the contemporary scene through lucid impressions of people, places, and, especially, politics. Having long contemplated applying the "inside" formula to his native land, Gunther threw himself into preparations for what would become a thirteen-month tour of the United States. In addition to contacting politicians, business people, and labor leaders across the country, Gunther spent a fair amount of time consulting the *American Guides,* and when he finally left New York in the summer of 1944 his suitcase was full of them. Though he quotes the series more than a dozen times throughout the book, it is difficult to parse the impact the *Guides* might have had on the conclusions Gunther put forth in *Inside U.S.A.,* which Arthur Schlesinger Jr. saw more as "vivid and acute reportage" than "profound analysis" in the manner of Alexis de Tocqueville.[50] They clearly informed Gunther's logistics, and, aside from obvious differences of content, one of the significant ways that the United States volume departs from the model of his other *Inside* books is the inclusion of a two-page map illustrating Gunther's road trips along large portions of such major federal highways as U.S. 1 and U.S. 101, on the East and West Coasts, and U.S. 30, 40, 70, 80, and 66 connecting the coasts and points in between. And while Gunther mentions taking airplanes, throughout *Inside U.S.A.*'s 900-plus pages it is car travel that is most essential.

Though Gunther calls the Merritt Parkway in Connecticut the most spectacular road he has ever driven, in general he avoids car-oriented superlatives in favor of meaningful description. Out west, on U.S. 40 in Colorado, "[Gunther] drove into Denver along the sharp steel-blue curtain of the divide," as U.S. 40 swept from the high plains toward the foothills of the Rockies. Back east, Gunther suggests that while taking a train from New York to Philadelphia might convey the industrial basis of "the American civilization," it was better to go by car because getting "lost driving in the Newark–Jersey City area, underneath the Pulaski Skyway" offered a firsthand experience of the place where "the fangs of industry really bite." Driving, then, was more than a means of navigation; for Gunther it functioned as a cultural touchstone for comprehending the autopian impulses of the country in the mid-1940s: "The United States is, as is notorious, a nation on wheels." That notoriety expressed itself almost clinically in the state-by-state data that Gunther selected for the charts that precede his text. Alongside statistics on population, income, rural households with telephones, and lynchings since 1882, Gunther included automobile registrations and automobile deaths for every state. The latter were placed next to each state's total of residents killed during World War II, presumably to emphasize the difference between what would have been understood as meaningful and meaningless deaths in a country whose citizens were "crazy about automobiles."[51]

The impact of the car appears in more poetic terms elsewhere and everywhere in *Inside U.S.A.* Thus, for example, Gunther asserts that in the United States good roads are part of "the essential landscape" of the country to the same degree as "bread or baseball." He also takes pains to describe "the concomitants" of the country's automotive orientation, evident in American individualism and isolationism, and, especially, in its giantism and nomadism (which also interested Wright). Gunther probes these in obvious ways, as they are manifest, for example, in the twin mania for road building and long-distance car travel. He notes how, particularly in the American West, these intertwined with unexpected results. Though the car and the highway assisted in "reducing distances" between far-flung western communities, they also "helped kill the old frontier," creating ghost towns in places like Nevada and Wyoming where Gunther observed that "the dependence on the automobile is of course enormous." In the Cowboy State, this car dependence was manifest most notably in per capita car ownership (the highest in the country) and in the fact that it was perfectly legal to drive in Wyoming without a license. In California, two decades ahead of Reyner Banham, Gunther offered an astute analysis of Los Angeles's decentralized and polycentric metropolitan form. There was no point comparing it negatively to San Francisco when their urban values were so profoundly different. So while he quotes epithets hurled at the city by the likes of Aldous Huxley and Frank Lloyd Wright (despite the latter's stated preference for the spreading city), Gunther argued that Angelenos, whom he calls "by all odds the most automobile conscious in the world," valued growth and mobility (along with their climate and their water), and that these were the factors propelling "the spreading out of the city." This, he proposed, had an important and largely overlooked consequence: because of "its monstrous size" Los Angeles was now dependent on "public highways" rather than private railways. As a result, its population had become "planning conscious and social minded"—at least as related to their desire and ability to move from one place to another.[52]

These observations about Southern California come in the early pages of *Inside U.S.A.,* but Gunther returns to themes of mobility, connectivity, and nomadism throughout the book, ultimately suggesting something fundamental about what he recognizes as an extant condition of American urbanism. While not denying the significance of outward migration from city to suburb to country, Gunther also interprets shifting populations to embody inter-urban migration, from one city to another city and from city to someplace-that-would-eventually-become-a-city-even-if-it-was-little-more-than-a-town-at-present. In his nuanced reading, American *nomadism* was not reduced to the centrifugal movement of migrating Americans, but was reified as "one of the chief centripetal forces, like chain stores and comic strips, that binds the United States into a country."[53] If Gunther leaves the automobile and the highway off that short list, it is not because he doesn't think they are as nationally binding as Woolworth's and *Dick Tracy,* but because their essential role in fostering the midcentury manifestation of what he calls our "national foot-looseness" was utterly self-evident, as even a cursory glance at a U.S. road map of the 1940s would have made clear.

Highway Cross Section

University of California, Berkeley, English professor George Rippey Stewart spent plenty of time looking at road maps in the 1940s. Best known as the man who gave tropical storms personal names, Stewart was an eminent toponymist whose now classic history of U.S. place names was published in 1945. In *Names on the Land,* Stewart offered an explanation of how some names came to "stand large on the maps" while others disappeared entirely. Though studying maps was critical to that project, no matter how detailed the maps were, their two-dimensional planarity could only hint at what the names, in Stewart's compelling narrative, actually revealed: the customs of the country in all their variety "of time and place, of blood and language."[54] Stewart confronted the limitations of the map-as-plan most directly in his next major work of nonfiction, a book whose novel subject attracted attention upon its 1953 publication, but sank into semi-obscurity in the following years. *U.S. 40: Cross Section of the United States of America* was a detailed pictorial and textual account of driving the 3,091-mile length of U.S. 40 from Atlantic City to San Francisco. For a number of years Stewart had contemplated producing what he called a "picture book" focused on federal forests or national parks. According to his biographer, it was Stewart's close friend, the novelist and environmentalist Wallace Stegner, who thought that a highway, U.S. 40 in particular, would be a much better subject for the extended photo essay with detailed captions that Stewart had in mind. Stegner was confident that Stewart could produce "something special" rather than, in a mild jab at the *American Guides,* "just another regional-folkways-geographical job." For Stegner, this was more than an idle suggestion since he had just become an editor at Houghton-Mifflin, which offered Stewart a hefty advance to begin working on *U.S. 40.*[55]

Unlike Katherine Kellock, who directed her *Highway Route* contributors to drive cross-country as guidebook documentarians in the service of motor tourists and armchair travelers, or John Gunther, who drove cross-country as a transportation means to a journalistic end, George Stewart drove cross-country in pursuit of "the basic structure of the continent itself." For Stewart, U.S. 40 was his means and his end: "Primarily and always, my subject has been the highway." Stewart's travels from New Jersey to California and back in the spring of 1949 and the summer of 1950 were a form of research, but the results of this research—the information Stewart gathered as he passed through fourteen states, one hundred five counties, hundreds of small towns, and eight of the country's most populous cities—could not be captured in plan, as a line on a map. Proper presentation of his findings required "cross-section." Stewart's cross-section was far more than the subtitle of the book; it was a guiding methodology. In the social sciences, a cross-sectional study is an observational one that seeks to make comparisons at a single point in time in order to produce what is frequently described as a snapshot of current conditions. This is precisely how Stewart described his own U.S. 40 project, calling it "a presentation, with the aid of photographs, of [the highway's] existing reality."[56] Stewart's book, then, was literally a snapshot of the highway circa 1950 and in this respect his was decidedly not a guidebook, despite the *New Yorker* dismissing it as a "pretentious" example of the genre. Rather, Stewart *used* guidebooks, the *American Guides* in particular, as a source for reliable information to include in the descriptions that accompanied his photographs. Still, the *New Yorker* was onto something when it argued that the reason Stewart had "inevitably" failed "to catch a likeness of the famous highway" was that U.S. 40 (or any highway for that matter) was "not an entity but merely a reflection of the regions through which it passes."[57] In denying the highway what might be called its ontological significance, the *New Yorker,* for all its literary sophistication, displayed profound conservatism with respect to this most basic territory of the automobile.

By 1953, when Stewart's *U.S. 40* appeared, the idea of highway-as-entity was not new, but neither was it widespread. Back in 1903, historian and poet Hilaire Belloc had identified "The Road" as a "primal thing," as fundamental to human need and desire as fire and shelter. That assessment came in Belloc's introduction to *The Old Road,* a physical and theoretical exploration of the 120-mile highway that served as a pilgrimage route connecting Winchester and Canterbury through the English Downs. When he expanded this study two decades later, Belloc argued that roads were so "fundamental to social existence" that they existed as "one of the great human institutions."[58] In 1950 architect and educator Jean Labatut reframed Belloc's institutionalization for the automotive age when he cited *The Road* in the introduction to *Highways in Our National Life,* the published proceedings of a conference he organized at Princeton University. Labatut joined Princeton's architecture faculty in 1927 and spent the intervening years developing an innovative pedagogy that sought to synthesize Beaux-Arts design principles with the realities of modern life, an approach would exert a profound influence on Robert Venturi, who was a student at Princeton during Labatut's tenure. Labatut drew parallels, for example, between the Beaux-Arts *marche* and contemporary traffic circulation, seeing both as forms of experiential and immersive movement. As Jorge Otero-Pailos has shown, Labatut's long-standing interest in mobility in the built environment led him to investigate not only how architecture and urbanism interacted with the automobile, but how they might be productively informed by it as well.[59] Labatut broadened this scope of inquiry in 1941 when he founded Princeton's Bureau for Urban Research to foster interdisciplinary scholarship and data collection on a wide array of topics related to urban studies and the so-called problems of cities as they existed at the time and in preparation for postwar developments.[60] That Labatut's Bureau regarded the car as an important dimension of the "different activities involved in urbanism" surely informed the bureau's decision to use a photograph of a Midtown Manhattan traffic jam to accompany an explanation of its work.[61] Traffic figured prominently in one of the bureau's first projects, a pilot study of public opinion and urban planning conducted in a small industrial town, where congestion, scarcity of parking, and the need for street improvements topped the list of local perceptions of current urban problems, regardless of whether or not respondents owned cars.[62]

The car's broad urban significance becomes even more explicit in *Highways in Our National Life,* with Labatut calling the automobile "the most influential nationalizing force in American society" and citing the 368 billion miles that Americans drove each year over 1.5 million miles of surfaced roads as baseline data.[63] For the symposium Labatut brought together four dozen specialists to consider the highway in historical and contemporary perspectives. Included were anthropologists, sociologists, economists, and historians; architects, landscape architects, and planners; highway and civil engineers, traffic safety consultants, and lawyers; and state and local commissioners, auto industry executives, and real estate experts—all of them offering what was, for the time, a comprehensive discussion of the highway's impact on human progress and its development from prehistoric footpaths to modern parkways. Though contributors ranged across epochs and continents, from the trade routes of the ancient Near East to Mayan sacred ways in the Yucatan, most of the book dealt with the urban, social, infrastructural, aesthetic, and economic consequences of highways in the United States in the middle of the twentieth century. This focus helps explain why Labatut's volume was reviewed so widely, and generally positively, upon its publication in 1950, not only in academic journals but even in the *New York Times.* Writing in the paper's book review when he was at the height of his road-building and slum-clearance powers, Robert Moses called the volume "a first-rate compilation to be thumbed through by the intelligent layman"—someone like George Rippey Stewart, who used *Highways in Our National Life* as his "general introduction to the whole subject" while he was working on *U.S. 40.*[64]

Highways in Our National Life influenced Stewart's approach to U.S. 40 in a number of ways, beginning, most obviously, with the cross-sectional methodology he derived, in spirit if not in letter, from essays like "The Highway and the Anthropologist" and "The Highway from the Point of View of a Sociologist." Anthropologist John Brew, then director of Harvard's Peabody Museum, proposed that roads be analyzed and interpreted from two distinct perspectives: as something conditioned by the culture, with respect to materials, layout, tools and technologies; and as something that effects the culture that it serves, with manifestations that Brew identified as historical, sociological, and psychological. He brings this into the present by offering an optimistic assessment of the highway in contemporary culture: "The Road is an instrument of democracy" vivified by both "the machines and the ideas" that travel on it.[65] The sociologists in Labatut's symposium offered insights that Stewart easily assimilated into his U.S. 40 analysis. Dartmouth sociologist Francis Merrill used the common perception of the highway as a "symbol of American mobility" as a starting point for examining how the automobile was shaping new social behaviors and dissolving established social patterns. For Merrill, automotive mobility was, literally, a vehicle of social mobility, from the *Grapes of Wrath*'s Joads to bank robbers Bonnie Parker and Clyde Barrow to joy-riding youths, and from wartime farm-to-factory migrations to postwar suburbanization spurred by the housing shortage that confronted returning veterans. For Merrill, tensions between the opportunities automotive mobility offered and the problems it engendered were inevitable, but in a country in which individual freedom had become inextricably linked to its status as "a nation on wheels," Merrill was pretty sure the scales would tip in favor of the "automobile-highway complex."[66]

Carle Zimmerman, who taught interdisciplinary "social relations" at Harvard, briefly examined "foot path" and "post road" societies before turning to an analysis of the "highway" society, the most recent societal type to emerge and, according to Zimmerman, the least understood. The United States was "the most typological manifestation" of a highway society even if, circa 1950, its highway system was still awaiting "perfection" and its highway "civilization" was still in formation. It was, nonetheless, sufficiently mature for Zimmerman to describe a society in which "the highway is partly cause, partly effect, and at all times a facilitating agent." In all three societal types, roads functioned like the blood vessels of living organism, "circulating the social blood" (of people and goods). In the United States, federal and main trunk routes, like U.S. 40, were "like the great arteries and veins leading directly from the smaller organic systems to the heart." In the highway society as a whole, this circulation system was so extensive, and its capacity for intercommunication so great, that it was utterly transformative: in physical terms, it produced more standardized and "semi-urbanized" patterns, not only on the coasts, but in the interior as well; in social terms, it caused the local to become regional and the regional to become national. The cumulative effect of this shift was the diffusion of "common systems of social values" that would ultimately, Zimmerman argued, give a new and mobilized meaning to the motto "e pluribus unum."[67]

Sociologists from the University of Texas and Michigan State University made the same observations about causation between the automobile and the highway and the increasing homogeneity of values, ideals, and standards in the United States, but they analyzed midcentury settlement patterns and land use to prove their point. For these authors, the mobilization brought about by the car/highway nexus had upended traditional geographic, social, and hierarchical relationships between what they called *field* and *center,* meaning the hinterland or periphery and the city or town, leading to the gradual obliteration of distinctions between them. Though their identification of the car as a "free agent" effectively contrasts its vehicular-to-route nimbleness with the mainline fixity of the railroad, it denies the reality of the roadway system as an infrastructure requiring enormous investments in financial and human capital. This point notwithstanding, George Stewart's on-the-road observations would soon verify their concluding analysis that the car and the highway had produced nothing less than "the fusion of urban and rural." Coming in 1950, this is a stunningly early recognition of autopia's broad significance—and the same can be said for most of the contributions to *Highways in Our National Life.*

Labatut himself was critical of what he saw as the disparity between "content and container," between the automobile and the highway in terms of technology, safety, and aesthetics, and he noted the absurdity and danger of driving high-horsepower vehicles on roads originally designed for horses. At the same time, Labatut was unstinting in praising modern motorways as designed environments that combined architecture, landscaping, and engineering to great effect. Though, in 1950, these were "too rare and too far apart" for Labatut's liking, they were, nonetheless, "among the greatest monuments of our time." Lest such monuments be regarded as too distant from the everyday realities of *our national life,* Labatut stated unequivocally that highways were "an integral part of the physical, intellectual, and emotional human trail," a summation that applies equally to George Stewart's interpretation of U.S. 40.[68]

Nowhere is the highway-as-trail more obvious than in the cartography Stewart included in *U.S. 40*. This was not the book's primary visual material, but it enhanced the cross-sectional conceit he derived from Labatut and his contributing authors, beginning with the book's endpapers, drawn by Erwin Raisz, a professor and curator at Harvard when he collaborated with Stewart. Raisz pioneered a type of hand-rendered physiographic representation using patterns and shading to depict landforms like plains, plateaus, mountains, and canyons in topographic perspective. For Stewart's endpapers, Raisz drew a dazzling two-page landform map showing the highway's entire length with a coast-to-coast cross section that revealed the continent's geological strata and periods beneath its landforms. Above the landform map was a band of vignettes depicting a vanished world of log forts and sod houses, of stagecoaches, Conestoga wagons, and steamboats, each rendered obsolete by the railroad long before the dawn of the automotive age. While the historicity gives these images a faintly nostalgic air, it also suggests a keen awareness of the successive infrastructures of continental transport on which Stewart's car-oriented midcentury analysis depended. Beneath the landform map were two additional cross sections showing altitudes and annual rainfall from the Atlantic to the Pacific. While these could be seen as visualizations of neutral data, they were in sync with Stewart's analysis since the effects of weather and road elevation were an important dimension of the work.

The same can be said of the other landform maps that Raisz prepared for *U.S. 40*, each one keyed to the ten geographic or regional sections of the highway that guided Stewart's journey. Each map and section is bounded by state lines, natural borders like rivers and mountains, important cities or, when appropriate, the start and end points of historic roads. Here, Raisz's topographic perspectives are particularly effective, as they allow the reader to comprehend the highway's path, and Stewart's journey across bridges and through town centers, skirting foothills, and climbing peaks. Place names, geological formations, and occasional points of interest are all highlighted on the maps, but far more important are the numbers keyed to the stops that Stewart made along U.S. 40.

Each stop on Stewart's journey, ninety-two in total, is represented by a narrative description and one of the author's own photographs. Stewart shot these photographs mainly from the side of the road, occasionally from an overpass, bridge, or

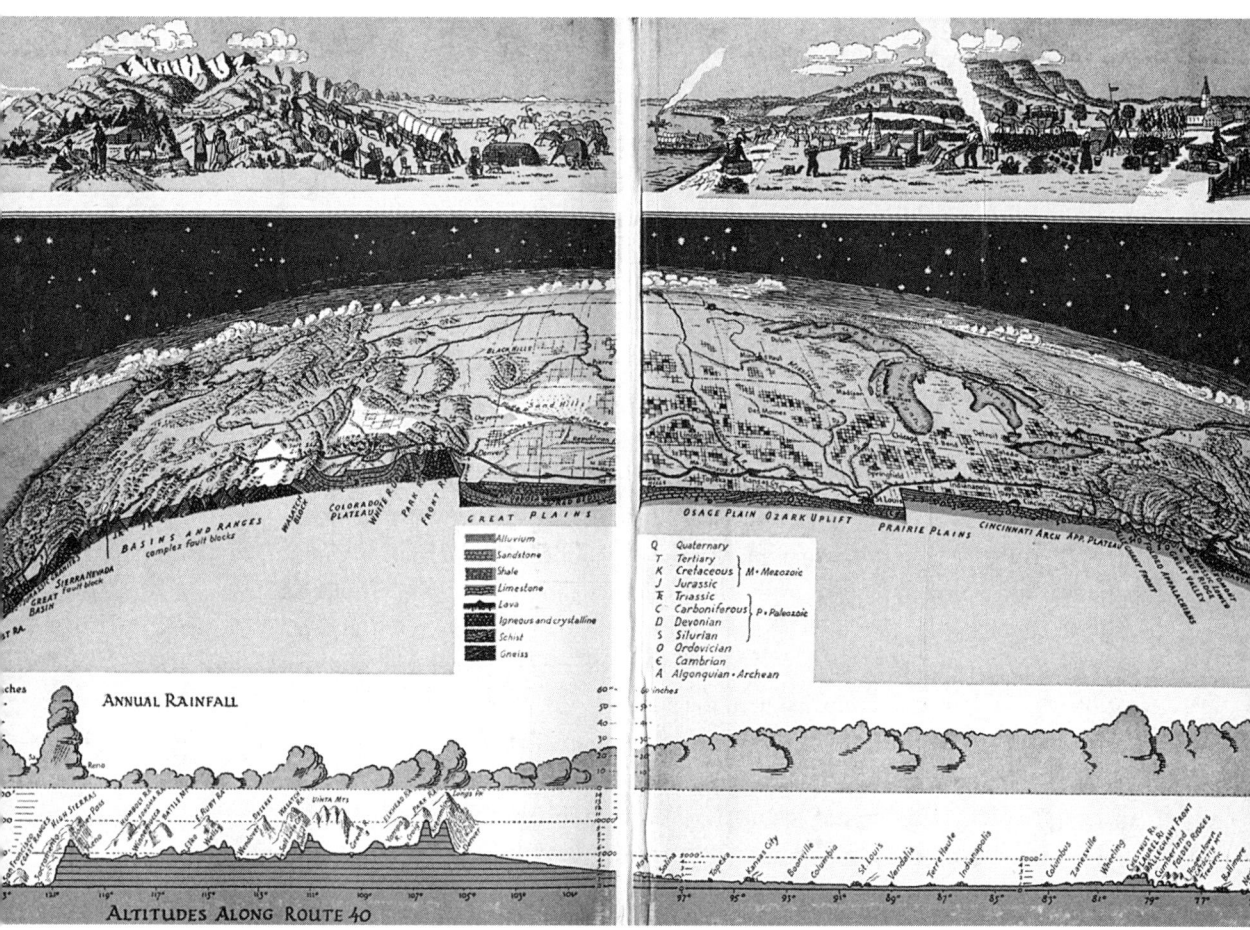

Figure 26. Erwin Raisz, landform maps used as endpapers in George Rippey Stewart's *U.S. 40: Cross Section of the United States*, 1953. (Permission courtesy of Raisz Landform Maps)

some other elevated point (a fire tower in New Jersey; a water tower in Missouri, a grain elevator in Kansas), and sometimes from what appears to be the driver's perspective, though steering wheels and windshields never appear in the frame. Each image presents a different stretch of the highway, and taken together they present a unified portrait of "a continuous strip of pavement that bisects a country." That simple description, from the book's dust jacket, belies the ambition of

Stewart's cross section. Like anthropologist John Brew, Stewart proposed a "two-way" analysis that dealt with the U.S. 40 as a *highway* and a *route,* as object and culture. His highway analysis posited the road as straightforward infrastructure, "a physical thing in space" expressed in terms of materials, dimensions, and course. Many of the stops on Stewart's descriptive itinerary present the diverse features of U.S. 40's highway morphology, its straightaways contrasting with its mountain passes (though the Rockies, Wasatch, and Sierras) and water crossings (notably the Mississippi River and San Francisco Bay), its raw cuts distinguished from its carefully sloped shoulders, its newest concrete and asphalt roadbeds juxtaposed with its older bituminous and brick surfaces. Stewart is particularly effusive when the road is "in full glory" as "a highly developed modern highway." As Stewart describes the details of double roadways and four- and six-lane stretches, neither oil stains nor scattered trash cans diminish his enthusiasm for a highway that "presents no flaws" along its most recently completed sections.[69]

Stewart's *route* analysis of U.S. 40 was more complex. Though route implied the expression of "distance and direction," it was more "in the nature of an abstraction," expressive of "an almost ineffable continuity, in time as well as in space." As Stewart recounts in two historical chapters that rely heavily on *Highways in Our National Life,* continuity in time stretched from the highway's early-nineteenth-century past, as a successor to the National Road authorized by Thomas Jefferson in 1806, to its mid-twentieth-century present as a federally designated roadway. In 1950 it is a "business-like modern highway" unimpeded, but for a few traffic lights and toll-bridges, in its direct line from the Atlantic to the Pacific, hugging the 40th parallel for much of its way. The efficiency of U.S. 40's path was, of course, directly related to the highway's embodiment of continuity in space along a line, as Stewart catalogues it, that sometimes followed the railroad, sometimes the emigrant trail, and sometimes was "wholly of the automobile period," thus linking the highway again to time. State lines flash by without the motorist realizing they've been crossed; truck routes, city routes, and alternate routes flow into one another from coast to coast. Unlike his highway analysis, Stewart's route analysis is largely perceptual as he attempts to convey what U.S. 40 "means to the man who drives along it." To organize his driving perceptions, Stewart establishes a three-part classification scheme, evident in the photographs and the descriptions, for sections of U.S. 40 when (1) the highway dominates the roadside, (2) the roadside dominates the highway, and (3) the highway and roadside are balanced or equal. Stewart's photographs of a six-lane "parkway" roadbed near New Castle, Delaware, and a congested intersection in the heart of Kansas City, Missouri, make the first two categories clear. Though Stewart conceded that parkways were beautiful, with their landscaped medians and rights-of-way, he objected to their artificiality; parkways were *dominating* highways that prevented the driver from seeing "the real United States of America."[70] On *dominated* highways, by contrast, there was almost too much of the real USA, as a street wall of buildings, a heavy flow of traffic, and parked cars crowded into the roadway.

Figure 27. "Equal highway": U.S. 40 in Funkstown, Maryland, from *U.S. 40: Cross Section of the United States,*1953. (Copyright © 1953 by George R. Stewart, renewed 1981 by Theodosia B. Stewart; reprinted by permission of Houghton Mifflin Harcourt Publishing Company; all rights reserved)

Stewart preferred the "equal highway" in which the driver perceived the road, the roadside, and the surrounding landscape as intimate and integrated. On an *equal* highway, the motorist's attention, interest, and focus were in happy flux across a roadscape continuum. Just west of Funkstown, Maryland, where U.S. 40 crosses Antietam Creek on a National Road bridge that dated to 1823 and survived Civil War skirmishes, Stewart observes visual balance in the historic architecture, the surrounding woods, and the power and telephone lines, which Stewart accepts as a "basic part of the American landscape." Only the billboards threaten the equilibrium because they assert themselves too aggressively into the viewer's consciousness. It is the size of the billboards to which Stewart objects: they are too big to "assimilate" completely into his cross section. His preference is for smaller billboards and signs, especially those advertising local businesses. These, Stewart argues, have a "certain rooting in the soil" that justifies their presence, while their more modest scale (when compared to the larger billboards) renders them "comparatively harmonious to the setting." Whether the stretch of U.S. 40 was dominated, dominating, or balanced, Stewart described his progression through the highway continuum as a "kinesthetic" experience. Driving across the country at the "speed of the modern automobile" produced a series of bodily sensations, from the exhilaration of acceleration to the reassurance of a whirring engine, from the irritation of rushing headlights to the anxiety of squealing tires.[71] Stewart doesn't explore the implications of this experience, but it anticipates the way designers in the 1960s began to reconceptualize highway driving as a way to improve the built environment (see chapter 4).

No less significant for Stewart than automotive kinesthesis were the "sobering" intellectual impressions the highway made upon the motorist. While he acknowledged that U.S. 40 passed through stretches of uninhabited desert and mountain that were staggering in their scenic beauty, these paled in comparison to the man-made environments that dominated the highway from New Jersey to California, "mile after mile, hundred mile after hundred mile." In an evocative illustration of the sociological contention of the country's ongoing urban-rural fusion, Stewart documented farm fields and oil fields, fine churches and houses, slums and skyscrapers, bridges and billboards, power lines and rusting beer cans, manufacturing plants and junkyards, shoestring towns and large cities. Though this urbanizing corridor became "gradually overpowering as one looks at it along both sides of the highway," it was also evidence to Stewart of "a highly populous and amazingly productive country." This then, was the nation, connected for more than 3,000 miles not only by the unbroken line of the coast-to-coast highway, but by the "ribbon development" that had grown up along it. Stewart did not necessarily approve of this development, but he understood it as proof positive of what Walter Firey, Charles P. Loomis, and J. Allan Beegle had observed in their review of *Highways in Our National Life:* that the car was "radically altering the settlement structure and community organization of the American continent."[72]

Of equal importance, Stewart took this development on its own terms as an essential part of the highway. What was part of the highway was part of the country itself: they had, to use Stewart's terms, developed and amplified together and would continue to do so into the future, until car travel was superseded by another means of conveyance. Thus, for Stewart, "only by considering it all, as we drive from the east or from the west, shall we come to know in cross section, the United States of America." Stewart repeats this point in the book's conclusion where it becomes a summary judgment on the state of the nation. Driving U.S. 40 meant "accepting the commonplace along with the spectacular, seeing the people and the country, too, taking the good with the bad and the beautiful with the ugly" in order to form a "balanced impression." In the American Autopia, acceptance of everything revealed in the highway cross section of the cross-country highway granted the driver-citizen a kind of national self-knowledge. In the opinion of geographer and landscape critic J. B. Jackson, that kind of knowledge was desperately needed at midcentury because most people were ignorant of the "wealth of the American landscape" that was revealed on U.S. 40. Jackson praised *U.S. 40* for the way Stewart paid attention to "diverse and apparently uninteresting subjects," and took the time to document and explain something as utterly familiar, but egregiously under-analyzed as the highway and its environs.[73]

Jackson commended *U.S. 40* as a welcome contribution to human geography in his 1953 review of Stewart's book in *Landscape,* the journal that Jackson founded two years earlier. In the reviews, editorials, and topical essays Jackson published in *Landscape* for the eighteen years he served as its editor, the car occupied a complex cultural position, and in his own writings for the magazine he rarely made black-and-white pronouncements about its influence (see chapter 4). That same withholding of judgment vis-à-vis the automobile characterized another contribution to human geography, dealing with another highway corridor, which also appeared in the pages of *Landscape,* five years after Jackson reviewed Stewart's *U.S. 40.*

Novus Ordo Seclorum

Though Jean Gottmann ends "Revolution in Land Use" with an impassioned plea for the expansion of geographical knowledge to make sense of explosive urbanization, when explaining the automobile as a factor of expansive urban growth the French geographer is utterly matter-of-fact: "The mobility allowing for such scattering is due to the motorcar [and] modern highways."[74] This 1958 article in

Landscape was one of the earliest in which Gottmann published the results of the research that would secure his place as a key thinker on the modern city, the man who helped to conceptualize and popularize horizontality as a form of urban density. Gottmann became interested in mass urbanization in the United States when he arrived at the Institute for Advanced Study in Princeton as a wartime refugee. Though he began preliminary investigations in the 1940s and lectured on the topic throughout the 1950s, it was not until he secured the financial support of the progressive Twentieth Century Fund that Gottmann was able to assemble his work into a single comprehensive study. Around the same time George Rippey Stewart was contemplating the breadth of east–west urbanized development along U.S. 40, Jean Gottmann was analyzing the extent of north–south urbanized development along the most built-up section of U.S. 1, the highway that, as noted earlier, was constructed largely in the 1920s and ran from Maine to Florida for over 2,300 miles. This was the research that would culminate in the 1961 publication that famously gave the name "megalopolis" to the 500-mile Boston-to-Washington urban agglomeration that dominated the northeastern seaboard of the United States. Gottmann's study is as rigorous and data-laden as Stewart's is impressionistic and observational, but there are compelling parallels, notably the degree to which both recognized how the country's pre-interstate highways provided the infrastructure—physically and symbolically—for the burgeoning roadside metropolis that Gottmann discerned.[75] It is not coincidental that these principal E–W and N–S routes were the first to be superseded by the earliest planned interstates: I-70 and I-95.

When Gottmann analyzes the intensity of land use in the Northeast, and its impact on employment opportunities, traffic circulation, and settlement and community patterns, he employs "metropolitanization" as an all-encompassing term for the processes that generated the structure of megalopolis. This he characterizes as the evolution of the nucleated city into the colloidal and nebulous city—a sticky, hazy mass of urbanization adhering to the concentric growth around those centers that used to have exclusive dominance in the region. More provocatively, Gottmann declares megalopolis "the Main Street of the nation" to explain how the services and functions of traditional compact downtowns were now distributed along a "continuous system of deeply interwoven urban and suburban areas."

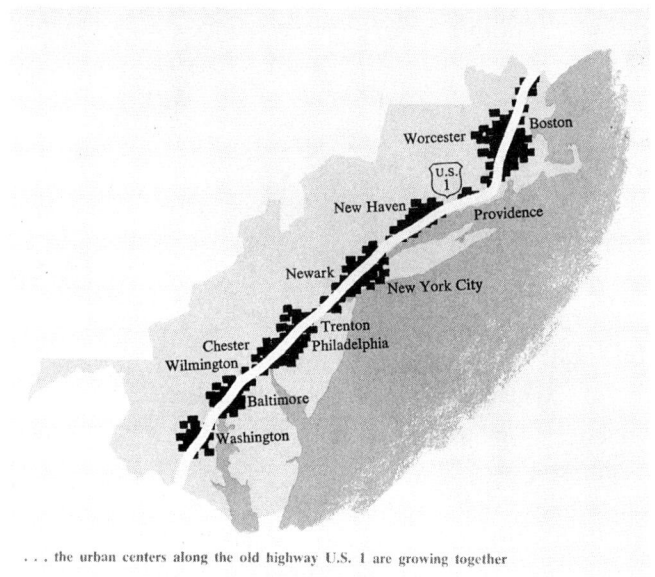

... the urban centers along the old highway U.S. 1 are growing together

Figure 28. "On the Eastern seaboard of the U.S. . . . the urban centers along the old highway U.S. 1 are growing together," drawing from Wolf von Eckardt, *The Challenge of Megalopolis: A Graphic Presentation of the Urbanized Northeast Seaboard of the United States, Based on the Original Study by Jean Gottmann*, 1964. (The Century Foundation)

As Gottmann readily points out, the central axis of that system is U.S. 1: "On the Northeastern Atlantic seaboard, from Massachusetts Bay to the valley of the Potomac, there is an almost continuous chain of impressive cities along the old highway known as U.S. 1."[76] Gottmann does not take the reader along the highway mile-by-mile in the manner of *U.S. One* (though he does cite the *American Guides* in his notes), because in studying the dynamics of urbanization his subject is the megalopolis as a whole. This does not mean, however, that an autopian perspective is not present in his study.

Everywhere in his *Megalopolis,* as Gottmann works to characterize this "Prometheus Unbound," he acknowledges the critical contribution of the highway and the car—though he is careful to situate them in an evolutionary chronology of "industrialization, mechanization, motorization, and automation" that obviously predates the internal combustion engine. Nonetheless, he offers a three-point analysis of the car's contribution to the development of Megalopolis: as a means of transportation ("the growth of Megalopolis owes much to the automobile"); as a shaper of culture ("the automobile has become very deeply imbedded in the American way of life"); and as a major force in the creation of what he calls "Megalopolitan sprawl." Gottmann carefully examines the socioeconomic push-pull cycles that brought this about: residences following industry and business out of the core; commerce and retail trade following residences toward the periphery. He, like George Stewart, is equally interested in its perceptual effects: "The scattering of buildings for various purposes along the roads has taken on such magnitude and frequency throughout most of Megalopolis that one seldom loses sight of buildings." At no point in *Megalopolis* does Gottmann suggest that it was the objective of *metropolitanization* that 38 million people should "exist in a world totally fabricated by man," but it is tempting to see in his descriptions of the "revolutionary changes" it produced in the environment a horizontal anticipation of Rem Koolhaas's *Delirious New York*. Megalopolis was so extreme in its 500-mile-long attenuation of density and congestion that it needed no adjective to qualify the ecstatic urbanism it embodied. As urbanism, Gottmann believed that Megalopolis embodied nothing less than the "novus ordo seclorum." Translated from the Latin as it appears on the Great Seal of the United States, this phrase means a "new order of the ages." For Gottmann at midcentury, the age of the automobile required a more precise translation: "a new order in the organization of inhabited space."[77]

Gottmann was a geographer, not a polemicist, and so throughout *Megalopolis* he refuses to pass judgment on the new order of urbanized concentration he so assiduously documents. Only at the very end of the book does he signal a mild cautionary note when commenting on the American tendency to seize material opportunity, with the Megalopolis as the result. That such critical evaluations were already underway is hinted at in the foreword to the book, written by August Heckscher, the future New York City parks commissioner and a regular commentator on arts and urban affairs: "I have found the almost universal impression among those who heard of [Megalopolis] for the first time to be that of a monstrous city, a kind of indefinite extension of Times Square up and down the whole Atlantic seaboard."[78] At the time, that is exactly what vast stretches of U.S. 1 in the heart of Megalopolis looked like, and neither the highway nor the attenuated urbanism it engendered had many defenders. U.S. 1, in particular, had been almost universally condemned for several decades. By midcentury, it may have been the *Main Street of the Megalopolis,* but there were few critics or scholars prepared to follow Gottmann's lead and take the new urban order on its own terms. Instead, as we will see in the next chapter, they mounted a sustained critique of the car and the buildings and landscapes it produced. Alternately sophisticated and heavy-handed, reformist and muckraking, these critiques offered a catalogue of Autopia's midcentury metropolitan discontents that was as sprawling and complex as the roadside metropolis itself.

3

AUTOPIA AND ITS DISCONTENTS

In the ten years after 1945, car ownership in the United States more than doubled from a wartime-restrictions-on-the-home-front nadir of 25 million in 1943. Whether the 52 million registered vehicles on U.S. roads in 1955 hastened suburbanization and the development of peripheral strips and subdivisions or were, instead, necessitated by decades-old patterns of decentralized growth, by the middle of the century, for many drivers, the autopian landscapes of the roadside metropolis still possessed a "brave new world" luster.[1] At the same time, however, from the moment urban populations began moving out of central cities, and with increasing frequency after World War II, those same landscapes provoked fervent critiques from foreigners and, especially, from Americans themselves. Ranging from smug amusement to moral outrage, from social commentary to reformist polemics, and from popular magazines to specialized journals, these critiques were united by their recognition that the car had spawned something new under the sun, and that the United States had finally produced a culture that was entirely its own. While some of these criticisms are well known individually, they have rarely been considered collectively, but when taken together they form a compelling midcentury parallel to that persistent strain of anti-urban critique focused

Facing page: detail of fig. 37, Alan Dunn's cartoon illustrating Lewis Mumford's "The Highway and the City"

on the central city and marking American thought from the late eighteenth century on. Historians Morton and Lucia White documented this anti-urbanism, in thinkers from Thomas Jefferson to Frank Lloyd Wright, in their now classic 1962 study, *The Intellectual Versus the City*. In revealing a variety of causes for antipathy and outright hostility toward the traditional American city—its corrupting influences, rampant commercialism, and density—along with a romantic attachment to a pastoral ideal, the Whites also shed light on the ideological underpinnings of the automobile-oriented "explosion into the suburbs" that was well underway by the time of the book's publication. As architectural historian William Jordy noted in a perceptive 1963 review of their work, it was that middle landscape, neither wholly urban nor wholly rural, that intellectuals who pitted themselves against the city idealized, despite the extent to which autopian impulses were transforming that pastoral realm into a place where, *pace* Ogden Nash, the billboards appeared to outnumber the trees.[2] The Whites also observed that many midcentury American intellectuals registered the rise of the suburb and the decline of the city by articulating a nostalgic tenderness for the latter, but it was beyond their purview to investigate whether this situation had caused those same intellectuals to mount any concomitant anti-suburban critiques.

In fact, many had, especially during the 1950s when diverse thinkers began to respond to the exponential growth of what popular historian Frederick Lewis Allen called the "motorized suburb" to distinguish these newer settlements from the older neighborhoods and communities spurred by railroads and streetcars.[3] John Keats in his satirical *The Crack in the Picture Window* (1957) and David Riesman in his more sober *The Lonely Crowd* (1950) both tracked suburban malaise as a rising social and sociological phenomenon. These bestsellers were a touchstone for sociologist Herbert J. Gans when he took up residence in Levittown, New Jersey, in 1958, becoming a champion of the motor suburbs—or at least an intellectual willing to refute the negativity of earlier critiques. But if Gans, in *The Levittowners,* defended the social reality of suburbia, finding an intellectual to defend its physical reality was a greater challenge. In the contest of the intellectual versus the motorized suburb, the attenuated commercial landscape of the roadside metropolis was a prime target. These attacks didn't start in the 1950s. They'd been around, as Sinclair Lewis and F. Scott Fitzgerald might have observed in the 1920s, for as long as a Ford car had parked in front of a Bon Ton store and the eyes of Doctor T. J. Eckleburg had been staring out from a billboard across the Valley of Ashes.[4]

Of Ribbon Development and Linear Slums

In 1938, the editors of *Life* magazine summarized the state of the autopian landscape, observing that "along 3,000,000 miles of highway" the country had created "the Supreme Honky-Tonk of All Time." Whether this was pejorative depended entirely on one's perspective, but it is probably safe to assume that for *Life*'s white, middle-class audience, it was a dubious superlative at best. The magazine left no doubt about its disparaging intentions when it selected U.S. 1 in the dense northeast corridor as its honky-tonk exemplar. The *U.S. One* volume of the *American Guides* had appeared earlier in the year, and *Life*'s editors seem to have paid particular attention to what the Federal Writers' Project had to say about the state of the highway, especially the 241 miles between New York City and Washington, D.C., where, despite its profound historical significance, it was "characterized by hideous shacks, enormous signs, dumps and raw cuts." *Life,* too, acknowledged the highway's multicentury importance as the nation's "greatest artery of travel and trade," along with its current condition between the country's financial and government capitals, which it disparaged it as an "unsightly" stretch of highway marred by miles of "roadside junk."[5] Most offensive in this regard was the signage, illustrated in *Life* by more than a dozen Margaret Bourke-White photographs. Whether guided by *U.S. One* or her editors, Bourke-White focused, in particular, on scenes in Maryland and New Jersey, including a segregated tearoom in Elkridge (MD) and an Esso filling station at the Bayway Refinery in Linden (NJ).

In her original proofs, the images are sufficiently wide-angled to capture the expansiveness of the roadside. In the Elkridge photo, the highway stretches from foreground to background on the right side of the image. In the Linden picture, a massive oil tank sits at the center, framed on either side by the pier of a modest Art Deco garage and the corner of a picturesque canopy shading the pumps.[6] As pub-

Figure 29. Margaret Bourke-White, photograph of a segregated tea room in Elkridge, Maryland, along the "Supreme Honky-Tonk" of U.S. 1, from "Speaking of Pictures," *Life*, 27 June 1938. (The LIFE Picture Collection/Getty Images)

lished in *Life,* however, the photographs were tightly cropped to direct attention to the signage. The headline made the editorializing intentions clear: "these signs make U.S. highways eyesores." Even worse, "Coca-Cola is everywhere," the editors noted with mild exasperation, as if the soda were responsible for the highway's generally unsightliness. The editors are unable to connect a profusion of commercial development—all that "roadside junk"—with the needs and desires of motorists in a country they acknowledged as "a nation that lives on wheels." In this same article, the editors use Bourke-White's photograph of a sign for Dutchland Farms dairy/restaurant (complete with neon windmill) as an example of commercial blight; twenty-seven pages later, in a different article, they promote its "32 flavors of ice cream" as a vacation attraction.[7] This unintentional irony, while probably an editorial oversight, highlights an underlying tension of autopia, between the ideal

Figure 30. Margaret Bourke-White, photograph of an Esso Refinery in Linden, New Jersey, along the "Supreme Honky-Tonk" of U.S. 1, from "Speaking of Pictures," *Life*, 27 June 1938. (The LIFE Picture Collection / Getty Images)

of an orderly, regulated environment and the pragmatic acceptance of free-market economics.

This tension was not new in the 1930s: by then roadside reformers had been dealing with it for nearly three decades. In the 1910s and 1920s, as Daniel Bluestone and Catherine Gudis have noted, the impulses of the City Beautiful movement found a corollary outlet in the countryside as anti-billboard forces crusaded against the commercialization of rural roadsides.[8] This proved an uphill battle. Though the theory of induced demand had yet to be applied to the highway, two things were already observable in the 1930s: first, as the mileage of hard surface roads increased, so did the number of cars driving on them; second, as roads and cars increased, so did commercial encroachments. J. M. Bennett, a park superintendent and road commissioner in Michigan's Wayne County (dominated by

Detroit, and one of the Midwest's most important highway hubs), called this type of development "mushroom growth" to indicate how quickly, seemingly overnight, "shacks and fantasies" sprang up along newly completed highways, whose roadsides he would have preferred to preserve as "the front lawn of the nation." Highway aesthetics were also an issue for the New England Regional Planning Commission when it described the "problem of the roadside" as "a straggling ribbon of commercial structures [that] destroy the pleasure of driving over an otherwise unspoiled country road." By 1939, as the commission knew only too well, there were few country roads left in New England that had no raison d'être beyond recreation and leisure. Indeed, many of them were already suburban commuter corridors, which is why the commission had long advocated the construction of Connecticut's Merritt Parkway as an inland, town-bypassing alternative to U.S. 1.[9]

In those parts of the roadside metropolis where the urbanizing process was most intense, along the Eastern Seaboard that Jean Gottmann would soon label Megalopolis, the rate of mushrooming commercial development prompted state highway and traffic safety departments to begin surveying existing roadside conditions in order to produce a body of data presumably more reliable than anecdotal visual evidence gathered behind the wheel of a moving car. Many of these studies focused, unsurprisingly, on U.S. 1 where, from New Haven to the New York state line (some 50 miles), surveyors found 2,900 buildings with highway frontage and access. There was a gas station every 895 feet and an eatery every 1,825 feet; other commercial establishments were an average of 425 feet apart. To the south, in New Jersey between Newark and Trenton (some 47 miles), surveyors found 300 gas stations, 472 billboards, and 440 other commercial concerns on the roadside. Still further south, on the 30-mile stretch between Baltimore and Washington, there were 618 commercial establishments intermingled with 665 residences and 2,450 signs and billboards, conditions that led highway officials to declare this section of U.S. 1 one of the "most dangerous and congested" roads in the country (see figure 31).[10] Highway officials were well aware of what had produced this situation. Beyond the increase in highway mileage and the number of cars on the road, they placed the blame on two long-standing highway practices related to access and zoning. Right of access, common law at midcentury, granted owners of property abutting most streets and highways the right to ingress and egress and the right of visibility. Contemporary land-use regulations tended to zone all property fronting major roads and highways for commercial use. Taken together, lawful access and lax zoning all but ensured a proliferation of roadside businesses that preferred drives cut directly to the highway and buildings and signs lining the highway or close enough to be visible from it. The result, in the argot of the day, was "insidious ribbon development" that produced "blight and decadence of property values." By the mid-1940s, highway analysts were arguing that the economic impact of ribbon development was so deleterious that a free-market approach was unsustainable. Public control of highway access and roadside development was put forward as the only workable solution. If it was not possible to implement limited access on existing highways, then it was time to advocate for an entirely new system.[11]

For most highway observers, the increasing quantity of roadside development was in direct proportion to its declining quality. Economist Stuart Chase conducted his own informal highway survey in 1930, driving from New York to Boston in order to grade scenery viewed through his car window as *pleasing, passable,* or *depressing*. Even though he confined his data collection to exclusively rural areas, Chase rated half those country miles as depressing, based on the "roadside eruptions" he encountered. Though he reserved most of his venom for what he called "movables"—garbage, abandoned automobiles, and the like—he was equally distressed by the state of "fixed properties," or buildings along the highway, which he labeled as "an acneous eruption [that word again] of filling stations, hot-dog stands, Tumble Inns, garages." Chase's inventory-cum-litany of architectural sins would become a staple of midcentury roadside criticism, as would his plea for "optical exercise in the everyday world," in which he exhorted his countrymen with the following questions: "Do you ever look at your America? Do you ever really use your eyes?" Writing in *Harper's* for a primarily elite readership, Chase offered up what *he* saw of America as evidence in support of autopian causality wherever highways and automobiles went, "which is practically everywhere save the tops of mountains and the middle of lakes." With still inaccessible territories diminishing, one found "the *extension* [his emphasis] of the metropolitan slum over most of rural America."[12] In 1930 Chase may not have been the first to apply the term "slum" to those areas outside the urban core that, according to critics, were adversely affected by the expansion of highways and motorcar use, but he was certainly among the earliest. And like his roadside inventory, this would become standard in the diagnostic language used to analyze the roadside in the coming decades, an attention-getting if not quite fear-mongering strategy that applied the polemics of urban crisis and urban pathology to territories increasingly far afield from the city center.

What Chase began in *Harper's* in the 1930s, Frederick Lewis Allen and Bernard DeVoto continued in the 1950s, using the magazine that Allen edited and to which DeVoto contributed a regular column as a platform for dissecting the rapidly changing midcentury roadscape. For Allen there was a "crisis in the suburbs," brought about by the "the great change," the automobile arriving in sufficient numbers to effect a total transformation. Allen, ever the American chronicler, carefully documented three distinct stages of motorized suburban evolution that followed the original horse-and-buggy era. In the 1920s the suburbs experienced "headlong growth" due to road building and what he called the developer's "field day." The Great Depression and World War II, despite economic decline and gasoline shortages, did not bring about a "hiatus in the suburban drift." Rather, Allen saw this as a period of consolidation in which the "fringes" further developed and the "chinks" filled in. Circa 1950, his current stage, suburbia had "gone into double quick" with the construction of large-scale housing subdivisions and "the discovery of the suburbs by business." This took the form of branch stores and shopping centers erected on "some hitherto open tract of countryside." This intensification in land use encapsulated the suburban crisis for Allen: "the automobile eats up space." Allen's tone was cautionary: "It would be a grave mistake," he wrote, "to think of the metropolitanizing of Suburbia as a phenomenon confined to the outskirts of a few big cities, mostly on the Atlantic seaboard." What happened to the suburbs of New York and Philadelphia as they grew into the Megalopolis would be repeated outside other cities, both large and small, from the Midwest to the Rockies. Allen contrasted the compact cities of the "elevator age" with those of the "automobile age," using Los Angeles as his obvious exemplar: "the motor age spreads things out."[13] Though a let's-do-something-before-it's-too-late ethos pervades Allen's writing on the suburban crisis, it is characterized by an editorial restraint his provocateur columnist eschewed.

Bernard DeVoto's "Easy Chair" column sometimes defied the relaxed mien implied by its title, especially when the subject was the state of the built environment in the mid-1950s. DeVoto was an ardent conservationist and an authority on Mark Twain who seized the opportunity his column provided to deploy Twainian colloquialisms while upbraiding the automotive consumerism he felt was wreaking havoc on the American landscape. DeVoto had been writing about the roadside in *Harper's* since at least 1940 when, in "Notes from a Wayside Inn," he offered pronouncements on the vagaries of driving while hungry and thirsty and detailed the state of eating and drinking establishments en route. Though "roadside lunch counters [were] an offense to the eye and a menace to the national health," DeVoto was more intrigued by a different roadside "institution" for which "the language has not yet found a name." The all-night restaurant and bar, which had initially catered to truckers and tourists, had long since established itself as "an important part of the local culture" wherever it was found in "small-town America." Serving "eatable food" ("you get good salads clear to the hundredth meridian") and providing "dances to the juke box," this kind of establishment fulfilled "an ancient purpose" of community gathering and "social health," which allowed DeVoto to overlook defects like "an offensively jocose name" or "neon tubes [that] are garish." DeVoto's evenhandedness is obvious when his observations are compared with British poet W. H. Auden's contemporaneous contemptuousness. In 1946, the same year the British poet became an American citizen, Auden wrote an introduction to a new edition of Henry James's *The American Scene* in which he bluntly described the U.S. interior as a place characterized by "unspeakable juke-boxes" and "insane salads" distributed across "the anonymous countryside covered with heterogeneous dreck."[14] DeVoto's critiques were always more nuanced, as in "Motel Town," a nearly anthropological follow-up to "Wayside Inn."

In the earlier essay DeVoto had noted that the "new in America" twenty-four-hour roadside institution, as yet nameless in 1940, originally emerged to serve the "trav-o-tels" and "tour-o-tels" clustered on the outskirts of towns across the United

States. By 1953, DeVoto discerned that these clusters had expanded into "drive-in" settlements of recognizable roadside typologies requiring further scrutiny. The all-night eatery he now identified as "what the vernacular calls a diner," and overnight accommodations responding "to the needs of the highway" he now referred to as "Motel," a coinage he called both folksy and functional. While motels represented a step up from tourist cabins, which he described as "the highway's slum structures," he found them frequently dingy and uncomfortable on the inside. When describing them on the outside, DeVoto is unable to restrain his sarcasm. With neon outlining and framing the motel's every element—facades, eaves, gables, windows—it was possible to read Gideon's Bible "without eyestrain" in the middle of the night with the blinds closed. And then there was the signage: "columns of neon" stood ten feet tall "before the suburb's proudest establishments," sometimes with added floodlights or multicolor flashing signs. DeVoto acknowledged that a motel "class structure" produced "annoying inadequacies" in architecture and furnishings, but failed to recognize that his own class privilege was informing his appraisal. DeVoto's disdain for much that he encountered on the roadside overwhelmed his perceptive urbanistic assessment of "Motel Town" as a "longitudinal metropolis" existing at the crossing of seemingly every trunk highway in the nation and frequently "more populous" than the village to which it was presumably attached. Near limited-access highways, development took the form of an urban "aggregate" on a straightaway at the end of a cloverleaf, utterly detached from existing settlements and unrelated "to any other factor, social, economic, or geographical."[15] Places that fit DeVoto's description had been around since at least 1940, when the construction of the Pennsylvania Turnpike gave rise to Breezewood, the unincorporated "town of motels" that grew up at exit 6 and U.S. 30.

For DeVoto, Motel Town was an urban form dedicated not merely to "a motorist's basic requirements" of gas, food, and lodging, but also including every possible "economic specialization of the highway." DeVoto catalogues myriad types discovered in "Texaco land" and "among the satrapies of Tydol [and] Gulf," from car washes and laundries to novelty and souvenir shops: "Besides the drive-in theater there will be a drive-in drug store and a drive-in church, which advertises redemption for miles down the highway and brings heavenly grace into competition with

Burma Shave." The sheer retail diversity of Motel Town may have amazed him, but its density was galling. So close was the average motel to the highway that the traveler might as well "spread a sleeping bag beside the pavement." DeVoto evoked the linear density of Motel Town by reciting the names of some three-dozen establishments supposedly cluttering the highway "in the province of neon."[16] Driving figuratively past Pal's Place, Steve's Place, and Cliff's Place, and onward toward the Hasty-Tasty Drive-In, Chief Glad-to-Mi-Chi's, and The La Fiesta Bowlaway, DeVoto's litany becomes a roadside rant rendered in bebop cadences.

DeVoto returned to the crowded highway in one of the last *Easy Chair* columns to appear before his death in 1955. In "Outdoor Metropolis," he analyzed the stretch of U.S. 1 north of Boston as it crossed into New Hampshire and up into Maine. Five years earlier another *Harper's* contributor had described the highway between Philadelphia and New York as having "clear title to the prize for uninterrupted architectural garbage."[17] Now, in DeVoto's view, it had some serious competition. Thanks to the northward seeping of the "metropolitan mass," what DeVoto had once viewed as the highway's vacationland corridor he now described as a "longitudinal slum" that had "Coney Islanded" the Maine Coast, especially south of Portland. The "blight of Vacationland" was spreading along roadsides and "plague spots" that were "jerry built, neon-lighted [and] overpopulated." After using the invective "slum" as often as possible, DeVoto had little to add to what was by then his decade-long critique, so he concluded with a dire warning that what was happening on U.S. 1 portended the "mass vulgarization" of New England as a whole.[18]

Sociologist David Riesman, in collaboration with another *Harper's* contributor, Eric Larrabee, seemed to suggest the opposite of vulgarity when they described the car as a "cosmopolitan influence" that acted to "net" communities together. Ultimately, though, in "Autos in America," which appeared in a 1957 issue of *Encounter,* the vaguely liberal (though CIA-funded) political and literary journal edited by the poet Stephen Spender and conservative journalist Irving Kristol, Riesman and Larrabee return to the standard analogies of squalor when they argued that community connectivity occurred principally through "ribbon-like roadside slums." That same year, architect and planner Carl Feiss, who claimed he was the first to use the term "land pollution" to describe "the linear hideous road towns," argued that geographic specificity was receding in significance as the country was built up with "our Route 1's and our Route 40's," embodying not just the "obvious superlative of bad taste" but "the epitomy [sic] of bad judgment" as well. For Feiss, "the honky-tonk automobile world" was perpetuating "obsolete patterns" of urbanized land use "over the countryside from central cities." Lewis Mumford made a similar observation when he discerned, presaging Jean Gottmann but without the geographer's detachment, the dissolution of distinctions that had once existed between urban and rural along the extent of the Eastern Seaboard, dismissing the development as "a drab, standardized, low-grade settlement, lacking both the advantages of the country and of the city."[19]

DeVoto's criticism of U.S. 1 prompted two defenses of the highway that were as rare as they were incisive. Writing in the *New Yorker,* like Lewis Mumford, essayist E.B. White offered a partisan riposte that focused on U.S. 1's mileage north of Portland (he was currently living 150 miles down east). With his typically wry humor, he conflates national gas station chains and the scenic appeal of the seaside: "like highways everywhere, it is a mixed dish: Gulf and Shell, bay and gull, neon and sunset." In *Landscape* J. B. Jackson conceded that U.S. 1 was "one of the most sensationally ugly roads in America" and that the stretch between Washington and Baltimore seemed "to epitomize the degradation which in the past few years has overwhelmed our highways." Nonetheless, in Jackson's view, the "modern highway and its margins" also possessed an "ambidexterity"—the potential for good as well as ill: aesthetic, social, and economic. Echoing his earlier comments on Stewart's *U.S. 40,* Jackson was disappointed that U.S. 1 and roads like it were scorned rather than studied, which is why, in the ensuing decades, he spent much of his professional life giving them the serious consideration he believed they deserved (see chapter 4).[20]

It was possible, of course, to scorn highways even while studying them. The same year that DeVoto's "Outdoor Metropolis" appeared, *Life* published "Dead End for the U.S. Highway" by staff writer Herbert Brean, who used U.S. 1 as a case study of congestion, chaos, and mortality illustrating "a discouraging tale of degradation and defeat." Brean reeled off the familiar national highway statistics about

Figure 31. Edward Clark, photograph of "Clog up on U.S. 1 in Maryland [College Park]," from "Dead End for the U.S. Highway, *Life,* 30 May 1955. (The LIFE Picture Collection/Getty Images)

increasing cars and mileage (claiming there were 60 million cars on 3.4 million miles by May 1955), but he also provided data-filled diagrams on U.S. 1 accidents, injuries, and fatalities in order to present "a horrible history" of unlimited roadway access. The fact that "anyone owning property along a highway has the right to cut as many entrances into it as he wishes anywhere on his land" had resulted in an incursion of "unregulated motels, pizza palaces, used-car or trailer lots, occasional private homes and beer joints that moved greedily to its very edge." All these driveways caused accidents; all these establishments distracted motorists. At midcentury, U.S. 1 was both a "hot dog highway" and a "hardened artery" that was best characterized as "obsolete, wasteful and murderous." Though Brean highlighted recent efforts to improve traffic flow on "the ancient turnpike," the article is unabashedly an endorsement of the Eisenhower interstate program as

Congress was debating it in the middle of 1955. The differences between proposed highways—with limited access, grade separation, and wide rights-of-way—and existing highways was illustrated by the two-page-spread Edward Clark photograph that opened Brean's article. This depicts U.S. 1 in College Park, Maryland (identifiable by the diner that still stands on Baltimore Avenue) and, despite a stand of dense trees in the background, the image is dominated by autopian-era ephemera: motels, gas stations, and ice cream stands, along with a discontinuous shoulder, narrow lanes, and too many signs and driveways to count. A few years later, the same photograph turned up in *Cities in the Motor Age,* a publication based on a 1957 symposium held at Connecticut General's new headquarters outside Hartford. What Herbert Brean called the U.S. 1 "clog up" was now presented in more socially ominous terms: inflected by the polemics of urban renewal, the highway was a prime example of "transporting slums to the suburbs," even though the overall tone of *Cities in the Motor Age* was supportive of car-oriented urbanism (see chapter 4).[21]

The View from across the Pond

Another study from the 1950s found the highway's northern extension, between New York and New Haven, so "littered with garages, eateries, junkyards, and factories" that motorists supposedly avoided it whenever possible. Here, U.S. 1 was surveyed to present the urban morphology of a New England city in "Man Made America," a special issue of the British journal *Architectural Review.* Supervised by Canadian planner and landscape architect Christopher Tunnard, a group of Yale students in a graduate course on the "visual effects of town planning" analyzed, in effect, what happened to the town when there was *no* planning. Though Tunnard claimed that American cities and towns were not "a standardized product like the American automobile," he introduced the case study by highlighting similarities rather than differences "from coast to coast," from "mass-produced" gridirons and Main Street storefronts to the city fringe with "Pepsicola billboards." While Tunnard finds moments of picturesque variety across the continent—the intense verticality of Manhattan and the rugged backdrop of Mount Hood in Portland,

Oregon—within "the broad mass of the urban landscape," he finds that "mobile America looks the same everywhere."[22] This is why their subject, though obviously New Haven, Connecticut, remains nameless throughout the case study. Tunnard and his students did not present an impressionistic highway portrait like George Rippey Stewart's *U.S. 40*. Rather, theirs was a clear and early example of Gordon Cullen's Townscape method.

Then serving as *Architectural Review*'s art editor, Cullen had recently developed a distinctive "pictojournalistic format" that used images and captions to make an argument about comprehending visual and spatial relations in the built environment. Here, in "Case Study: City," Tunnard used forty-seven images, accompanied by detailed captions, to present what Cullen would eventually call the optics, place, and content of the town.[23] The first three images are perspective site plans depicting the "specimen" city in 1650, 1850, and 1950, in the river and railroad eras and then at midcentury when the "automobiles, mass production, and the telephone have led the city to expand on every side." The rest of the visual essay is organized into nine photographic sections that illustrate how the city spread out beyond its original nine squares and central green. Throughout, the reader assumes the motorist's point of view: progressing from *highway* to *approach, outskirts,* and *entrance;* into the town *center* and its *residential* areas, both old and new; and then back out again from *periphery* to *shore*. In every section, the car is inescapable: on highways, roadsides, parking lots, and even junkyards—all of it evidence of the relentless transformation in land use that accompanied the city's extension "to the horizon." An independent town on the urban periphery before World War II has now "been absorbed into the city," its Main Street reduced to "a shopping centre for what is now a suburban district." What was vacant land and market gardens, circa 1940, is now recognizably "the edge of town," occupied by residential subdivisions and strip commerce. Though the case study is presented as a straightforward and neutral analysis, Tunnard's introductory comments suggest a pointed cultural interpretation. He sets the tone by quoting Henry James's observation that American cities were like scandalous women: though they lacked proper form and decorum, they possessed a certain "something." There were limits to this titillation, as Tunnard made clear by quoting Napoleon: "Du sublime

1650 The town was first laid out for the founders in 1638. This plan was an area half a mile square, subdivided into nine equal squares. The central square was set aside as the 'public market' and has remained common ground ever since. Today it is called the green. All the wealth of the town in these early days came from shipping and farming. The town continued to grow around the harbour until 1793 when a gun factory was started up river near the present dam. This was the first step towards converting the town into a manufacturing centre.

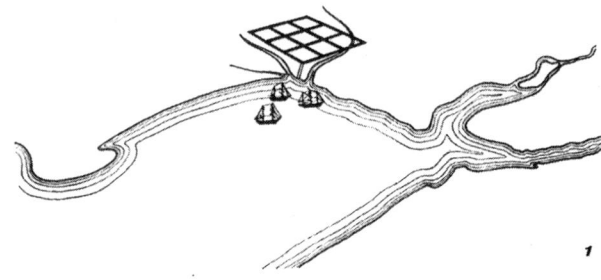

1850 The coming of the railway and the location of its tracks along the waterfront cut off the nine squares from the sea. The city turned its talents to manufacturing and overland trade. Great expansion followed and people crowded into the town to work and build at random without plan or foresight.

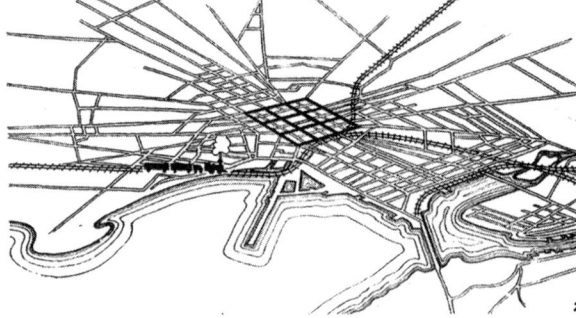

1950 After 1900 the automobile began to overcome the influence of the railway. Now the nine squares are losing their power as a centre. The motor car has made travel so easy that more and more people are moving out of the cities to live in the adjacent communities. Automobiles, mass production and the telephone have led the city to expand on every side.

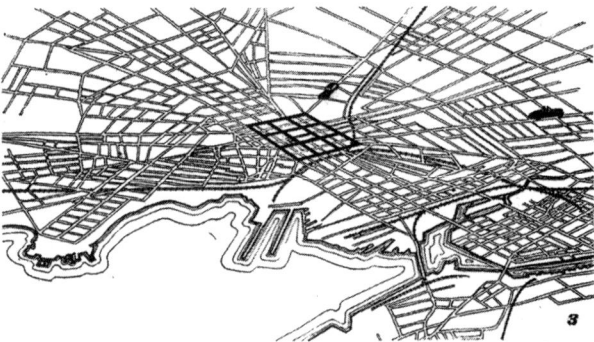

Figure 32. Christopher Tunnard, diagrams of three stages of urban development, from "Man Made America," *Architectural Review,* December 1950. (Christopher Tunnard Papers [MS 1070], Manuscripts and Archives, Yale University Library)

au ridicule, il n'y a qu'un pas." In the "environment of the mobile citizen," which Tunnard and his students call "as characteristic of the country as the skyscraper," there was (paraphrasing Bonaparte's aphorism) but a single step from the sublime to the ridiculous.[24]

A shift in scale from urban field to urban artifact marks the other Cullen-influenced visual essay in the "Man Made America" issue. "Case Study: Details" considers the "mass of objects and effects" found on American roads, including parking lots and meters, sign lettering and symbols, and billboard and poster advertisements. These are arranged in tightly framed photographs that remove the objects from their context to highlight how they contribute to "the everyday scene" and "the character of the real" and to suggest how they might be redesigned or reassembled to create "a functional, beautiful, and specifically twentieth century townscape." A photograph of U.S. 1 in New London, Connecticut, illustrates the degree to which this had not yet been achieved in America, at least from the editors' perspective. A fluted cast-iron utility pole dominates the picture, flanked by filling station pylons for Tydol and Gulf; in the background, the nineteenth-century buildings are barely visible under a dense signage superstructure. Presented as neither unique nor extreme in the United States, the image depicts the "haphazard, and all too often squalid, fantasies called streets." The editors take the country to

Figure 33. Street and signage in New London, Connecticut, from "Man Made America," *Architectural Review,* December 1950. (Photograph by Ian McCallum; Architectural Press Archive / RIBA Collections)

task for failing to solve the problem of supposed visual blight, arguing that without Saul Steinberg—whose illustrations appears on the cover and throughout the issue—it "would possess no critic of the community art of townscape." They concede, however, that perhaps because the United States had so much "acreage of good land to smudge," it was easy for "visual experts" to overlook seriousness of the roadside situation.[25]

For Gordon Cullen, the town represented architecture's "wider field," but individual roadside buildings were not overlooked in "Mad Made America." In the "city" study, Tunnard and his students earnestly explained to British readers such American typologies as the diner, the drive-in theater, the gas station, and the motel.[26] The last two, according to the Yale team, were said in the main to draw inspiration from regional architecture, though in stylistic interpretations that grow "increasingly strange on inspection." Historian Henry-Russell Hitchcock picks up on the theme of architectural peculiarities, offering a lively critique of roadside types as one half of his "the way things are" survey that also included postwar campuses, the car and the college embodying the two spheres of design activity, which for Hitchcock "characterize the entire architectural scene in 1950." While a four-page photographic spread accompanies his analysis of campus architecture, including buildings by Alvar Aalto, Walter Gropius, Frank Lloyd Wright, and Skidmore, Owings and Merrill, Hitchcock handles the roadside in a different manner.

When assessing the state of the "urban complex" at midcentury, Hitchcock foregrounds the automobile, citing traffic as the chief concern of planners and planning authorities. He notes the differences between parkways, with their encroachment controls and limited access, and all other highways lined with either "spotty ribbon development" or "roadside agglutinations." These, despite degraded aesthetics, possessed a "symptomatic actuality" that made them a ubiquitous part of the American scene. Hitchcock couches his remarks on auto-oriented architecture with a disclaimer that he knows them personally "only from the outside." This suggests a sort of anthropological detachment apparently necessary when scrutinizing "the *terrain vague* that surrounds the cities," as if the habitats of the mobile citizenry were occupied by an alien race. Nonetheless, Hitchcock wrote enthusiastically about drive-in theaters, which he regarded as formally spectacular, and he analyzed motels with great care, as a significant "modification of an existing functional type" that had evolved formally and programmatically from cabin to motor court to full-blown motor hotel. None of this should be mistaken as a break with modernist formalism on Hitchcock's part: when he turns to the issue of style, he derogates the "silly archaism" of roadside picturesque, whether of the log cabin, Cape Cod, or Spanish variety, while cautiously praising "simple Builders' Modern." Hitchcock clarified this position a decade later, in an unexpected aside in his revised edition of *The Architecture of Henry Hobson Richardson and His Times*. Though he regards the "strict functionalism and bold symbolism of the best roadside stands" as the popularization or "vernacular acceptance" of Corbusian modernism (derby-hat and ice-cream-carton buildings "with ribbon windows for outside service"), Hitchcock dismisses them as "incidental to our culture." This echoes his earlier argument in *Architectural Review* that such roadside buildings were "largely outside the conventional range of capitalized Architecture." This for him is an important distinction: these buildings are merely a phenomenon, "receiving almost unconscious formulation without benefit of architect."[27] Thus, for Hitchcock, such buildings were largely beyond the reach of capitalized History and Criticism as well, a connoisseurship approach that dominated aesthetic assessments of autopia until, mostly in the 1960s, new standards of evaluation emerged (see chapter 4).

Though Hitchcock conceded that larger commercial establishments on highways were sometimes architect-designed, he argued that such buildings were not, properly speaking, "roadside architecture" because they were located on "the edge of built up areas." Hitchcock makes no attempt to parse this supposed difference between the roadside and the urban fringe, which he had conflated in his discussion of motel design. It is surely significant that here, unlike in his analysis of midcentury campus design, he doesn't mention a single architect by name. The editors correct this omission by supplying one architect-designed example to illustrate Hitchcock's discussion of these larger-scale roadside/highway buildings: Milliron's Department Store, designed by Victor Gruen and Elsie Krummeck in 1949 (see figures 45 and 46). The editors describe the building as "outside Los Angeles," probably to make clear to British readers that it was not in the city's downtown (where Milliron's main store was located), but in fact it was within the city limits on the far west side of town. Either way, the editors added it to Hitchcock's piece as a rare example of architecture that rose above the "highway muddle." Thus, it "put paid to the idea that the motor-car is inseparably connected with a squalid environment." In the larger context of the "Man Made America" issue, Milliron's seemed more like the exception that proved the rule, because in their reading the U.S. highway was a place where "anarchy, often at its least attractive, is still triumphant."[28]

Exploring that anarchy as subject and object was the heart of this special number of *Architectural Review:* "It is the purpose of this issue to investigate the mess that is man-made America," the editors declared in the introduction, and by "mess," as they make clear in the conclusion, they meant "a hygienic, but visually scrofulous waste-land which is the universal embodiment and symbol of Progress, twentieth century style." It is not clear is whether the editors objected more to the wasteland itself, born of an unholy union between the "potentialities of the machine" and the "bottomless appetites of human beings for material things," or to fact that it was a symbol of progress. In either case, the editors let it be known that they targeted the United States because it, in effect, was targeting the rest of the developed world: "The technocracy, as we see it, is the pistol the U.S. holds to the stomach of western civilization," in the form of inevitable and outsize influence. And the technocracy's most visible manifestation of "infantilism and arrested development," they argued, was its built environment. At the same time, the editors acknowledged that the United States had created "a great Popular art" defined not only by jazz and movies, but by elements of that same built environment: "Main Street [and] Highway Culture." If there was an apparent ambiguity in saluting popular culture while simultaneously condemning the popular landscape, they justified it by insisting that "a huge chasm divides Popular from Fine art." That chasm, they continued, was the same one dividing "specialists ... sitting in ivory towers" from the "secular world," which seemed to include everyone responsible for constructed environments *except* architects and town planners, a group of "glossy gentlemen" whom the editors accused of deliberately ignoring what was being created "out there" in the world around them. Attempting to provoke the specialists, the editors asked two startlingly direct questions: "Is there the will to realize a new kind of world?

Is there even the will to visualize a new kind of world?" Here, the editors' word choice is telling: not desire or disposition, but *will*.[29]

Earlier, when arguing that the "man-made" landscape was "a more realistic self-portrait than many of us like to admit," the editors analyzed ineffable concepts like the American Dream and the American Way of Life before proclaiming that the landscape was, ultimately, a three-dimensional expression of the nation's "form-will." It didn't matter whether the haphazard arrangement of roads and railways, wastes and wilds, ornamental parkways and ribbon developments was "created consciously or unconsciously, by acts of commission or omission"—all of it was a "realization of its will to shape life in a certain way." There may be an echo here of one of Mies van der Rohe's aphorisms of the 1920s, which Philip Johnson had recently translated into English: "Architecture is the will of an epoch translated into space." Or perhaps the *Architectural Review*'s editors, Nikolaus Pevsner among them, were riffing on Aloïs Riegl to suggest a sort of car-centric *Kunstwollen,* which may not have manifest itself as a particular style, but certainly gave rise to a distinctive form. Either way, from the editors' perspective, it was a "theory" that helped to explain the built landscape of the United States in the middle of the twentieth century and would, the editors hoped, stimulate "informed analysis" of the same. This gets at the ultimate purpose of the *Architectural Review* special issue. It was a "sweeping accusation" intended to provoke American citizens "to look less at themselves and more at America." This was an ambitious goal, given what we can suppose was the limited American and nonprofessional readership of *Architectural Review* in 1950, but the editors' concluding quotation was surely meant to emphasize their seriousness of purpose, at least for the cognoscenti. A few sentences after sarcastically observing that Americans "hate to be reminded" they've moved beyond the cowboys-and-Indians phase of national development, the editors turn solemn: "Si monumentum requires, circumspice."[30] Providing neither a translation of the Latin nor a source for the phrase, borrowing this inscription from Christopher Wren's tomb in St. Paul's Cathedral was little more than an inside joke for the architecturally inclined. Condescension aside, it was not unreasonable to suggest that one might indeed seek the monuments of midcentury America by looking around the nation's highways, as a younger generation would soon discover (see chapter 4).

Looking at Ourselves

Stateside, the most immediate response to the provocations from across the pond was a humorous rejoinder that appeared in *Time* magazine in February 1951. "Poor Old U.S." offered up the *Review*'s choicest dismissals of the nation's built environment ("a combination of automobile graveyard, industrial no-man's-land and Usonian Idiot's Delight"), while reminding readers, in a tone of so-it-was-ever-thus resignation, that the British had long been appalled by what constituted the American *civilization*. A more pointed reply came two months later in another Time Inc. publication, when *Architectural Forum* published a thoughtful refutation written by its editor, Douglas Haskell. In 1937, *Architectural Review* had published Haskell's "Architecture on U.S. 40 and 66," in which he sought to dispel the idea that "this country is a series of dreary Main Streets."[31] Fourteen years later, Haskell found himself in a similar position, but he was less interested in defending the "mess" than in explaining how it got that way.

Haskell was no mere apologist (as we will see in the next chapter): though he complained about the Eurocentrism of the *Review*'s contributors, he claimed to be thankful for their "sharp reminder" about the state of the American built environment, which forced the thoughtful American to reconsider "his Continent in its most basic relationships." In contemplating those relationships, Haskell did not take issue with the *Review*'s basic critique of the impact of American technological determinism on the landscape, but he argued that it failed to take proper account of the actual significance of development spurred first by the railroad and then by the automobile—namely "its scale and tempo." To explain the influence of these factors, Haskell playfully spoofed the *Review*'s cowboy condescensions, observing that you "spoil more grass" busting a bronco than riding a trained steed in a show ring. He concluded with a more subtle critique of the *Review*'s evaluation. Putting forward Walt Whitman rather than Henry James as the native literary voice most appropriate as commentary on the current American scene, Haskell challenged the assumptions of the *Review*'s monolithic aesthetic judgment; "What *is* ugly?" he asks, with an emphasis as telling as his answer, which itself hinted that there were lessons to be learned from autopia: "There are great reservoirs of vitality even in honky tonk." Four years later, and still smarting from what he believed was the *Review*'s misreading of architecture and urbanism predicated on a distinctive American experience, Haskell offered the same answer to a different question, in another *Architectural Forum* editorial: "Can Roadtown Be Damned?" Noting that the ubiquitous highway landscape was "catching hell" from thinkers outside the United States, Haskell conceded that Roadtown was "crude, ugly, vulgar," but he asserted again that it was "vital."[32] Roadtown, Haskell implies (thus tacitly agreeing with the theory of "Man Made America") was the form-will of the United States.

Haskell refined this critical position in "Architecture in America," a series of *Forum* articles that constituted a further rebuke of *Architectural Review*, but was really aimed at the American architecture profession, which he implored to dedicate its skills and creativity to saving Roadtown—and hence the country—from its worst impulses. Throughout the series, which appeared intermittently in *Architectural Forum* from September 1955 to February 1957, Haskell himself only rarely groused about autopian discontent, spending most of his editorial energies setting out a reformist agenda intended, in part, to show architects how they might productively engage with the landscapes of the automobile. This agenda, which we'll explore in chapter 4, was woven throughout Haskell's broader goal of "exploring where architecture stands in America and what is happening to change its future." Though Haskell claimed to be surveying the influence of architecture's "men and methods"—not only designers and engineers, but realtors, bankers, contractors, builders, and manufacturers—he and the other contributors to the series also probed architecture's "deepest contexts," looking at an array of influences seemingly external to architectural design, but nonetheless exerting a profound influence on it.[33] These included zoning codes, loan regulations, material distribution networks, and consumer demands in the marketplace. The latter occasioned the most stridently polemical text in Haskell's "Architecture in America" series, which picked up literally where *Architectural Review* left off. The author, Mary Mix Foley, used *Review* as a point of departure in her trenchant critique of the "laissez-faire environment" of the United States.

Foley's background made her an ideal writer for what Haskell promised would be a "controversial article." After an early stint at the popular women's magazine

McCall's, Foley became an associate editor at *Architectural Forum,* remaining there for most of the 1940s. When Haskell tapped her to contribute to "Architecture in America," she was a publicist for the American Institute of Architecture, where she clearly mastered the art of the attention-grabbing title and the punchy hook. For her 1957 *Architectural Forum* article she did not mince words: hers was not a gentle survey of masses and markets and she made no pretense of journalistic balance as she investigated contemporary consumer desires: this was "a vigorous counterattack" on "The Debacle of Public Taste." But while Foley takes potshots at what she views as American aesthetic vulgarity, her analysis is supported by a thoughtful engagement with the politics of class and consumerism as embodied in the built environment—the same considerations she would shortly bring to a collaboration with sociologist Janet Abu-Lughod researching the intersection of social values, consumer preferences, and suburban housing for a project funded by the Ford Foundation. Their concluding assessment shows more restraint than Foley displays in *Architectural Forum,* though she would cite her "Debacle" essay: public taste with respect to housing is merely "laggard" rather than being a complete fiasco.[34] The difference is not merely semantic because Foley directs her greatest scorn not at split-levels and subdivisions, but at the commercial excesses of autopia.

Foley uses popular taste as her lens for analyzing the constructed environment of the United States because, she argues, popular taste is what informs, motivates, and generally shapes "the great bulk of American building." She divides this bulk into three general "mass market" fields: subdivisions, stores, and the roadside. Her *subdivisions* category includes the mass-produced housing of the merchant builders; *stores* encompasses downtowns, Main Streets, and the newer shopping districts of the urban/suburban periphery; the *roadside* is the "conglomeration" of highway retail dedicated to supplying gas, food, lodging, and everything in between. Thus, Foley does not just distinguish between residential and commercial; she parses the commercial realm in order to make certain qualitative differences clear. At first glance, though, Foley appears catholic in her dislikes, seeming to object equally to suburban ranch houses, Main Street's modernized storefronts, and roadside ice cream stands decorated with "concrete icicles." Her stylistic critiques are similar: pseudo–Cape Cod cottages and pseudo-Mediterranean gas stations are as offensive to her as pseudo-modern ones, especially when they display attributes of the streamlined moderne or "borax" modern. Still, she seems to take particular umbrage at what she considers faux modern, mainly because it moved from high style to popular so quickly, becoming, in her terms, a "monstrous hybrid" appearing on the landscape like a "specter." But whether the buildings were modern or traditional, commercial or residential, as far as Foley was concerned, they all contributed to the "raucous ugliness which is taking over our land."[35]

To probe the emergence of this supposed ugliness, Foley begins by arguing that subdivisions, stores, and the roadside constitute the "modern vernacular" of the twentieth century in that they served the "average man"; emerged, on the whole, "without benefit of architect" (here, she reiterates Hitchcock's position); and reflected contemporary cultural values and priorities. As a modern vernacular, these buildings were the legitimate successors to the rural cottages, wayside inns, and blacksmith shops of the eighteenth and nineteenth centuries. But for Foley a *legitimate* vernacular is not the same as a *satisfying* vernacular. In the past, she argues, the American vernacular possessed "an integrity and a dignity which we call beauty," and she implies this was the case across all popular typologies. Yet, when she draws a parallel between dignified nineteenth-century buildings and vulgar twentieth-century ones, Foley uses apples-to-oranges comparisons that undermine her logic. Iowa farmhouses and Shaker barns are hardly the equivalents of the restaurants she mentions in this context, those occupying buildings both modernized ("jazzy with glass brick and shiny metals") and mimetic (like Brown Derby restaurant she references in the text and the Hoot Owl ice scream stand she includes as an illustration). Foley doesn't need them to be equivalent; she needs them to be emblematic—of American culture before and after the Industrial Revolution. Significantly, Foley does not only focus on the shift from handicraft to factory production, but also on the distribution networks and promotional apparatus that supported it. Her goal is to trace the emergence of the mass market, its impact on popular taste, and, by extension, its implications for the built environment as manifest in the commercial buildings she designated as the modern vernacular.[36]

Foley makes some astonishing observations along the way, arguing, for example, that prior to the industrial age (i.e., "before the machine"), Americans

Figure 34. "Raucous ugliness...taking over our land": Hoot Owl Café, Los Angeles (1926). (Security Pacific National Bank Collection, Los Angeles Public Library)

had "never created ugliness" because they "possessed an intuitive grasp of line, color, texture, proportion." With logic redolent of A. W. N. Pugin, William Morris, and the like, Foley states that the division of labor led to loss of craftsmanship, disconnection from place, and the erosion of traditions in buildings and furnishings. When the "chaos of plenty" was set loose on "rails and highways to transport these things anywhere at any time," it "destroyed an esthetic sense in the vast majority of people." By the middle of the twentieth century, Foley concludes, the debacle of popular taste was a fait accompli: "The people who build, buy, sell, live and work in the suburbias, the Main Streets and the roadtowns of America" were not only "eminently satisfied with the established ugliness... they do not even know it is ugly." From this perspective, cultural depredations followed in short order. Everywhere in the modern vernacular, Foley saw "unbridled license" evident in forms, materials, and stylistic clichés devoid of any meaning beyond advertising their own "right to vulgarity" (a term she borrows from philosopher José Ortega y Gasset). This was bad enough in the individual stores and subdivisions; in "roadtown" as a whole it was another appalling order of magnitude. Here was the "freest display" of popular taste, where "the former peasant, cut off from tradition and from his once meaningful way of life, goes a little mad." For Foley, the delirium was exacerbated by the average American's lack of interest in authority or expertise in matters of architecture and design. Describing the results, Foley was her

148   AMERICAN AUTOPIA

most condescending: "To this has human symbolism fallen," she icily observed of a hot dog stand shaped like a hot dog bun (see color plate 5). Along the roadside, Foley witnessed the country's most execrable—and visible—manifestations of popular taste. Embodied in these "worst forms," popular architecture had become "obscene," and this obscenity was characterized by "arrogance."[37] In a catalogue of cultural offenses, this was perhaps the most egregious of all.

In Foley's analysis, popular architecture in the past was modest: "it knew and kept its place." Now, in "a new and peculiarly twentieth-century phenomenon," it was the opposite—especially in roadtown where the rate of travel in a moving car coupled with the density of commercial competition produced a vernacular that was loud, brash, and struck "the man of taste like a blow in the face." As a woman of taste, Foley took the blow just as hard, but the sting gave her the clarity to call a spade a spade. At one end of the spectrum (the one Foley presumably occupied), it took "a sophisticated taste to be truly simple and an even more educated palate to achieve richness without monstrosity," but on the other, the modern American, an unequivocal "twentieth-century primitive," had "created popular architecture in his own image." It is tempting to think that Foley knew Adolf Loos's "Ornament and Crime," even though Reyner Banham's reintroduction (and English translation) of Loos to the discourse of modern architecture appeared in *Architectural Review* exactly contemporaneous (February 1957) with Foley's "Debacle" in *Architectural Forum*. There are distinct parallels between Foley's assertion of American primitivism evident in exuberant popular architecture, particularly of the "chrome, glass and neon" variety, and Loos's equating of ornamentation with cultural regression. In the U.S. context, this primitive was neither a criminal nor a degenerate, like Loos's tattooed modern man, but in Foley's terms he was just as dangerous, for though he worked hard and meant well, he would, inevitably, impose "his taste across the land."[38]

Douglas Haskell reprinted "The Debacle of Popular Taste" with minor, though significant changes when he compiled the essays of his "Architecture in America" series into a book entitled *Building, U.S.A.* later in 1957. In *Architectural Forum*, the essays reached a mainly professional audience. Now, repackaged as "Building, U.S.A. by the Editors of *Architectural Forum*," a slim hardcover retailing for $3.95, the essays were aimed at a broader audience. Alongside chapters devoted to the architect, the engineer, the contractor, and the corporation, Foley's essay was positioned to explain the role of "the public" in "the beguiling enterprise of building" in the United States, and to provide readers with the opportunity to locate themselves within that process and production. This probably explains Haskell's decision to drop Foley's original contentious title in favor of an opening provocation that was leading rather than alienating: "Why are there so many bad buildings in America?" It is difficult to imagine Foley's complex answer to that question—her analysis of the inverse relationship between the rise of mass production and the decline of taste as embodied in everyday architecture—resonating with a popular audience. It wasn't overly sophisticated; it was just abstruse. It's debatable whether the text's comprehensibility was improved by substituting the mimetic hot dog and frozen custard stands that originally accompanied Foley's essay with Andreas Feininger's 1947 photograph of U.S. 66 as it passes through the dusty town of Seligman, Arizona.[39]

Alongside the book's other illustrations, of exceptional buildings like Rockefeller Center, the S. C. Johnson Research Tower, and the GM Technical Center, Feininger's shot of Route 66 may have been intended to give readers a shock of the familiar as they read the chapter's opening gambit, its text superimposed on the everyday environment of the automobile—all those Texaco and Mobil and Coke and Pepsi signs, plus a couple of late 1940s sedans and even a few hitchhikers. But the picture is expanded to the book's only two-page, full-bleed spread, a layout that draws attention to its low horizon line and dominating big sky and seems more like a celebration of the highway landscape than a condemnation of "public taste, or the lack of it." If, however, Feininger's expansive view of the Route 66 stayed with the reader all the way to the end of the chapter, Foley's conclusion resonated more in the book than it did in the magazine. "The march of roadtown," she observed with great resignation, "goes on and on . . . extending yearly the dominion of the hideous." From that vantage point, what readers of *Building, U.S.A.* might have discerned in Feininger's picture was something greater than the Mother Road, an intimation, or perhaps a foreboding, of her progeny—two lanes of asphalt, two lines of buildings stretching endlessly toward the horizon.

Figure 35. Andreas Feininger, photograph of Route 66 in Seligman, Arizona, in 1949, from "Architecture in America," *Architectural Forum,* September 1955. (The LIFE Picture Collection / Getty Images)

As we saw in the last chapter, such an interpretation of the highway known as "The Main Street of America" was not really an overreach by the late 1950s. Indeed, in 1956, the *Forum* had already proclaimed that "the American city virtually *is* a Roadtown." Urbanism, the magazine noted, always followed trade routes and, at least since the 1920s, those trade routes were shaped by "a motorized centaur... the American man and his mobile mania." In a nation where, as Foley argued with mild sarcasm, washing one's car on Saturday afternoon was "the one remaining ritual act," her twentieth-century primitive was raised to mythic status. With its condemnation of public taste so explicitly and forcefully stated, Foley's analysis of the forces shaping popular architecture at midcentury stood apart from the rest of *Building, U.S.A.*—though, in truth, corporate clients, manufacturers, and real estate operators (the subject of the other chapters in the book and the other articles in Haskell's series) were just as implicated in her critique of how "the machine [had] shattered [modern life] into pieces." And they were just as responsible as "the public" for creating what Foley interpreted as the attenuated monstrosity of the American roadtown. If Foley didn't take them to task for "the relentless march of the steamroller" and "implacably eating up our rolling wooded farmland," there were others on deck who would. *Life* magazine noted as much when it gave Foley's essay its first popular exposure in a June 1957 editorial.[40]

"America—the Beautiful?" was most likely written by John K. Jessup, the magazine's chief editorial writer and a twenty-year Time Inc. veteran who drew on a number of articles published, like Foley's piece, in magazines that were part of the Time/Life universe. Reviewing a litany of recent complaints about all that was wrong with America, Jessup found much to agree with in assessments that were both imported (*Architectural Review,* again) and homegrown, and he seems to have taken particularly to heart "the bitter indictments" that Americans themselves were leveling at America. He starts with Mary Mix Foley, reprinting some of her most scabrous comments from *Architectural Forum,* and then moves on to lengthy quotes from, and sly references to, a veritable who's who of social commentators on the physical and emotional wastelands of suburbia: social critics John Keats and Vance Packard, cultural critic Russell Lynes, management psychologist Robert McMurry, and sociologists C. Wright Mills and David Riesman. Jessup borrows key phrases from the latter's "Autos in America" (discussed earlier) to effectively summarize a hypercritical perspective on the American built landscape: "ribbon like roadside slums . . . man-made rural ugliness . . . the endless aesthetic atrocities of the cities." Though not Jessup's intention, those ellipses suggest a sort of continuum of built form across multiple domains of settlement, from the city to the country to everything in between. Jessup himself put it in terms of building up rather than stretching out, calling the United States "a great swarming ant heap of a country."[41] Accretion and attenuation were, in fact, accurate ways to describe the changes taking place in midcentury urban form, and they became a preoccupation for another critic whose work, the bestselling *The Organization Man* of 1956, was referenced explicitly in "America—the Beautiful?"

Exploding and Scattering

William H. Whyte, journalist, social analyst, and urbanologist, was an editor at *Fortune* when he began the research that would become *The Organization Man,* his acclaimed study of the postwar culture of conformity that had replaced the United States' original self-mythology of rugged individualism. Whyte's examination of a new "Social Ethic" was primarily concerned with the dominating bureaucracy of American business in the 1950s and the pressures this exerted on the white-collar employees of an expanding middle class of middle managers. After exhaustively scrutinizing the ideology and practices of corporate culture, Whyte turned his attention to "Organization Man at Home." Focusing on the "packaged villages" of new suburbs like Park Forest in Illinois and Levittown in Pennsylvania, Whyte analyzed how socially prescribed belongingness was manifest outside the workplace in the family lives of Organization Men. Whyte deals with the automobile only in passing, noting, for example, that within the "inconspicuous consumption" of "new suburbia" the car, far from being a luxury, was "accurately described as a necessity." Twice, he references the Buick Special as a kind of cultural shorthand for Organization Man's taste, the status quo as embodied in a bland sedan squarely in the middle of the General Motors fleet (more premium than a Chevrolet, less luxurious than a Cadillac). Beyond this, Whyte takes measure of Organization

Man's transience, his daily routines and leisure activities in a world where "the new highway [was] broad and flat" and husbands regularly "stopped off at the giant supermarket" on the way home from work. For the most part, the car's ubiquity and the extent of its influence were too obvious to need mentioning.[42]

In Park Forest, in an early demonstration of the observational skills that he would later and famously apply to small urban places, Whyte mapped "the web of friendship" evident in activities like holiday parties, picnics, and potluck dinners, using this information to analyze the relationship between Organization Man's social networks and the physical design of his suburban habitat. Unsurprisingly, he found that subdivision superblocks, courts, and cul-de-sacs were tremendously important in enhancing or diffusing community cohesion, depending on their scale, as well as the layout of their lawns, driveways, and parking areas and the traffic flow through the neighborhood. The impact of the "organization way of life" on the built environment outside the new residential suburbs was largely beyond Whyte's purview in *The Organization Man,* but when he considers the growing importance of mobility on a national level, he hints at what its effects might be. Calling mobility under the contemporary regime of corporatism "the whole drift of our society"—this was the era that gave rise to the joke that IBM stood for "I've been moved" rather than International Business Machines—Whyte observed that "the more people move about, the more similar the American environments become, and the more similar they become, the easier it is to move about."[43] The physical and socioeconomic implications of this were already clear to *New York Times* chief book critic Orville Prescott when he reviewed *The Organization Man* in December 1956. What Whyte called the "momentum of mobility" was evident to Prescott in the changes wrought by "superhighways, split-levels, and color television," and he wondered whether these were fundamental or superficial with respect to how they were transforming "the American civilization." From Prescott's perspective, no one in America was better qualified to suss out the answer than Whyte, "a brilliantly gifted student of the customs of the country and an awesomely industrious investigator."[44] While *The Organization Man* was climbing to the top of the bestseller lists in 1957, Whyte turned his attention to what the culture of mobility was doing to the American landscape. By 1958 he had emerged as one of autopia's most ardent critics, publishing cogent analyses of, and increasingly urgent pleas about, the devastating effects of the uncontrolled automobile-oriented development that we know today as sprawl.

Whyte did not invent the term *sprawl,* but he most assuredly added it to the American popular lexicon. As Robert Bruegmann has shown, it was in Great Britain in the 1920s that "sprawl" was first applied to the built environment, and it was most likely Lewis Mumford who introduced it into urban discourse in the United States the following decade.[45] In the postwar period, sprawl came into wider use as the scale and speed of urban, suburban, and exurban growth increased. In 1948, when Regional Plan Association President Paul Windels used the term to describe the future of greater New York, he felt the need to characterize and qualify the kind of development he was discussing. New York City and the seventeen counties surrounding it were becoming indistinguishable parts of "the great metropolitan sprawl" that was spreading across the tristate area "like a solid flow of lava." It wasn't just the rate of the flow that concerned Windels; the fact that growth consisted of "formless sprawls" [*sic*] was even more worrisome. "Aimless" and "directionless" and "disorganized," this sprawl had costs that were emotional as well as physical. As strips, grids, and curvilinear patterns were "perpetuated and extended," older streets became "gasoline alleys for through traffic" while the houses lining them became "rooming houses and funeral parlors." Their inhabitants, assuming they had the means, were transformed into "urban wanderers" dedicated to seeking places that were "less obsolete, but ever more remote." The effect on their mental life was extreme: overcome by "anti-social mass emotions," these urban wanderers—automotive-era equivalents of Georg Simmel's blasé metropolitan characters—were subsumed by the anonymity of the "formless mass developments" in which they were now, inevitably, living.[46] Though the descriptors Windels used to depict sprawl's postwar features and effects would become commonplace in the 1950s and 1960s, his portrayal of its psychological impact was distinct in these decades, even if it had shades of the supposed soullessness that some commentators would use to critique life on the suburban frontier.

By the time William H. Whyte took on sprawl as a serious large-scale problem, the ideas put forward by planners like Windels were circulating widely in architecture and urbanism circles. In 1956, planning theorist and housing advocate Catherine Bauer, who was then teaching at Berkeley, went so far as to suggest that it would be better for the country if planners, along with government officials and developers, turned away from urban renewal programs altogether and instead made it their "first job [to] control new city sprawl." Staring down 1976, when there were projected to be 56 million more Americans and 50 million more cars, Bauer thought it was absurd to spend so much energy "fixing up the past rather than shaping the future." The continuous outward expansion of the central city across existing suburbs and into the "giant sponge" of the rural fringe was the "city pattern" on which planners should be focused—precisely because it did not exist as a conventional urban pattern at all. "Growth of the hinterlands," Bauer argued, "just happens," shaped only by "fate and ad hoc decisions" on the part of developers and lenders. When design was a factor in guiding growth circa 1956, it was usually limited to the work of road engineers whose route-planning priorities were girded by the passage of the Federal Aid Highway Act and the gradual implementation of the Interstate System. As Bauer noted, patterns of urban expansion were always shaped, "for better or worse, by inevitable public decisions about transportation." When those decisions involved the federal government paying 90 percent of the cost of the construction of highways leading to ever more far-flung peripheries, a new level of intentionality and purposefulness was introduced into the *it just happened* scenario that Bauer argued had long been dominant. The result was the same, but with greater intensity as "scatteration," Bauer's other term for "chaotic sprawl" continuing unabated.[47]

Writing in *Architectural Forum,* Bauer reviewed a number of alternate urban growth scenarios that would have been familiar to the magazine's professional readership, based as they were on well-known planning models from the first half of the twentieth century, but she sorted them into useful categories-cum-taglines and assessed their viability for midcentury conditions: Ebenezer Howard's Garden City, Frank Lloyd Wright's Anti-City, Le Corbusier's Super City, Great Britain's New City. While many of these ideas were applicable in the United States in the 1950s—"the noncity, or anticity" is the only one that promotes "communication only by automobile"—Bauer believed they would all remain utopian dreams until planners accepted the essential American reality that urbanism did not look the same everywhere. Bauer makes this explicit by acknowledging something that "may sound like heresy": despite being "at opposite poles of density and centralization" (and reliance on the car), New York and Los Angeles were both undeniable models of "modern urban organization," however "primitive or vulgarized" Bauer thought L.A. actually was. Ultimately, though, Bauer concluded that even this acceptance might not be enough to control rampant growth through thoughtful planning. While she was confident that political and economic hurdles could be overcome, for Bauer the "biggest potential obstacle" was cultural: "do we want real cities and real country—or do we actually prefer rurban sprawl?" If, as Bauer seemed to think, preference was for the latter, this raised other critical questions: How to save America from itself? How to restore a sense of "visual and social identity" to American places, whether they were cities, suburbs, or the strips in between, all of them "shapeless, endless [and] overlapping"? Bauer thought that preserving open space "for profit, recreation, and general amenity," might be the place to start. William H. Whyte agreed, and used the idea as the basis for his "Plan to Save the Vanishing Countryside," published in *Life* in 1959.[48]

By the end of that decade, with the Interstate System expanding and the highway beautification movement intensifying, *Life* quietly began to champion a new wave of roadside regulations that would "set our esthetic tone for a generation."[49] This position was articulated most convincingly when Whyte introduced the "disease of urban sprawl" to *Life*'s readership with an article whose manifesto-like tone and policy-oriented content were clearly a novelty for the pictorial weekly. He began by condemning the usual suspects, among them "billboards, neon signs, [and] frozen custard spas," but he also focused blame: the expansion of the "American standard of living," rampant development as a synonym for progress, and the "speculative land rush" set off by the federal highway program. After articulating the causes of sprawl and its effect on landscapes both natural and built, Whyte proposed a program of conservation easements and land trusts, carefully explaining their implications for taxes and development. Whyte exhorted *Life*'s readers to look again at the roadside: "Your instincts will tell you that anything that looks this terrible cannot be good economics, that it is not progress, that it is not inevitable."⁵⁰ Uncharacteristically for the photo-oriented *Life,* there was little visual evidence of *terribilità* in the mostly small-scale, black-and-white illustrations that accompanied Whyte's lengthy article—as if images of the nation's sprawling roadsides might have distracted readers from the author's "seriousness of purpose"—something that was being intensely discussed at the time, in realms both rarified and popular. President Eisenhower had recently organized a Commission on National Goals to establish consensus on U.S. social and economic priorities in the 1960s, and, in response, *Life* launched an eight-part series dedicated to "the National Purpose." In both cases, likely influenced by Whyte's "Plan," urban sprawl was identified as a pressing national problem.⁵¹ This article was only the latest volley in what emerged as Whyte's multiyear anti-sprawl crusade.

As a Time Inc. editor with a growing interest in urbanism, Whyte had been keeping abreast of city and suburban planning at least since the middle of the 1950s, especially coverage in *Architectural Forum, Fortune*'s sister publication. In 1957, he and *Forum* editor Douglas Haskell convened a two-day roundtable to study urban sprawl from the perspectives of governance, economics, land use, taxation, transportation, recreation, and planning, including Catherine Bauer among the nineteen participating experts. Whyte and Haskell published preliminary results of the meeting simultaneously in the January 1958 issues of their respective magazines: Jane Jacobs's "The City's Threat to Open Land" in *Forum* and Whyte's "Urban Sprawl" in *Fortune.* In his essay Whyte was unequivocal in bemoaning sprawl as a pernicious threat to America's quality of life and standard of living, as manifest in, for example, "life on the cloverleaf" in the new territories being generated by the interstates, which he illustrated with an aerial view of the Baltimore Beltway and the extensive development its construction generated. Whether flying from Los Angeles to San Bernardino or from New York City to Philadelphia, Whyte witnessed "an unnerving lesson in man's infinite capacity to mess up his environment." He warned Americans not to be deceived by any illusion of remaining green space they might spy from the air: "outlying supermarkets and drive-in theaters are omens of what is to come." And he cautioned them against complacency derived from any lingering fantasies of Manifest Destiny: "Open land in Wyoming is not going to help the man living in Teaneck, New Jersey." Beyond such

Figure 36. "Another new way of life on the cloverleaf": Baltimore Beltway under construction in 1955. (Permission from *The Baltimore Sun;* all rights reserved)

dramatic statements, Whyte presented data that was starkly unadorned—like the one million acres required for the right-of-way to build the 41,000 highway miles proposed for the Eisenhower Interstate System. He also quoted what appeared to be a straightforward declaration of the program's intentions: "To disperse our factories, our stores, our people; in short to create a revolution in living habits."⁵²

In fact, this, too, was a rhetorical flourish because Whyte edited the original text for polemical purposes. In the conclusion to its 1955 report, the President's Advisory Committee on a National Highway Program (headed by General Lucius Clay) wasn't claiming that the *new* interstates would instigate the revolution. The committee believed the revolution had already happened, that *existing* federal and state highways had already effected the dispersal: "our cities have spread into suburbs, dependent on the automobile for their existence." The purpose of the Interstate System was to *maintain* U.S. auto-dependence, and the "way of life" it engendered. "We are indeed a nation on wheels," the Clay Committee concluded, "and we cannot permit these wheels to slow down."[53] Writing for a business-oriented publication like *Fortune,* it is easy to understand why Whyte selectively quoted the Clay report, lest he be accused of slowing down the nation's progress at a moment when it was tied explicitly in socioeconomic terms to the momentum of the automobile. Instead, he subtly undermined the very definition of progress as tied to the consumption of greenfields at a rate of 3,000 acres per day: "You can't stop progress, they say, yet much more of this kind of progress and we shall have the paradox of prosperity lowering our real standard of living."[54] In this sense, "Urban Sprawl" was less anti-automobile than pro–open land. A bias against the car was more explicit when Whyte reproduced "Urban Sprawl" in an edited volume aimed at a popular audience, studying "the assault on urbanism and how our cities can resist it." Though Whyte didn't change the text, he placed it the company of essays that called out the automobile's role in producing the eponymous *Exploding Metropolis.* In "The Car and the City," though Whyte's *Fortune* colleague Francis Bello conceded that there was "something irrational" about the place of the automobile in U.S. society, he regarded it as "the most powerful and insistent" of the numerous forces "reshaping" the metropolis at midcentury. Dismayed by this transformation, Whyte defended conventional notions of pedestrian-oriented urban form, as did Jane Jacobs in her contribution to the volume, "Downtown Is for People." At the same time, Whyte acknowledged theirs as a quixotic urban position because "the norm of American aspiration" was no longer in the central city; it had shifted (at least for the time being) to the exploding territories of the automobile.[55]

By the time *Exploding Metropolis* was released in the fall of 1958, the relationship between the car and sprawl was already front-page news. Early in 1957, the *New York Times* explicitly linked them when investigative journalist Charles Grutzner reported on "the rise of the urban region." Across the country, these "urban complexes" were not only "fostered by auto," but required the car to tie them all together—from "flat factory" to "king-sized shopping centers." The impact of the car, Grutzner evenhandedly stated, was "something other than an undiluted blessing."[56] As a result of this expanding interest in expanding urbanization—and its negative effects—the *Times* reviewed Whyte's *Exploding Metropolis* volume in both the Sunday and daily editions of the paper, having already announced its impending publication as a "warning... of the coming chaos." Charles Poore implicated the car in his "Books of the Times" review: "The automobile, which has done so much to cause the exploding metropolis to explode, raises more problems of transportation than it settles." In the paper's other review, Harrison Salisbury moved beyond chaos to "the grip of revolution," calling *Exploding Metropolis* an "iconoclastic study" that demonstrated that the real menace of those Cold War years was not Communism but "social mutation and technological change" that was spreading like cancer "remorselessly along the arteries of the great motorcar routes."[57] It is an indication of a new scope of autopian discontent that a book "from the Editors of *Fortune*," a byline intended to convey all the authority and gravitas Henry Luce's conservative-leaning media empire could muster, was being saluted for questioning the sanctity of what had once seemed like an unassailable institution. This is all the more remarkable for coming at a moment when what came to be known as "the greatest public works project in history" was just getting underway with the commencement of interstate construction, when General Motors had produced its 50,000,000th car and had assumed the mantle of largest corporation in the world, and when former GM CEO, Charlie *"what's good for General Motors is good for the country"* Wilson was serving as secretary of defense.

Mono-Transporation and the Delusion of Progress

Around the same time, French critic Roland Barthes recognized the profound power of the automobile as institution when, in 1955, he took a moment from waxing poetic about the new Citroën DS, the "goddess," to provocatively situate the automobile in contemporary culture: "I think that cars today are almost the exact equivalent of the great gothic cathedrals: I mean the supreme creation of an era, conceived with passion by unknown artists, and consumed in image if not in usage by a whole population which appropriates them as a purely magical object."[58] When Henry Adams paired the automobile and the dynamo with the virgin, two generations earlier (see chapter 1), he understood the machine as a generative cultural force. When Barthes paired the car and the cathedral fifty years later, he understood the machine as culture itself. Yet both commentators grasped a medieval Christian metaphor to explain how thoroughly their respective machines saturated their respective societies, just as the church—its buildings, people, networks, and rituals—dominated the West in the middle ages. For Barthes, automobility was more than a constituent fact of life; like Christianity, it grew from an isolated phenomenon into a world-dominating force and a car-oriented worldview—especially in the United States where, by some estimates in the mid-1950s, roads were being paved at a rate of two hundred miles per day.[59] Some might have argued that in America a more secular comparison was preferable: David Riesman and Eric Larrabee made a similar analysis using sociological terms, but even they couldn't help but reveal the idolatrous dimensions of the nation's complex car-dependence: the car, as a repository of values, had meaning that extended beyond its significance as a discreet object. It was a shaper of social habits, a dictator of cultural norms, a transformer of physical environments, and a creator of new cities.[60]

Single-minded devotion to the car was particularly troubling to an urbanist like Lewis Mumford, who had been reckoning with the impact of the automobile on American landscapes and cityscapes since at least the 1920s (in his work with the Regional Plan Association and his support of projects like Radburn, New Jersey, the town for the motor age). Rejecting Barthes's critical detachment and embracing iconoclasm far more forcefully than the editors of *Fortune,* Mumford was strident in his judgment of the car as deity. "The current American way of life," he wrote in "The Highway and the City" (published in *Architectural Record* in 1958), "is founded not just on motor transportation but on the religion of the motor car." The implications were clear: through its organizations and influence, the car had cultivated something akin to blind faith in the supposed efficacy of privatized mobility, which in turn generated fervent intolerance for everything except what Mumford called a system of "mono-transportation." Though Mumford surely intended the theistic implications of this term, he also used a gendered and sexual analogy. The American enthralled with the automobile was like a man "demented with passion" for a "capricious" lover, willingly throwing over his marriage and his income to satisfy his desire. "Our motorized mistress" had brought the United States to the brink of ruin, "promis[ing] delights" that we could now "only occasionally enjoy." Try as he might to flee the congested center, when the motorist reached the edge of the metropolis, he found that because of the highway, the countryside he sought had disappeared. Lest Mumford's readers miss the point, a cartoon by Alan Dunn made this clear by depicting a traffic-clogged surface road lined, out to the horizon, with billboards, giant ice cream cones, and a typical array of gas-food-lodging signs, but also accompanied by the looming roadside presence of a circa-1958, standard-issue low-rise shopping center.[61]

At a basic level, Mumford was disgusted by individual American drivers indulging in what he decried as the "swollen imaginations" and "infantile fantasies" of the "indecently tumescent chariots" coming out of Detroit.[62] Mumford was not alone in this regard: Frank Lloyd Wright disparaged Detroit's late model offerings in a 1957 speech to the Michigan Society of Architects. By then, Wright, a

Figure 37. Alan Dunn, cartoon illustrating Lewis Mumford's "The Highway and the City," *Architectural Record,* April 1958.

AUTOPIA AND ITS DISCONTENTS

dedicated automobile aficionado, had become dissatisfied with U.S. cars, dismissing the tailfin era as "evidence of bad design." With less reserve than Mumford, he declared that they looked like nothing so much as "a ferryboat coming down the street, gnashing its teeth at you for no good reason" and "shriek[ing] to heaven" while disturbing "the quiet beauty of the environment." Of the numerous critics in the 1950s who associated the automobile with environmental blight, Wright and Mumford might have been the only two in that decade to make explicit that they were as offended by the design of the cars as they were by the design of the roadside. Both men refused to place blame on the growing power of car stylists like Harley Earl, assigning culpability instead to the American consumer. "Why do you buy the things?" Wright asked. "Why do you go on from here to there with your streets becoming more and more crowded and your cars getting bigger and bigger with no consideration ever given to the *nature of the thing* . . . the nature of mobility in a car."[63] More was at stake in these critiques of car design than mere consumer preference. For Wright, it was a choice between quantity, conformity, and mediocrity or quality, freedom, and democracy—and he used all of those terms for dramatic ends in his speech in Detroit.[64] Mumford understood that, on their own, the cars were inconsequential; the real danger was in their aggregation. In Mumford's view, the midcentury driving public had become zealous, if not fanatical: "The sacrifices people are prepared to make for this religion [of the motor car] stand outside the realm of rational criticism." So irrationally enthralling was the culture of the car in the 1950s that, in Mumford's view, the American people were sacrificing nothing less than the polis itself, "wip[ing] out the very area of freedom the private motor car promised to retain for them."[65] Democracy was being cast onto the pyre under the guise of, well, democracy—or at least the operations of the republic—as embodied for Mumford by the $25 billion congressional appropriation to fund the construction of Eisenhower's Interstate Highway and Defense System in 1957.

As Mumford knew only too well, the automotive industrial complex had deployed (or manipulated) the rhetoric of freedom and democracy for as long as there had been cars on the road, and it was no different in the 1950s. When Riesman and Larrabee scrutinized the consumer psychology used to market the latest models from Ford, Chrysler, and General Motors, they were led, unsurprisingly, straight back to those putatively American values the car had come to embody over the preceding half century: "an intrinsic appeal to freedom"; "a manifesto of self-definition"; an affirmation of "one's democratic impulse." The Big Three had long exploited these values to increase car sales, and in the mid-1950s they manipulated them to even greater effect to make the interstates a reality. General Motors, in particular, lobbied hard for the establishment the system and threw the full weight of its media apparatus into the effort. *Give Yourself the Green Light* (a GM promotional film of 1954) picked up where *To New Horizons* (a GM promotional film of 1940) left off, which made sense since both were produced by the Jam Handy Corporation, the nation's leading maker of motivational movies. The earlier film used scenes of Norman Bel Geddes's Futurama from the 1939 World's Fair to *imagine* a nation of "magic motorways" offering "freedom of movement from place to place." The later film finds that "the American dream of freedom on wheels" is largely unfulfilled because "Futurama's free-flowing channels of concrete and steel" are limited to a few scattered miles "across the friendly face of our land." And these, alas, are not sufficient "to carry the mounting traffic of our growing greatness." A manifest destiny of "motorized mobility" is clearly in jeopardy: "we're running out of roads [because] we didn't dream big enough."[66] This stirring Burnhamesque rhetoric, combined with scenes of mid-1950s urban congestion in large cities and small towns alike, was a deft piece of corporate propaganda, precisely the kind that Mumford sought to undermine in "The Highway and the City."

Like Whyte, Mumford insisted that the automobile and its infrastructure had perverted conventional notions of social and economic progress. Policies and practices now emanating from Detroit and Washington were not progress; they were "regression" and the expressways themselves were "pyramid building with a vengeance." Mumford was not unilaterally condemning all highway building. He was too sophisticated a critic not to acknowledge that sometimes they were "consummate works of art" (with Gilmore Clarke's Taconic State Parkway as an example). Instead, Mumford was decrying the ruthlessness of the supposed efficiency of contemporary interstates. In urban centers, the interchanges, parking lots, and garages were like "a tomb of concrete roads and ramps covering the dead corpse of a city." Outside the centers, they effected "a brutal assault on the landscape." In both cases, the new highways were laying waste to everything in their paths, not just woods and streams, but "human neighborhoods." Looking at the scale of transformation in 1958, when the end of World War II was still within living memory, Mumford permitted himself a painfully timely analogy: the highway produced "about the same result [as] the blast of an atom bomb."[67] That Mumford would compare the destruction wrought by highway building to the force of a nuclear weapon indicates how high autopia's critics believed the stakes were in 1958. Previously, it might have been possible to pretend that the automotive transformation of the country had been achieved principally through the inexorable operations of the free market. After 1957, and especially as the rate of interstate construction increased during the 1960s, it was impossible to ignore that direct government action was effecting the transformation and that the scale of change was of a previously unimaginable magnitude. In confronting autopia's depredations, many critics believed it was well past the time for gentlemanly commentary.

Surveying the Junkyard

Peter Blake was a European émigré who departed Germany for the UK after the Nazis came to power and arrived in the United States in 1940 to attend architecture school at the University of Pennsylvania. Blake spent the 1950s and 1960s as an editor at *Architectural Forum* working under Douglas Haskell. During that time, in addition to becoming an intimate of the American architectural elite, he began fulminating against "Ugly America." When he looked out at the same landscape of the automobile where Haskell discerned possibility, Blake saw only the spires of Howard Johnson's, deeming them "an accurate reflection of today's relative values." When he acknowledged the significance of the new typologies of the automotive age, he interpreted them with unmitigated cynicism: "Another of suburbia's 'symbolic' buildings is, of course, the shopping center—which is certainly symbolic of *something*." Blake continued this kind of analysis with funding from the Graham Foundation, publishing his study of "the planned deterioration of the American landscape" in 1964. By Blake's own description, *God's Own Junkyard* was a "muckraking book," one written not "in anger, but "in fury."[68]

Blake complained loudly about the state of U.S. cities, denouncing in particular the American custom of tearing down fine historic buildings in the name of progress. He also complained about the construction of modern buildings if they were of poor quality or if he considered their presence detrimental to the historic fabric. But Blake's loudest, most howling jeremiads were against the vast territory he identified as the "interminable wastelands dotted with millions of monotonous little houses . . . and crisscrossed by highways lined with billboards, jazzed-up diners, used-car lots, drive-in movies, beflagged gas stations, and garish motels." All of these were amply illustrated in the 157 photographs that accompanied the text. Blake chose most of these from predictable sources: agencies like Magnum, Black Star, and UPI, along with the work of well-known photographers like Berenice Abbott, Balthazar Korab, Ezra Stoller, and Elliott Erwitt and including both of Roy Stryker's major documentary efforts for the Farm Security Administration and Standard Oil of New Jersey. His selections include locales well known for their hypercommercial development at midcentury, from Times Square to Miami Beach (Morris Lapidus–designed buildings were particular targets) and from U.S. 1 to U.S. 30, notably in the vicinity of Admiral Wilson Boulevard in Camden, New Jersey, then experiencing its most intensive automobile-oriented development.

In a book designed by Elaine Lustig Cohen, the images were presented as full-page bleeds or in strategic pairs that did much of the heavy lifting for Blake's polemic. Clearly influenced by the work of Ian Nairn and Gorden Cullen (the latter discussed earlier in this chapter), whose "Outrage and Counter-Attack" in *Architectural Review* critiqued what they called the taxonomies of British "subtopia," Blake organized the images into five picture sections in which the text was limited to a single introductory page. From townscape and landscape to roadscape, carscape, and skyscape, these sections depicted the scale and repetition of interstates and older federal highways, housing subdivisions, automobile graveyards, commercial strips, Main Streets, and other "roadside junk," all of it contributing to the "uglification" of the country. By 1963 these were familiar sins, and Blake's register

Figure 38. Admiral Wilson Boulevard, Camden, New Jersey in 1952, from Peter Blake's *God's Own Junkyard,* 1964. (Photograph by Walter Sanders; Standard Oil [New Jersey] Collection, SONJ 7266OM-5, Archives and Special Collections, University of Louisville)

of roadside offenses is both expected and unsurprising. Indeed, in a memoir published thirty years later Blake acknowledged that his argument was "more than a little narrow and obvious," but such was his need to rage against the machine and its deleterious effects.[69]

Echoing critics from Mary Mix Foley to Lewis Mumford, *God's Own Junkyard* also offered a political analysis of the contemporary situation. Under the mantle of democracy, Blake argued, the free market, coupled with a cultural impulse toward novelty, had produced a "complete and unrestricted freedom of esthetic choice." Any attempt to restrict this freedom "went against the popular grain." Blake particularly resented how difficult it was to escape the "degraded ugliness," unlike pornography or avant-garde art which, he reasoned, people could view or avoid as they wished, noting that "the trouble with most of the eyesores created in America in recent years is that they are impossible to ignore." For Blake, the responsible parties were "public uglifiers" in clear violation of the social contract.[70] Like Foley and Mumford, Blake, too, blames his "fellow citizens" for lacking pride of place,

1. Disneyland's "Autopia" ride shortly after the theme park's opening, July 1955. (Photograph by Loomis Dean; The LIFE Picture Collection/Getty Images)

2. Robert Venturi and Denise Scott Brown driving south on Las Vegas Boulevard, near Sahara Avenue, in 1968. (Photograph by Learning from Las Vegas Research Studio; The Architectural Archives, University of Pennsylvania by the gift of Robert Venturi and Denise Scott Brown)

3. John Steuart Curry, painting of "gimcracks" on the highway from "The Great American Roadside," *Fortune,* September 1934. (Permission courtesy of Kiechel Fine Art and John Steuart Curry Estate)

4. John Steuart Curry, painting of gas pumps and highway signs from "The Great American Roadside," *Fortune,* September 1934. (Permission courtesy of Kiechel Fine Art and John Steuart Curry Estate)

5. "To this has human symbolism fallen": John Margolies, 1981 photograph of Tail o' the Pup Hot Dog Stand (Milton Black, 1946), Los Angeles, 1981. (John Margolies Roadside America photograph archive [1972–2008], Library of Congress, Prints and Photographs Division, LC-MA05-7406)

6. John Margolies, 1967 photograph of the Big Duck, a roadside building on Long Island from 1931. In Peter Blake's *God's Own Junkyard* it is intended to illustrate the degraded state of the U.S. built environment. (John Margolies Roadside America photograph archive [1972–2008], Library of Congress, Prints and Photographs Division, LC-MA05-6708)

7. Continued development of "auto territoriality" and "other-directed" architecture: typical commercial strip, circa 1970 (probably U.S. 1 in Woodbridge, Virginia). (Chris Wilson Collection of J. B. Jackson American Slides [Series 3], Center for Southwest Research and Special Collections, University of New Mexico Libraries, 000-866-10-035)

8. "Blight blossoms on the American highway": Speedway Boulevard in Tucson, Arizona, from *Life*, 24 July 1970. (Photograph by Michael Rougier; The LIFE Picture Collection/Getty Images)

9. Allan D'Arcangelo, *U.S. Highway 1, No. 3,* 1962, acrylic on canvas. (Smithsonian American Art Museum, © 1962, D'Arcangelo Family Partnership, Museum purchase made possible by the American Art Forum, 2011.13; © 2018 D'Arcangelo Family Partnership/Licensed by VAGA at Artists Rights Society [ARS], NY)

10. West End of Glitter Gulch (Fremont Street) at night, circa 1953. (UNLV Libraries Special Collections)

11. Melvin Zeitvogel, sign for a Buick dealership at El Cajon Boulevard and 34th Street, San Diego, 1959, from Tom Wolfe, "The New Life Out There," *New York Magazine,* 9 December 1968. (Photograph by Mike Salisbury; permission courtesy of the photographer)

12. Motorists line up at a Texaco gas station on New York's Long Island, summer 1973. (Copyright Associated Press)

13. Installation view of *Signs of Life: Symbols and the American City,* Renwick Gallery, 1976. (Photograph by Tom Bernard; The Architectural Archives, University of Pennsylvania by the gift of Robert Venturi and Denise Scott Brown)

14. John Margolies, 1977 photograph of Tascosa Drive-In Theater, Amarillo, Texas. (John Margolies Roadside America photograph archive [1972–2008], Library of Congress, Prints and Photographs Division, LC-MA05-311)

15. Shell Service Station (1930) in Winston-Salem, North Carolina. (Photograph by Carol M. Highsmith, 2005; Carol M. Highsmith's America, Library of Congress, Prints and Photographs Division, LC-DIG-highsm-04862)

16. Signs on Las Vegas Boulevard, near Sahara Avenue, in 1966. (Photograph by Denise Scott Brown; The Architectural Archives, University of Pennsylvania by the gift of Robert Venturi and Denise Scott Brown)

for being indifferent to the country's "man-made heritage," and for not seeming to "care a hoot about what their [insert list of commercial typologies here] do to the streetscape."⁷¹ Significantly, Blake also condemned his fellow architects and other members of "our supposed 'intellectual elite,'" for abdicating their responsibility to guide the public in matters of taste and beauty. Blake assumed that the American intellectual elite shared his definition of taste and beauty, and for the most part they did, but by the mid-1960s change was in the air and such cultural certainties were about to be challenged. Indeed, one of the most attentive readers of *God's Own Junkyard* would shortly turn Blake's argument completely on its head.

In a contrast worthy of Pugin, Blake begins his "townscape" chapter with a pair of images: Thomas Jefferson's Lawn at the University of Virginia is contrasted with Canal Street in New Orleans, running between the French Quarter and the Central Business District. Blake intended the pair to represent "the decline, fall,

Figure 39. Canal Street in New Orleans, from Peter Blake's *God's Own Junkyard*, 1964. (Photograph by Wallace Litwin; ©Stanley B. Burns, MD & The Burns Archive)

AUTOPIA AND ITS DISCONTENTS

169

and subsequent disintegration of urban civilization." For Blake, Jefferson's Lawn, with its balance of open space and ordered pavilions, embodied a utopic, urban ideal, while Canal Street, with its hodgepodge of buildings and signage superstructure, embodied the defilement of America.[72] Within the muckraking pages of *God's Own Junkyard* it would have been inconceivable for him to interpret these images in any other way. But in 1966, in what, retrospectively, we can now describe as a postmodern act of appropriation, Robert Venturi republished this pairing in *Complexity and Contradiction in Architecture* and drew very different conclusions. Harkening back to Douglas Haskell, Venturi found "vitality and validity" in Canal Street's "honky-tonk elements." In Venturi's misreading of Blake, he observes that "the pictures in the book that are supposed to be bad are often good" and "besides the irrelevancy of the comparison, is not Main Street almost alright?" Blake's earnest opprobrium becomes Venturi's "ironic interpretation."[73]

God's Own Junkyard was hardly free of irony. How else to explain Blake's quoting of Vitruvius next to a photograph of the Big Duck on Long Island (see color plate 6), a building Blake knew because he summered in the Hamptons? We can assume he found no eurythmy in the shop that William Collins designed for poultryman Martin Mauer near Riverhead, nor anything remotely comparable to the pastoral beauty depicted on the facing page of the book—children, ducks, and water features in Greenbelt, Maryland, and the green necklace of the Minneapolis park system.[74] Venturi was uninterested in whether or not the Duck satisfied the Vitruvian triad, and when he and Denise Scott Brown appropriated the building in their famous collaboration, Peter Blake's "commercial vandalism" was transformed into "commercial heraldry," as they made an argument about buildings in which the architecture is made subordinate to symbolic form. In theorizing the duck in 1968—in "A Significance for A&P Parking Lots," in "On Ducks and Decoration," and in their Las Vegas studio at Yale—Venturi and Scott Brown guaranteed its architectural immortality, along with *God's Own Junkyard,* prompting roadside documentarian John Margolies to photograph it a few years later and eventually leading to its listing in the National Register of Historic Places (see chapter 5).[75] But when they repurposed the duck within architectural discourse, Venturi and Scott Brown also decontextualized it within that discourse, severing

Figure 40. Marion Post Wolcott, photograph of children feeding ducks at Greenbelt, Maryland in 1938, from Peter Blake's *God's Own Junkyard*, 1964. (Farm Security Administration—Office of War Information Photograph Collection, Library of Congress, Prints and Photographs Division, LC-USF33-030037-M4)

it from a particular historical moment of autopian discontent. Though Blake deployed the building for his own polemical ends, to serve his trenchant critique of the commercial landscape, it was one image of more than one hundred, with no more significance than any of the others. The theoretical afterlife of the Big Duck has overshadowed the larger argument of *God's Own Junkyard*—that Blake intended it, idealistically, to spur his fellow citizens to action. This becomes clear if we follow Blake's critical trajectory a moment longer, to the year after the book's publication.

In December 1965, in a double issue of *Life* magazine focusing on the city published just two months after Lyndon Johnson signed the Highway Beautification Act into law, Paul Ylvisaker, a planner and policy expert with the Ford Foundation, followed Blake's lead in taking aim at the sprawling landscapes of the attenuated American metropolis. Though he argued that "sometimes even the gargantuan whole of urban America can be a thing of beauty," especially by air at night, the real issue for Ylvisaker was that most Americans had "to contend with grubbier

Figure 41. "A corroding artery": Alt-U.S. 90 around Houston, from "The Villains Are Greed, Indifference—and You," *Life,* 24 December 1965. (Photograph by Bill Ray; The LIFE Picture Collection/Getty Images)

realities below." For this reason, he refused to pull any punches when identifying what—and who—was responsible for all those miles of grubby "slurbs and junk," illustrated by the "corroding artery" of Alt-U.S. 90 through Houston: "The Villains Are Greed, Indifference—and You." Replace Ylvisaker's "villains" with Blake's "vandals," and this prodding contempt could have come straight out of *God's Own Junkyard*. Blake supplied a guest editorial for that same issue of *Life;* by then he was editor of *Architectural Forum,* so his contribution to another Time Inc. publication makes sense. In that brief essay, having vented his spleen in his own book the previous year, Blake is conciliatory—after all, in *God's Own Junkyard* he suggested that it was not too late "for us to learn to see again." A year later, in "Astride the Open Road," a frustrated Peter Blake lamented that architects had failed as yet "to make their peace" with the habits of the car. To Blake, the reasons were clear: they were spending too much time trying to pretend that the United States was Europe, instead of accepting the obvious differences between attenuated urban corridors (like those of Houston) and compact urban cores of older cities. What piazzas were to Florence and vistas were to Paris, highways were to the American city, and the time had come, Blake declared, for architects "to come to terms with the automobile and the highway."[76] At that moment in 1965, with the critiques of Venturi and Scott Brown still nascent, Blake could hardly have anticipated what form that acceptance would take, but by the mid-1960s and with growing intellectual force, a coming to terms with Autopia was well underway; indeed, as we will see in the next chapter, it had been there all along.

4

LEARNING FROM AUTOPIA

In 1950, the U.S. Bureau of the Census updated its statistical classifications to better reflect the geographic and demographic realities of a nation changing rapidly at midcentury, an objective that underscored the significance of the American Autopia as a physical place and a cultural condition. Though *rural* and *urban* remained the principal census categories for territories, people, and housing, the bureau introduced a key refinement to its urban definition. Prior to the 1950 census, places outside incorporated cities and towns were always classified as rural, regardless of population density or settlement patterns. As a result, the bureau admitted, the census was failing to provide an accurate picture of residential and commercial development beyond municipal corporate limits; this had been the case for thirty years, since the 1920 census first enumerated the United States as a majority urban nation. Since then, decentralization had gained momentum, aided by the increased automobile ownership and expanding automobile infrastructure that critics accurately blamed for exacerbating sprawl. From the bureau's more neutral perspective, the problem was that the 1930 and 1940 counts had no means of characterizing the in-between places that constituted what it now identified as "suburban territory" and "urban fringe." Beginning in 1950, these places—neither

Facing page: detail of fig. 44, Paul Rudolph's rendering of Temple Street Garage, New Haven, Connecticut

wholly rural nor traditionally urban—became, in bureau parlance, "urbanized areas," frequently bounded by little more than a census tract and an arterial highway, with at least 2,500 people per square mile. What this definition lacked in precision, it made up for in currency when the bureau's preliminary analysis found that one-third of all Americans lived in these *urbanized areas* circa 1950. For the 1960 census, the bureau expanded its definition to include "linking corridors" connecting one urbanized area to another, provided these corridors contained at least 1,000 people per square mile. For the 1970 census, the bureau went even further, replacing "urbanized areas" with an "extended city" concept that flattened the urban hierarchy of core and periphery to capture the circumstances of the country's consolidating metropolitan regions.[1]

While a numbers-do-not-lie pragmatism made it easy for demographers to discern the primacy of car-centric urbanization in the extended city, when architects, planners, and their broader professional sphere considered its formal and semantic implications, they looked beyond the baldly numerical. Nonetheless, when the American Institute of Architects turned its attention to these issues in the mid-1950s, one particular number had surprising resonance with urban attenuation: the nearly 25,000-mile circumference of the earth. Assessing the status of "the architect at mid-century" through a survey of its membership and roundtable discussions among practitioners and other experts, the AIA related the magnitude of the earth's circumference to the "population shifts, migrations, and decentralization" shaping building activity inside and outside central cities. Tallying the quantity of this activity, the AIA observed that if it consisted entirely of continuous one-story structures, it would encircle the equator eighteen times, thus constituting a developed strip 450,000 miles long! As it pondered the *quality* of this activity, the AIA sounded a familiar note of autopian discontent, wondering if it was "compatible with the best potentialities of modern life." While buildings like skyscrapers and detached houses seemed to exemplify the "enterprising individualism" reflective of "our national character," the U.S. landscape as a whole was characterized by "a savage litter" that produced "discord rather than to aid the citizen." This, the AIA implied, resulted from architects failing to reckon with the scale of the new metropolis and to conceptualize buildings as "components of the whole community," whether that community was morphologically compact or elongated. Sociologist William Goode, an expert on family patterns in industrialized societies who seemed to echo Census Bureau reports when he participated in an AIA discussion in New York, came to a similar conclusion: architects and planners had no choice but to respond to the reality of "urbanization in all directions," even in once remote rural areas that were "becoming citified" through increased automobile usage and a car-oriented built environment.[2]

Elizabeth Gordon, the influential *House Beautiful* editor, went even further at the New York meeting, chiding architects for adhering to outmoded hierarchies, anticipating Catherine Bauer's comparable admonition in *Architectural Forum* in 1956 (see chapter 3). Why, Gordon asked, were architects still paying so much attention to the downtown core instead of "driving literally hundreds of miles around the fringes of cities to know what goes on?"[3] Gordon, an ardent Frank Lloyd Wright supporter, was in sync with the basic premise of Wrightian automotive urbanism in which "every Broadacre citizen has his own car." Though Wright's "gift of the motorcar" had begun to seem more like a burden by the 1950s, the architect who called himself Gordon's godfather still believed in the possibility of redemption in the attenuated metropolis, along "the great architectural highway." When Wright declared "the car is architecture" around this time, it was not a Fordist updating of his "art and craft of the machine" credo from half a century earlier. The car was architecture for Wright in the 1950s because it was as fundamental to "the way you live" as the clothes Americans wore and the food they ate.[4] When Gordon, at that AIA roundtable, suggested the urban fringe as a key site for comprehending contemporary urban form, hers was a Wrightian proposition for the acquisition of autopian architectural knowledge as essential as census statistics.

To *know* autopia, not as an unavoidable fact of American life, but as the subject of thoughtful scrutiny and deliberate inquiry—this was a critical first step for architects attempting to intervene in the new American city. Though a dedicated anti-modernist like Gordon would have disavowed the comparison, there was something Corbusian in her suggestion of exploring the urban fringe, an extension of his "eyes that do not see" parallel beyond the car and the building to the territories they occupied. Standards had been established, in the strips and subdivisions, along the highways, at the exit ramps. In the automobile utopia it was time to face the problem of perfection, especially with Eisenhower's interstate program promising (or threatening) to radically alter urban and urbanized areas. While autopian perfection remained elusive in the 1950s and 1960s, that did not stop a diverse assortment of architects, planners, and critics from engaging the contemporary built environment of the automobile in a more conciliatory manner than those discussed in chapter 3. These roadside observers were neither intellectual outliers of metropolitan discourse nor apologists for an autopian status quo. Nor, given their varied interests, outlooks, and agendas, were they part of an organized intellectual movement or school of thought. Nonetheless, they did constitute what we can now recognize as the vanguard of thinkers who were ready to learn from autopia, and their approaches to the maturing territories of the automobile would have far-reaching consequences, in theory and in practice.

Motorized, Yet Civilized

If autopian perfection existed anywhere on the urban fringe in the 1950s, it may have been amid the rolling hills and former tobacco fields of Bloomfield, Connecticut. Frazar Wilde certainly thought so, which is why, in the fall of 1957, the insurance company president brought four hundred urban thinkers five miles northwest of downtown Hartford to introduce them to Connecticut General's new corporate headquarters on the occasion of an urbanism symposium he convened to mark the dedication of the complex. More accurately, Wilde bused his guests out, allowing them to observe the transition from Hartford's congested business center to its less dense residential districts and on through an urban periphery scattered with commercial establishments, farms, and churches. Arriving at Connecticut General, they encountered a bucolic, 280-acre campus designed by Skidmore, Owings and Merrill and lauded as a "palace of industry" where "Colonial gives way to the Bauhaus and the Bauhaus to U.S.A. 1957." This distinction was as much geographic as stylistic. With respect to Wilde's conference, both charateristics contributed to what participants and *Life* magazine recognized as the setting's portentousness, as they circulated between sleek interiors and landscaped

Figure 42. Aerial View of Connecticut General Life Insurance Company Headquarters (Skidmore, Owings and Merrill, 1957), Bloomfield, Connecticut. (© Ezra Stoller/Esto)

courtyards, contemplating the "challenges of the new highways" and the "tangled problems of metropolitan growth" with nary a car in sight.[5] Whether this was ironic or acceptable depended on one's relationship to autopian urbanism.

To James Rouse, real estate developer, urban renewal advocate, and early promoter of enclosed shopping malls and suburban new towns, Connecticut General was both "a symbol and a symptom." In his symposium talk, Rouse argued that its "magnificent" buildings and landscapes were a response to the "obsolete" state of the central city and to the general condition of "scatteration" outside the urban core. While Connecticut General was a manifestation of "human aspiration," more typical exurban development—built with "less boldness, imagination and taste"—gained significance from its "magnitude," its sheer quantity indicating the "massive reorganization of the metropolitan area" then underway. Despite obvious qualitative differences, both reflected "the way we want to live and work," away from the "maelstrom" of the urban core, in those burgeoning realms of casual mobility dominated by "station wagons [and] blue jeans." Historian and critic John Burchard, serving as MIT's humanities dean when he took the podium at Connecticut General (as noted at the end of chapter 1, he had earlier participated in *Architectural Record*'s fiftieth-anniversary roundtable), was reluctant to include himself in Rouse's "we," but he recognized the limitations of a highbrow perspective when characterizing urbanism in the expanded field. Though Burchard personally preferred "center" and "symphony" to "strip" and "juke box," he conceded that "people lolling in their cars while a car hop brings them chicken in the rough and a chocolate malted" with 45s playing in the background were, in fact, "living an abundant life."[6] In Burchard's description of a roadside fried chicken joint, there was little veiled condescension, mainly a bemused evocation of the simple pleasures of the motoring public.

Lewis Mumford—unsurprisingly given the views discussed in the last chapter—was more skeptical of this public in his "summary and outlook" comments that *Architectural Forum* described as concluding the symposium "with fireworks." Though he saluted Connecticut General for creating "an intellectual center for Hartford and for the nation," he mocked defenders of sprawl who might have been tempted to claim the corporate campus as legitimizing "limitless suburbia." To Mumford, Connecticut General existed as a *center* only because it was legible as a *place,* one clearly defined by the "limited space" of its buildings and grounds. The rest of Mumford's comments were the anti-autopian complaints that became the basis for his 1958 article "The Highway and the City." Mumford bemoaned the fact that so many fellow Americans had rejected Emerson's transcendentalist commandment to "give all to love" by publicly sanctioning giving "all to the motor car." In practical terms, this "one-dimensional thinking" meant a bewildering eagerness to replace "thy woods and templed hills" with "parking lots, big cloverleaves, and traffic knots," all of them unredeemable from Mumford's perspective. Though he took aim at recent congressional authorization of the Interstate Highway System, calling out the falsity of its defense rationale, Mumford's real target was the automotive single-mindedness that made it possible: "instead of planning motor cars to fit our life," Mumford stated bluntly, "we are trying to plan our life to fit the motor car."[7] For Mumford in 1957, equivocation was not an option, but there were those among his urbanist colleagues, including many in attendance at the symposium, who saw a form of critical accommodation as a reasonable way forward. They were not interested in condemning the automobile, and, like Rouse and Burchard, they had not traveled to Bloomfield to spend three days problematizing the car's impact.

Instead, they came to reflect upon, not rail against, the current state of (much of) the United States: "Americans have made up their minds to live in metropolitan areas and ride in automobiles." Such was the matter-of-fact assessment of Wilfred Owen, the Brookings Institution senior fellow who organized Frazer Wilde's symposium. A transportation economist and contributor to the automobile section of the *New York Times,* Owen freely accepted the necessity of "adapting to the automotive age." In his work at Brookings, Owen advocated for intermodal transportation policies that treated public carriers and private cars as equal parts of comprehensive metropolitan planning. While he recognized that congestion and decentralization predated the automobile, Owen acknowledged the car's role in intensifying outward growth and roadside blight. Though unabashed in his "defense of the automobile," he approached the car's impact with even-handedness: "supply side" transportation solutions (i.e., the seemingly perpetual construction of car, bus, and train infrastructure) had to be balanced with "demand side" retooling of land use and density, traffic flows and economic activity across urban centers, suburban fringes, and outlying areas. From Owen's macroeconomic perspective, all planning initiatives required this supply-and-demand double thrust to produce anything resembling "a satisfactory urban environment."[8] Though Owen implied that unanimity existed, what kind of environment qualified as *satisfying* and *urban* was highly contested, even among those committed to learning from autopia. With metropolitan forms and customs in flux due to expanding car usage, another issue arose. As Owen phrased it when parsing the symposium proceedings for publication, "Is it possible to be urbanized and motorized, yet civilized?"[9] This was not rhetorical; it was a fundamental cultural question that reflected the United States' continued evolution as an advanced industrialized society.

Though critic Douglas Haskell and architect Victor Gruen applied distinctly different criteria when evaluating autopia as culture and place, both would have answered Owen's question affirmatively when they agreed to participate in the Connecticut General symposium. Gruen was the symposium's keynote speaker, and his 1954 Northland Shopping Center near Detroit was featured prominently in the glossy précis-cum-brochure that circulated in advance of the gathering, along with Edward Clark's ubiquitous view of U.S. 1 outside Baltimore (see figure 31). Haskell, then editor of *Architectural Forum* and a member of the symposium advisory group, clearly influenced the selection of panelists, many of whom were *Forum* contributors; for months after the symposium, Haskell used the pages of *Architectural Forum* to promote its content, publishing excerpts of some papers (by Mumford and Rouse) and articles based on others, including Gruen's on "Highways and the American City." Haskell featured the proceedings and outcomes in the *Forum* because the symposium was timely and appropriate for his readership, but a professional kinship was also at work, since its cities-in-the-motor-age theme was aligned with Haskell's ongoing intellectual project.

A Roadside Methodology

As we saw in previous chapters, by the 1950s Haskell had spent nearly two decades as an intellectual independent, and even a maverick, using his practice as a critic and editor to interrogate the American autopian order and to thoughtfully consider the nation's urbanizing landscapes. In his earliest view-from-the-road architectural reporting from the 1930s, he explored buildings and settlements deemed appropriate for "a country of the automobile" and he made the first of many manifesto-like declarations that encouraged designers to move beyond studying European precedents in order to get "the American scale into their bones." This meant eschewing the standards of compact urban centers in "bicycle-riding England or Germany" in favor of cities where the "main growth" had occurred "since the use of cars became widespread." In the western United States, Haskell argued in 1937, architects and planners would find the model for the twentieth century. Overlooking its streetcar past for rhetorical effect, he declared that "Los Angeles is a city built on the automobile as Boston was built on the sailing ship." Though L.A. might appear to the casual viewer as "a series of parking lots interspersed with buildings" or as "a string of semi-independent communities" lacking coherent form and so large that the city limits seemed to extend as far as Alaska, Haskell astutely comprehended it as "a modern American city" that might generate "a modern architecture of movement and spaciousness."[10] As urban form evolved in the 1940s and 1950s, Haskell drew a parallel between Roadtown and Main Street, recognizing the former as the midcentury car-centric version of the latter, a place both symbolic and real, a social and cultural archetype as well as an economic and physical infrastructure. Highways, Haskell argued, "set our overall building pattern today just as forts set the pattern of the Middle Ages." The consequences were clear to even "Joe Bloke American," who understood that a country with 50 million people "must live along roads." As he summarized a half-century of auto-oriented evolution, Haskell offered a more cogent assessment of the situation than, as he put it, the oft-repeated, over-simplified idea that "the 20th century is making a slum of the entire countryside." The origins were familiar enough: a barn at a highway crossroads becomes a painted signboard, a gas station, a diner, and a tourist court. The mom-and-pop scale eventually gave way to corporate enterprise: "The sign companies put sappier advertisements on better frames. Bankers are taking over the motels, and chains the restaurants." Haskell continued his timeline right up to the exurban developments of the 1950s, situating the new large-scale structures sheltering decentralized work (including Connecticut General), shopping, and leisure as the typological descendants of Roadtown's earliest forms: "The big brains now put department stores in shopping centers along the road; the big brains now build insurance company headquarters out on the road too; and bigger showmen have superseded the roadside juke-box joint with Disneyland and Frontier Villages." With this level of capital investment and this scale of real estate development, social and aesthetic recriminations over Roadtown were pointless. "Sensitive people," he argued, needed to stop despairing and accept Roadtown as "a formidable fact" of an economy and culture predicated on "endless movement and transportation."[11]

Just as the car (and capitalism) expanded Haskell's definition of urban culture and city form, it also stretched his concept of architecture. In 1955, Haskell suggested that architecture was no longer an individual pursuit of the "art that insures human quality in a building"; it was now part of a larger whole, existing at multiple scales along a social and physical continuum of place and patronage—an "environment" that became *architectural* wherever and whenever humans intentionally changed their surroundings. In the old days, Haskell claimed, Charles McKim sat down with Alexander Cassatt to hash out the details of Pennsylvania Station over a glass of Madeira; now, "long ribbons of superhighway and throughway [*sic*] drop suddenly into place, and instantly the rubber-borne parade begins thundering over them." If Haskell failed to acknowledge the continued role of power brokers in shaping the midcentury built environment, it was because his point was metabolic: at the current rate of development, the country was approaching an era of "*total* architecture" as far-reaching and "radical" as the concept of "*total* war" (a term that gained currency during World War II). In this scenario, "the Market" was the locus of architectural power, and "highbrows" who refused to recognize this (here Haskell borrowed Russell Lynes's new formulation of cultural stratification) doomed architecture to regression and obsolescence. To make this clear, Haskell analyzed the relationship between architecture and two midcentury icons of mass production and consumption: houses and cars.[12]

Writing while the postwar homebuilding boom dominated by large-scale outfits like Levitt & Sons was in full swing, Haskell noted the increasing importance of "ready-made" houses marketed to "en masse" homebuyers. The automobile industry offered a comparable model of how to curry "public favor" by attempting "to clothe its great services in allurement." This was not as straightforward as it seemed because "the lure of the automobile is complex." For Haskell, the power and the perils of the car lay not only in the visual seductions of its design and marketing, but, more significantly, in its ability to enable car owners to drive away from "dingy areas of building," meaning away from the congested central city to those (for the time being) less-developed areas at and beyond the periphery. The trouble, Haskell recognized, was the car's "after effects," specifically its innate ability to make the new areas as dingy as the old. In addition to generating traffic congestion, automobiles generated environmental congestion through "miles of signs and jukebox roadside building." Haskell knew that by the mid-1950s it was well beyond the time when traditional architecture and city planning might be called upon to "restore civilization," as Lewis Mumford, whom he quoted, would have put it. Haskell also knew that "the mass of buildings can never be better or worse than the institutions which have shaped them." Architects needed to figure out how to design buildings for car-oriented places that had the same "romance" as the cars themselves, the kind of allure that would "stir people's imaginations" like the newest models out of Detroit. In effect, Haskell asserted, architects needed to learn from the autos, if not from autopia. "America," he wrote a few years later, "is the land where fashions swing en masse, and if this is true of the sack dress and the elongated automobile, why should it not be true of architecture?"[13]

In "Architecture in America," Haskell deployed a contrasting pair of photographs to drive this point home as a visceral visual critique: an aerial view of Los Angeles emphasizes the freeways and subdivisions of the expanding postwar metropolis that was rapidly subsuming what remained of farm fields and citrus groves, while Andreas Feininger's roadside view of Arizona emphasizes the gas-food-lodging honky-tonk of prewar Route 66 as it passed through the already dusty town of Seligman (see figure 35). Here, Haskell implied, were the two extremes that typified America: "vast clean dullness" versus "Roadtown clutter." The former was the product of calculated efficiencies and standardizing regulations; the latter emerged "innocent of all architecture and of any plan." The only way to mediate these extremes, Haskell believed, was for architecture in America to locate alternative "fulcrum points," those extra-architectural pivots that might prompt midcentury designers to demonstrate the relevance of humanistic practice even when servicing expanding consumerism and a car-oriented culture. Haskell lauded Victor Gruen, for example, for leveraging the ideal of community as *his* particular fulcrum when planning shopping centers and shopping malls in suburbs throughout the country (discussed shortly).[14]

Earlier, when examining the relationship between "Architecture and Popular Taste," Haskell had celebrated John Lautner's commercial work in Los Angeles for effectively deploying symbolism and exhibitionism as another sort of fulcrum. "Googie," as Haskell famously dubbed this approach (after Lautner's 1949 design for the eponymous West Hollywood coffee shop), embodied how designers could appeal to popular taste without architectural compromise. As Haskell continued to entreat architects to acknowledge the existence of "vitality in America's popular building, even in its roadside honky-tonk," he likewise promoted Googie as a method for putting on "a good show"—and thus satisfying public desire for drama—while still producing modern architecture. Honky-tonk, too, was another means of establishing "rapprochement" between the excesses of the roadside and the refinements of high-style modernism, as Haskell saw in the improvisation and variety of buildings lining highways the basis for establishing "an architectural counterpart to jazz." Haskell did not intend these parallels between roadside buildings and capital *A* architecture as mere polemics.[15]

As he explored architecture's limits and possibilities in the midcentury confluence of modernism and the automobile, his was an operative criticism in the service of an architectural methodology in and for autopia. In another "Architecture in America" article (the series in which Haskell included Mary Mix Foley's scathing critiques, discussed in chapter 3), Haskell celebrated the New Jersey Turnpike across the Hackensack Meadows (NJ Department of Highway Engineers with consulting architects Fellheimer & Wagner [Roland Wank], 1951), noting that the tapering concrete piers had already become an instant icon of the newly opened "superroad [*sic*]"—even if they were invisible to drivers on the turnpike. For Haskell, this did not really matter because the piers represented not only the turnpike's most formidable engineering challenge in crossing the wetlands, but also its most spectacular photographic opportunity, evident in an image by Eliot Elisofon widely circulated in Time-Life publications. Within Haskell's totalizing definition of architecture, the piers were significant in and of themselves, offering a vision of what autopia might become if architects took seriously the "vast horizontal spread of our society." What might happen, Haskell challenged his contemporaries, if architects applied the Vitruvian triad whenever approaching the "environment as a setting"? If the result gave "visual pleasure by its fitness and harmony," then the result would qualify as architecture, whether it was infrastructure or a roadside stand.¹⁶

Only a few American architects accepted Haskell's challenge in the 1950s, in passing references to autopian perfectibility that seem to come out of nowhere, but for the car's ubiquity in U.S. culture. Such was the case of Paul Rudolph, whom Haskell described as "that perspicacious architectural teacher of the younger generation," when hinting that Rudolph was sympathetic to his ideas about taste. In "The Six Determinants of Architectural Form" of 1956, Rudolph's reevaluation of modern architectural theory is decidedly not premised on an autopian analysis, but cars keep turning up in his argument.¹⁷ While a modernist desire to make city squares and public spaces "more human" was admirable, Rudolph wonders how architects should handle the "acres of cars" they encountered there. Though frustrated that architects too often ignored "the scale of vehicular traffic," Rudolph observed dryly that it should be possible to "find ways of seeing our buildings above the automobiles." This comment captioned Rudolph's own photograph of a shopping center parking lot, a typology that prompted continued speculation, a decade ahead of Venturi and Scott Brown taking in the view from the parking lot of an A&P. "Is it not possible to make parking lots agreeable?" Yale's newly appointed dean of architecture asked an audience of architectural educators in 1958. In "To Enrich Our Architecture," Rudolph was proposing a way out of the functionalist sterility of form that he believed characterized mainstream modernism, but he directly discussed autopian space as well, noting that in "relationship to the terrain," buildings and cities had "changed tremendously because of the automobile." Rudolph was optimistic that because "an American's peculiar love for his automobile makes him spare no ex-

Figure 43. Eliot Elisofon, photograph of the New Jersey Turnpike in Hackensack Meadows (NJ Department of Highway Engineers with Fellheimer & Wagner [Roland Wank]), from "Architecture in America," *Architectural Forum,* October 1955. (The LIFE Picture Collection/ Getty Images)

pense where it is involved," the country would soon charge its architects with unlocking "the innermost potentialities of the automobile," in terms of built form, planning, and development. For Rudolph, the nation's superhighways proved that Americans could build exceptional spaces for moving cars. Why couldn't they build exceptional spaces for parked cars as well? Parking was an opportunity as much as a problem for Rudolph, and he believed it might become "a major and exciting architectural form" rivaling bridges from the Ponte Vecchio to the George Washington. Once parking became properly architectural, it might even restore dignity to the urban fringe, creating gateways for areas lacking "focal points" because they were dominated by undifferentiated strips and subdivisions.[18]

The difficulty in Rudolph's view was that most designers had not yet "faced the facts" of present-day realities, which he described in terms that anticipate Gottmann's Megalopolis: "One is hurled through space at ever-increasing rates, over and through cities which will shortly be several hundred miles long." Yet, he observed, "we produce endless streets in which buildings disappear behind advertising and motor cars." For Rudolph, dealing with this condition meant formulating a new concept of space, scale, and ornament, but his critique is situational because in architectural terms neither advertisements nor automobiles were intrinsically problematic. In some instances, advertising was even worthy of serious consideration. Times Square appears in both of Rudolph's essays, first illustrating the "spirit of the times" and then lauded as "the most dynamic outdoor room in America." There, the density and bigness of the signs heralded the possibility of a new monumentality in which enrichment was understood spatially and graphically.[19] In projects like Connecticut's grandiose Temple Street Garage in New Haven of 1960 and the seductive (if notorious) scheme to transform the engineer's route for the Lower-Manhattan Expressway into *City Corridor* (1967–72), Rudolph offered ample evidence that he eventually followed his and Haskell's own advice.[20] For New York, Rudolph produced a "topographic architecture" in the form of a monumental megastructure whose "hierarchy of building types" was derived from the notion that transportation should include "much more than the highway" and, concomitantly, that a highway should be much more than transportation.[21] In New Haven, though Rudolph was careful about sidewalk access and the inclusion

Figure 44. Paul Rudolph, rendering of Temple Street Garage, New Haven, Connecticut, 1959–63. (Paul Rudolph Archive, Library of Congress, Prints and Photographs Division, LC-DIG-ppmsca-03522)

of commercial space, he took his cue from the form and scale of thruways like the Oak Street Connector, newly completed as part of planner and public administrator Edward Logue's massive redevelopment of the city's downtown. On Temple Street, Rudolph designed a garage whose form and materiality announced it unmistakably as a building that "dealt with cars and movements." This aspect of the design, in addition to its, "glory, bulk, and impressiveness," led Victor Gruen to praise the garage effusively in *The Heart of Our Cities* (1964). In that "diagnosis and cure" of midcentury urban ills, based on Gruen's unrealized plan for Fort Worth, Texas, parking was the Gordian knot of contemporary urbanism.[22]

Scapes of the Auto Age

Parking was also directly related to what Gruen saw as the central charge of the architect at midcentury: to convert chaos into order and ugliness into beauty. Throughout his three decades in the United States, Gruen remained undaunted by this task, and like Douglas Haskell, he lit out for the territory of the car when most architects and critics were, in effect, still walking around downtown. In this pursuit, Gruen was equally unabashed: "if we don't want to get trapped, doubtful and actionless, at the co-merging of the clover leaves, we have to stop looking and listening around and get on the road." On that necessary voyage of discovery architects would realize their discipline needed to concern itself with more than buildings "in the conventional sense." Gruen came by his equivalent to Haskell's total architecture through a methodology more clinical than intuitive, as he analyzed "all man made elements which form our environments, with roads and highways, with signs and posters, with outdoor spaces as created by structures, with cityscape and landscape." In the landscape, nature dominated the environment; in the cityscape, human interventions did. Between those environmental extremes was a sprawling middle zone that became Gruen's utmost preoccupation, as he demonstrated in a 1955 address to the International Conference of Design in Aspen that served as a teaser for his much-heralded Fort Worth Plan. Gruen argued that before you could transform the modern metropolis, you had to understand it, starting with its attenuated complexity, which he dissected with formal and functional categorizations while documenting metropolitan socioeconomic development and devolution in light of mass production and consumption. Gruen was particularly interested in the "various species" of midcentury cityscapes that had emerged because of (or been transformed by) automobile proliferation. The *technoscape* and *transportationscape* were principally infrastructural, and included the diverse apparatus of mass communication, be it electric, telephonic, or automobilic. *Suburbscape* encompassed residential districts outside the center and across the socioeconomic spectrum, especially the rapidly growing subdivisions produced by the "mass housing industry" of the 1950s.[23]

The *subcityscape,* whose name indicated its hierarchical status, was defined by "commercial slums" that were the focal axes of metropolitan "vulgarity and ugliness." For Gruen, the subcityscape was "the degrading façade of suburbia, the shameful introduction to our cities, the scourge of the metropolis." Encompassing more acreage than the other scapes and combining their worst elements, the subcityscape was an extended corridor of blight created and exacerbated by the car, and defined by its built ephemera and detritus: billboards, gas stations, diners, and the like. In Gruen's analysis most of these structures lacked even rudimentary architectural ambitions, and those that were consciously designed were lost behind "an ugly rash of blatant signs [and] blinking cascades of neon." As unplanned individual elements clung "like leeches" to American roadsides, the chaotic subcityscape as a whole "spread its tentacles" across all known boundaries, be they local, regional, or national. Here, in a "wild sea of anarchy" was "commercialism at its worst."[24] Commercialism at its best was central to daily life: "Buying and selling," Gruen would soon argue, "is as old as mankind." More than that, it had long been an "invigorating part of urban life," but as automotive suburbia disrupted this tradition, an "amorphous conglomeration" had supplanted once dynamic commercial centers and merchants found it difficult "to integrate [their] activities with the local scene."[25] Gruen's critique was not new; indeed, it echoed standard autopian complaints, but his dissection of autopian metropolitan form was exactly precise and this precision served his larger agenda as a modernist reformer fighting a "personal battle against the suburban commercial slum." Importantly for Gruen, the subcityscape was redeemable, and like Douglas Haskell, who would give him an important platform for circulating his ideas in the pages of *Architectural Forum,* Gruen saw it as a site of endless cultural and architectural potential. Nowhere was this clearer than in Gruen's efforts to perfect the typology of the "integrated shopping center," in which he deployed architecture and planning as a vehicle for delivering civic and communal values to the farthest reaches of the motorized metropolis.[26]

Gruen's analysis of car and commerce interaction revealed itself earliest in projects like Milliron's of 1949 (see chapter 3), designed with his then-partner Elsie Krummeck. Located in Westchester on the far west side of Los Angeles, not far from the airport, the building still anchors the northwest corner of Sepulveda and La Tijera Boulevards. As Richard Longstreth has noted, it is sufficiently set back from the street to accommodate a wide sidewalk and originally featured three pedestrian-oriented entrances.[27] It also had a series of broadly projecting display pavilions set at angles from the main facade, increasing visibility for north- and southbound motorists. Similar reasoning motivated the architects' placement of

Figure 45. Julius Shulman, photograph of Milliron's Department Store (Gruen and Krummeck, 1949), Los Angeles; view of front ramp to rooftop shops and parking. (© J. Paul Getty Trust; Getty Research Institute, Los Angeles [2004.R.10])

a tall pylon, flush with the building's north facade, but projecting up and outward toward Sepulveda, where it functioned as a signboard and incorporated an exterior stair connecting the sidewalk to the store's so-called "terrace" level. Here, on the roof of the building, Gruen and Krummeck placed a beauty shop, children's playroom, and a lunch counter with outdoor seating under a covered portico. The terrace level also featured rooftop parking, which was probably superfluous, given the size of the rear lot, but provided drive-up convenience.

It also offered an opportunity for a bravura architectural display—as long as one viewed the building from the parking lot at ground level, where the designers extended the west facade with a pair of dramatically crisscross automobile ramps that provided access to and egress from the terrace level. When photographing

Milliron's on commission from the architects, Julius Shulman captured the sculptural quality of those ramps in a wide-angle view across the expanse of the nearly empty lot. The building all but disappearing behind the giant *X* of the low-slung ramps, this was the most abstract of Shulman's photographs of the department store, which may explain why *Architectural Review*'s editors selected this image to accompany Henry-Russell Hitchcock's roadside critique in "Man Made America" of 1950 (see chapter 3) and why Reyner Banham, who was probably introduced to Milliron's by the *Review*, reproduced it in *Los Angeles* two decades later. Banham, looking at Milliron's form, characterized the ramps as "futurist." *Architectural Review,* looking at Milliron's program, noted how the building satisfied the activities of "auto-mobile shopping." Gruen devoted much of his practice to the proper accommodation of that activity, and his commitment to it culminated in two justly famous projects in the Upper Midwest from the mid-1950s: Northland Shopping Center and Southdale. In these, he resolved the tension between commerce and the car by inserting *cityscape* values into zones dominated by *subcityscape* chaos.[28]

Figure 46. Julius Shulman, photograph of Milliron's Department Store (Gruen and Krummeck, 1949), Los Angeles; view of rear ramps from parking lot. (© J. Paul Getty Trust; Getty Research Institute, Los Angeles [2004.R.10])

Figure 47. Northland Shopping Center (Victor Gruen, 1954), near Detroit, Michigan; aerial view. (Detroit Historical Society)

With more than a mile of storefronts and parking for 7,500 cars, Northland Shopping Center, outside of Detroit, was the largest such facility in the country when it opened in 1954, and it received extensive coverage in the popular and professional press. Responding to Gruen's coordinated control of signage, fixtures, plantings, and artworks, *Life* celebrated Northland as a "20th century bazaar" that combined "modern efficiency" with "fine architecture and pure gaiety." Though Haskell's *Architectural Forum* focused on the center's technical aspects and planning dimensions, its assessment was equally glowing. Northland was a "classic," as typologically significant as Rockefeller Center was to the skyscraper and Radburn was to the suburb, and the "yardstick" by which all future retail facilities would be measured. Gruen's success, according to *Forum,* lay in his rejection of the status quo, embodied in the "vehicular tradition" (the strip street) and the "village tradition" (the common), and his embrace of the "market town" as an appropriate model for the urban periphery. In essence, as David Smiley, Jeffrey Hardwick, and Alex Wall have shown, Gruen effectively reinvented pedestrian and commercial density for the age of the automobile. If, as Gruen would eventually claim, the automobile destroyed "the last vestige of community coherence," the architect might restore it through the integrated shopping center—not by ignoring cars (and buses and trucks), but by giving them their proper place, in this case through surface parking, including reserve space for 4,500 additional vehicles directly connected to new and widened collector roads and bi-level drives for deliveries and passengers.[29]

When Gruen's Southdale opened near Minneapolis in 1956, *Life* dubbed it "the splashiest shopping center in the U.S.," stressing those features that made Southdale "fancier" than contemporary retail complexes: its three-story Garden Court of Perpetual Spring, its twenty-one-foot-tall bird cage, its fifty-foot-high Harry Bertoia sculptures.[30] *Architectural Record* focused on what made Southdale typologically distinct as a shopping *mall,* namely ten acres of retail space fully enclosed in "a controlled climate for shopping." The more news-oriented *Time* focused on its economic implications, calling Southdale (along with James Rouse's Mondawmin outside Baltimore, designed by Pietro Belluschi) one of the "most advanced shopping centers in the U.S." from a retail planning perspective. Emphasizing their size and diversification, *Time* argued that these "pleasure domes with parking lots" were not only able to "vie on their own terms with city retail districts," but were poised to "siphon shoppers from an entire region." Anticipating this economic impact, Gruen hoped it would stimulate retail (and architectural) hypercompetitiveness among the commercial denizens of the subcityscape. In terms of design, the advantages of these centers were obvious: they saved drivers "the fender-bending frustration" of downtown and, because they were "insulated" from suburban sprawl, they offered a respite from "the sight, sound and smell of traffic"—at least until you had to confront the parking lot. To emphasize the superiority of the "decentralized centers," *Time* gave developer Rouse the last word, in comments that anticipated his talk at Connecticut General the following year. The significance of planned shopping centers extended far beyond the retail sphere:

Figure 48. Southdale Center (Victor Gruen, 1956), near Minneapolis, Minnesota; view of Garden Court of Perpetual Spring. (Victor Gruen Papers, American Heritage Center, University of Wyoming)

they represented "a massive reorganization of the urban community," as conditioned by the car.³¹

Gruen's awareness of that ongoing reorganization was precisely what prompted his initial "cityscape and landscape" analysis and this remained an important point of reference for his subsequent interventions in the subcityscape. Strangely, though, as influential as his shopping typologies became, Gruen's parsing of autopian scapes never gained much discursive traction. While his functional categories accurately reflected the layered complexity of the extended metropolis, they did nothing to help restructure its geospatial realities. Revisiting this analysis in 1956 for *Architectural Forum*'s "Crisis before 1976" report, which provided the basis for his subsequent Connecticut General address, Gruen simplified his "urban organization," replacing six distinct scapes with a continuous "fabric" that stretched out "in an over-all weave" across the entire metropolitan region. "Tightly woven here, loosely woven there," the density of the fabric correlated to "congestion downtown" and "scatteration outside of town." Gruen argued that regardless of location or density, the pattern was the same because of the consistency of the "fibers"—that is, roads, streets, and highways serving all manner of human occupation. The trouble, as Gruen saw it, was that the fibers were doing double duty, serving automobiles and buildings without any distinction between the needs of transportation and inhabitation. This severely compromised both: at one extreme they became a hopeless knot, at the other a frayed string.³²

Gruen repeated this model in the picture-heavy "what city pattern" study that framed his diagrammatic proposal to replace existing chaos and anarchy (his terms) with urban clusters that served pedestrians and cars equally. *Forum*'s editors, including Douglas Haskell, whose editorial influence is obvious, defined urban organization as the outward, though not concentric, growth of three distinct and evocatively named domains: *centertown, fringetown,* and *roadtown.* The essential dilemma of centertown was how to prevent concentration, a source of urban strength, from becoming congestion, with its enervating implications, especially when traffic—cars, trucks, transit, and pedestrians—was the cause. In fringetown, the danger was in reproducing the central city and "all the same old built-in problems" of congestion and commuting. As was already evident in 1956, fringetown was no longer a "dormitory suburb"; it was "a working town itself," albeit one spread out across an "amorphous mass" whose "random" organization was enough to "drive visitors crazy." Fringetown's overdevelopment had a domino effect on roadtown, transforming it from "a motorized fairyland" solely in the service of "the great American excursion" into a coast-to-coast continuum of "strip cities" for "people by the million." A combination of Main Street and Coney Island had "exploded into the country," as the original gas-food-lodging enterprises of the prewar period were joined by drive-in institutions, including markets, banks, and even churches, that served residents rather than tourists. Large-scale enterprise followed in the form of shopping centers, industrial parks, and housing developments that favored clusters rather than ribbons. Following Gruen's lead, the editors suggested that such a cluster development, far from signaling future chaos, might become "the nuclei of really organizable cities"—as long as architecture and planning would "grow up to Paul Bunyan size."[33] In the mid-1950s, it was not clear if this was a winking reference to the scale of professional growth required to tame the automotive metropolis or an exasperated acknowledgement that such a feat was more tall tale than achievable.

Underlying this analysis of the physical form of centertown, fringetown, and roadtown was a nuanced exploration of their social dimensions. The particular conditions of roadtown, for example, arose because the highway was "being treated like a street"—as a focal point of multiple activities—rather than as a mere conduit for long-distance or through travel. Gruen's social analysis was attuned to this distinction: urban form should be understood as "habitat," a locality whose "sympathetic environment" allowed a species to "feel at home," even when the species was mechanical. The car, Gruen argued, deserved its "lebensraum." With construction of the interstates already underway in late 1956, Gruen's expansionist attitude toward what he implied was the automobile's natural range may have been timely, but it was also necessary to ensure "peaceful coexistence" between four wheels and two legs. Significantly, however, Gruen believed that the only way to accomplish this was, ultimately, "to separate the warring forces." In Gruen's vision of an autopia reformed, there was one "natural habitat for human beings" and another one for cars.[34]

Toward Odology

With its careful scrutiny of the complex environmental interactions of cars, people, buildings, and highways, Gruen's habitat analysis would have appealed to John Brinckerhoff Jackson, though the influential writer, editor, and publisher of *Landscape* would have disagreed with the architect's conclusion. Gruen saw an inherent tension in the automobile-human nexus and, like so many of his modernist confreres, wanted to resolve it by designing separate domains. Jackson was interested in what that nexus revealed about how car-driving humans were shaping an environment in which they chose to live with, in, and among automobiles. While he conceded that Gruen's shopping centers were beautiful and modern, Jackson regarded them as "bloodless places" whose tidiness and tastefulness embodied a "lopsided view of urban culture." This critique embodied the fundamental character of Jackson's approach to the roadside. Whereas Douglas Haskell's approach was operative and Victor Gruen's was reformist, Jackson's was interpretive and philosophical—which is one reason he was skeptical of "expanding metropolis" symposia like the one at Connecticut General that opened this chapter: people, like himself, "whose business it was to interpret the modern city" generally stayed away. This didn't mean he was at odds with those who attended such events: like Haskell and Gruen, Jackson looked at roads in physical and social terms, but he also examined what he described as "the subjective relationship" between humans and the environment. Unbounded by architecture's professional sphere, Jackson also devoted himself to *odology,* the study of roads (and trails and paths), "how they are used, where they lead, and how they come into existence." To Jackson, it made no difference if they were federal highways, state or county routes, or thoroughfares at smaller scales; it mattered little whether they were precisely engineered or barely paved, if they were lined with thoughtfully designed buildings or flimsy and haphazard structures. In the automotive era, Jackson argued, "roads no longer merely lead to places; they *are* places."[35] That precise declaration of road-as-place came in one of his final essays, "Roads Belong in the Landscape" of 1994, but Jackson had been making similar assertions for more than four decades, in publications, lectures, and seminars that were critical in establishing the American roadside as a cultural landscape of intrinsic significance.

Jackson's reputation as an autopian thinker emerged during the eighteen years he was editor of *Landscape,* the journal he founded in 1951. As historian Timothy Davis has noted, Jackson used *Landscape* as a platform to test out sociospatial theories about the American scene: virtually every issue between 1951 and 1969 dealt with the changing values of buildings and landscapes in the territories of the car.[36] Jackson published his own work on this subject and that of his contemporaries: in addition to Jean Gottmann (see chapter 2), architects Geoffrey Baker and Bruno Funaro on shopping centers as new town centers; journalist geographer Grady Clay on the future of Main Street in the age of the interstate; city planner Roland Rainer on urban space and the modern highway. The contrasting attitudes of Clay and Rainer demonstrate Jackson's editorial catholicity where autopia was concerned. Clay, reporting on a 1957 conference that was not the Connecticut General symposium but also focused on urbanism and the interstates, expressed frustration with what he perceived as the absence of regional cooperation and community input of the new highway program. Though to Clay the scale of land-use transformation wrought by the interstates staggered the imagination, he believed the professionals who claimed that Main Street might yet be rescued from "the automobile tyrant." (Clay was no anti-autopian crank: under Jackson's influence he learned "how to read the American city" in all its environmental diversity, giving pedestrian and automotive realms equal consideration.) Rainer, in contrast, refused to view the car as a tyrannical destroyer of existing cities; citing precedents like Radburn and Le Corbusier's Ville Radieuse, he argued the opposite: the automobile was "a force creating a new and better city, and a new type of spatial experience in architecture, urbanism, and highway design."[37] Given Jackson's insatiable curiosity about all forms and dimensions of the landscape, his own views rarely expressed such black-and-white certainties.

When Jackson studied the automobile's impact on urban form, he had little interest in better-or-worse evaluations, especially if they were too distant from the everyday experience of place. And place, too, required qualification: "We like to think of ourselves as an urban people," Jackson noted in 1967, attuned to similar demographic subtleties as the Census Bureau, "but much depends on what we mean by urban." Scale was important, but as a marker of similarity rather than difference, from city to town to village. As for the supposed newness of autopian urbanism, from Jackson's perspective the social continuities were just as important as the disruptions. Throughout his career Jackson explored these transformations—which were not always car-caused, but were generally car-complicit—in useful and nearly archetypal terms that made them immediately recognizable at national, regional, and local levels. As Jackson observed, named, documented, and interpreted autopia, he was attuned to spatial reorganizations of "layout, morphology, and architecture" that were major and minor, sudden and incremental: a bank installing a drive-in window, a housing development growing in a cornfield, horizontality emerging as "the national style, a universal American characteristic." Whether he was looking at gridirons, tenderloins, subdivisions, or strips, Jackson balanced the generic and the specific to emphasize the ubiquitous and "essential" in the urban landscape, as it existed in "most cities" or "almost any small American city" or "in every large community."[38] What those places had in common by midcentury was something Jackson labeled "auto territoriality," a broad term intended to capture the fullness of car's implications for life in the United States.

Moving through the public realm detached and isolated within the confines of a personal vehicle, drivers and passengers occupied "a completely private world unequivocally defined by physical boundaries." These internalizing impulses also animated car-oriented building types: the motel, for example, did away with "public and often spatially ambiguous realms" like the lobby and internal corridors, allowing direct passage from personal vehicle to private room. "Whatever the psychological role of the automobile," Jackson observed, "we do not like being separated from it for very long." Drive-in restaurants and drive-in movie theaters functioned in similar ways, but were even more extreme in their elimination of liminal public space: in these most autopian of building types, car and driver were never separated. However disconcerting these developments were with respect to traditional notions of community as a civic ideal, Jackson argued that they were motivated by an almost primal urge to mark boundaries as a way of identifying self, thus "fulfilling deeply rooted concepts of human territoriality." The primacy of the car as private space in the public realm did not mean that community no longer mattered in the United States. In accepting the automobile, Americans had not rejected "shared existence," and they still occupied what Jackson called "the social landscape." But with rising car usage, "favorite places of social interaction" had shape-shifted. Though traditional spaces and institutions, like the public square and the church or lodge, remained focal points for "special occasions," across autopia their everyday significance diminished as the highway strip emerged as a new, and "specifically American," social condenser. In the way it attracted a "mixed public" and seemed to offer "almost complete freedom of conduct and dress" (which formal institutions did not), the strip became "the chosen area of brief informal communication and social interaction." In Jackson's analysis, highway strips across the country grew into important "centers of sociability" for a simple reason: they were "entirely adjusted" to cars and drivers.[39]

Jackson's auto-territoriality was a nuanced extension of an analysis of the modern (pre-interstate) highway he began a decade earlier with "Other-Directed Houses" of 1956. Published in *Landscape,* Jackson's essay was the most cogent assessment of the highway as "a thriving American institution" since James Agee's "Great American Roadside" appeared in *Fortune* in 1934 (see chapter 2). Agee's text was an ode to a new phenomenon; Jackson's was a Whitmanesque plea for giving a familiar landscape the "love" and "understanding" he thought it deserved, if only because it had grown in stature with the passage of time: "What a complex thing the modern highway has become; how varied its functions and how varied the public that makes use of it!" Jackson paid special attention to all of that complexity and each of those functions as he distinguished between the highway's workaday and leisure functions and examined the strip in relation to changing community values and expectations. Among his most significant conclusions was pointing out the wrong-headedness, if not the absurdity, of evaluating motorized landscapes by pedestrian standards. As in the contemporaneous critiques of Haskell and Gruen, but with a much keener eye, Jackson looked beyond the highway as a transportation corridor to examine it as a place that served the daily life of the driver. This allowed Jackson to perceive the highway as analogous to those older commercial and civic spaces that served the daily life of the walker. Connecting the supermarket to the subdivision, the Dairy Queen to the drive-in, or serving as cruising strip in itself, the modern American highway was equivalent to "Main Street or the Park or the Court House Square," even if it looked nothing like them. Jackson's shift in focus revealed the "human landscape" of the highway as a part of the complex social order of automobility.[40] His geographer's assessment was confirmed a few years later when sociologist and *Landscape* contributor Herbert Gans, then at the University of Pennsylvania (where he influenced Denise Scott Brown), compared the city of the pedestrian to the city of the car in similar terms. Based on his field research in Levittown (now Willingboro), Pennsylvania, Gans observed that the differences between walking to the corner drugstore and driving to its suburban strip equivalent were inconsequential as long as one evaluated the "emotional, social, or cultural impact" of the latter in terms of "a wholly auto-based way of life."[41] Jackson intended other-directedness as precisely this kind of evaluation, especially as he moved beyond the social to consider the architectural implications of car-centrism in American life.

A few years before "Other-Directed Houses" appeared in *Landscape,* the critic and Barnard American Studies professor John Kouwenhoven observed in *Harper's* that "the highway landscape, debunked at one end and glamorized out of existence at the other, is badly in need of calm appraisal for what it really is—a commercial, exuberant, and unpredictable burst of construction along the roadside."[42] That 1950 request for evenhanded evaluation anticipated Jackson's analysis of "other-directed architecture," which at its most basic existed in direct opposition to what we would now regard as autonomous architecture, conceived as "a self-justifying work of art." Roadside buildings were other-directed because they existed to "woo the public" at 40, 50, and 60 miles per hour. This, Jackson acknowledged, was "not always easy to do," hence the desire for buildings possessing more than simple eye appeal. Other-directed architecture was assertive and flamboyant in its forms and visual effects, manipulating color and design so successfully, when measured by the attention-getting metrics of commercialism rather than the aesthetic standards of "civic reform groups," that it produced buildings of "real vitality." Even more sensitive to vitality's potential for relativistic interpretation than Haskell, Jackson noted that other-directed architecture was "creating and at the same time reflecting a

Figure 49. J. B. Jackson, drawing depicting aerial view of highway at night, from "Other Directed Houses," *Landscape*, Winter 1956–57, 35. (Permission courtesy of Collection of J. B. Jackson Pictorial Materials from Various Sources, Center for Southwest Research and Special Collections, University of New Mexico Libraries)

new public taste." In any event, this vitality was most apparent to Jackson in the treatment of roadside lighting and signage, which, he noted a decade before Venturi and Scott Brown, tended to become brighter and bigger as highway speed increased. For Jackson, illuminated signs at highway scale represented the strip's "most original and potentially creative elements" (light and signage, along with compositional "flashiness," comprised the highway's main architectural features). Neon especially captured his attention, and he observed that only a blind person could fail "to respond to the fantastic beauty of any neon lighted strip after dark," which Jackson attempted to convey in an accompanying drawing: an abstracted, aerial nighttime view of a highway lined with blinking signs and steady lights that create a celestial aura resembling nothing so much as an autopian sublime. With equal enthusiasm, Jackson speculated on how Gothic and Baroque designers might have exploited neon's potential for theatricality and illusionism, almost predicting the postmodern neon classicizing of Charles Moore's Piazza d'Italia in New Orleans, completed in 1978. Demonstrating his familiarity with contemporary design, Jackson wondered why modernists who celebrated the synthesis of the arts preferred static and traditional fresco and mosaic to dynamic and pulsating neon and fluorescents. He also wondered why "advertising experts" had not devised universal roadside symbols to replace the "nightmare of words" that afflicted so many illuminated signs, despite their potential for poetic communication. Playfully referencing Victor Hugo's "ceci tuera cela" declaration from *The Hunchback of Notre-Dame,* Jackson noted that while the word had yet to kill architecture in America, it was definitely threatening to overpower it.[43]

Jackson was not indiscriminate when praising the other-directedness of the highway. Similar to anti-autopian crusaders, he complained loudly about billboards adding to "the highway jungle," but, characteristic of his critical nuance, Jackson did not condemn billboards simply for creating roadside blight and unsightliness; he called for their elimination because they obscured the "unsuspected architecture and urbanist values" he believed the highway strip inherently possessed. At the scale of the individual building, while Jackson insisted on the overarching need for "intelligent and artistic" handling of the roadside, he distinguished between the "shock treatment" visuals of establishments erected by "the owner with no sort of guidance but his own limited experience and taste" and those designed by "imaginative and skillful architects." While the latter in Jackson's estimation were too few and far between, when he looked at the strip as a totality, he was impressed: after only a few decades it embodied "folk art in mid-twentieth-century garb." On the American roadside, Jackson found "a flowering of a popular architecture." The gerund is important: this architecture was still in the process of becoming, of evolving, and its final form—assuming such a thing was possible within the restless precincts of car and consumer—was far from clear. From Jackson's perspective, changeability meant potential. Surveying the highway scene a decade later, he found the roadside amplified by the mid-1960s into "a remarkable aesthetic style of its own." In its exhibitionist forms, dramatic lighting effects, and bright materials, Jackson even discerned a growing American appreciation for "a new kind of beauty," defined by crisp geometry, primary colors, and smooth surfaces—in effect, mainstream modernism refracted through the lens of popular taste. While Jackson celebrated the continued development of what he now emphasized as "the art and architecture of the strip," he was concerned about its ability to fulfill a very traditional cultural role—to provide "symbols of permanent values" and "landmarks to reassure us that we are not rootless individuals without identity and place." Here, Jackson was hardly striking a blow for the *new monumentality* that circulated in postwar architectural discourse; indeed, he had little faith that the midcentury architectural establishment could be counted on not to throw the baby out with the bathwater, eliminating the "merits and charm" of the roadside while introducing "order and harmony." Already in 1956, Jackson was frustrated that "we have become entirely too fastidious, too conformist, in architectural matters," and he recognized that the highway's continued socioeconomic-aesthetic evolution promised more of the same, in the guise of "urban improvement" and the shift from small roadside entrepreneurs to large corporations retaining professional designers. With the federal government poised to commence construction of the interstates, Jackson prepared himself for the worse: however problematic the highway strip was, however vulgar and tawdry and chaotic, the alternative was more troubling—"the sterilizing of our roadsides."[44]

Though Jackson didn't define sterility in "Other-Directed Houses," he makes it clear that it was dullness he dreaded, not control. In other words, monotonous and homogeneous roadsides were just as numbing as chaotic and congested ones. If sterility was to be avoided, which strip characteristics were worth preserving and replicating? Jackson's critiques of existing highway landscapes provided the answer, suffused as they were with visual and spatial qualities that embodied what he regarded as sterility's opposite: roadsides that stimulated drivers through varied color, texture, light, shadow, expanse, and enclosure (see color plate 7). In 1959, Jackson noted with satisfaction contemporary investigations that studied how variety in layout, sightlines, signage, and other features increased the pleasure and safety of highways and expressways (meaning old right-of-access arterials and new limited-access interstates). In retrospect, this research was important for several reasons: not only did it validate Jackson's insistence on the significance of "aesthetic sensory experience" in car-centric landscapes, it also demonstrated that designers were learning to appreciate—and even understand—the strip's social and formal values, something Jackson believed was essential to the roadside's nonsterile development. By making those values legible, Jackson's critical scrutiny of the highway strip helped to codify what we might call roadside analytics, which architects and planners fruitfully deployed in the 1960s, pushing Jackson's odological project forward even as autopia transmogrified in the interstate era. In his own investigation of this "landscape metamorphosis" in 1972, Jackson cautioned that such work should only be undertaken "in the proper frame of mind." This, Jackson explained, was "largely a matter of recognizing and accepting our national landscape for what it is: something very different from the European."[45]

That frame of mind was essential to the authors of *Face of the Metropolis*. Planner Martin Meyerson was vice chairman of the American Council to Improve Our Neighborhoods (ACTION), a business-friendly nonprofit organization that developer James Rouse founded in 1954 to promote the urban renewal policies of the Eisenhower administration.[46] Meyerson was also director of the Harvard/MIT Joint Center for Urban Studies and was about to become dean of Berkeley's College of Environmental Design, where he was likely to encounter Jackson, who circulated among the faculty and students of Carl Sauer's geography department before he began teaching there in the 1960s. Planner Jaqueline Tyrwhitt also taught at Harvard, and was a close associate of historian Sigfried Giedion and architect Constantinos Doxiadis. *Face of the Metropolis* shares many of their ideas, seemingly merging Jackson's approach to human landscapes with Team X's concept of humanistic habitat and the human settlement studies of Ekistics, to stimulate public interest in architecture and urban design in the United States. The goal was not simply to enlighten the public (i.e., the design laity), but to expand "the knowledge of the electorate" so that its members might make informed decisions about the cities where they lived and worked. Meyerson and Tyrwhitt believed that before the public could engage with the built environment, "the people" needed to be able to look at their surroundings and evaluate what they saw, distinguishing, for example, between "contrast and diversity [and] monotony." To give them the skills they needed, Meyerson and Tyrwhitt offered an introductory lesson in "the American vocabulary" of urban form. Acknowledging its initial dependence on European precedent, they began by surveying U.S. urban design, from the New England common and the republican grid, to courthouse squares and row house blocks, to model towns and modern skyscrapers. The goal was not to cultivate nostalgia for earlier forms, but, *pace* Jackson, to enable citizens to discern the persistence of older patterns in the contemporary metropolis, despite three centuries of drastic change in scale and form.[47]

To combat what they saw as a crisis in legibility and comprehensibility in this "changing cityscape," they also sought to explain its spatial realms. In contrast to Victor Gruen and Douglas Haskell, when Meyerson and Tyrwhitt organized the metropolis into center, middle, and outer cities, the schema was locational and not hierarchical. Downtown did not exist in opposition to suburbia, but only as a different zone of metropolitan inhabitation. The same is true of the projects they include in each zone: Connecticut General's headquarters (see figure 42), the GM Technical Center, Southdale Center (see figure 48), the Wellesley Row Houses (public housing for veterans outside Boston), Lankenau Hospital on Philadelphia's Main Line, and Boston's Route 128 corridor, among others. Rather than isolating them functionally, Meyerson and Tyrwhitt present them together as the urban landscape of the "outer city of today." Temporality was key: assuming continued decentralization, these sites would become "the middle city of tomorrow," and were definitely where "the form of the future metropolis [was] being set." As such, it was also where "modern usage of the native vocabulary" was clearly on display, even if, beyond their exemplary selections, intensive land use and the scale of new development caused by "widespread reliance on the automobile," as they stated without judgment, strained its expression. Like others learning from autopia, Meyerson and Tyrwhitt were not interested in cataloging the negative effects of a transformation they interpreted as an assertion of social and spatial freedom by individuals and industries liberated by the car and truck. Even when highlighting an emblematic corridor of congestion like U.S. 1 between Baltimore and Washington, illustrated in *Face of the Metropolis* by Edward Clark's often reproduced photograph of 1955 (see figure 31), they avoided calling out signs and access ways as commercial blight. Instead, they focused on how order might be imposed on existing highway landscapes without impinging on the personal preferences of those owning and operating roadside businesses—an autopian vision in which the free market is regulated by little more than the guidance of an educated public. To that end, they posed a question to their readers and "see-ers" (the book's visuals and graphics were "as important as the text") that was intended to prompt serious reflection on the midcentury metropolis: "For whom do we design the city? Man in an airplane, man in an automobile, man on his feet?" Each required a different interpretation of scale relations. Their survey of historical projects demonstrated how well the United States had mastered "the art of urban living" for the pedestrian age. It was time to do the same for the age of mass transportation, and to ask whether or not the contemporary forms of the roadside metropolis successfully embodied earlier values: "What can the motorist see through his windshield to make his journey to work, to shop, to play pleasant?"[48] In the 1960s, some of autopia's keenest observers were already working on the answer, building on J. B. Jackson's behind-the-wheel analysis at the intersection of social habits and spatial patterns, but with a deliberate shift from observation to intervention.

Seeing through the Windshield

Like Jackson, planners Christopher Tunnard and Boris Pushkarev fully understood the importance of drivers as urban stakeholders in the United States, and they addressed them directly in *Man-Made America*. This winner of a 1964 National Book Award is a monumental examination of what its authors perceived to be the acutely degraded state of the built environment in the United States. The subtitle to *Man-Made America* makes this clear: "Chaos or Control?" is obviously a rhetorical question, as it is unlikely that the authors, respectively, a Yale professor and Regional Planning Association researcher, would have needed five hundred pages if their intention was to condone chaos. They underscored this by acknowledging their debt to *Architectural Review*'s 1950 "Man Made America" issue (see chapter 3), in which Tunnard first published the city-growth case study that stimulated his interest in automotive urban transformations and convinced him of the need for planning intervention as a means of "civilizing the American roadscape." In addition to laying the foundation for *Man-Made America*, that earlier work also set the book's tone, but only to a degree. Though Tunnard and Pushkarev parted ways with autopia's harshest social critics by accepting it as the contemporary metropolitan condition, they were not aligned with typical reformers, and did not just want to improve the "visual sphere" of the roadside through, for example, proper control of setbacks, building heights, and billboards—all standard correctives by the mid-1960s.[49]

Tunnard and Pushkarev wanted to move the roadside to a more advanced stage of development. *Man-Made America*'s second subtitle explicated this broad project as "An Inquiry into Selected Problems of Design in the Urbanized Landscape." Significantly, their approach to those problems was more conservative than many others on the *learning from* end of the autopian spectrum. This is evident in the way they situated the roadscape in a hierarchical spatial matrix that was critically outmoded by the time the book was published. Though their bibliography included Jackson's *Landscape* (to which Pushkarev had already contributed), as well as Gottmann's *Megalopolis,* they ignored the nebulous structure of the geographer's sprawling city type and adhered, instead, to a rigidly concentric model even when analyzing the "emerging American landscape"—meaning the landscape "attributed to the rise of the automobile." In their analysis of "the morphology of the urban fringe," they depicted both strip and subdivision as subordinate to the central city, and when they begin to assess the commercial roadside their critique aligns with the discontents: they characterize it as "visually aggressive" and use U.S. 1 in Connecticut as their predictable illustration. At the same time, much like J. B. Jackson, they also regard some of that supposed aggression positively, as "folk architecture," including two mimetic buildings reproduced using their own photographs: the 1954 Premium Tex gas station, shaped like a cowboy hat and boots, and Bob's Java Hut, occupying a colossal coffeepot built in 1927, both of them standing along what was then U.S. 99 in Washington, on the outskirts of Seattle and Tacoma, respectively.[50]

Throughout their discussion of the roadside, Victor Gruen is an important point of reference. Their description of "a mindless juggernaut of subtopia" builds upon Gruen's notion of the subcityscape, here defined by its "ubiquitous" drive-in typologies. Like Gruen, Tunnard and Pushkarev acknowledged that these types emerged from the functional necessity of attracting and serving car-driving customers, which explained their "oversize signs and garish displays," and that they

Figure 50. "The entrance to a city cluttered up with billboards... a suggestion for improvement," from Tunnard and Pushkarev, *Man-Made America*, 1964. (Permission courtesy of Yale University Press)

became chaotic through the coupling of excessive commercial frontage and intense retail competition. When asserting "the need for visual control," they used Gruen's work, notably his Northland Shopping Center outside Detroit (see figure 47), as an illustration of successful efforts to control so-called roadside blight.[51] Gruen also promoted roadside interventions like the planned shopping center as a way to cultivate community values. Here, however, Tunnard and Pushkarev distanced themselves from Gruen; by their own admission, their concerns were principally aesthetic. They proposed a "framework of order" for the roadside, not for social reasons, but to allow structures and signage to mediate the extremes of chaos and control, which they softened rhetorically by advising architects to balance "cheeky, colorful gaiety" and "tasteful restraint." These they represented with views of Ernie's Hamburger Heaven and the Boardwalk. The former was a drive-in festooned with "too many signs," mostly set perpendicular to U.S. 66 in Missouri and emblazoned with menu items and brand names; the latter was a community shopping center with "one large sign," originally made of redwood planks and set parallel to CA-131 in Northern California. The signage was not the only point of contrast between the buildings, despite being roughly contemporary. Ernie's opened in 1957 in a former ice cream stand built in a modestly Googie style, with a striped canted roof, situated just off a cluttered stretch of the historic "Mother Road" in what was then the outer limits of the Saint Louis suburbs. The Boardwalk opened in 1955, anchored by a grocery store and a library in a complex designed in the Bay Regional style by architect John Lord King and landscape architect Thomas Church. It was a new shopping center for an area of southern Marin County just then being developed as part of the Bay Area's broad metropolitan extent. Tunnard and Pushkarev were not explicit about these urbanistic differences, though Ernie's and the Boardwalk embodied what, by the early 1960s, were clearly divergent conditions in the autopian landscape.

They were more interested in the viewpoint of the driver, contrasting "the passing motorist" with "the motorist who approaches the building as a visitor." Because the former used the road as a through route, driver behavior was predictable; because the latter used the road for everyday activities, driver behavior was unpredictable, as he/she searched for a sign or access way. They also studied the

Figure 51. "Chaos and control": Ernie's Hamburger Heaven, on U.S. 66 west of Saint Louis, Missouri, and the Boardwalk (John Lord King and Thomas Church, 1955) in Marin County, California, from Tunnard and Pushkarev, *Man-Made America*, 1964. (Permission courtesy of Yale University Press)

moment the passer-by became the visitor—when driver attention was captured by a conspicuous roadside landmark and, in a perceptual-to-physical chain reaction, he/she impulsively turned off the highway into the parking lot of a commercial establishment. Those "turning movements" to which the driver/shopper was continually subjected on a typical "commercial ribbon" created "psychological friction" that had a deleterious effect on the person behind the wheel. Those turns also generated compelling graphics: three reverse figure-ground diagrams depicting driver-vehicular movement toward and around roadside buildings with white arrows against a black field that rendered the typical highway strip as a composition of multi-directional distractions pulsating like Mondrian's *Broadway Boogie Woogie* set free from the confines of the grid. However appealing formally, this was hardly positive for driver concentration, but neither was the static, nearly mono-directional condition of the limited-access highway with commerce (of the gas-and-food variety) restricted to the median, as on older parkways in the American Northeast. In that scenario, the white arrows of driver movement were relentless in their forward motion because there was very little friction. Tunnard and Pushkarev offered these extremes as the rationale for replacing existing highway strips and median services with an alternative that combined the strip's built and visual density, and its retail mix with the regulated and orderly facilities of a limited access highway, creating retail islands on the lobe-like interstices of grade-separated interstate/freeway interchanges. Tunnard and Pushkarev do not speculate on the economics of these retail islands, and only begrudgingly acknowledge that the redevelopment they suggested for the nation's unruly, auto-centric commercial landscapes would require exact placement "by some all-powerful designer on a tabula rasa." Beyond omnipotence was their gobsmacking suggestion that zoning restrictions, reductions in building permits, and even eminent domain might be used to curtail the growth of commercial strips in America. Though this seems like regulatory overreach, they regarded it as a sensible response to the conclusion they drew from a sharp analysis of autopian retail: "vehicular movement and shopping are incompatible," because they represented such disparate modes of visual perception and spatial occupation.[52]

Their most detailed analysis of driver and car in motion and space occurred in

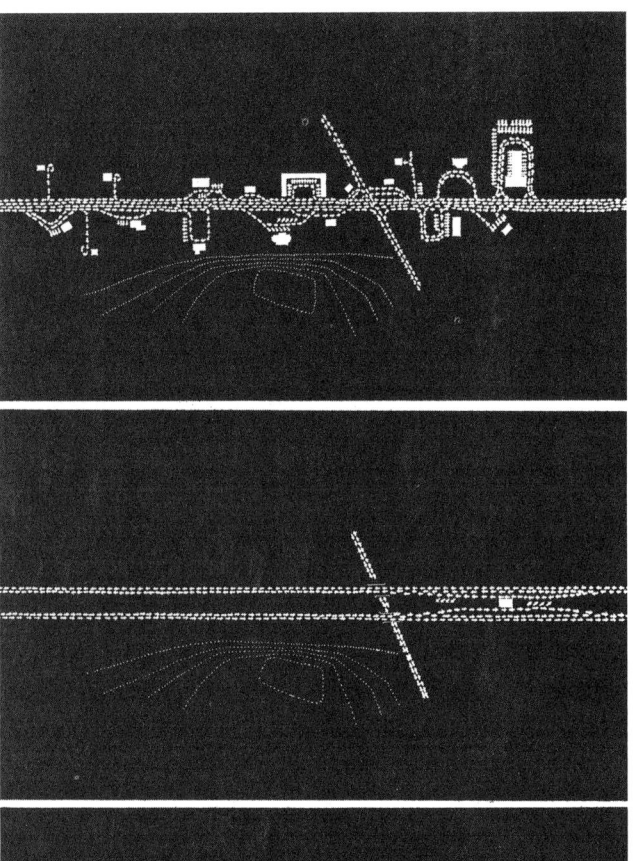

Figure 52. Past, present, and "possible" of highway commerce: typical strip, median strip on limited-access road, and service loop development, from Tunnard and Pushkarev, *Man-Made America,* 1964. (Permission courtesy of Yale University Press)

"The Paved Ribbon" section of *Man-Made America*. The "driver" is still a "consumer," but now of the highways themselves rather than the businesses lining them. More precisely, the driver is a consumer of highways *without* businesses lining them because now Tunnard and Pushkarev focus exclusively on limited-access, grade-separated, divided highways of the interstate type. They hoped to teach members of the driving public how to appreciate beautiful highways and to regard ugly highways "as detrimental to the American spirit as the in-city slums we are now all committed to remove." In text and diagrams predicated on behind-the-wheel documentation, they sequentially present all aspects of the visual design of the highway (categorized as structure, function, and form; internal and external harmonies; and micro- and macro-environments), but they begin with an exploration of the various factors that influenced "vision in motion." Using principles derived from a growing accumulation of "psycho-physiological data" related to the motorist's experience in "a multidimensional world of space, time, and energy," they offer clear explanations of why "seeing takes time" (as drivers perceive at an average rate of three-quarters of a second the objects that appear to be moving all around them) and why "seeing is limited in space" (as drivers attempt to discriminate detail at great distances and within a limited scope of vision).[53]

They also consider what happens to drivers' concentration and vision as speeds increases (one goes up the other goes down) and the impact of increased speed on perceiving foreground detail and extended space. They diagram this with great clarity in a manner that recalls George Stewart's study of U.S. 40 (see chapter 2), using white, hatching, and black to show how drivers would see the sky, roadside, and roadbed under typical conditions through the windshield of a typical 1960 model American car. On a two-lane highway the roadside dominates; on a freeway, traveling at a speed of 60 miles per hour, the sky dominates, but the roadbed itself is increasingly prominent. This leads Tunnard and Pushkarev to conclude that these "ribbons of pavement define the visual space of the road." Given this prominence, the roadbed should be designed for aesthetics as well as engineering, but it was not sufficient to treat the roadway as "sculptural form" and "plastic abstraction." The person behind the wheel had to apprehend it as such. The consideration of the driver's point of view continued in their discussion of freeway "focus, interest, and drama" relative to the design and siting of highway landmarks. To enhance the driver's concentration, these should have the clarity of discrete objects placed in relation to the carriageways and the sight lines. To explain, Tunnard and Pushkarev compare these landmarks to the spires of Chartres visible across the wheat fields of Le Centre, as well as a more recent example, the Conoco Glass House restaurant across the Will Rogers Turnpike (now I-44) in Vinita, Oklahoma. Completed in 1957, this bridge restaurant, supposedly the first across a public highway in the United States, offers drivers a dramatic counterpoint to the flat prairie landscape.

"The road must aim the eye," they argue, offering a final example to emphasize the point. In a collage diagram, they placed Max Bill's 1951 sculpture *Tripartite Unity* in two different roadway locations. When the sculpture is adjacent to the lanes, driver attention is directed, inappropriately, away from the highway. When

Figure 53. "Restaurant in bridge as landmark": Conoco Glass House on I-44 in Vinita, Oklahoma, from *Man-Made America,* 1964. (Oklahoma Turnpike Authority)

LEARNING FROM AUTOPIA

Figure 54. Freeway diagram with Max Bill's *Tripartite Unity* (1948–49), from Tunnard and Pushkarev, *Man-Made America*, 1964. (Permission courtesy of Yale University Press)

it is placed in between the lanes on a median expanded to an island, a smooth flow of uninterrupted sight lines directs driver attention, correctly, in their analysis, toward and beyond the landmark.[54] To maintain internal harmony, such landmarks should be treated as modernist abstractions in sync with the dynamic plastic forms of the road itself. They demonstrate this potential by comparing *Tripartite Unity* to an aerial view of I-80 at Vallejo, California, just before it crosses the Carquinez Strait: the elongated curves of the elevated roadway visually parallel the sinuous arcs of Bill's Mobius-like sculpture. Of course, I-80 did not sit in abstract space, but its actual context, due north of San Francisco, made it even more compelling. In the California Highway Department photograph that Tunnard and Pushkarev reproduced (which Superstudio would deploy to memorable effect in *Continuous Monument* of 1969), the interstate crosses a landscape in which subdivisions and car-centric development dramatically give way to canyons and unimpeded nature. The image is also a reminder of *Man-Made America*'s conceptual reach and its jump in scale and ambition, from attempting to intervene in the "esthetic

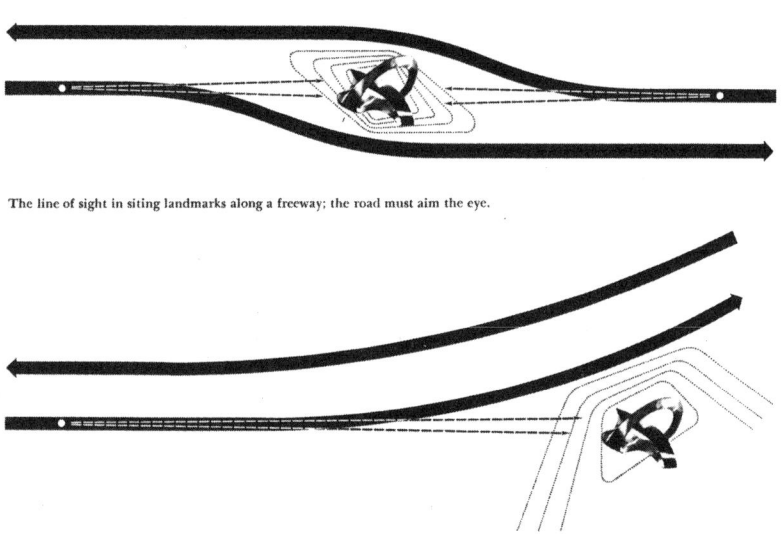

AMERICAN AUTOPIA

of commerce in the landscape"—what Jackson had called the art and architecture of the strip—to trying to influence "the esthetic of freeway design." This shift reflected the difference between the highway landscape that had long existed when the book appeared in 1963 and the one then under construction, which would soon render the roadscapes of the 1930s, 1940s, and 1950s as the outmoded, if not yet obsolete, corridors of an earlier autopian age.

Landscape architect Lawrence Halprin demonstrated that he was keenly aware of the difference in his 1966 book *Freeways,* a spirited, even emotional riposte to Tunnard and Pushkarev's coolly detached and self-professed formalism. Though such well-known Halprin-designed projects as Nicolett Mall (Minneapolis; 1968)

Figure 55. Interstate 80 at Carquinez Strait in California with U.S. 40 at right, from Tunnard and Pushkarev, *Man-Made America,* 1964. (Photograph by California Highway Department, 1959; courtesy Federal Highway Administration)

and Lovejoy Plaza (Portland; 1971) were still in the future—as was Freeway Park (Seattle; 1976), a commission Halprin secured because of *Freeways,* the book—he had already completed the adaptive reuse of Ghiradelli Square (begun 1962) in San Francisco, showing how traditional urban form might be reconfigured for pedestrians and cars—through a plaza above an underground garage—without sacrificing traditional urban values. In *Freeways,* Halprin's modernist values were clear in his espousal of views similar to those of Tunnard and Pushkarev. Like them, he considered the modern superhighway "a form of art" and "sculpture for motion," and he acknowledged the existence of "magnificent examples" like the Baltimore–Washington Parkway completed in the early 1950s. (Halprin called all highways built to interstate standards "freeways," which reflected his West Coast orientation and his work as a consultant to the California State Division of Highways.) Halprin's autopian values were clear in his giddy enthusiasm for "the spin of the wheels and the feeling of 'go'" while driving and in his ardent declaration that the car on the freeway symbolized "the intense dedication of our age to motion." Not only did he view freeways as "among the most beautiful structures of our age," he also saw them, along with the skyscraper, as "the most typical of our civilization." More sedately, Halprin reviewed nine formal principles related to driver sightlines and stimulation that were applicable to new highways in undeveloped, lightly developed, and newly developed areas, and these are not very different from Tunnard and Pushkarev's ideal characteristics. In each highway context, the designer would ideally have "a clean slate" to develop either a single roadway or an entire system "forming the backbone of a plan geared to the automobile."[55] Ultimately, however, urban freeways were Halprin's particular concern, as he demonstrated in his celebration of the new and frequently controversial highways that had been under construction in major American cities for nearly a decade by the time *Freeways* was published.

After a straightforward discussion of six different types of urban freeways, including depressed, at grade, and various species of elevated, Halprin described his utterly exhilarating experience of driving on them. A sports car enthusiast, Halprin is as effusive as Filippo Marinetti in the Futurist Manifesto: "The great vivid skylines of the city can be seen, all of a sudden, not as a static picture, but as a series of constantly changing impressions which move by like the frames of a motion picture." Surpassing their function as transportation corridors, these freeways became, in Halprin's view, "some of the greatest new urban experiences," offering drivers panoramic vistas of skylines and a new, and even intimate, knowledge of the city through which the highway passed. Halprin's language is flush with the thrill of shifting urban scenography, especially at night: the driver passes through "a vast lightmobile" and witnesses a "brilliant kaleidoscope of motion" generated by illuminated cars, signs, and buildings, each illustrated with nighttime freeway photographs in which long exposures produced gyrating light trails.

Figure 56. "A vast lightmobile": freeway approach to San Francisco, from Lawrence Halprin, *Freeways*, 1966. (Lawrence Halprin Collection, The Architectural Archives, University of Pennsylvania)

Halprin also considered urban context and how freeways were experienced not by drivers on the highway, but by everyone else off of them. Initially, he was enthusiastic, describing the underpasses of grade separations and the undercrofts of elevated roadways in glowing, environmentally immersive terms: "In cities, the great overhead concrete structures with their haunches tied to the ground and the vast flowing cantilevers rippling above the local streets stand like enormous sculptures marching through architectonic caverns." A two-page spread of stop-action photographs shot in Novato, California (in Marin County) demonstrated how the man-made canyons might be occupied, at least in a place that was not densely urban. In eighteen sequential images Halprin's wife, the experimental choreographer Anna Halprin, dances beneath the overlapping undersides of U.S. 101 and CA-37, her torso and gesturing arms emphasizing the megastructure of powerful piers and girders. While Anna Halprin's dance aestheticized what might be understood as the freeway's interior environment, Lawrence Halprin's analysis also examined the freeway's exterior environment.[56]

Figure 57. Embarcadero Freeway as seen from the street, with the Ferry Building in background, from Lawrence Halprin, *Freeways*, 1966. (Lawrence Halprin Collection, The Architectural Archives, University of Pennsylvania)

In other words, Halprin was just as interested in the aesthetics of what was *around* the freeway, assessment of which occasioned more sober observations about priorities of urban land use and hierarchies of urban actors. He noted, for example, that a typical cloverleaf exchange occupied nearly the same acreage as a midsize downtown, generally in areas in which the inhabitants were unable to influence route planning or to prevent their displacement. Too often, Halprin argued, new highways observed the principles of *freeway* design while violating the principals of *urban* design. Nowhere was this clearer than in depressed roadways like the Dan Ryan Expressway in Chicago (completed 1962) and in elevated roadways like the Central Artery in Boston (completed 1959, demolished 2003) and the Embarcadero Freeway in San Francisco. The latter, part of I-80, was a small but notorious fragment of a much larger urban interstate that was planned but never completed due to the "Freeway Revolt" of 1959. What was finished in 1958 (and demolished in 1991) was a 1.2-mile stretch of elevated roadway from the Bay Bridge to Broadway, coming between the city and the waterfront, most conspicuously where the Ferry Building sat at the foot of Market Street. Halprin returned to the Embarcadero frequently throughout *Freeways*, using it as a negative exemplar of the "confrontation" between the city and the highway. Regardless of what it felt like to be astride the Embarcadero, walking or driving beneath it was another matter entirely. Occupying the space beneath a typical urban elevated freeway, or alongside a depressed one, was dispiriting at best. There, Halprin discovered landscapes devastated—physically, socially, and economically—by the roadways passing through them. In Halprin's analysis, urban freeways did not only destroy neighborhoods and communities; they also destroyed community values. Contemplating these environments prompted not outright condemnation, but something closer to an autopian lament: "Do we have to ban the freeway from the city and thus ultimately, the automobile, which has meant so much to us?" Halprin's use of the third person plural is telling, as an acknowledgement of his conflicted status as an urban driver, an urban dweller, and an urban diagnostician.[57]

As an urban designer, Halprin was not ready to support the car-free city. Urban freeways were "not inherently bad," but they were badly designed and badly sited. While the city, as a complex social and physical "organism," should always prioritize human relationships, "the fun and excitement and mobility that comes with the car also [had] its rightful place." Halprin hoped *Freeways* would contribute to the discourse of balanced "civic building," and serve as a corrective to mistakes already made. (This same impulse led him to serve as an "urban advisor" to the Federal Highway Administrator and to coauthor a report to the transportation secretary that borrowed heavily from *Freeways*.) Significantly, however, most of Halprin's analysis considered the road itself and not the urban "havoc" it wreaked. While Halprin conceded that "major changes" were an inevitable part of inserting a new freeway into a densely built city, he believed that designers could "exercise judgment and creativity in guiding the change rather than try to arrest it." The solution was for highway designers to pay more attention to "urban aesthetics and the qualities of movement through space." Too often, Halprin argued, highways were designed in plan and profile, rather than in section. As a result, relationships in the urban strata from sidewalk to roadbed to roofline were ignored, and designers did not treat highways as the "intense spatial compositions" they actually were. Nor, by extension, did they consider the "architectonic environment of the structures as seen from their surroundings," because the standard planometric approach privileged the driver's through-the-windshield perspective. Halprin was not faulting the engineer-designers and, as we've seen, he was enthusiastic about the behind-the-wheel urban prospect; rather, he believed designers were handicapped by their tools of analysis and composition. Because these tools were developed for static forms of design, they failed to account for essential aspects of highway design: motion through space and perceptions of change at a fluctuating speeds. To drivers, these were not "abstract conceptions"; they were "a vital part of our everyday experiences."[58] Highways, Halprin concluded, needed to be designed the same way they were experienced, bodily as well as mentally.

Because it is experienced in time, architecture is frequently compared to music. While Halprin might reasonably have extended this comparison to his investigation of automotive infrastructure, instead, under Anna Halprin's influence, he saw dance as the relevant art form. To Lawrence Halprin, driving on a freeway was "an exercise in choreography in the landscape." If a driver on the highway was like a dancer on the stage, the highway designer, like the choreographer, needed a way to document all aspects of environmental experience: "movement quality, character, speed, involvement with other mobile (or static) elements and progressive spatial relationships." His solution was a method of movement notation intended as an aid to studying existing highways or routing new ones. Using dance notation as a foundation, the Halprins had been collaborating since the early 1960s to develop "a technique for designers working kinesthetically" (i.e., designing for movement). As described in *Cities,* Lawrence Halprin's 1963 investigation of open space in the contemporary city, they were searching for a way to choreograph the city and to capture every feature of urban mobility, from flying pigeons to spraying fountains to speeding cars.[59]

By the time *Freeways* was published in 1966, the Halprins had perfected a system of motion notation, or MOTATION. As a descriptive shorthand, MOTATION provided a set of symbols and a simple columnar template for recording, frame-by-frame, according to the vehicle's acceleration, the elements drivers perceived horizontally and vertically as they drove along highway corridors and city streets. The major symbols represented static objects encountered while in motion, including structures and landscapes. Variations on a square indicated low-, mid-, and high-rise buildings or groups of buildings; variations on a semicircle did the same for topographic features and vegetation like hills, valleys, and trees. MOTATION also allowed simple directional ticks to indicate other elements, be they vertical, horizontal, or diagonal. There were also symbols for objects in motion, principally people and cars, and for indicating distance, direction, speed, and time. To make these more comprehensible, MOTATION also employed photographs and a narrative description of the journey. When brought together as a descriptive system, MOTATION became a tool that allowed the student of the freeway to "visualize the highway experience" and create a representation of the motorist's point of view.[60] Halprin demonstrated the utility of MOTATION by documenting his own journey south on the Embarcadero Freeway, which is captured most basically in nine sequential photographs that document his progress, frame-by-frame, approximately every quarter mile along the waterfront. In that MOTATION diagram, even for those unfamiliar with the city through which the infamous freeway "stub" cut (or not referencing the photographs), the prominent horizontals and verticals of the San Francisco skyline are instantly legible—the arcing cables and extending decks of the Bay Bridge are a constant, represented by one vertical symbol, one horizontal symbol, and two diagonals; the slim silhouette of the Ferry Building and the squatter form of the Embarcadero YMCA pass by more quickly, but Halprin captures them, too, with the MOTATION symbol for "tower." As a tool for evaluation and conceptualization, Halprin claimed that what made the MOTATION system distinctive was that it recorded movement itself, rather than recording the environment of movement.

This was Halprin's way of distinguishing MOTATION from techniques pioneered by planners Kevin Lynch and Donald Appleyard and architect John R. Myer in *The View from the Road* (1964). In the context of autopia, the differences are less important than the similarities. Both recording techniques were motivated by interventionist agendas dedicated to understanding how city dwellers perceive urban form. Indeed, as the authors of *The View from the Road* explain in the book's preface, their study of automobility was an attempt to put the methods of urban analysis that Lynch developed for *The Image of the City* (1960) literally into the driver's seat. Lynch's earlier study had not completely ignored the automobile. In the book's Los Angeles case study, Lynch reported that traffic and the road system dominated his interviews there, even though his area of study was the old (walkable) downtown core along Broadway and around Pershing Square. Several of his observations about legibility in the car-centric city also informed the later study:

Figure 58. MOTATION (in photographs) applied to the description of a trip on the Embarcadero Freeway, from Lawrence Halprin, *Freeways*, 1966. (Lawrence Halprin Collection, The Architectural Archives, University of Pennsylvania)

even when driving, Lynch's research showed, Angelenos perceived vivid urban images, oriented themselves at local and regional scales, and sometimes regarded driving as an exciting, even thrilling experience.[61]

The View from the Road focused on these experiences to produce, in essence, "the image of the highway," or, as the authors put it, "applying the general heritage of the design professions [to] a new subject"—driving in the context of the "new metropolitan scale." Like Halprin, they focused on urban freeways, hoping to stimulate the creation of a midcentury equivalent of the suburban parkways and scenic highways that characterized an earlier automotive era. Funded by the Rockefeller

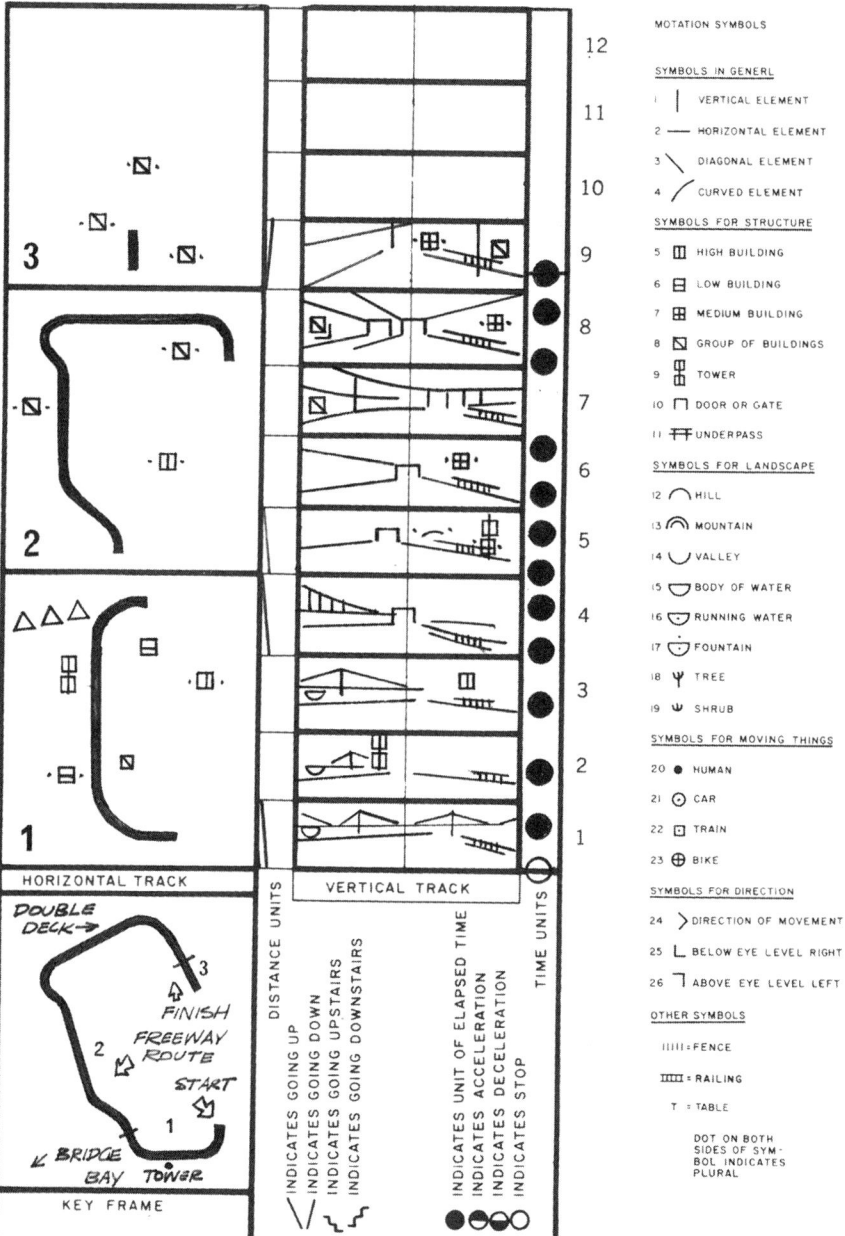

Figure 59. MOTA-TION (in diagrams) applied to the description of a trip on the Embarcadero Freeway, from Lawrence Halprin, *Freeways*, 1966. (Lawrence Halprin Collection, The Architectural Archives, University of Pennsylvania)

Foundation, the research for *The View from the Road* was conducted out of the MIT/Harvard Joint Center for Urban Studies, which also sponsored Meyerson and Tyrwhitt's *Face of the Metropolis*. Like them, and other urbanists learning from autopia, the authors of *The View from the Road* rejected the notion that "ugly roads are often taken to be one price of civilization." More fundamentally, they also rejected the notion that U.S. cities ought to be redesigned "so that everyone could walk to work." In their view, this was not only impractical, given the realities of urban and suburban growth, it also overlooked the possibility that cars might make a positive contribution to twentieth-century life and environments. Like Tunnard and Pushkarev, they believed in the highway's potential to become a work of art, which they explored by provocatively comparing the scenographic variety of select examples of Japanese, Islamic, and Chinese architecture to the experiential sequencing of a typical highway. Like Halprin, they focused on the immediacy of the highway experience, contending that "road-watching is a delight" — even when the road in question, reproduced on the book's cover and in their initial discussion of "the highway landscape," was an unlovely stretch of the East River Drive (now FDR Drive) in Midtown Manhattan. Even ugly roads had "special visual qualities" that drivers and passengers perceived every day, including "a dramatic play of space and motion, of light and texture, all on a new scale." On the East River Drive, shifting views of the Waterside generating station and the United Nations campus provided "pleasurable tensions" for drivers as they apprehended stacks, conveyors and brick arches, elevated carriageways and, most prominently, the marble-clad slab of the UN Secretariat Building. The driver's progress toward these "goals" added a frisson of excitement to even a routine trip. By recognizing the view from the road as continual visual sequences, it was possible to make the car-oriented metropolis legible in Lynchian terms, revealing to the driver "how the city is organized, what it symbolizes, how the people use it, and how it relates to him."[62]

Creating legibility required a means of expressing legibility, so it was necessary to devise a "technique for recording, analyzing, and communicating its visual sequences." Some of these were the conventional techniques of representation that Lynch had already deployed in *The Image of the City:* annotated maps, sequential and oblique photographs, and quick perspective sketches. Like storyboard vignettes, these sketches helped driver documentarians eliminate the details and exaggerate the effects in order to mimic mobilized vision. They understood, however, the limits of static representations, acknowledging as Halprin did that they incompletely captured the experience of highway driving. Scale models offered apparent completeness, but communicating texture and detail would make them prohibitively expensive to produce. Motion pictures were less expensive and they recorded sequences that could be sped up to convey the "major visual effects" of the roadway. A major drawback, however, was the differences between the camera and the human eye, which leaps from object to object, perceiving them with varying levels of focus, especially when driving. By contrast, with its "uniformly acute vision," the camera recorded too much.[63]

It was to overcome these shortcomings that Appleyard, Lynch, and Myer developed "an abstract notation of motion and space," a graphic shorthand that borrowed heavily from *The Image of the City* and its emphasis on recording subjective perception of places, rendered as paths, edges, nodes, landmarks, and districts with specific symbols for each (parallel lines, hatch marks, stars, triangles, and dots). When forward-directed highway travel was introduced, these elements were mobilized into a sequential system for documenting "approach and attainment" that was further enhanced with notations for recording changing speeds, stops and starts, and the varied locations where visual elements were apprehended along with varying degrees of visual intensity. They provided a way to notate a range of perceived motion in the driver's visual field: of views that were unbounded or constricted and of surfaces and objects passing alongside or overhead, whether they were well-defined or indistinct, backlit, or cross-lit. All of this was rendered in sequence diagrams arranged in thin strips to be read from bottom to top or combined into diagrams that represented the entire route in plan or highlighted specific visual elements. As with MOTATION, this was a system for recording the experience of highway motion and space that attempted to capture the driver's overall orientation toward, or image of, the road and the environment through which it passed. While the authors were eager to deploy their system to design new highways—and they directed *The View from the Road* to highway engineers, in particular—they first demonstrated its efficacy by analyzing existing highways representing the

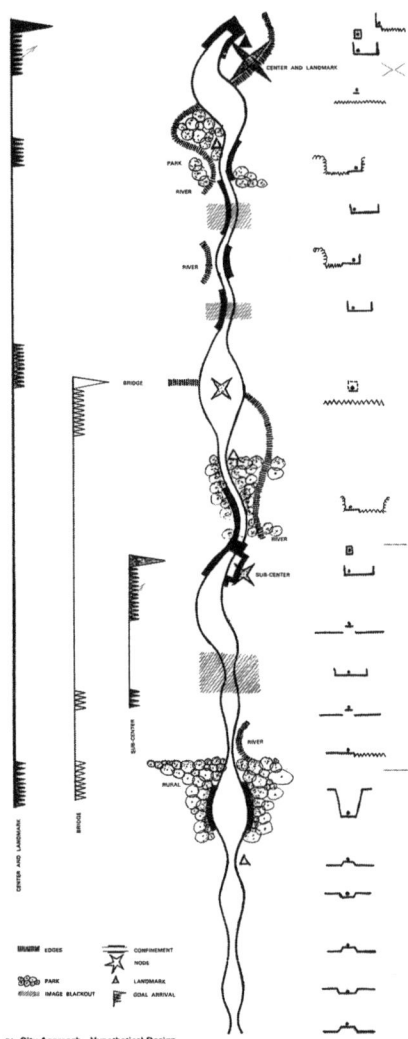

Figure 60. "Abstraction notation of motion and space," from Donald Appleyard, Kevin Lynch, and John R. Myer, *The View from the Road*. (© 1965 Massachusetts Institute of Technology, by permission of The MIT Press)

typical road morphologies of the United States in the 1960s. They considered parkways, arterials, interstates and urban freeways, especially on the East Coast, but also including several in the Midwest and California. As they studied such dimensions of highway experience as attention, motion, space, alignment, and rhythm, they referenced roads as dissimilar as the Rockefeller Parkway in Cleveland (begun 1894) and the New Jersey Turnpike in the Meadowlands (begun 1949), interpreting their distinct qualities both choreographically and cinematically.[64]

To test the notation system's utility, they documented in detail a daytime, non–rush hour seven-mile trip on the Northeast Expressway, a widened swath of U.S. 1 in Boston, travelling south from Revere through Charlestown to the downtown waterfront. They presented their own "subjective evaluation," and that of twenty mostly middle-class commuters, using maps, sketches, photographs, and strip diagrams that registered the dynamic procession of the sequential highway landscape in the foreground and in the distance: bridges and rail yards, traffic signs and billboards, and fixtures on the Boston skyline like the Bunker Hill Monument and the Custom House tower. The accompanying textual description captured visual impressions and sensual responses: the pleasure, confusion, dizziness, and distraction of driving the expressway. The accompanying quantitative analysis mined those impressions to reveal "the rhythm and locus of attention," with reference to the features and meanings of the roadscape as drivers interpreted them. As a data set, the value of these coded and counted impressions (532 in total) was mainly speculative, since, as the authors admitted, the Northeast Expressway's engineers, preoccupied with cost, capacity, and safety, had probably not considered them when designing the route.[65]

But what if they had? Might it be possible to design highways as "conscious works of art" that would transform driving into "a coherent and delightful aesthetic experience"? The authors of *The View from the Road* answered with an unqualified yes, and offered as proof "an imaginary design" for Boston's Central Artery, the elevated freeway that infamously cut off downtown from the North End and the waterfront. In *The Image of the City,* Lynch described the Central Artery as "a special kind of automobile land," because its hermetic path detached drivers' perception from the surrounding city, even as it enabled "fast and undisturbed movement." In *The View from the Road,* Lynch and his coauthors were interested in how this "misalignment" might be corrected by prioritizing "the visual and esthetic experience of driving on the road" rather than "the cheapest or most efficient layout"—the expedients that guided urban freeway construction in the interstate era. Deploying their notation system to great effect—at least in visual terms—they presented an improved highway route in a series of maps, sketched vignettes, self-motion strips, combination diagrams, and travelogue-like commentary. Taken together, text and image conveyed almost a sense of wonder at the road and the city revealed through the windshield by the car's choreographed movement past natural and constructed features: the river on one side, gas tanks on the other; flanking brick walls giving way to arching trees; close-up advertisements balanced by water features at a distance. Paying attention to *the view from the road* also meant that this ideal route avoided objects and landmarks the authors considered undesirable or unimportant, including the municipal incinerator, sitting

Figure 61. Quick perspective sketch with overpass, from Donald Appleyard, Kevin Lynch, and John R. Myer, *The View from the Road*. (© 1965 Massachusetts Institute of Technology, by permission of The MIT Press)

Figure 62. Quick perspective sketch with vertical sign, from Donald Appleyard, Kevin Lynch, and John R. Myer, *The View from the Road*. (© 1965 Massachusetts Institute of Technology, by permission of The MIT Press)

on axis with the highway as built. Beyond the route itself, their scheme also imagined a cityscape transformed by a carnivalesque curation of existing and proposed illumination, as captured in a stunning night diagram of "nocturnal landmarks" along the route. This proved one of the most influential images in the book, exerting considerable impact on Robert Venturi and Denise Scott Brown in their analysis of the Las Vegas Strip. The "chaotic skyline" of the daytime city disappeared into a luminous field, and, through the deliberate plotting of the highway's curves and straightaways, the route heightened perception of urban luminosity by exposing points, strips, and nodes of maximum intensification: not only the beaconlike lantern of the North Church, the floodlit dome of the State House, and the illuminated thermometer atop the John Hancock Tower, but also paths of circulation defined by car headlights, street lamps, and "the clamor of lights on the commercial avenues."[66]

As this scheme makes clear, and the authors stressed repeatedly, the literal view from the road—drivers' perception of the city's "visual resources"—was the study's exclusive focus. The authors are explicitly *not* concerned with "how the highway looks from the outside, i.e. in the city itself."[67] This position is remarkable given the trauma that urban freeways visited on the neighborhoods through which they

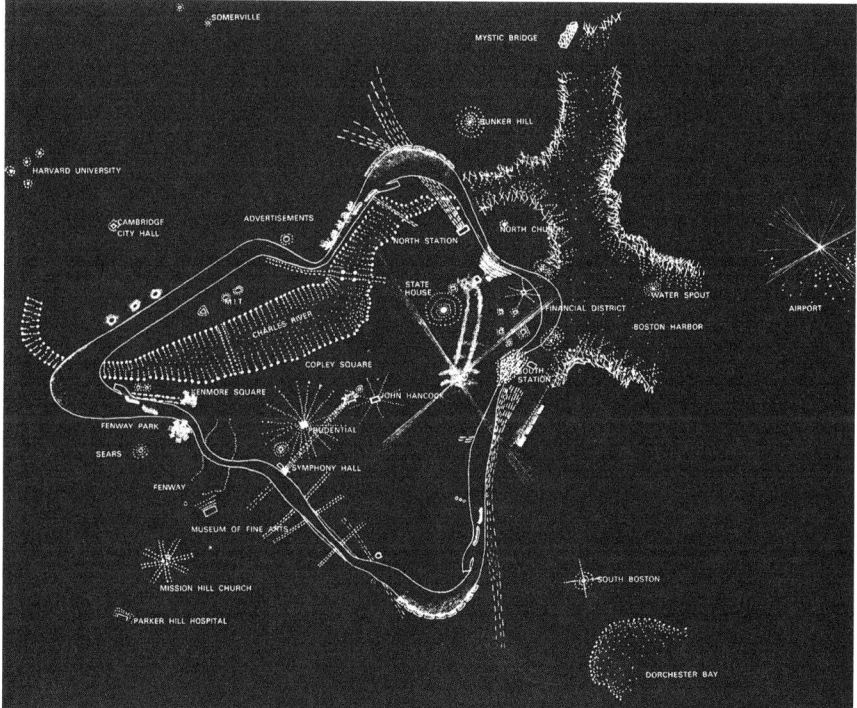

Figure 63. Night diagram of Central Artery in Boston, from Donald Appleyard, Kevin Lynch, and John R. Myer, *The View from the Road*. (© 1965 Massachusetts Institute of Technology, by permission of The MIT Press)

LEARNING FROM AUTOPIA

passed (a condition that was rectified in Boston only in 2007 when the Big Dig finally buried the Central Artery). Other planners, they claimed, were already attempting to mitigate the urban impact of urban freeways, but so great were the design challenges of these roadways that, they contended, the only way to deal with them was to separate the handling of internal and external conditions. In hindsight, it seems like the authors struck a Faustian bargain as urban planners, but they saw their work in a positive light, even as a form of advocacy—for the roads and the city as a whole, if not for the immediate locales of the highways themselves. If, from the outside, the view *of* the road exposed a monolithic form imposed on the existing urban fabric, the view *from* the road revealed a dizzying combination of "kinesthetic sensations" of large-scale architecture. In a clear intensification of Stewart's experience on U.S. 40 a generation earlier, these were now likened to a roller coaster ride that seemed to combine elements of music, cinema, and dance. The automobile was guide and "filter" for this hyperstimulating world; it framed sight even as it diluted one's sense of smell, sound, and touch. What the car's occupants received in compensation was acute perception of the "speed, scale, and movement" of the trip itself; this, the authors argued, had consequential urban effects. As the car propelled them through the vast domain of urban space, it was as if the whole of the metropolis was under the driver's control, which "neutralized the disparity in size between man and the city." J. B. Jackson had called this "autoterritoriality." Appleyard, Lynch, and Myer were more blunt: driving the highway was an "extension of self." They were not fetishizing the automobile or valorizing the autopian flâneur; they were recognizing that the changes wrought by the car went far beyond the physical transformation of the built environment.[68]

One of the stated ambitions of urban freeways, regardless of their urban consequences, was to enhance automotive circulation between cities and suburbs, binding them together into an extended motorized metropolis. The nature of the roadside had changed drastically since the pre-interstate era, becoming by the 1960s the expanded field of the corridor through which the highway passed, rather than the accumulations of its increasingly denuded margins. But limited access did not mean limited perception, as Tunnard and Pushkarev, Halprin, and Appleyard, Lynch, and Myer so thoroughly demonstrated. And though they largely failed in their efforts to improve highway design by providing a system for analyzing it, they achieved something else: they brought J. B. Jackson's notion of the road as a human landscape into the interstate age. And in so doing, they revealed an uncomfortable truth: as a socially signifying place, the Main Street sidewalk was eclipsed by the commercial strip which, in turn, was eclipsed by the freeway—though, of course, all three continued to exist, if not always to thrive. What the evolution and persistence of these spatial domains had to say about American culture was a question their highway analytics were not able to answer.

Toward an Aesthetic of the Hi-Way Culture

By the late 1960s, an increasing number of critical voices were attempting to find meaning in the American Autopia from inside and outside architectural and urban discourse. The expanding highway metropolis, with its distinctive buildings and spaces and artifacts, had seemingly irresistible appeal to the generation that matured into, or witnessed from afar via movies and glossies, the booming consumer culture of the United States at midcentury. Nonetheless, the prevailing attitude among observers of the car-oriented American scene was grave concern about that culture's environmental impact, which the 1965 passage of the Highway Beautification Act did little to assuage. "Blight blossoms on the American highway," *Life* staff writer Loudon Wainwright commented dolefully in 1970, after an extensive tour "down that loathsome road." Everywhere he turned was "the plastic homogeneity of trash and hucksterism." Signs shouted "a garble of messages nobody needs" and made "almost every place look like somewhere you've just been." Across eight pages, Michael Rougier's color photographs displayed the fulsome fullness of this roadside excess, nowhere more vividly than on Speedway Boulevard in Tuscon, Arizona, which the city's mayor declared America's ugliest street, with its the physical congestion of cars, visual congestion of signage, and stark contrast between the expanding commercial domain and the shrinking natural realm[69] (see color plate 8). *Life* undoubtedly intended its readers to find the pictures shocking, even obscene, but by 1970, younger roadside observers were rejecting the establishment's automatic equating of roadside with blight. Uninterested in fomenting autopian discontent, they concerned themselves with, as Venturi and Scott Brown put it, finding a significance for A&P parking lots. Looking beyond the beer cans littering the highway toward the signs and strips, the gas stations and drive-ins, they didn't see what critic Walter McQuade bemoaned as "the great banal plastic jungle of popular taste."[70] What the younger generation saw on the roadside was the genius loci of America.

British curator and Independent Group member Lawrence Alloway was one of the earliest critics (Gilbert Seldes was another) to offer a theoretical basis for what would become a profound cultural reappraisal. In an oft-quoted 1958 essay "The Arts and Mass Media," Alloway attempted to identify the fundamental characteristics of the popular arts of industrialized societies. Emerging from mass communication, mass production, and mass markets, these arts possessed a "sensitiveness to the variables of our life and economy" that enabled them to anticipate, influence, and accompany rapidly changing values, interests, and tastes. As a result, existing critical standards for evaluating and judging disparate art forms were now in flux. In a direct riposte to visual art critic Clement Greenberg, Alloway argued that distinguishing between supposedly *genuine* and *ersatz* cultural forms (be they high and low or avante garde and kitsch) was irrelevant because the "expanding framework" of media made a static definition of culture impossible. In the twentieth century, he wrote, "our definition of culture is being stretched beyond the fine art limits imposed on it by Renaissance theory." By the late 1950s, it referred "increasingly, to the whole complex of human activities"—including, of course, the production and consumption of the popular arts themselves.[71]

When Alloway wrote this essay, he had not yet visited the country whose "mass-produced folk art" had largely occasioned his analysis, but shortly after its publication in February 1958 he traveled the United States for nearly a year on a grant from the State Department, settling in the country permanently in 1961. Before 1958, Alloway consumed American culture at a distance through movies, magazines, and pulp fiction; after 1958, Alloway experienced American culture up close, in three dimensions, behind the wheel of a car. This stateside immersion produced a key shift in critical perspective as he came to terms with both the vast space of the American landscape and the dense symbols with which it was laden, as he explained in "City Notes" of 1959. Though he admired those places and buildings that could be characterized as "architect-controlled"—including the Flatiron Building, Rockefeller Center, General Motors Technical Center, and the Lake Shore Drive Apartments—Alloway was more interested in what he saw as the totality of the larger urban places that contained these one-off "monuments." These were "messy configurations" of "patched-up, expendable, and developing forms" that conventional architectural terms inadequately described. For Alloway, much like J. B. Jackson, the "popular environment" was a more useful descriptor because it could embrace a range of modern urban forms and phenomena—from the "neon spectacle" of signage and lights to everyday commercial typologies of bars, restaurants, drug stores, and the like, to the inadvertent soundscapes created by Muzak and sidewalk speakers—all of which would confound "the categorists" and anyone else trying to understand the popular environment through "permanent formal principles" that, regardless, were already giving way before the demolition, construction, and expansion he witnessed everywhere in the United States.

This dynamic evolution was an important dimension of the popular environment, but so was dynamic experience, as he observed firsthand. Driving here, Alloway had a critical epiphany: American cars perfectly matched "the scale of American streets" in terms of "design symbolism" and "spatial experience." Writing for a British architectural audience ("City Notes" appeared in *Architectural Design*), Alloway explained this by analogy to CinemaScope, the wide-screen technology then at the height of its short-lived popularity: just as CinemaScope's extended screen seemed to expand the movie experience into the "real," that is, the physical environment of the theater, so the wrap-around windshield of a 1950s sedan— Harley Earl's 1958 Cadillac Coupe de Ville had an eighty-inch width—created a "panoramic view" of the environmental continuum flashing by on the other side of the safety glass. The windshield, like the movie screen, was a "communications device" that allowed drivers and passengers to comprehend the totality of a "communications-saturated environment."[72]

Buildings, billboards, signage, traffic signals, lights, words, shapes: for Alloway these constituted the "symbol-thick environment of American cities and highways." There was, he argued, a "Great White Way" stretching virtually uninterrupted and "with only marginal regional differentiation" for 3,000 miles, from Times Square in New York to Market Street in San Francisco (whether metaphorically or literally, along the route of the Lincoln Highway or the future Interstate 80), but also extending southward to, inevitably, Los Angeles, that "flat city . . . built for cars" whose importance as a "mass communications centre" had as much to do with its distinct metropolitan space as with the presence of Hollywood film studios. It was because of that distinct urban form, Alloway observed seven years before Reyner Banham, that Angelenos used their cars "like a cowboy uses his horse, as a natural adaptive extension of his legs." Alloway's measured appraisal of continental urban diffusion stands in marked contrast to British disparagements of nearly a decade earlier in *Architectural Review* (see chapter 3). Indeed, Alloway took the *Review* to task for recoiling in knee-jerk intellectual horror at "the mess that is man made America." The establishment clung to this old-guard position, Alloway argued, because to do otherwise was to admit that the architect "exaggerated the significance of his contribution to the city." A vibrant popular environment had developed despite, not because of, the profession—though he conceded that Skidmore, Owings and Merrill had created a "pop architecture" by disseminating "the Mies's vernacular" in skyscrapers and ground-scrapers throughout the country, and he applauded Victor Gruen for attempting to plan the unplannable in his shopping centers.[73] Alloway also pointed favorably to Douglas Haskell's call for a "reciprocal interchange" between architecture and popular taste.[74] At the same time, much like J. B. Jackson, he cautioned architects against "adopt[ing] playful and odd forms without their spirit [and] without their precise functions," lest they "make a travesty of the environment in which pop art naturally thrives." Significantly, Alloway had no such admonition for painters, whom he championed (along with photographers and sculptors) for work he regarded as not simply a reflection of the popular environment, but as a validation of its centrality to contemporary American culture.[75]

After he moved to the United States in 1961, Alloway had ample opportunity to refine his ideas about the American popular environment and to formulate them into a theory that sought to explore the implications, artistic and otherwise, of an autopian nation. At the same time, his post-1961 professional positions—as a Guggenheim curator and art critic for *The Nation* and *Artforum*—provided Alloway with direct access to the art world activities that he and others would soon identify as pop. These interconnected interests came together in an article he published in *Arts Magazine* in February 1967. Though his subject in this instance is highway culture, Alloway's title is "hi-way culture." Clearly demonstrating his pop art credentials, Alloway used the roadside slang spelling ubiquitous to motels, drive-ins, and carhops. This culture referred to the "hardware and sociology generated by automotive transport," balanced between "specialization and proliferation on and off the road." In other words, highway culture had moved well beyond the construction of roads and other infrastructural accommodations to the car to encompass a full range of social attitudes, activities, and practices, becoming a vast and richly "folkloric" domain. This was evident in the range of artifacts Alloway documented, from pony cars like the Plymouth Barracuda, which he saw as "symbolic of intimacy with the road, speed, and kicks," to hot rod and drag race comics that contributed "vroom vroom" and other car-derived "onomatopoeic words" to the common language of the nation. The folkloric quality of highway culture was, obviously, most evident in the environment, where Alloway briefly observed the typological transformation of gas stations and Howard Johnsons, analyzing how changes in form and program reflected shifting market demands and tastes in the second half of the twentieth century. These caused the former to add "consumer temptations" like soda and cigarettes and the latter to shed a "Disneyesque Colonial profile" in favor of more abstract forms that retained, nonetheless, the chain's familiar turquoise-and-orange color scheme.[76]

Here, with greater precision than in his "City Notes" essay, undoubtedly because he was no longer merely a tourist, Alloway catalogued the perceptual impact of viewing the country "through the windshield." His was not the thoroughgoing analysis attempted by Halprin or Appleyard, Lynch, and Myer, who developed their notation systems for recording how drivers experienced the city in motion with a goal of improving highway design. Rather, as befits an art critic, Alloway's is an *aesthetic* analysis of automotive visuality, one infused with a pop criticality predicated on a thoughtful response to the work of such artists as Allan D'Arcangelo and Ed Ruscha. D'Arcangelo's *U.S. Highway 1* paintings (beginning 1962) depicted the commercial spine of the Eastern Seaboard as a continuum of signage, scenery, and infrastructure produced by the mobilized vision of the driver behind the wheel (see color plate 9). On the opposite coast, Ed Ruscha's *Standard Service* series (beginning 1963), and books like *Twentysix Gasoline Stations* and *Thirtyfour Parking Lots in Los Angeles,* reflected not only the laid-back cool of the L.A. School, but the startling transformation of the physical form of Southern California in the decades after World War II. D'Arcangelo's work distilled the roadscape into a soporific corridor as eerie as it was uncluttered. Striking a balance between realism and abstraction, these pictures captured the zoned-out state that sometimes accompanies long distance or nighttime driving (now recognized as *highway hypnosis*). Ruscha's work, by contrast, refused psychological engagement, especially in the photographs he started shooting in 1962 when driving the 1,300-mile stretch of Route 66 between Oklahoma City and L.A. Passing gas stations, mile after mile, they became, Ruscha later reflected, "like a musical rhythm to me," and in case that sounded too lofty, he added a modifier: "cultural belches in the landscape."[77] The stations seemed less like burps and more like monuments when Ruscha put them on canvas, sometimes as large as ten feet wide, with a perspectival flourish enhanced by the klieg light lines cutting across the sky.

Making a gas station look like a monument and claiming it *as* a monument were two different things, and, Ruscha and D'Arcangelo left it to the critics to explore their work's larger meanings, assuming those critics could get beyond their stupefaction at finding gas stations and everyday elements of the roadside in work regarded as avant-garde rather than latter-day American Scene Painting or Regionalism. Indeed, as Alloway noted, most critics were "so amazed to see [the highway] as the subject matter of art that they noticed almost nothing else." For his part, Alloway seemed to notice almost everything relating to the highway, at least in terms of visual perception from inside the car. Through the windshield, drivers experienced the roadscape as "sliced open [and] fanned out," while passengers were treated to "terrific sequences out of side windows." Fleeting images passed by in quick succession, though not in regular or predictable order since apprehension depended on one's position in the car and the direction of one's gaze. Alloway replaced his earlier CinemaScope analogy with an everyday reality of the mid-1960s:

viewing the roadscape from inside a moving car was "like flipping the station control on TV," as glimpses of "Hi-Way Kulchur" flickered past like momentary images of changing channels. What most caught Alloway's attention was commercial content: the advertising superstructure he described as "the baroque progeny of old merchant signs" rendered at the sci-fi scale of "Flash Gordon super-cities," and the strip's commercial vernacular he catalogued in a celebratory fashion like a Beat Poet urbanist: "Alamo Plaza, Leaning Tower of Pizza, Pizza Palace, Tiki Room,

Figure 64. Ed Ruscha, *Twentysix Gasoline Stations: Standard, Amarillo, Texas,* 1962, gelatin silver print, 11.8 × 12.1 cm. (The J. Paul Getty Museum, Los Angeles, © Ed Ruscha)

Figure 65. Ed Ruscha, *Twentysix Gasoline Stations: Standard, Figueroa Street, Los Angeles,* 1962, gelatin silver print, 12.4 × 14.6 cm. (The J. Paul Getty Museum, Los Angeles, © Ed Ruscha)

Holiday Inn, Flamingo, Glamour Cottage, The French Room, Crab Orchard Motel, Gulf, Giant City Lodge, Heritage Motel, University Drugs, The Moo and Cackle, Hub Cafe, Don's Body Shop, Elroy 'Butch' Grob [*sic*], Pirate's Cove Inc., House of Fabrics, Air Conditional Chapel, Serv-U Mobile Homes, The Parasol." As we have seen in the writings of Bernard DeVoto and Peter Blake, lists like this were a familiar trope in autopian discourse of the 1950s and 1960s, representing an attack on or celebration of the highway landscape, depending on the author's point of view. For Alloway, the list was the textual equivalent of pop art's visual iconography, capturing those elements of the "familiar man-made environment" that were of abiding interest to artists like Ruscha and D'Arcangelo, but were taken for granted by almost everyone else. This rendered highway culture effectively "invisible," Alloway argued, despite its outsized continental presence. Though Alloway acknowledged that some architects and planners were learning from autopia, outside limited and mostly professional debates, highway culture was ignored "except by those who don't like it."[78] With a notable exception, as Alloway surely knew: Tom Wolfe had already published two articles in *Esquire* that, in addition to virtually inventing New Journalism, fostered the hipster cognoscenti's appreciation of the same aspects of the highway culture that had long interested Alloway, and Haskell and Jackson, too.

In "There Goes (VAROOM! VAROOM!) That Kandy Kolored (THPHHHHHH!) Tangerine-Flake Streamline Baby (RAHGHHHH!) around the Bend (BRUMM-MMMMMMMMMMMMMMM . . .)" of November 1963, Wolfe explored the drag racing and hot rod culture of Los Angeles, profiling car customizers George Barris and Ed Roth as the Pablo Picasso and Salvador Dali of the field. In "LAS VEGAS (What?) LAS VEGAS (Can't Hear You! Too Noisy) LAS VEGAS!!!!" of February 1964, Wolfe turned his attention to the casinos in the Nevada desert, reporting on a city that was so committed to 24/7 "electronic stimulation" that it had elevated into "an institution" what was "a quixotic inflammation of the senses" in most American towns. Both pieces are replete with sharply observed details and descriptive flourishes sketching the neon and chrome roadscape of Glitter Gulch and the Strip (see color plate 10). In Las Vegas, Wolfe noted that signs occupied the same place on the skyline as towers in New York and trees in New England. Neon signs, especially those of the Young Electric Sign Company, had become "the architecture of Las Vegas," and he placed them on par with "the most whimsical, Yale-seminar-frenzied devices of the two late geniuses of Baroque Modern, Frank Lloyd Wright and Eero Saarinen." Next to the bigger-than-building-scale signage of "designer-sculptor geniuses" like YESCO's Herman Boernge and Kermit Wayne, Wolfe wrote, the work of Wright and Saarinen seemed "rather stuffy business." Significantly, Wolfe also noted that while the casino signs were the largest and most elaborate, comparable "motifs" existed throughout the city, adorning a range of lesser institutions: gas stations, car washes, and motels, but also "funeral parlors, churches, public buildings, flophouses, and sauna baths." Like the automobile-oriented types, in terms of their built form, these, too, were modeled on the "The Look" of the casinos. As a result, Wolfe suggested (attempting to prompt outrage), Las Vegas was "one of the few architecturally unified cities in the world." To describe this unified architecture, Wolfe invented a specialist's vocabulary for the commercial "aesthetic" he witnessed. With terms like "Boomerang Modern," "McDonald's Hamburger Parabola" and "Mint Casino Elliptical," he seemed to take special pleasure in riffing on the language of formalist art history and criticism in order to thumb his nose at the high culture establishment. Throughout both of these articles, however, Wolfe carefully maintained his own elite cultural distance from the places he observed, sprinkling the text with "wink-wink" references that drew a parallel between the signs and buildings of Las Vegas and the built environments of Miami Beach and New Jersey, implying analogous gaucheness of form and culture.[79]

In 1968, in an article entitled "The New Life Out There: Electro-Graphic Architecture" that Wolfe published nearly simultaneously in the *Los Angeles Times* and *New York* magazine, he toned down the elitism while making his critique of the establishment even more pointed. "I drove around Los Angeles and its [sic] crazy!" he proclaimed, "the art world is upside down." Here, the article's form is as important as the content: the entire text is written as a drive-by, short paragraphs and ellipses conveying a sense of Wolfe driving around Southern California pointing things out to readers-cum-passengers, and balancing pop enthusiasm with erudite interpretation. "The existing vocabulary of art history is helpless before what commercial artists are now doing in the western United States," Wolfe declared, extending his account of signage in Las Vegas to the work of designers in Los Angeles and San Diego, particularly Melvin Zeitvogel of the California Neon Company, to whom Wolfe seemed attracted as much by his non-WASP name as by his "baroque rocket" aesthetic sensibilities. In Zeitvogel's hands, neon tubes and pulsating bulbs, especially when combined with sculptural structure, amounted to an "electro-graphic architecture" and a "car fantasy architecture" that upended existing hierarchies of form and space, as Mike Salisbury's accompanying color photographs made abundantly clear. Wolfe also extolled the swoopy concrete and fluorescent-lit virtues of Gin Wong's Union 76 gas station "pagoda" in

Beverly Hills (designed 1960; built 1965)—though he rendered the given name of William L. Pereira & Associates' lead designer as "Jim." Describing the canopy as a "huge spherical triangle resting on three piers with curving soffits," Wolfe noted that Wong's now iconic scheme replaced an existing Union 76 on the same site and produced a 50 percent increase in business in its first month of operation. This, he said, demonstrated the commercial value of architecture that privileged three-dimensional representation—in this case, what Wong saw as the motion of cars and airplanes. As for the gas station's aesthetic value, Wolfe used it as the starting point for a rant against art and architectural establishments too wrapped up in a nostalgia, "de la château" and "de la Lincoln Center," to pay heed to the forms, materials, typologies, infrastructure, and urbanism of those West Coast and desert cities that, he argued, were usually regarded as "sprawl, chaos, madness, [and] strangled by the automobile."[80]

In fact, Wolfe insisted, regardless of this "intellectual snobbery" and willful misreading of the autopian landscape, Los Angeles, Las Vegas, and San Diego had produced "something wild enough and baroque enough to express the new age of motion and mass wealth." This was most obvious to Wolfe in Zeitvogel's signs, like the eleven-story space-age pylon (complete with atomic orbitals) he designed in 1959 for a Buick dealership in San Diego (see color plate 11). In Wolfe's reading of Zeitvogel's work, the coloration, kinetic movement, and composition, however satisfying in themselves, also served to reverse the terms by which art was comprehended as avant-garde or derivative. Regardless of what was taking place in New York galleries or on the pages of *Progressive Architecture*, Wolfe argued, Zeitvogel and others like him, who "have been building not to catch the eye of the art world but

Figure 66. Jack Colker's Union 76 gas station, Beverly Hills, California (William Pereira & Associates [Gin Wong], 1965), from Tom Wolfe, "The New Life Out There," *New York Magazine,* 9 December 1968. (Photograph by Mike Salisbury; permission courtesy of the photographer)

of people driving by in cars"—in other words "designing for the eyes of people moving"—were the "classicists," while the "serious" artists and architects were "the primitives," reduced to borrowed motifs and pale imitations of the originals.[81] Wolfe's evaluation of car-centric design was as sophisticated as it was shrewd, but however much he championed the bravado form-making of Zeitvogel and Wong et al., his interest in autopia extended only far enough to jab a few colored plastic tubes in the collective eyes of the high culture gatekeepers. But that may have been enough, because his comments, however condescending, caught the attention of Scott Brown, Venturi, and Banham.

If Wolfe remained an elitist in populist drag, Lawrence Alloway was the opposite. His evaluation of commercial aesthetics in "Hi-Way Culture," while equaling Wolfe's in enthusiasm, displayed none of Wolfe's smugness, though he, too, happily took a swipe at the design community's holier-than-thou handwringing about finding a "platonic Esperanto" to replace the physical and symbolic "sprawl of urban chaos." Alloway suggested that designers would do well to avoid Aspen (site of the International Design Conference) and simply get out on the road, echoing Elizabeth Gordon's comments to the AIA in the previous decade (discussed earlier). Commercial signage might communicate imperfectly and unevenly, but traffic signs were nearly universal and, with a hint of satisfaction, Alloway observed that pop artists realized this long before most architects were even paying attention. It seems clear that, to Alloway, artists "taking highway culture as subject matter" for their work represented something more significant than merely "an expansion of iconography" as an alternative to heroic abstraction. In Allan D'Arcangelo's work, the painter's obsessive imagery of oblique and fragmented vistas capturing roads, overpasses, and signs represented an essential cultural condition as much as an insistent point of view, both succinctly expressed as "implicitly that of man at the wheel."[82]

Denise Scott Brown and Robert Venturi went even further than Alloway in arguing for the broad cultural importance of pop art's autopian imagery and they, too, discussed D'Arcangelo's work in "A Significance for A&P Parking Lots." In that now classic essay, which they published in *Architectural Forum* in March 1968, a year after Alloway's "Hi-Way Culture" appeared in *Arts,* they reproduced the artist's "Red Arrow" of 1965. In that print, a large blocky arrow points to the left while a superimposed and stylized manicle points to the right. To Scott Brown and Venturi this image was a poignant evocation of the spatial and perceptual contradictions, if not confusions, the driver encountered in the contemporary highway landscape. Unlike on the crossroads of old, where a left was a left, on cloverleaf interchanges, "to turn left [the driver] must go right." To the architects, D'Arcangelo perfectly captured a directional ambiguity that had become so routine by the 1960s that it was generally overlooked, despite its impact on (they would soon argue) "the psychology of the driver."[83] D'Arcangelo's work also appeared in *The Highway,* a 1970 exhibition at the University of Pennsylvania's Institute of Contemporary Art (ICA) to which Scott Brown and Venturi contributed a catalogue essay. Curator Stephen Prokopoff claimed the ICA show was the first to survey the highway's impact on visual art, and it included not only contemporary pop work, but also paintings and photographs from the 1930s and 1940s by Edward Hopper, Ralston Crawford, Dorothea Lange, Walker Evans, and others. Also on display at the ICA were maquettes produced by YESCO for the Flamingo and Desert Inn casinos on the Las Vegas Strip. These were likely selected by Scott Brown and Venturi, who had visited the sign company during the field research portion of their fall 1968 Yale studio. Though presented as anonymous pop-culture-folk-art objects, the signs were, in fact, the work of a specific designer: Herman Boernge, whom Tom Wolfe had already identified as one of Las Vegas's most creative graphic artists. Scott Brown and Venturi don't mention Boernge (though the lack of design credit in the exhibition catalogue probably had more to do with YESCO than with curation), but they do acknowledge Tom Wolfe, whose observations on Las Vegas urbanism they had also quoted in "A Significance for A&P Parking Lots."

"The Highway" is very much a reprisal of that earlier essay, synthesized for a non-architecture audience, and containing, as a result, a useful summation of its major arguments: that as "sculptural and symbolic" architecture, memetic roadside buildings gave meaning to the environment; that "the roadside commercial vernacular of the 1960s" had the potential to inspire contemporary architecture the way the industrial vernacular inspired modernists in the 1920s; that the Las Vegas Strip itself was "archetype for all commercial strips, but prototype for none."

They bookend this digest of their earlier polemic (which they would shortly expand in *Learning from Las Vegas*) with a consideration of the evolution of the roadside vernacular from folk art to fine art that hews more closely to Alloway's criticism than to Wolfe's reportage. They argue that in making "the highway and its paraphernalia" the subject of their work, pop artists like D'Arcangelo, Ruscha, and Robert Indiana "help us through their translation to see ourselves as we really are." Continuing the artist's historical role of interpretation, pop's practitioners validated "Auto City USA" by making it "acceptable to and usable by ourselves." In this regard, the exhibition was equally important, since, "by putting the highway in an art gallery," it provided a critical "new context" for considering how painters, sculptors, and photographers were "creatively elaborating" on the reality of highway and roadside. As such, it served to "jolt our aesthetic ruts and enable us to learn from its vitality." The roadside, they assert, offered contemporary designers "useful lessons in the functional problems of relating auto and architecture." But this would occur only when the highway was "accepted on its own terms" and its artistic interpretations were more generally understood.[84]

Making pop art's highway iconography comprehensible was one of Alloway's goals in "Hi-Way Culture," particularly the "Notes on D'Arcangelo" section of the essay, but equally critical in this regard was the way Alloway chose *not* to interpret D'Arcangelo's work. The autopian perspective was so essential that he refused to draw a parallel between D'Arcangelo's highway depictions and landscape painting. Even if he had wanted to make such a comparison, it would have been necessarily limited, because, Alloway claimed, D'Arcangelo's canvases depicted schematic, not dramatic vistas.[85] A half-century on, it is easier to see this pop work in the artistic tradition of Frederick Church and Albert Bierstadt. While the pop artists claimed to be interested in their subjects on purely formal grounds (e.g., regularity and repetition, even as these characteristics exemplified mass production and standardization), they were also intrigued by the apparent placelessness of the places they depicted, and those *places,* as places, defined the midcentury American environment as emphatically as the natural scenery captured by Church and Bierstadt a century before. If sameness and even banality had replaced the singularity and majesty of earlier depictions of the landscape, this had less to do with the aesthetic sensibilities of individual artists than with a paradigmatic shift in the culture. In between the Hudson River School and pop art, members of the Ash Can school and the Photo-Secession viewed the skyscrapers of New York as man-made mountains, and so did the broader culture. What the Adirondacks and the Rockies were to the middle of the nineteenth century, the Flatiron and Woolworth Buildings were to the turn of the twentieth—and the American avant garde continued to regard them as such right through the 1930s. If, after World War II, groundscrapers like the GM Technical Center and Connecticut General Headquarters never quite displaced the skyscraper in the American imagination, this was because they were not as visible, hidden away amid the rolling hills of suburban campuses. But the autopian landscape still managed to capture the American imagination. As roadside observers from the 1930s to the 1960s implied, as the metropolis extended outward along seemingly endless highways, it was as if the doctrine of Manifest Destiny had been revitalized and redeployed for the age of consumerism and the car. Whether found on local arterials, federal routes, or interstates, the popular environment had produced a new set of human-made icons, and engendered an enduring aesthetic of the highway culture.

The Accepted Monuments of Autopia

Reyner Banham embraced that aesthetic almost from the moment he started poking around American streets, strips, and freeways during his first visit to the United States in 1961. Like Lawrence Alloway a few years before, he came to relish direct experience of the country's buildings and landscapes. Every inch the "observational" historian equipped with stenography notepads and rolls of Ektachrome, he was also an "archetypical British tourist armed with credit car and rented car."[86] Driving was key to Banham's analysis of American urbanism, architecture, and design, and a through-the-windshield POV is a leitmotif in much of his writing. Driving also established a direct link with distinguished literary forbearers like Alexis de Tocqueville, Frances Trollope, and Charles Dickens, who traveled the nation in the nineteenth century much like Banham in the twentieth, interpreting the American civilization for Europeans back home. While none made claims for the

American originality of the stagecoach, steamboat, or railroad, they all observed a keen native interest in movement, distance, and speed, in cutting canals and laying out roads to establish communication between the country's vastly dispersed settlements, connections that, by Banham's day, had become a basic fact of life in the United States. Though the existence of good roads did nothing to mitigate what he called the "boring, sweaty, interminable miles" stretching between the coasts, those miles also represented "the lure of sheer distance" that, for Banham, was equally characteristic of the United States.[87] The more miles Banham drove, the more he argued for the cultural and architectural significance of the places the car produced, as he became convinced that autopian buildings, billboards, and highways had de facto importance, with or without high art mediation.

Perhaps it was inevitable that the historian who established his reputation with *Theory and Design in the First Machine Age* (1960) would turn his scholarly and critical attention to the territory of the automobile: the car was minor character in that trailblazing work of modernist revisionism (Banham deals briefly with cars designed in the 1930s by Walter Gropius, Buckminster Fuller, and Harley Earl), and Banham concluded his study by suggesting that the architect circa 1960 might do well to "discard his whole cultural load."[88] Though he was referring to what he saw as expanding disciplinary incompatibility between architecture and technology, a comparable tension existed between the discipline of architecture and the culture of the car, at least within architecture's power centers. Five years later, Banham made precisely this point when he chastised the Museum of Modern Art for what he considered a serious sin of omission in the 1965 exhibition *Modern Architecture, USA*. Curated by Arthur Drexler, the show surveyed sixty-five years of built work, with a particular focus on architecture since 1950, when, in the curator's words, "the American imagination was dominated by the inspired method of Ludwig Mies van der Rohe."[89] The show wasn't all glass and steel; Drexler included a fair representation of modernism's increasingly disparate strands, from the shingled regional eclecticism of Bruce Goff and Herb Greene in Oklahoma to the new ornamentalism of Minoru Yamasaki in Detroit. He even included two projects that were car-oriented and car-dependent, respectively: Paul Rudolph's Temple

Street Garage in New Haven, Connecticut (see figure 44) and Victor Lundy's IBM Garden State Office Building in Cranford, New Jersey.

These were not sufficient to satisfy Banham, who aired his grievances in a BBC radio broadcast. Subsequently transcribed for the network's periodical, *The Listener,* as "The Missing Motel," Banham republished the piece in J. B. Jackson's *Landscape* with a pointed subtitle: "Unrecognized American Architecture." Drexler may have believed that "architectural excellence has many forms" (as he stated in a wall text in the exhibition), but those forms were not, apparently, to be found along the American highway. When Banham pressed him about why, in effect, the motels were missing, Drexler conceded that "people might build such things, and they might be culturally significant," but, he claimed, they could never be shown at MoMA, given the museum's committed to "'quality' in design." What irked Banham about this bland justification was how subjective it was. Goff's Bavinger House, to Banham's eye, was basically "a pure supermarket dream," and while Lundy's IBM might not have been "faced in plastic artificial brickwork in the motel mode," the real bricks on its facade were treated in a comparable superficial and decorative manner, in a pattern Drexler viewed as suggestive of Mayan architecture and computer punch cards. Banham posits that these buildings made the cut while "a host of witty and inventive" roadside buildings did not because they possessed conventionally monumental exteriors, because they satisfied "a purely stylistic definition of 'quality,'" or because they were designed by architects whose professional status (as innovators or form-givers) was legible "in the European sense [of which] Mr. Drexler seems to approve." In Banham's assessment, this explained Drexler's inclusion of Eero Saarinen's TWA Flight Center, the merits of which the historian probed on an entirely different basis. To Banham, TWA, which opened in 1962 at New York's Idlewild Airport, was "a genuine 100-per-cent, Big-A, all-American building" not because of its engineered concrete shells and glass curtain walls, but because of its sculptural expressionism, which embodied "the frank and pleasurable emotional engineering" he found so frequently and convincingly on U.S. highways. Banham sees an indisputable parallel between the terminal and a range of roadside buildings "conceived in this mode of emotional engineering," including hamburger stands, gas stations, motels, supermarkets, and bowling alleys, and he argues, as J. B. Jackson had earlier, that such buildings were akin to Roman Baroque churches (of Bernini, no less). Banham explains how this worked in practice by documenting the visual-spatial progression to and through a typical highway restaurant, as a driver might encounter it on the urban periphery: from road, past sign, into parking lot, under porte-cochère, out of car, and into foyer, before arriving, finally, at the dining room, with each moment in the composition calibrated to the "environment or atmosphere" appropriate to the specific function or theme. Something similar happens at the TWA terminal, itself a highway building on the urban periphery connected by car to New York's population centers via the Van Wyck Expressway. There, the progression went as follows: leaving the expressway for the airport's inbound access road, drivers approached the terminal directly on axis before swinging south around a parking island. Continuing past the airline's illuminated plastic sign (with TWA's windswept logo mounted on a muscular concrete pedestal) as the building's bird-in-flight silhouette came into view again, drivers pulled up to the terminal's twin entrance portals, exiting their cars beneath the attenuated overhang of the canopy and between plastically articulated columns. For Banham, the wingspread-toward-airborne forms of TWA's concrete vaults were "as plainly eye-catching as the neon signs that twinkle and twitch along the freeways." In contrast, historian and critic Vincent Scully, who championed the work of Venturi and Scott Brown, dismissed those same forms at around the same time as "whammo" exhibitionism.[90]

Banham's comparison between the now iconic midcentury modernist TWA terminal and quotidian roadside buildings occasioned one of his most audacious assertions, that the motels and "other drive-in installations" of the middle of the twentieth century constituted the "radically new building types" the United States had bestowed upon "world architecture since 1900." Thus, even more emphatically than Scott Brown and Venturi (and slightly ahead of them), Banham placed these commercial buildings on par with the industrial typologies (daylight factory and grain elevator) that exerted such an influence on the first generation of modernist architects. This was of far more than historiographic significance, and it reflected an important dimension of Banham's critique of *Modern Architecture, USA,* as

Figure 67. View of TWA Flight Center (Eero Saarinen and Associates, 1962), Idlewild Airport, New York City, exterior towards the northeast. (© Ezra Stoller/Esto)

he tried to figure out what, specifically, was American about the work on display. With what Banham regarded as characteristic Eurocentrism, Drexler anointed Mies as his "chosen vessel of the spirit of Modern Architecture USA." Banham, by contrast, but without facetiousness, chose the motel. And he was confident enough to predict that "the hindsight of the year 2000" would prove him right. In 1965, however, the historian was not yet prepared to trace the aesthetic and technological evolution of "the real architecture of America," because, by his own admission, he had not yet given car-centric types the scrutiny they deserved. But "ignorance" of key designers and buildings was not an acceptable excuse, not when "this huge unexplored territory accounts for perhaps 95 percent of the buildings put up in the United States." If only in terms of sheer quantity, these buildings called out for "investigation and understanding" by historians, curators, critics, architects, and students. Banham noted with approval that Tom Wolfe was already paying attention to roadside types, and his own call to arms seems intended as a continuation of Wolfe's project, with what he hoped would be a key difference: Banham would *not* "patronize the designers" as the journalist had. Banham knew, however, that most U.S. intellectuals would react to his autopian polemic the same way they reacted to American food. Ask to eat a hamburger, and they'll take you to "some amusing little Swiss place on Third Avenue"; ask to study a hamburger stand as architecture, and they'll talk to you about "Le Corbusier or Gropius instead." Undaunted, Banham initiated his own scholarly and critical inquiry into the "unprecedented development" of these new building types, pursuing this emergent "pop architecture" across the country, "in the Nevada desert, on the Pacific beaches, among the tall corn of the prairie States."[91]

Figure 68. Johnie's Coffee Shop (Armet & Davis, 1956) on Wilshire Boulevard, from *Los Angeles: The Architecture of Four Ecologies*. (Copyright © 1971 by Reyner Banham, reproduced by kind permission of Mrs. Mary Banham)

It was on the West Coast that Banham's hamburger analogy finally, in effect, came full circle: though it was "a non-Californian invention," the hamburger "achieved a kind of symbolic apotheosis in Los Angeles." And so did the hamburger stand, as Banham explained in the second architecture chapter of *Los Angeles: The Architecture of Four Ecologies*.[92] Pursuing the emotional engineering analysis he began in "The Missing Motel," Banham studied in great detail buildings like Johnie's on Wilshire Boulevard, designed by Armet & Davis in 1956, not only as "the architecture of symbolic assemblage," but as representative of the distinctive cultural forms of a highly mobile consumer society. Banham observed that Johnie's "butterfly roof," with its sharp angles and broad blue and white stripes, is "purely notational," and that the massive signpost that appears to be part of the building's structure was actually supporting an unrelated billboard. These features prompted neither derision nor condescension toward the design; instead their presence led the Banham to probe their economic origins and to conclude that across the commercial landscape, though dependent on the owner's "financial substance and cultural pretensions," it frequently made sense "to buy a plain standard building shell" from a systems manufacturer and then hire a designer to "impose your commercial personality on it with symbolic garnishes." The *architecture* emerged from the challenge of balancing "commercial frugality" with "cultural or aesthetic status," whether in a coffee shop, a motel, or a hamburger stand.[93]

By 1971, Banham had given roadside buildings enough consideration to declare, with apparent canonical certainty, the existence of "the accepted monuments of Autopia," evident in such buildings as the Ships Coffee Shop in Westwood (1958, demolished 1984), even if—in those early days of autopian scholarship—he incorrectly attributed it to Armet & Davis rather than Martin Stern Jr. Erroneous attribution aside, Banham's declaration has historiographic significance, for though he failed to specify who, besides himself, even recognized, much less accepted, car-oriented structures as possessing sufficient architectural and urban interest to be regarded as monuments, his thinking was clearly informed by the work of architect Charles Moore. In 1965, during his first year as head of the School of Architecture at Yale, Moore contributed to *Perspecta* 9/10 an essay that Banham cited in the "drive-in bibliography" that concludes *Los Angeles*. "You Have to Pay for the Public Life" is, today, regarded as a key text of postmodernism, and the essay is justly famous for Moore's detailed analysis of Disneyland as public space, as literal theme-park urbanism. But "You Have to Pay" also contains an extended examination of monumentality in the attenuated metropolis as Moore ruminates on the diverse ways that drive-ins, strips, and subdivisions marked place in the middle of the twentieth century, despite their apparent lack of conventional means of legibility. Along the way, Moore challenged the conceit that sprawling urbanism meant formless urbanism and a nonexistent public sphere. Instead, he argued, in the highly mobilized realm of the expanding city, where centers and edges were continually in flux, traditional monuments were irrelevant. Monumentality, along with urbanity, needed to be reimagined in order to function "for our own society and not of some other one." Though, for example, he commended the verticality of the Los Angeles City Hall as a gesture toward "making a center for a city that had none," Moore conceded that within the hierarchy of a horizontal urbanism, the freeways were of far greater public importance as public space—even if they were, as yet, imperfectly understood as such. Of equal importance were any number of commercial ventures since, Moore argued, they offered activities that "elicit[ed] public participation," or at least what passed for public participation in an era characterized by hypermobility and hyperconsumption. As exemplars of this type, he highlighted such Californian roadside landmarks as the Nut Tree Restaurant on U.S. 40 (now I-80) in Vacaville, designed by Don Birrell, and Disneyland off the Santa Ana Freeway in Anaheim (see color plate 1). Moore also situated these sites in a formal and programmatic evolution that embraced icons like the Brown Derby restaurant and Grauman's Chinese Theatre. These, Moore conceded, represented "an enlargement of the public realm" that was still in the process of becoming, but he was cautiously optimistic that the United States might yet develop a modern monumentality characterized by "visual delights at the scale of the automobile."[94]

Two years later, Moore explored these issues further in another *Perspecta* article, using the au courant tropes of plug-in networks and electronic space, with a dash of titular pop hipsterism. In "Plug It in, Rameses, and See if It Lights up. Because We Aren't Going to Keep It Unless It Works" of 1967, Moore scrutinized the further flattening of conventional urban hierarchies—and, thus, of conventional urban monuments—not only in Los Angeles, which "had poured itself unhierarchically across the landscape," but throughout the urbanized United States of the Automobile, even as most architects and planners were, myopically in Moore's opinion, preoccupied exclusively with the "super-high-density pedestrian urban core." Meanwhile, far out beyond that core, Moore observed that "the commercial strip which [the architects] abhor has arrogated to itself more vitality, more power of growth, indeed more inevitability of growth, than the whole of their tiny output put together." In Moore's analysis, the commercial strip is a starting point for discussing what architects like Donlyn Lyndon (his erstwhile design partner) and Robert Venturi (whom he would hire to teach the Las Vegas studio at Yale the following year) were learning from autopia with respect to form and symbolism, as they studied "popular roadside manifestations of our own time" to produce what Moore called "commercial formalism." Though Moore considered Venturi's Guild

House (Philadelphia, 1963) and Lyndon's Seaside Professional Building (Seaside, California, 1962) in great detail, there is another building in "Plug It in, Rameses" that hovers, literally, over Moore's entire argument: running as a banner across all but two pages of the essay is a strip of photographs of a strip of stores. Shot at night from a low angle, the photograph(s) emphasize the building's low-rise elongation, its glowing signage and plate-glass fronts, its street-side parking and planted buffer. This building, which Moore fails to mention in the text or identify in the captions, despite its outsize presence in the essay, is the Connecticut Post Center, a 500,000-square-foot complex with three dozen stores and parking for 5,500 cars. Propitiously located at the junction of U.S. 1 and a newly completed section of the Connecticut Turnpike (now I-95) in Milford, it was the largest shopping center between Boston and New York when it opened in 1960. Moore may have known it firsthand, since it was only six miles south of New Haven; he might even have known that it was designed by architect Jesse James Hamlin, but the lack of attribution and location (or photo credit) suggests that Moore was more interested in deploying the Post Center for polemical purposes, as the embodiment of "the commercial strip vernacular" and "the architecture of inclusion," as the kind of building that, he would have us believe, almost genetically possessed that "special vitality" that marked place along the American highway. As such, Moore was positing it as the kind of building that embodied a "coming to grips with our civilization" as it demonstrated the transformed organizational matrix of American urbanism at midcentury.[95]

Moore's argument that it was outmoded and even retrograde to define cities spatially—that is, to determine architectural importance by scale and proximity to the center—clearly resonated with Banham, who remained attentive to Moore's ideas as he shifted from consideration of individual "monuments" to evaluating autopian landscapes at urban scale. In "Roadscape with Rusting Nails," written for the BBC and subsequently expanded for *Los Angeles,* Banham, like Moore, takes pains to position himself 180 degrees from those he calls the "planning propagandists" as he considers the environmental impact of billboards and large-scale commercial signage. Explicitly rejecting the idea that such signs were blight, Banham heralds their contribution to urban character and he problematizes viewing them

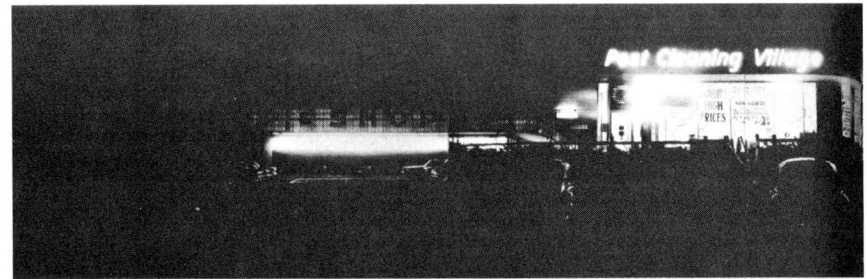

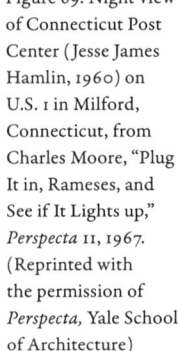

Figure 69. Night view of Connecticut Post Center (Jesse James Hamlin, 1960) on U.S. 1 in Milford, Connecticut, from Charles Moore, "Plug It in, Rameses, and See if It Lights up," *Perspecta* 11, 1967. (Reprinted with the permission of *Perspecta,* Yale School of Architecture)

(and all forms of advertising) as "visual pollution" when, from his perspective, this evaluation was mainly "a question of cultural taste." Like Jackson and Alloway before him, Banham, far from decrying billboards and signage on roadside buildings, interprets their presence on the skyline through a pointed historical parallel that invites comparison with Moore's observations in "Plug It in, Rameses." Moore argued that the distributive systems and networked communication that characterized the social and physical structures of the twentieth century would never produce a "contiguous hierarchic visual order." This was the reason "the pyramidal hierarchy," evident in such world monuments as the mortuary complex at Giza and the Forbidden City at Beijing, remained a planning ideal no matter how obsolete and inappropriate it was with respect to midcentury environmental realities. Though Moore failed to suggest that visual order might be found in the discontinuous and nonhierarchic (an odd omission given his awareness of Robert Venturi's search for complexity and contradiction in mannerism and the baroque), Banham isolates precisely the historical precedents that offered a model for comprehending visual order within the supposed "chaos" of the multinucleated urban structure of the Los Angeles in the 1960s: Christopher Wren's post-1666 City churches and the Tuscan tower-houses of the Duecento. Across the flatlands and into the valley, the billboards and road signs did for L.A. what the steeples did for London and towers did for San Gimignano. Signage in Los Angeles, and in Las Vegas, and on myriad American commercial strips, created urban identity and made urban places. Banham goes further than Moore when he extends place-making powers to the Los Angeles freeways as well, arguing, in a justly famous comparison, that they were rivaled as urban interventions only by those of Pope Sixtus V in sixteenth-century Rome and Baron Haussmann in nineteenth-century Paris. Regardless of what aspect of the roadscape Banham analyzed, he demonstrated a keen awareness of the specificity of place in the auto-oriented landscape (even if he, like Moore, was generally tone-deaf on the impact of racially motivated spatial segregation). When, for example, he turns his attention to Wilshire Boulevard, he does much more than simply relate the story of Arthur Ross's development of Miracle Mile. Banham also provides a thoughtful consideration of its urban morphology as a 1920s-era shopping district that straddled the city's premotorized and motorized eras in the

front and rear orientation of its spaces for strolling, entry, display, and parking. While many of these observations could have been divined from looking at plans, what emerges in his analysis is the degree to which Banham's experience of driving on Wilshire has directly informed his study.⁹⁶

The same is true in his exploration of autopia as a whole. Banham introduced this last of L.A.'s four ecologies with an astute observation of a seemingly inconsequential driving habit: the quick check in the mirror to adjust hair and makeup as the car takes an off-ramp and descends to surface streets. For Banham, this simple gesture had large urban import: "coming off the freeway is coming in from

Figure 70. "Chaos in Echo Park," from *Los Angeles: The Architecture of Four Ecologies.* (Copyright © 1971 by Reyner Banham, reproduced by kind permission of Mrs. Mary Banham)

Figure 71. "Commercial Non Plan on Sepulveda Boulevard," from *Los Angeles: The Architecture of Four Ecologies.* (Copyright © 1971 by Reyner Banham, reproduced by kind permission of Mrs. Mary Banham)

outdoors."[97] While this interpretation is informed by a strong dose of smog-in-your-eyes romanticism, it also suggests Banham's familiarity with sociological techniques of urban observation. And with respect to quantitative analysis, Banham asserted that he had witnessed this occurrence frequently enough, in various forms, to assign it more than anecdotal value. This analysis of freeway-to-surface-road etiquette offers an important insight into the social life of large urban spaces. In fact, it is nothing less than a mobilized, hands-on-the-wheel version of the feet-on-the-sidewalk point of view promoted by "downtown is for people" advocates like William H. Whyte and Jane Jacobs. Like all of the architects, planners, and critics discussed in this chapter, Banham had absorbed autopia's most important urban lesson. Though not repudiating the downtown-and-sidewalk perspective, Banham and his autopian fellow travelers were willing to accept something that Whyte and Jacobs could not: there was more than one kind of American city, and in the automobile-oriented city, the one that expanded rapidly in the middle of the twentieth century—the autopian city, whose social, architectural, and infrastructural legacy we are still grappling with in the twenty-first century—the *driver* was an urban figure every bit as authentic as the *walker*.

Banham hinted that this point of view was bound to gain wider acceptance as autopian discontents were outnumbered, not only by the "indifferent," but by those who found something "to admire" in the buildings and signs of the roadside, especially "their flamboyance, and the constant novelty induced by their obsolescence and replacement."[98] In architectural and urban discourse, and in popular culture as well, those autopian admirers were poised to become a more commanding majority, especially in the aftermath of the 1970s oil crisis, when the American Autopia was forced to slow down for the first time in decades.

5

THE TWILIGHT OF AUTOPIA

The scene captured in the Associated Press photograph is somewhere on Long Island, but it could have been anywhere in the United States during the oil crisis of 1973 (see color plate 12). Dozens of cars sit bumper-to-bumper at a gas station in four long lines, inching slowly toward two sets of pumps, just visible in the distance under a couple of butterfly lights. The cars are American, mostly full-size sedans from the late 1960s, gas-guzzlers distinguished mainly by their V-8 engines and overall lengths. The station is a Texaco, one of more than 30,000 such outlets operating in all fifty states at the time, but the branding is oddly out of sync. Though the sign facing the highway is up-to-date, with the hexagon logo that was the company's standard by 1968, the building is an aging prewar model, a white box trimmed with green speed lines that years before stopped heralding an optimistic future.[1] When it was new, the station must have gleamed like a harbinger of modernity, dominating its low-rise landscape on the expanding urban periphery. But now, crowded on all sides by the postwar strips and subdivisions that are visible at the edge of the frame, it is just one more stretch of one more mile of one more American roadside. With its leafless trees and almost violet sky, something of

Figure 72 (*facing page*). Night view of Mels Drive-In, from George Lucas (director), *American Graffiti*, 1972. (© Dennis Stock / Magnum Photos)

The Course of Empire hangs about the picture, after *Destruction,* before *Desolation.* It's the twilight of Autopia.

Autopia in Crisis

By the fall of 1973, scenes like this one were commonplace across the country. Already in the spring, as demand for fuel gradually outstripped supply, drivers in cities, suburbs, and small towns experienced with a shock the nation's first-ever peacetime gasoline shortage. Given the realities of energy production and consumption since 1945, it was bound to have happened eventually. The United States was using more oil than it produced domestically and was relying on greater amounts (nearly 30 percent) of imported crude. Its refinery capacity was insufficient to meet the country's seemingly insatiable desire for gasoline (as well as fuel oil for electricity and heating). There were more than 100 million cars on 3.8 million miles of U.S. roads and their gas mileage was lousy (averaging only 13 miles per gallon); after 1970, when amendments to the Clean Air Act mandated equipping them with anti-pollution devices, these cars were burning more fuel than ever before.[2] But that was OK, because before 1973, gas was cheap and abundant—at least as dispensed at the nation's 220,000 filling stations.

Exacerbating the situation were the monopolistic practices of the country's largest oil companies, which continued to own or control their own oil reserves, refineries, and retail outlets, despite the breakup of Standard Oil all the way back in 1911. In March 1973, they augmented this long-standing vertical integration with "conscious parallelism," following each other's lead in establishing quotas for crude oil processing and curtailing deliveries to independent refiners. This last action slowly closed the spigot for the independent service stations that accounted for 45 percent of the retail gas market. Within a few months, 1,200 independents were permanently out of business; thousands of others were operating on limited schedules depending on when, and if, they could replenish their supplies of gas. Name-brand retailers, meanwhile, were experiencing brisk business and increased profits, whether they were Mobil stations in New Jersey or Conocos in Colorado.[3]

In May, the Nixon White House announced a voluntary allocation system with a goal of forcing even distribution of crude oil and gasoline to all segments of the market. In July, the Federal Trade Commission issued a damning report that placed most of the blame for the expanding gas shortage at the feet of big oil.[4] Neither did much to relieve the squeeze on the independents, and the mounting shortage allowed Exxon, Gulf, Shell, and other companies to stoke consumer fears through restricted business hours, ten-gallon purchase limits at stations on highly visible roads (like the New York State Thruway and the New Jersey Turnpike), and alarmist full-page newspaper ads that played up the looming crisis. Taken together, these ploys seemed to portend even more serious shortages to come. At the height of the summer driving season between Memorial Day and Labor Day, "no gas" signs were legion on roadsides coast-to-coast.[5] The final blow came in late October, with the oil embargo spurred by Saudi Arabia and supported by Arab OPEC members in direct retaliation for recent U.S. support of Israel in the Sinai. Since 1945, when President Franklin Roosevelt met secretly with King Abdel Aziz Ibn Saud on his way home from the Yalta Conference, the United States and Saudi Arabia had enjoyed a special relationship predicated on economic exchange and security guarantees and founded on the common bond of oil—the Saudis had it, the Americans needed it. For both countries, oil was an essential ingredient of postwar prosperity and geopolitical power. With the embargo, and the artificial oil shortage it created, Saudi Arabia demonstrated how powerful it had become. From October 1973 to March 1974, the price per barrel of crude quadrupled, from $3 to $12. Stateside, though the United States only received 10 percent of its crude oil from Arab countries in the Middle East and North Africa, the embargo intensified existing shortages, and consumers with cars felt the pinch almost immediately. Over the course of the embargo, gas prices rose nearly 50 percent, from 38 cents to 55 cents per gallon.[6]

Though motorists were apparently unfazed by gas shortages during the summer, consuming a record 200 million gallons on a typical day, the embargo produced five months of "panic at the pump" as prolonged "gasoline fever" set in. With dwindling supplies of petroleum pushing gas prices skyward and extending gas lines toward the horizon, news reports multiplied about drivers waiting for hours in queues that stretched for miles. Aggravating the actual shortage was its psychological impact, not only the fear of running out of fuel, but mounting frustration against conservation measures like gasless Sundays and a 55 mile-per-hour speed limit for cars on all roads and highways—both of which the Nixon administration put in place in November. Accompanying the immediate effects of the embargo were long-range government tactics that coupled dire pleas for fuel conservation with the specter of driving bans and gasoline rationing, limitations that Americans had not experienced since the restrictions of World War II. Though state-imposed rationing would not begin until the spring, irate motorists turned violent even earlier, subjecting perceived line cutters, gas siphoners, and especially service station attendants to verbal as well as physical abuse. Angry truckers were blockading interstates; deranged drivers were shooting up gas pumps; concerned citizens were installing locks on their fuel caps.[7] While these occurrences offered mounting anecdotal evidence of the impact of the energy crisis, they also augured deeper disturbances of the American status quo.

There was an obvious ripple effect, radiating outward, both literally and metaphorically, from a car with an empty tank. First were the gas station closures that threw thousands of small business owners and their employees out of work during the summer and fall; the first layoffs in the automobile industry, and in manufacturing sectors related to it, came in December. With roughly 20 percent of all American jobs connected directly or indirectly to Detroit, this was understood as the leading edge of the intransigent stagflation that would ultimately characterize the decade. "If people drive less," *Time* magazine observed in November 1973, "companies that rely on car-borne customers are likely to be hurt." To underscore the gravity of the situation, the article named three companies likely to be affected: McDonald's, Holiday Inn, and Walt Disney.[8] It wasn't necessary to name any others because these purveyors of fast food, motor lodging, and family escapism were ubiquitous landmarks of the American roadside and emblems of the autopian transformation of the midcentury landscape.

McDonald's was in a period of hyperexpansion in the early 1970s, with more than 2,600 franchises in operation and a massive modernization campaign underway to replace its original circa-1960 hamburger stands with mansard-roofed eat-in restaurants. This was also a period of hyperprofitability for the Golden

Arches, with record sales through the spring of 1973 despite rising inflation.[9] The same was true of the Nation's Innkeeper: some 200,000 driving travelers stayed every night at a Holiday Inn. By 1973, with more than 1,400 motels in the chain, each equipped with an iconic fifty-foot "Great Sign," Holiday Inn had become "inescapable on American highways"—typically the nation's older state and federal routes rather than newer limited-access expressways. With new Holiday Inn units supposedly opening every three days, they were already recognized as "a catalyst and a reflection of the age of mass travel."[10] Disney World had opened two years earlier on 27,000 acres of swampland outside of Orlando and midway between Tampa and Daytona Beach on the recently completed I-4. At a time when 80 percent of Florida tourists arrived by car, the theme park's easy-on/easy-off location was critical to its success—and to the success of the hotels, restaurants, and resorts that immediately surrounded the park, which, unlike in California, were Disney-owned or -controlled.

By the time of the embargo, the outlook of car-dependent businesses was increasingly gloomy. In November, McDonald's, Holiday Inn, and Disney, along with other publicly traded companies that investors believed would be hurt by gas shortages, rationing, and driving restrictions, got caught in the sharpest Dow Jones plunge in more than a decade.[11] Fears of a "domino effect" seemed confirmed by what was called a "chilling" winter for the travel industry, when declining attendance caused Disney World to layoff 750 of its Florida employees and Holiday Inn and other motel chains endured lower occupancy rates and last-minute cancellations of group reservations.[12] Though many analysts viewed plummeting stock prices as evidence of steeper declines to come, one securities expert sneered at the panic: "It's kind of silly season on the Street . . . We may come to realize the relative unimportance of kiddie cars and greasy hamburgers."[13] What the analyst overlooked was the possibility that "relative unimportance" was itself relative: what was insignificant on Wall Street might be consequential on Main Street and the Strip, where Americans were beginning to grapple with the social consequences of driving less. Thus, as grave as the economic impact of the energy crisis was, its cultural consequences were even more severe. Technology historian David Nye has described the 1970s energy crisis as a "cultural crisis" because of the way it destabilized the foundations upon which modern U.S. society was built, thus challenging the so-called "American way of life." In keeping with his critique of technological determinism, Nye argued that the energy crisis, in effect, revealed the ugly face of human agency in creating, over a half century, but especially in the years after World War II, social and spatial systems organized almost entirely around the car.[14]

Nye's analysis is not merely the result of hindsight; indeed, the degree of contemporary recognition of the situation is remarkable. "The phrase [energy crisis] is misleading," the *Los Angeles Times* declared in April 1973, "not because there is no energy crisis but because the crisis involves so much more than mere high gas prices and rationing of automotive gasoline," and what it involved was "just about every aspect of every American's daily life."[15] It was sobering to realize, as the media regularly reported, that from the spectacular to the quotidian, nothing would be untouched by the crisis. In Las Vegas, the lights of Glitter Gulch and the Strip were dimmed to save electricity, and with the signs turned off the sheds appeared considerably less decorated. This was a largely symbolic gesture intended "merely to set an example," but to many observers it also seemed to be a tacit acknowledgement that fewer cars were cruising Fremont Street and Las Vegas Boulevard than before the gas shortage.[16] Outside Chicago, suburban housewives whose daily routines of school, sports, and shopping were made possible by the family station wagon considered the impossibility of life without wheels. Of the forty-three errands she completed one week in her 1966 Oldsmobile Vista Cruiser, Bunny Orkin observed, in the fashion of William H. Whyte and Herbert Gans, that these car trips were far from "unimportant . . . in the context of a family's life out here." They were also an "accepted necessity of life" given the distances between her house, her children's high school, the grocery store, and "that metropolitan center of motordom"—the shopping center. According to the *New York Times*, 76 million other suburbanites shared Orkin's plight.[17] In Los Angeles, in particular, this plight was most acute. The *Los Angeles Times* reported that the typical Los Angeles housewife generally traveled more than 10,000 miles a year conducting the business of daily life, as did thousands of laborers and office workers, all of them oriented to those "distinct and dependent forms of retailing, wholesaling, journey to work, recreational and industrial patterns" that had emerged in a city "built to the scale of the automobile."[18]

As daily papers, nightly newscasts, and weekly magazines made abundantly clear, the energy crisis confirmed just how significantly dispersed patterns of postwar development had intensified the nation's reliance on cars and its autopian self-image. In contrast to the country's physical state in the previous era of gas shortages during World War II, "today, rambling suburbs have spread out of urban areas, and millions of Americans drive to work by car," *Time* declared in November of 1973, a fact it repeated at least once a month well into 1974.[19] Demographic data and geographic analysis back up these journalistic assertions. Writing in the *Annals of the Association of American Geographers* earlier in the year, John Hudson noted that growth in "suburban fringes [of] major metropolitan areas" had been so intense in the past few decades that new analytical models were required to understand existing distributive patterns of settlement and density.[20] Of course, residential, commercial, and industrial decentralization, along with proliferating car ownership, were well underway *before* the war, but after two decades of mortgage insurance, accelerated depreciation, and highway subsidies, this federal trifecta, along with local efforts to dismantle streetcars and inter-urbans, had turned the United States irrevocably into Autopia with a capital *A,* or "Car Country" in environmental historian Christopher Wells's apt phrase.[21] Whatever one called it, the impact of the energy crisis was unmistakable. As existing routines were disrupted, "sweeping changes [. . .] to the way people work, travel, and spend their leisure time" were inevitable. Even the newest roadside landmarks, businesses clustered at interstate exits, were threatened with obsolescence.[22] There is a rueful tone to much of this coverage, an awareness that an era was coming to a close, even if commentators rarely agreed on what, specifically, was ending. To some, it was as grandly ideological as the end of a belief in Manifest Destiny and a unilateral equating of growth with progress, no matter the cost, which, as we have seen, Lewis Mumford and William H. Whyte had been critiquing for years. If the size of the continent had prompted an American "doctrine of bigness" in the nineteenth century, Henry Ford's "profligate invention" gave an "ethic of unbounded growth" new life in the twentieth—until, that is, the energy crisis offered "a painful, overdue comeuppance."[23]

At the opposite extreme and out on the American roadside, local responses to the most obvious effect of the crisis—the accelerating rate of service station closures—varied sharply. Some expressed concern about the visual and psychological effect of abandonment, claiming that blight had reached the suburbs for the first time since the Great Depression, notwithstanding what by then were decades-old complaints about roadside slums. From Long Island to Los Angeles, there were discussions about ordinances to prohibit gas stations from operating within 1,000 feet from each other. New zoning rules were enacted in many places, but they were only minimally effective in controlling roadside development because, irrespective of quality, the strip malls that replaced the gas stations were so numerous they looked like one more form of wayside overbuilding.[24] Others mourned the passing of the gas station as "a way of life" and an institution that serviced more than automobiles and operated as a de facto community resource, a suburban counterpart to the West Village shopkeepers Jane Jacobs celebrated in *The Death and Life of Great American Cities* (1961). As a representative of a gasoline trade association described it, "[the gas station operator] is the unpaid information center of the country, the lubricator of baby carriages and kids' bicycles, the keeper of the nation's toilets [and] the community Joe who sponsors Little League teams." But now, the trade rep concluded, because of intense competition, high-prices, and fuel shortages, these local entrepreneurs were suffering from "future shock," this reference to Alvin Toffler's 1970 bestseller underscoring the speed and extent of the economic *and* social changes the energy crisis was bringing to the American Autopia.[25]

A year before the energy crisis hit, former secretary of the interior Stewart Udall warned in *The Atlantic* that the United States had finally reached the tipping point where the social costs of the country's car-oriented way of life would outweigh its benefits. Arguing for a "less is more" ethos and borrowing the contemporary language of birth-rate regulation, Udall wrote of the need to place "a limit on the automobile population" while supporting mass transit, denser communities, and preservation of open space.[26] Udall's arguments in "The Last Traffic Jam" were prescient, and at least some of his predictions seemed confirmed the following summer when Congress approved a compromise three-year extension to the Highway Trust Fund, the taxation accounting mechanism that financed the construction of the interstates. Since its establishment in 1956, the Trust Fund had been used exclusively for automobile-oriented infrastructure, a fact that led the *New York Times* to describe it as having had "more to do with determining the physical character and social style of American cities and suburbs than any other Government program." The Trust Fund was predicated on a basic philosophy that the automobile was "sacrosanct," as a *Times* editorial put it, and so were its highways. But the extension ratified in July 1973 permitted states, for the first time, to use a small portion of its revenues to finance mass transit instead of interstates.[27] While Stewart Udall would likely have welcomed this as a modest sign of a return to sanity where the car was concerned, "The Last Traffic Jam" makes clear that he was also a realist, and he offers a wary caution, briefly quoting James Roche, the retiring head of General Motors, to assess the current state of affairs: "I think the average American today would give up about anything before he gives up his automobile."[28] In the midst of endless rending of garments and gnashing of teeth over the energy crisis, the car's place in American culture and American life was inviolate, but blind faith in the automobile was going to be sorely tested.

On the last day of 1973, *Time* published a cover story that seemed like nothing so much as Autopia's eulogy. It mistily recalled the pleasures of the automobile and dutifully catalogued its deleterious side effects: the simple exhilaration of barreling down a highway at top speed and the unbounded geographic mobility that many people equated with social mobility, but also air pollution, traffic congestion (in cities and suburbs alike), longer commutes, mounting consumer debt, increasing traffic fatalities, and "a blighted landscape of junkyards, filling stations and hotdog stands." Even as the negatives piled up, and car dependency was dissected both statistically and socially, it was never really questioned. Challenges to the existing order that were already underway, like the freeway revolts that were becoming more frequent in urban centers, especially in San Francisco, went unmentioned. For *Time,* there was a literally larger concern: the nation's "gigantic geographic dispersion" was too great, its "drive-in economy" was too important, and too many of its citizens had no alternative means of transportation. It was possible to imagine that "there could be a movement of middle-class whites back to the city, where they [could] get away from auto dependence" (as did happen by the century's end), and to speculate that this might, concomitantly, help "contain suburban sprawl," but at best this was a hazy dream, not a practical reality.

Such was the nation's conundrum as the energy crisis worsened. Though the country was either unable or unwilling to give up automotive transportation, it was at least ready to acknowledge it had a problem with the car. More precisely, like the functioning addict it had become during the past half-century, the nation was ready to acknowledge the *car* had a problem. Which car? The "classic, distinctively American, roomy, powerful, glittering family car" that was "built for an age when 50-m.p.h. speed limits, gasless Sundays and talk of rationing would have seemed like blasphemies." The United States did not need to end its love affair with the car, only its love affair with the "big car." This distinction was not as inconsequential as it might seem. For the American public, there was "a painful change to thinking small," as citizens were forced to reevaluate vehicles that were status symbols, objects of desire, and frequently the largest single purchase aside from a home. Now, in direct response to the energy crisis, the "two-ton eight-cylinder behemoth" was to be sacrificed on the altar of fuel efficiency.[29] The shift in market demand brought on by the gas shortages of 1973 prompted Detroit to finally produce smaller, fuel-saving models to compete with Japanese economy-class imports.[30] It didn't matter that the pre–energy crisis gas guzzler never quite died—millions of them continued to roam the highways for the rest of the decade, through the oil shortage of 1979 and even as the sun rose on Ronald Reagan's "Morning in America" of the 1980s. Fuel efficiency was a zero-sum game in the landscapes shaped by the car because the post-1973 automobile did nothing to lessen traffic congestion or environmental blight. Whether it was a Honda Civic or a Chevy Chevette, these cars became, in effect, enablers of American auto-dependence, of its dispersed settlement patterns and its drive-in cultural practices. The United States would remain Car Country for the foreseeable future, but something *had* definitely changed in the automobile utopia.

In the Rearview Mirror

As the oil crisis intensified in the early 1970s, a diverse range of commentators attempted to give a name to what many regarded as a distinct period coming to a close. Stewart Udall, typifying the ethical environmentalism of "The Last Traffic Jam," wrote of "the end of automania," an era characterized for him (as it had been for autopia's long-standing critics) as much by its consumption of land as by its consumption of oil. The Joint Congressional Committee on Atomic Energy referred to "the deepening twilight of the fossil fuel age," acknowledging the lingering social and economic effects of the era of cheap and abundant fuel.[31] John Jerome, a former editor for *Car & Driver* who subsequently renounced his ties to Detroit, went so far as to pinpoint "the death of the automobile" to these years, evident to him in the nexus of the stylistic and mechanical excesses of the *big car*, their overproduction despite a glutted marketplace, and the "ancillary disasters" of pollution, congestion, and environmental degradation. Jerome looked back, not happily, on what he now viewed as "the Golden Era," when the car grew from "pervasive element to absolute necessity in American life." Though the car remained a necessity, the early 1970s were a turning point for Jerome because U.S. society finally began to "audit the books" on the "supercorporation" the automobile industry had become. He also made an important historiographic prediction about those years: "When the history of the automobile is written, scholars will necessarily focus careful attention on this crucial period."[32] The only thing Jerome got wrong (aside from exaggerating the automobile's death) was that scholars were *already* focusing on this crucial period.

One of the first to recognize the end-of-an-era significance of the oil crisis was James J. Flink, a historian teaching in the comparative culture program at the University of California, Irvine. Flink's first book, *America Adopts the Automobile, 1895–1910* was important as an early social history of the car that studied its impact on everyday life before World War I. In 1970, when the book was published, automotive history was confined to the great men and great machines (Henry Ford, the Model T, etc.), so Flink's work was clearly a departure.[33] The following year, at the annual meeting of the American Historical Association, in the AHA's first-ever session devoted to the automobile, Flink expanded his purview beyond the car as a vehicle to study its broader and more ineffable cultural effects, namely the collective image of the car in American consciousness as this had changed over the course of the twentieth century, evolving as the car proliferated. As published in *American Quarterly* in 1972, Flink's three stages of automobile consciousness were modeled, indirectly he claimed, on those of Charles Reich's *The Greening of America*—a best-selling meditation on the transformative power of the counterculture that staged U.S. history as three distinct shifts in consciousness.[34] Flink's stages of automobile consciousness also have an uncanny relationship to Elisabeth Kübler-Ross's stages of grief, which emerged in public discourse around the same time, except that they operate in reverse: beginning with acceptance and ending with anger and denial.[35] In the first stage, roughly from the earliest automotive experiments to the increase in car production brought about by the assembly line at Ford's Highland Park factory starting in the mid-1910s, Americans embraced the car, or at least recognized the inevitability of its influence on social and physical structures. In the second stage, they idolized the car and transformed existing institutions to accommodate it, as we saw in chapters 1 and 2; according to Flink, this stage begins with the expansion of consumerism in the early 1920s, which was led in no small part by the automotive industry; it endures through the Depression and World War II, and then regains strength in the postwar period.

In Flink's final stage of automobile consciousness, Americans shift gears and regard the car as a major social, economic, and environmental problem.[36] Flink originally dated the commencement of stage III to the late 1950s when critiques of the auto industry—both its products and its effects—first gained traction. But as discussed in chapters 3 and 4, even through the 1960s, and even as the full consequences of the interstate system were becoming apparent, those critiques either remained outside the mainstream of popular opinion or went hand in hand with solutions predicated upon a belief that autopia was perfectible, that the problems could be fixed. A few years later, his book *The Car Culture* (1975) demonstrates the value of hindsight. Flink's chronological scope now extended from the 1890s right up to Richard Nixon's resignation in August of 1974. Though Flink recognized the perils of attempting "contemporary history," by writing the energy crisis into the historical narrative, he was able to periodize the 1950s, 1960s, and 1970s to conclude, erroneously as it turned out, that he was finally witnessing "the ending of the age of automobility." *The Car Culture* is as polemical as it is historical, with Flink committed to seeking the origins of the problematics of the automobile and, hence, the beginnings of the third stage of auto consciousness. And though he highlights evidence of social, economic, and environmental dissatisfaction with the car all the way back to the 1920s, what he calls "the disenchantment"—the era when the car was no longer a progressive force of change—is his own, present-day moment in history.[37] Thus 1973 was to Flink, what 1890 was to Frederick Jackson Turner. The oil crisis (and the other auto-related socioeconomic dynamics conveniently identified with it) had effected the twentieth-century equivalent of the closing of the frontier, or at least provide a useful historical milestone.

In his famous and influential paper "The Significance of the Frontier in American History," presented at the 1893 meeting of the American Historical Association, Turner argued that the continual process of western settlement, of introducing "civilization" into the "wilderness," was the decisive shaper of a distinctly American culture and character. When the 1890 census demonstrated that, in effect, no unsettled land remained in the continental United States, Turner concluded that the "first period in American history" had ended.[38] To Flink, the Turner/frontier comparison was neither dramatic nor historical license, though he must have enjoyed the AHA parallel. His argument, seconded at the time by other historians of culture and technology, was that the car as fact and idea had a more profound influence on twentieth-century Americans than the frontier did on nineteenth-century Americans. In establishing a chronological climax for automobile consciousness stage III, Flink's goal was not to update Turner's frontier thesis. Though the thesis's influence on U.S. historiography in the first half of the twentieth century was profound, as was its contribution to the nation's popular mythology, scholarly revisions had already taken place and Flink willingly acknowledged their significance, particularly George Pierson's contention that it was the "m-factor" of movement, migration, and mobility, rather than the frontier, that most profoundly shaped the American character, assuming such influences could be authoritatively defined.[39] Instead, Flink's purpose was to emphasize the cultural significance of automobility and to ponder the meaning of what he believed was its unequivocal end in 1973, when it became impossible to ignore the fact that "the automobile culture and the values that sustained it are no longer tenable."[40] It seemed clear to Flink that the United States was entering a new phase of its historical development, even if its outlines were as yet indistinct. By the late 1980s, Flink realized that reports of the car's death were greatly exaggerated, and this prompted him to declare, now correctly, that "there can be no doubt that the automobile will continue into the twenty-first century to be the dominant mode of personal transportation in the [developed and developing] world." What did not change was his view of "the automobile age" as a distinct historical period whose parameters were as immutable as those of the era of westward expansion.[41]

Given Flink's emphasis on a historical parallel between the end of automobility and the closing of the frontier, it is not surprising to find nostalgia for the not-so-distant past in the early 1970s as keen as the one that elevated the cowboy—whether in a Remington sculpture or a Hollywood western—to mythical status several generations earlier. And just as that earlier nostalgia was intensified and complicated by expanding industrialization and its dramatic social and environmental effects, so too in the 1970s did additional mitigating factors emerge: deindustrialization, the Vietnam War, Watergate, chronic inflation, and the aftershocks of social unrest in the 1960s all played a role in provoking, at this particular moment, a particular longing for a supposedly more innocent age in America's recent history. This longing is epitomized by the popular and critical success of the 1973 film *American Graffiti,* George Lucas's not quite–coming-of-age story that takes place at the end of summer 1962 in the Modesto, California, of the director's youth.

In his influential 1983 essay "Postmodernism and Consumer Society" Fredric Jameson argues that *American Graffiti* inaugurated a new genre, "the nostalgia film." What separated nostalgia films from other movies about the past, Jameson asserts, was the way they attempted to recapture "specific generational moments," in this case "the atmosphere and stylistic peculiarities" of what still seemed like the Eisenhower era, which Lucas rendered in something that amounted to a "collective spiritual autobiography," as the *Los Angeles Times* described it.[42] This is evident most obviously in the cars, but also in the culture those cars engendered. Over a twelve-hour period from sunset to sunrise, a group of white, mostly middle-class, and presumably heterosexual teenagers cruise the strip, hang out at a drive-in, drag race on the edge of town, and diffidently discuss their future. Cars are both subject and object in the film, serving as mis-en-scène, trope, and very nearly dramatis personae: an elusive Thunderbird, a reliable Impala, an aging Deuce Coupe hot rod.[43] The mobilized spatial domain these cars occupy is central to what film critic Stanley Kauffmann, writing in *New Republic,* called *American Graffiti*'s "quintessence." For Kauffmann, the casual motorized mobility the film depicts was one of its most striking aspects, but its overall effect was "realistic abstraction." The streets, storefronts, and parking lots were real enough (the film was shot on location mostly in and around Petaluma, standing in for Lucas's hometown of Modesto), but a decade's remove from 1962 had distilled them into an archetypal landscape of a "preserve[d] commonplace."[44] A decade after Kauffmann, Jameson offered a harsher assessment in "The Cultural Logic of Late Capitalism," viewing *American Graffiti*'s nostalgic milieu as "a desperate attempt to appropriate a missing past."[45] That the past it depicted was already missing in the early 1970s was something that was not lost on commentators at the time.

In 1974, the *New York Times* sent a reporter to Modesto to see what had changed in the past decade, and he observed almost wistfully that the easy downtown cruising depicted in the film was now relegated to the city's northern periphery along a two-mile, low-rise, traffic-choked artery it called "the ultimate esplanade of modern America, with clusters of shopping centers, motels, and service stations interspersed with 61 restaurants and fast food shops."[46] *Time,* citing a Harris report that found that more than half of all Americans believed the nation's quality of life had deteriorated since the early 1960s, pointed to a "wave of nostalgia" that explained why "by the millions, they crowd into movies like *American Graffiti.*"[47] Film critic Roger Ebert had a more precise diagnosis in the *Chicago Sun-Times:* "No sociological treatise could duplicate the movie's success in remembering exactly how it was to be alive at that cultural instant."[48] While the cars, clothes, and music are essential to the film's depiction of that distinct cultural moment, so is its principal location, a drive-in called Mels. Given the film's focus on movement—cars passing each other on Main Street, pulling away from stoplights, disappearing around corners—it is unexpected that one of the most enduring images from *American Graffiti* is a building (see figure 72).

Mels Drive-In appears in the first frame of the film, behind the opening credits; as the sky gets darker just after dusk, the principal characters cruise by, pull in, park, and converse next to their cars. Though they drive around town relentlessly throughout the film, they always return to Mels, which serves the narrative as the characters' home base, continually shifting between foreground and background. If it served as a local landmark within the film, Mels functions as a *cultural* landmark beyond the film. Though Mels was a real place—the original San Francisco location of a drive-in restaurant with several outlets in the Bay area—Lucas shoots it to transcend the particular, rendering it, in Stanley Kauffmann's apt phrase, "an oval neon temple." This description refers as much to the structure's glowing presence on film as to its centrality in early 1960s U.S. youth culture. Though drive-ins like Mels had been a regular feature of the American landscape since the 1930s, especially in California, by midcentury their "rock n' roll style" (as a trade manual described it) made them irresistible to teenagers with wheels.[49] In *American Graffiti*, against the backdrop of a blazing Technicolor sunset, the establishing shot of Mels looks like nothing so much as an autopian update of Edward Hopper's *Nighthawks* (1942), with big sky and a parking lot replacing buildings and sidewalks. Mels, too, had an expanse of plate glass revealing a curved counter, but curbside carhop service was the draw when the drive-in opened in 1947. By the time filming began twenty-five years later, Mels already seemed like a relic from another era. As *American Graffiti*'s producer acknowledged in an interview in the *Los Angeles Times,* "circular drive-ins . . . the favorite stomping grounds for teenagers and their hot rods in those years had virtually disappeared."[50] And though period photographs reveal that Mels was definitely showing its age, looking like a run-down greasy spoon on a seedy block South of Market, through careful visual styling and strategic camera work the *American Graffiti* crew returned Mels not so much to its original appearance as to George Lucas's memory of how a drive-in like this one, whether in the central city or the suburban fringe, would have looked in the early 1960s.

In truth, there was nothing all that remarkable about Mels, which occupied a workaday modern structure designed and built by the carpenter father of one of the restaurant's founders.[51] A two-story rectangular block housed the kitchen, served as a signboard, and anchored a one-story circular pavilion containing counter and booth dining areas. Though broad, neon-trimmed canopies cantilevered from the block and a pavilion sheltered in-car patrons, Mels lacked the formal exhibitionism typically associated with Googie. Nonetheless, at night, with bubble pendants shining through the plate glass and up-lit stanchions illuminating the underside of the canopies, the drive-in possessed a modest flying-saucer aura and a modicum of Atomic Age cool. And that's how we see it almost exclusively in *American Graffiti,* where, through Lucas's lens of nostalgia, the drive-in functions as a historical marker of a fondly remembered recent past, one that, to use Jean Baudrillard's terms, has been utterly "aestheticized by retro."[52] This phrase was more appropriate than the cultural critic could have imagined.

Had George Lucas not immortalized it in celluloid, Mels Drive-In would have been forgotten long ago. The franchise was sold just before the South Van Ness location was scouted for *American Graffiti;* the new owners went bankrupt a few years after the movie's release; by the late 1970s, the building was gone and the site remained vacant for the rest of the century.[53] Mels was an inevitable and insignificant casualty of real estate and retail restlessness caused by forces at work not only in Northern California but across the United States: continued erosion of urban industrial areas, shifting traffic patterns caused by freeway and interstate construction, and changing demographics of burger consumption as related to auto-oriented eating establishments. "The death knell has already sounded for another manifestation of the car-crazed society," the *New York Times* observed in 1978, placing the blame on the rise of fast food along with the maturation of 1950s-era teens, who now preferred to sit inside instead of eating in their cars. Even in Los Angeles, a city "so car-mad that it still boasts a drive-in church," the number of drive-ins had declined from around 800 in the 1950s to fewer than 10 in the 1970s. An executive at Bob's Big Boy quoted in "Meanwhile, Drive-In Restaurants Fade Away" captured the essence of that late-1970s moment: "I'm sorry to see them go. But maybe I'm just being nostalgic."[54]

A few years later, that nostalgia had intensified sufficiently for Steven Weiss, son of the eponymous Mel, to relaunch what he hoped was a recognizable brand, or at least a registered trademark. After opening a single restaurant in San Francisco in 1985, Weiss now has eight Mels Drive-Ins in Northern and Southern California, including two (in the San Fernando Valley and Hollywood) that occupy original, though significantly remodeled, Googie coffee shops designed by well-known midcentury modernists, including Armet & Davis. There are two additional Mel's, with the apostrophe, at Universal Studios theme parks in Los Angeles and Orlando because *American Graffiti* was a Universal picture. Though these are described as "replicas" of the drive-in that appeared in the film, like Weiss's Mels, beyond the signature neon sign, they have little in common with the original, unprepossessing Mels on South Van Ness, and the differences are instructive of the way nostalgia for a golden age of autopia operated beyond cinematic space.[55] These are less reproductions than representations, overloaded with whatever "period" chrome and neon details are necessary to suggest an image of "Where were you in '62?" car culture; the world of the drive-in is understood principally through the mediation of *American Graffiti*. Another not insignificant difference between the original and the reproduction is equally reflective of the changed cultural climate that commenced in the 1970s: though a few have outdoor seating, these are walk-in or drive-up-and-park restaurants. In other words, despite the name, none of the retro Mels/Mel's Drive-Ins are actually, typologically, drive-ins. Nostalgia triumphs as simulacra.

At the End of the Road

In his classic 1964 study *The Machine in the Garden,* Leo Marx argued that in U.S. culture in the nineteenth century, manifestations of pastoralism were either popular and sentimental or imaginative and complex, and that both operated as forms of nostalgia for a past idealized as a middle landscape neither purely agrarian nor fully industrial.[56] It may seem a stretch to view nostalgia for the 1950s as a latter-day version of the pastoral ideal, but from the vantage point of the post–Vietnam-Watergate-energy-crisis 1970s, it was possible to imagine a car cruising the strip as the ne-plus-ultra machine in the garden of a postwar autopian age. While the broader culture's nostalgia for this golden age was mostly rose-colored, as just discussed, there emerged at the same time in the 1970s a backward glance that was less obviously sentimental, and that was, in fact, more imaginative and complex, though hardly critically detached. Here, the urge was not to recapture the aura of a lost era as a salve to present discontents, but to study autopia as a distinct landscape in order to document its places and spaces with something approaching verisimilitude, and while the oil crisis did not trigger this work—much of which relied on the critical foundation of autopian inquiry of the 1960s discussed in the last chapter—it did provide a moment of cultural and chronological clarification. This work was not, at first, precisely scholarly, but it had a methodological thoroughness that meant it could easily (eventually) be deployed in the deliberate production of historical knowledge about the *recent past*—a period that historian and preservationist Richard Longstreth defines not only chronologically, but also as one characterized by "attitudes and practices" that are no longer current but are still within "living memory."[57] This excludes the work of Reyner Banham and Robert Venturi and Denise Scott Brown, since, as we have seen, they approached autopia as a contemporary (i.e., existing at the same time) condition of the twentieth-century city. *Los Angeles: The Architecture of Four Ecologies* (1971) and *Learning from Las Vegas* (1972) were critically important and highly influential attempts to theorize the present day of the late 1960s and early 1970s, and not to analyze the recent past (despite Banham's chapters on the history of L.A. architecture). The strip, the freeway, and the environments they produced were clear evidence of "signs of life" in the contemporary American city.

Venturi and Scott Brown chose *that* title for the exhibition they organized with Steven Izenour at the Smithsonian's Renwick Gallery, revisiting ten years of their architectural and urban research on the occasion of the U.S. Bicentennial. While historical artifacts and photographs appeared throughout *Signs of Life: Symbols and the American City,* these were mostly overshadowed by objects and images from the 1970s, which documented, as the *New Yorker* put it, "everything . . . the firm sees as representative of contemporary Americana." While they dealt with both domestic and commercial spheres, the curators' *presentist* orientation was provocatively on display in the Renwick's long, narrow West gallery on the first floor, where two sets of post-1968 florescent McDonald's golden arches (a pylon topper and drive-thru sign, respectively) literally outshone the red-and-white neon of a Mobilgas Pegasus from before World War II, a juxtaposition Ada Louise Huxtable described as "startlingly beautiful in the perverse way of Pop." Framed between the arches, and between the gallery's paired Corinthian columns, was a full-scale replica of a 1920s-era roadside billboard rendered in state-of-the-art molded plastic, complete with faux lattice fascia, and featuring hundreds of photographs and supporting text on color transparencies composed as oversized broadsides (see color plate 13). Devoted to "symbols and signs on the strip," one side of the billboard summarized the big-sign-little-building and building-as-sign analyses of *Learning from Las Vegas*. The other side of the billboard presented a seventy-five-year evolution of roadside typologies and iconographies that resolutely focused on the present—the domestic turn in gas station imagery, the double-loaded corridors of motel chains, all with a goal of explicating what Huxtable called "the country's inescapable reality"[58]—illustrated with vintage postcards and especially contemporary photographs, many commissioned for the exhibition from John Baeder and Stephen Shore, among others.

In the mid-1970s Baeder was already becoming known for his photorealist paintings of diners and roadside eateries. Shore's interest in the ordinary realm, evident in projects like *American Surfaces* (1972) and *Uncommon Places* (begun 1973), paralleled the architects' desire to learn from the everyday environment, even if his goal was art and not theory. As text and photographs came together in the exhibition, however, the objective was explicitly didactic: to teach Americans "to understand our symbols and signs" in order "to understand better ourselves and our landscapes." If they were interested in reckoning with the past, it was only in the service of the future because for Scott Brown and associates, this was "a necessary prelude to improving the landscape." It was true, as Huxtable observed, that the exhibition was "full of historical insights," but she overstated the case when she claimed that *Signs of Life* was "the definitive dissertation on the forms, symbols and sources of the American way of life" and "one of the most significant contributions to the writing of art history since the identification of Mannerism." *Signs of*

Life, like Venturi and Scott Brown's larger contribution to architectural discourse, was not a historical project because, from their vantage point, autopia was not yet history.[59] But in the work they most immediately and directly influenced in the 1970s, it assuredly was. By the end of the decade this new historical perspective resulted in a sufficient quantity of roadside publications to necessitate a roadside historiography.

John Margolies's first monograph, *The End of the Road,* was published in 1981 as the catalogue for a solo exhibition of 125 of his photographs. Included were color pictures of gas stations, diners, drive-in theaters, motels, ice cream stands, and other roadside attractions. At first glance, and when viewed in isolation, the pictures are not that different from Stephen Shore's contemporaneous work—indeed, during the road trips he took to produce images for *Signs of Life,* Shore shot some of the same roadside buildings as Margolies. But while their subject matter occasionally overlapped, their intentions utterly diverged. For Margolies, these photographs portrayed the buildings and signs that collectively constituted "vanishing highway architecture in America," as he noted in *The End of the Road*'s subtitle. This work was the result of a project Margolies began in 1973, which would become his life's work. With funding from the National Endowment for the Arts, he embarked on a five-year, 100,000-mile road trip across the continental United States, producing in excess of 10,000 Kodachrome images. For Margolies his titular highway terminus was temporal more than locational, because he was attempting to capture seven decades' of roadside buildings before they fell victim, depending on the location, to either growth or abandonment. Though well known at the time as a critic and curator, Margolies approached those seven decades with a historian's sensibility, dividing them into four distinct periods of roadside development. As he defines each period, he demonstrates a keen awareness of the ephemeral character of automobile-oriented architecture, as well as very particular aesthetic preferences informed by his long-standing skepticism of modernist hegemony. For Margolies the "golden age" of the roadside was 1920 to 1955, the period most represented in his photographs and bracketed historically by the rapid expansion of U.S. automobile ownership after World War I and the fixing of routes and locations for the interstate system in 1955. The following period, 1955–73, was one of decline, he argued with drastic oversimplification, because interstate construction and the concomitant corporatization of the roadside brought an end to the era of the individual entrepreneur. For Margolies, it was the one-off businesses that produced the unschooled, frequently eccentric roadside buildings he clearly preferred to the "homogenized nationwide uniformity" of mainstream and modernist commercial design of the 1960s, exemplified for him by the architecture of national franchises and chains.[60] In previous decades, Douglas Haskell and J. B. Jackson had expressed parallel concerns.

The trajectory of Margolies's work, as a member of the pop avant-garde and especially as a founder of the art collective Telethon, had been tending toward the study of the commercial landscape for several years before he embarked on the project that resulted in *The End of the Road*. In presentations, installations, and publications like "The City Experience as a Day-to-Day Reality [New York and Los Angeles]" and "Roadside Mecca," Telethon documented the contemporary environment by focusing on commercial forms both ubiquitous and idiosyncratic.[61] Gradually, however, Margolies also began to distinguish between the commercial present and its past, and he became increasingly interested in what lay beyond the centers of "vital cities." Whether on secondary highways and by-passed routes or on Main Streets and strips that were no longer main drags, Margolies found roadsides lined with the architecture "we are so nostalgic about today" (see color plate 14). Unsurprisingly, Margolies locates the origins of this nostalgia in the energy crisis that "caught us up short" and "predicted the end of it all"— meaning, he speculated, the end of gas, of driving, and "ultimately, it seemed, the end of roadside architecture."[62] Though there was a certain irony in undertaking a project requiring large quantities of gasoline at precisely the moment when gasoline was least available, the energy crisis gave Margolies's work undeniable urgency and intensified his underlying polemic about the end of the autopian era.

This is reflected in the book in image and text, both of which emphasized the passage of time and the historical distance between the metaphorical end of the road in the 1970s and its beginning in the 1920s. Margolies achieves this not through chronological arrangement (which he eschews in favor of formal and programmatic groupings), but through his photographic selections: the architecture depicted in *The End of the Road* is worn, weathered, and sometimes already abandoned. It is also highly individualized, despite the repetition of mimetic forms like teapots and teepees and of building components like railroad cars, screen towers, and dwelling units. Throughout the book, Margolies's pictures highlight customization rather than standardization: hand lettering and painting, sheet metal cutouts, plaster and chicken-wire ornamentation, and neon signs for one-off local establishments featuring place-based iconography like oil towers and evergreen trees more often than national logos. At the same time, because he tightly frames each photograph to eliminate contextual references, the individual buildings and signs transcend regional specificity to occupy an almost mythological roadside of Anyplace, USA. This is reinforced by Ivan Chermayeff's book design: thick black bands border every page like miles of asphalt lined with Margolies's selectively photographed highway architecture.

Margolies's language and the book's overall tone were equally subjective. More than one critic noted the rueful quality of his prose, manifest as "Salingeresque self-pity" and a "sense of cultural grievance" at what had been lost over the years and at the failure of the academy and "professional architects and planners" to understand its significance. Margolies even upbraided himself for allowing his education to undermine his love of the roadside: "it was intellectualized out of me." Others critics complained about his overweening nostalgia and uncritical enthusiasm for the subject of the roadside, thus missing an essential point of Margolies's project—to foster enthusiasm for the lost "golden age" that was as keen as his own.[63] With references to screaming billboards and hypnotically spinning gas-pump gauges Margolies's text is passionate and excitable, revealing his intentions and ideology in a way that the photographs alone do not. He declares roadside architecture not only "very important," but also the country's "definitive contribution" to twentieth-century design, a level of critical bombast several degrees more intense than Banham's. Refuting critical condemnations of the roadside, he argues that "it is not blight and ugliness and bad taste. It proves that what we are really best at is being tacky and commercial." Along the nation's highways, Margolies found manifestations of "American capitalism" that he regarded as "statements expressing pride in product," concluding finally with echoes of earlier autopian observers, that "this is splendid, wonderful folk architecture." Margolies's declaration is full of contradictions: the roadside is not bad taste, but it is nonetheless tacky; it exemplifies folk traditions, but it is also a definitive contribution to design. Nonetheless, this statement shows how Margolies transformed simple nostalgia into a culturally operative project that moved the work of Haskell, Jackson, Alloway, and Banham forward by continuing to push at the boundaries of what had constituted art, design, and architecture in the United States in the middle of the twentieth century. Less clear is what audience Margolies was targeting. Though he had been a regular contributor to the national architecture press during the 1960s, after curating a controversial show on the hotel designer Morris Lapidus in 1970 he considered himself at odds with both the modernist mainstream and the postmodern avant-garde. Into the 1970s, what he called his "public assertions" about everyday architecture in the realm of the automobile exacerbated his perception of outsider status. In retrospect, this had more to do with his methodology than his subject matter, since there were a number of other photographers, Shore among them, who, in the words of critics Andy Grundberg and Julia Scully, were "redemptively" making "works of art from subject matter that most Americans would characterize as trivial, ugly, kitschy, banal or worse" (building on the foundation of work by artists like D'Arcangelo and Ruscha.)[64] Margolies's work was topographical, but he was not aligned with New Topographics; his subjects were pop, but he was not an artist; his pictures were documentary, but not comprehensive; his research had breadth, but was largely anecdotal. Ultimately, *The End of the Road* was a heartfelt appreciation of the roadside more than more than an incisive analysis of its evolution, form, or meaning.

This distinction was a point of contention when *The End of the Road* was reviewed in the *Journal of the Society of Architectural Historians* alongside two other books (Richard Gutman and Elliott Kaufman's *American Diner* and Paul Hirshorn and Steven Izenour's *White Towers*) that embodied the emergent consideration of autopia as the recent past. Though the reviewer found them to be "uneven in quality," he considered them sufficiently coherent as a body of work to constitute "the early literature on such a relatively new subject."[65] In terms of historiography, however, their differences are far more interesting than their similarities.

Neither *American Diner* nor *White Towers* are as polemical as *The End of the Road*, and their authors are far more engaged than Margolies with buildings as material and architectural objects. This is partially the result of their deliberately narrower focus. Whereas Margolies took on the entirety of highway architecture, Gutman and Kaufman and Hirshorn and Izenour each examine a single typology. By the time *American Diner* was published in 1979, Richard Gutman, the book's lead author, was something of an authority on the eponymous building type—in 1972 the *New Yorker* called him "the important architectural historian of the diner," as a reporter followed him to Lower Manhattan to inspect a 1945 model built by Kullman Dining Car Company of New Jersey. Here, we must assume that tongue was planted at least partially in cheek since Gutman had only just graduated from architecture school at Cornell, and the *Talk of the Town* column in which the *New Yorker* article "Fast Food" appeared was known for its gently mocking humor.[66]

More serious was Gutman's contribution to *Perspecta* 15 in 1975; this issue of the student-run Yale architecture journal was dedicated to "backgrounds for an American architecture" and sought "to identify some aspects of the vernacular worthy of reconsideration." Despite this stated interest in reassessing the vernacular (in an issue that featured plenty of non-vernacular work, much of it now regarded as canonical, including the *Arts & Architecture*–sponsored Case Study Houses and Albert Kahn's factories), the editors introduced *Perspecta* 15 with what amounted to a high culture and Ivy League disclaimer that would have amused Tom Wolfe. They cautioned that in publishing essays on diners, resort hotels, and southern houses they "did not intend to assign undue significance" to any of these buildings. Rather, they strove to be "documentary without being pedantic."[67] Gutman's essay is thoroughly documentary, perhaps the earliest to trace the diner's development as a manufactured structure that grew in complexity as it evolved from movable wooden lunch wagons of the late nineteenth century into permanently sited railroad/streetcar models of the 1920s and from 1930s all-steel streamliners to 1950s modular prefabs. In addition to introducing readers to companies like Worcester Lunch Car and characters like Charles P. Gemme, Worcester's design-build supervisor for half a century, Gutman catalogues a range of material and fabrication technologies, including welded frames and interchangeable wall panels, illustrated

Figure 73. Day and Night Diner (Worcester Lunch Car Diner, 1923), Palmer, Massachusetts. (Historic American Buildings Survey, Library of Congress, Prints and Photographs Division, HABS MA-1231)

with construction details and patent drawings, as well as stylistic and programmatic permutations from Art Deco to Googie to colonial, from counter to booth to dining room. And while he convincingly argues that diners possess "overlooked sophistication," Gutman heads off any perception of pedantry with a few critical qualifications: diners represent "indigenous architecture"; as architecture their intentionality exists "on a totally vernacular or craft level"; and "no architects ever designed diners." The validity of these statements is questionable: diners are certainly indigenous, but in the same way the steel frame and the automobile are, as products of an advanced, urbanized, industrial society; conversely, given the diverse outlets architects found for their skills during, say, the Great Depression, it tests credulity that no one with architectural training ever designed a diner, and that they resulted exclusively from "native ingenuity" of diner entrepreneurs.[68]

What is more important is that Gutman felt compelled to offer these caveats, particularly in a publication from the school that sponsored Venturi and Scott Brown's Las Vegas studio. Though arguing for diners as a legitimate subject of architectural study, Gutman nonetheless minimized their architectural significance. The roadside, even in historical perspective, was still intellectually suspect. This may explain why in *American Diner* Gutman appears less as a diner apologist appealing to architects and more as a diner enthusiast engaging a popular audience. Though the book contains a greatly expanded version of his *Perspecta* essay, which details each episode of diner evolution, its focus is less architectural and more broadly social, with a greater emphasis on personalities and gimmicks. The diner is no longer an unexamined *typology* and an underappreciated *vernacular;* instead it is "something totally familiar, as comfortable as the language we speak or the everyday food we eat."[69] In the context of the book, the diner has, in effect, ceased to be architecture.

In their 1979 book *White Towers*, Paul Hirshorn and Steven Izenour make the opposite point about hundreds of hamburger stands built mainly on the East Coast in the middle of the twentieth century, situating them in a broad architectural middle, between the work of the "famous architect" and what they call the "unconscious folk vernacular," similar to what *Architectural Forum* called "minor" in the 1930s (see chapter 1). Mostly the work of a single architect, Charles Johnson, White Tower's in-house designer for forty years, the buildings are "limited architecturally," according to Hirshorn and Izenour, but only because of their narrow programmatic requirements: to sell hamburgers as efficiently and effectively as possible. As those needs changed over the decades, so did Johnson's White Towers, responsive as they were to retailing, to marketing, and to location. As a group, Hirshorn and Izenour argue, the White Towers "represent a strong architectural idea," mainly the deployment of "signs and symbols" in the service of commercial design. That phrase reveals *White Towers*'s impeccable avant-garde credentials. When they became interested in hamburger stands, Hirshorn and Izenour were working in the office of Venturi and Scott Brown where, the authors noted, "roadside awareness was in the air," as their architect/theorist bosses were in midst of the multiyear study of the architectural character of the commercial strip that would become *Learning from Las Vegas* (with Izenour as a coauthor). Hirshorn and Izenour began photographing White Tower buildings casually in and around Philadelphia in 1970, and became more determined about documenting them the following year, when they met Johnson, almost by chance, in Camden, New Jersey. After he invited them to the White Tower corporate headquarters and shared the company's photographic archive, they decided to "attempt a serious study of these little buildings."[70]

They published the initial results of this study in 1973 as a brief survey of the chain's "remarkable architectural history" accompanied by a number of their own color photographs, including several nighttime, neon-saturated views that made the towers appear anything but white. The article appeared in *Architecture Plus*, a short-lived progressive architecture journal. Founded by former *Architectural*

Forum editor and roadside muckraker Peter Blake, *Architecture Plus* was dedicated to interpreting architecture "in the broadest possible sense," which may explain Blake's willingness to feature *White Towers* in the journal's fifth issue, despite his own critical misgivings about roadside buildings (see chapter 3). He expressed these concerns in the editorial note that introduced the article, inevitably titled "Learning from Hamburgers": "The authors are both Philadelphia architects who lunch frequently at Philadelphia #14. This deadpan dissertation may earn them an Honorary Doctorate in Pop History—or it may not."[71] This insistence on the authors' humorous intentions says more about Blake than it does about Hirshon or Izenour, though they remained straight-faced long enough to publish their White Towers research in book form. *White Towers* was a more complete case study of nearly half a century of commercial architecture presented in an analytical essay tracing the development of the "White Tower System" and a photographic portfolio depicting the chain's architectural evolution between 1926 and 1972. The study begins with the opening of the first White Tower in Milwaukee and ends with the company coming to terms with the fast food, auto-oriented revolution of the McDonald's era. Hirshorn and Izenour carefully examined White Towers from the perspectives of hygiene and food service, architectural prototyping, and the promotional value of standardized design. They pay particular attention to the impact of shifting social patterns as the chain followed its customers from sidewalk to roadside, from storefronts to freestanding buildings with parking. In tone, Hirshorn and Izenour are far more restrained than either Gutman or Margolies; they are critically distant, even detached from their subject. Beyond a quiet acknowledgment in the introduction of a "fondness" for the buildings they study, they adhere to Venturi and Scott Brown's admonition in *Learning from Las Vegas* to use "withholding judgment" as "a tool to make later judgment more sensitive."[72] In *White Towers,* this produced a bloodless analysis, and the book's layout reflects this bias.

White Towers is a trim volume with a spare modernist design by Muriel Cooper, the MIT Press art director who was also responsible for the design of the first edition of the *Learning from Las Vegas.* Cooper's page layouts for *White Towers* have much in common with the schema of *Learning from Las Vegas,* which in turn borrows heavily from the art books of Ed Ruscha, whose deadpan, serial photographs of quotidian structures in and around Los Angeles were formative to Venturi, Scott Brown, and Izenour's framing of the commercial landscape (see figures 64 and 65). It is tempting to think of *White Towers* as "169 hamburger stands"—equivalent to Ruscha's *Twentysix Gasoline Stations* or *Thirtyfour Parking Lots in Los Angeles*—except that Hirshorn and Izenour approached their hamburger stands with documentary rather than artistic intent. The result is akin to a collection of specimens for an architectural morphological classification, at least as presented in Cooper's design for the book's introductory essay: its columns of stacked thumbnails and location-and-unit-number captions render nearly illegible any trace of individuality in the buildings depicted, whether they are presented as exteriors, interiors, or plans. As a result, although it was Venturi and Scott Brown's postmodern ideology that prompted their study of popular architecture, Hirshorn and Izenour end up presenting the White Towers as exemplars of modernist seriality, middlebrow commercial versions of a Bauhaus dream of the factory-built house. As Hirshorn and Izenour put it, the architectural strength of the White Towers "lies in their numbers."[73]

The book's photographic portfolio is an accumulation of standardized compositions: it presents one towered white box after another, as the crenellations and modernistic detailing of the 1920s give way to the streamlining of the 1930s and 1940s and then the more austere modernism of the 1950s and 1960s. Here, however, a strange transformation takes place: although Hirshorn and Izenour assert that the White Towers are not "self-conscious Architecture" (capitalization theirs), they present them as self-conscious capital *A* Architecture by depicting them almost exclusively through photographs from the White Tower corporate archives. No grease, no grime—these hamburger stands are iconic, frozen in time at their moment of completion. Also frozen in time are the cars and clothing captured in the photographs along with the buildings. Though their project is largely devoid of nostalgia, Hirshorn and Izenour allow that such period details have "amusement" value, but this, in a way, merely adds to the utility of *White Towers* as a historic record. Though only a few were included in the book, Hirshorn and Izenour's own photographs circa 1970 serve the same purpose from our vantage point in the twenty-first century: to capture the commercial ephemera of a particular moment in the recent past when the midcentury roadside still retained the artifacts if not the aura of autopia. In a lecture he gave at SCI-Arc shortly before *White Tower*'s publication, Izenour nodded to the end-of-an-era zeitgeist of the 1970s by acknowledging the near obsolescence of these artifacts. They were, he said, already "historical objects to a great extent."[74] Exactly thirty years later, Paul Hirshorn picked up this thread in the preface to a reprint edition of *White Towers* released in 2007. Commenting both on the absence of Steven Izenour (who died in 2001) and on the destruction of so many White Tower units in the intervening decades, Hirshorn observed that "I am guessing [Steven] would be surprisingly unsentimental about the disappearance of these little buildings that we liked so much, once they no longer had a collective purpose. Don't preserve them, just record them for posterity, I think he would say. And that's just what we did."[75]

Recording the White Towers for posterity was not without preservation consequences, and what was true of *White Towers* was also true of *American Diner* and *The End of the Road*. Through these books, roadside commercial buildings gained an enduring place in the nation's cultural memory, a commencement of legitimization that was amplified by the inclusion of some of the extant buildings the books documented on the National Register of Historic Places during the 1980s. The register was authorized in 1966 by the National Historic Preservation Act (NHPA), which emerged "in the face of ever-increasing extensions of urban centers, highways, and residential, commercial, and industrial developments." At the same time, the NHPA broadened eligibility criteria to include buildings and sites that were of state and local impor-

Figure 74. White Tower New York #10 (Vitrolite Company, 1933) on West 168th Street and Broadway, New York, reproduced in Hirshorn and Izenour, *White Towers,* 1979. (Photograph by Wurts Bros. [New York, N.Y.]/ Museum of the City of New York, X2010.7.2.5531)

tance rather than exclusively national significance; the goal here, according to one historian, was to move away from "museum-quality" sites to be inclusive of those understood to embody "contemporary social concerns." Thus, though the register was intended to encourage preservation "of the rich heritage of our Nation," at least in part to ameliorate the cultural impact of the rapid changes brought about by car-oriented decentralization, the buildings and landscapes the car produced were now eligible for consideration as "historic places."[76]

First, though, the ephemeral landmarks of autopia had to last long enough to become the recent past, either to meet the fifty-year rule or demonstrate sufficient significance to waive this requirement. The iconically shaped Shell Service Station, built in Winston-Salem, North Carolina in 1930 (see color plate 15), is the only survivor of eight originals; it was added to the National Register in 1976. Two years later, the 1940 Modern Diner in Pawtucket, Rhode Island, joined it, the first diner on the register. The nomination form credited Gutman with providing authoritative information about this rare extant Sterling Streamliner. Margolies photographed the diner the same year it was listed (1978) and included it in *The End of the Road,* adjacent to an image of the Miss Bellows Falls Diner in Bellows Falls, Vermont, a circa-1942 Worcester Lunch Car model with an approved nomination report (1983) that cited Margolies's book.[77] A comparable citation occurs in the designation report for the White Tower that Hirshorn and Izenour identify as Boston #5 from 1932. Actually located in Cambridge, the structure at 25 Central Square is now a contributing building to the Central Square Historic District and a protected city landmark, even though falafel in the fryer replaced hamburgers on the griddle a few years before White Tower Boston #5 achieved that status.[78]

The Historian on the Highway

The work of Margolies, Gutman, and Hirshorn and Izenour may have helped to catalyze burgeoning popular and professional interest in the midcentury roadside, but the 1970s were a ferment of comparable research and documentation activities, many of them motivated by parallel social awareness, intellectual concerns, and nostalgic enthusiasms. In the preface to his frequently cited *Americans on the*

Road (1979), Warren James Belasco recalled how, during his initial research, the impact of the energy crisis, environmentalism, and growing anti-car sentiments caused him to view the emerging consequences of the car between 1910 and 1945 through the lens of the early 1970s. Without checking this inadvertent presentist perspective, he had "projected this attitude back into the early years of the century," which meant he was looking at the new landscapes of the automobile in almost exclusively negative terms. Only after a series of "sudden breakdowns and forced detours," did the historian embark on a more neutral assessment of the period. As completed, his study of recreational motor touring attempts to "look at what Americans actually did *with* their cars rather than judge what cars did *to* Americans." By recognizing that the values and priorities of autopia were not the same as his own, Belasco effectively solved his intellectual crisis. Refusing to criticize the car's historical context did not mean he was uncritical of the car in the present. Belasco described his shift in perspective as the conceptual flash that ultimately changed the direction of his work, moving it from what he anticipated would be a contribution to environmental history to what he viewed as an investigation of motorist behavior rather than effects. The latter, he claimed, were "unanticipated and hard to measure," but that reveals him still thinking like a man of the 1970s, about congestion and pollution and injuries and fatalities, because his thoroughgoing account of the evolution of auto camps and motor hotels *was* about effects: the emergence of spaces set aside for the car and designed specifically for it, which he discovers in the archives just as Albert Frey and James Agee had discovered on the highway (see chapters 1 and 2). At the same time, Belasco was also thinking very much like a historian of material culture, evident not only in his reliance on travel magazines, trade journals, and other period sources, but in his establishment of nuanced chronologies tracking how "gypsying" with a horse-drawn carriage gave way to car camping, and driving to recreational sites replaced taking the train. His historian's agenda was equally obvious in the book's detailed notes and its extensive "Bibliographical Guide," one of the earliest on the subject, in which Belasco, in effect, shares the research roadmap he created out of necessity when, "despite the car's major role in American life," he confronted a dearth of scholarly literature and archival collections relating to the automobile in general and auto-tourism in particular. That Belasco's book would help fill this void was regarded as one of its leading virtues upon its publication. A reviewer in *Winterthur Portfolio,* Folke Kihlstedt, felt that by the late 1970s the time had come "for evaluating the car's impact with at least a degree of detachment," and he called this "a scholarly imperative" that had emerged even as the automobile's socioeconomic value was still being debated. Despite Belasco's explicit discussion of his intellectual struggle with the car as a subject of historical inquiry, Kihlstedt complained that he lacked "a skeptical or theoretical framework" and even accused him of being an automobile apologist—a complaint lodged with regularity against those who attempted to study autopia with condemning it.[79] Whether because of these critiques, or despite them, methodological self-awareness characterized the work of many roadside scholars in the 1970s.

Longtime collaborators John Jakle and Keith Sculle have also recalled their own dawning awareness of the roadside's cultural significance in the 1970s, prompted by the state historical surveys undertaken nationwide in response to the NHPA's mandate to expand the National Register. It was the summer of 1973 in southern Illinois. Though they were driving along U.S. 40, the old coast-to-coast highway documented by George R. Stewart (see chapter 2) and about to be rendered obsolete by I-70, the geographer (Jakle) and the historian (Sculle) weren't looking for autopia. They found it anyway, in the form of a derelict Classical Revival gas station complete with Doric columns, an entablature, and dentil molding.[80] What were they to make of this? While their academic training had prepared them to study such a building—they were skilled in fieldwork and material and morphological analysis—their academic training had not acknowledged that such a building might exist. Though it was torn down a few years later, that gas station in Casey, Illinois, left an indelible mark on Jakle and Sculle, setting the course for their subsequent historical and geographic research. Since then they have produced scores of articles and, beginning in 1994, nearly a dozen coauthored books charting the evolution of the built typologies the automobile spawned. These include a "gas, food, lodging" trilogy, as well as studies of signage, garages, parking lots, and the highways themselves. Reflecting on the trajectory of their careers, Jakle and Sculle also point to the serendipity of when they were born as a key factor in determining the direction of their work: "We can think back now and recognize that we were born [in 1939 & 1940] at the end of an era." In demographic terms, they were children when the so-called Silent Generation was giving way to the Baby Boom. In experiential terms, they came of age in the midst of accelerating postwar change. They were old enough to remember when Main Streets were vital community centers and drive-in restaurants were relative novelties; they were young enough to have been dazzled by the expanding scale of the strip, the shopping center, and the interstate. Because, when they began to study these landscapes in the 1970s, there was "no scholarship to fall back on," they filled the void themselves.[81]

By 1978, Jakle had published "The American Gasoline Station, 1920–1970" in the *Journal of American Culture*, where it appeared alongside studies of American cookbooks, high school mascots, and real estate advertisements as the only article to deal directly with the built environment. Jakle's essay is a solid introductory survey of the building type, not unlike those that architects published in the 1920s and 1930s. Beginning with the emergence of standard programmatic features (canopies, pumps, etc.) after World War I and ending with the gas station's point of highest market saturation (in terms of number of retail outlets) just as the era of cheap fuel was coming to an end, Jakle concentrates on the evolution of station morphology, especially the building's relationship to the street and its spatial accommodation of the car as curbside stations gave way to those pushed back from the road to make room for additional pumps, canopies, and service bays. Missing from this analysis is a consideration of the sociocultural implications of spatial dispersal, though that would emerge in Jakle's later work. What was clearly more important, given the visual focus of so much research in the 1970s, was his downplaying of mimetic and "unique designs" in order to emphasize typological consistency, regardless of formal characteristics.[82]

However useful the essay's content, Jakle had larger methodological aims. The first, based on his use of *National Petroleum News* as a primary source, was to encourage scholars, as Banham had done in the 1960s, to broaden the archive to include trade journals and other commercial and industrial publications as a serious part of the historical record.[83] Jakle's second and more critical aim, which also made explicit what would become his life's work, was to urge scholars of the built environment to give the American roadside the "serious attention" he believed it deserved. To a degree, Jackle was preaching to the converted by publishing this essay in the *Journal of American Culture,* where previous issues included a special feature on fast food with two lengthy articles about the spatial domains of contemporary McDonald's. As the official publication of the Popular Culture Association, the *JAC* was dedicated to "the study of American culture in the broadest sense of the term, from 'elite' to popular and folk culture as a continuum."[84] Jakle is careful to situate the gas station within this continuum, particularly as it applied to the whole of the designed landscape, which, he argues, had as much to teach us about the "American experience" as all other architectural expressions, whether they are "monumental, vernacular, or folk." That Jakle had to explain this intellectual position—like Alloway explaining the iconography of highway culture in art—affirms its novelty within certain disciplines, namely those filled with scholars to whom it "may not be very obvious" why anyone would spend time researching the American roadside. Included in this group were historical geographers, architectural historians, and others whom Jakle described as suffering from "a well developed sense of 'good taste' in landscape."[85]

The issue of taste—good or bad—as equated with cultural and scholarly value was nearly inescapable in roadside historical studies of the 1970s—though, as sociologist Herbert Gans observed in *Popular Culture and High Culture* of 1974, it was all but ignored by the majority of "social scientists and humanists" at the time.[86] In work on the roadside, taste was something of a two-way street, with scholars raising the issue as frequently as critics of the work they produced. In the 1979 book based on his thesis in historic preservation at Columbia, Daniel Vieyra drove straight into the fray. His title, *Fill 'er Up: An Architectural History of America's Gas Stations,* is reminiscent of Alloway and Wolfe in the way it unabashedly conjoined roadside slang with disciplinary specialization. Vieyra had already struck a blow for the gas station's respectability when he presented a portion of this work in a session on "Architecture and Sculpture in America" at the annual conference of the Society of Architectural Historians in 1978, where his paper on gas stations must have seemed either original or laughable depending on one's perspective. It certainly placed the gas station in good company, alongside talks on the collaboration of modernists Gordon Bunshaft and Isamu Noguchi (on projects like Lever House and Connecticut General) and the nineteenth-century eclecticism represented by the public monuments of Henry Van Brunt and J. Q. A. Ward.[87] If, in the other papers, there was a clear distinction between the building and the sculpture, in Vieyra's contribution the building was the sculpture, whether (following the precepts of Venturi and Scott Brown) it was an oversized oilcan or a Brutalist cantilever. His title, "Fantasy and New Forms," reflects the stylistic themes upon which *Fill 'er Up* is predicated.

Vieyra organized the entire history of the gas station, from the 1910s right up to the 1970s, into four categories, ranging chronologically through the Fantastic (which shows his debt to Banham's *Los Angeles*), the Respectable, the Domestic, and the Functional. Methodologically, the book is best described as old-fashioned, descriptive formalism, but Vieyra deploys it almost subversively within the disciplinary context in which he is operating. As James Marston Fitch, the distinguished preservationist, noted rather diplomatically in his foreword, "architectural historians have not yet found auto-generated structures worthy of more than peripheral study."[88] A decade earlier, in "Where Architectural Historians Fear to Tread," John Maass identified some of the factors that held sway over scholarly practice in the field circa 1969, among them the bourgeois standard, the genteel tradition, the isolated building, and the isolated discipline. Any one of these was sufficient to keep timid architectural historians away from the landscapes and buildings of the automobile, as Reyner Banham had already discovered. In that article, Maass quotes Charles E. Peterson, one of the founders of the Historic American Buildings Survey and editor of the "American Notes" section of the *Journal of the Society of Architectural Historians,* who described the gas station as "an all too conspicuous feature of the American roadside [that] deserves further investigation" on the occasion of the 1960 publication in *JSAH* of a brief essay on Frank Lloyd Wright's Lindholm Service Station in Cloquet, Minnesota (1958).[89] That investigation was a long time coming, as Paul Goldberger observed when reviewing Vieyra's book in the *New York Times* and seeming to echo Maass, Peterson, and Fitch: "Not so very long ago, no architectural historian would dream of looking even casually, let alone seriously, at the commercial architecture that lines the roads and highways of this country." The buildings of the roadside were "viewed as objects of contempt—if their existence was acknowledged at all." Acknowledging changing taste and zeitgeist nostalgia as the reason for this scholarly reversal of fortune, Goldberger still has difficulty taking the subject seriously. Gas stations, and studies of them, are a sentimental pleasure, he argues, and the buildings themselves are "amusing and friendly." But it is only with apparent reluctance that Goldberger concedes that Vieyra's book (along with *White Towers* and *American Diner*) makes a "reasonably convincing case for the value of considering these roadside places as real works of architecture."[90]

Though he begrudgingly grants the roadside a degree of architectural authenticity (while failing to define realness), Goldberger underscores why Vieyra's book, like so many others of this period, needed to be an explicitly legitimizing project—one that sought, as Fitch put it, to accord this roadside typology "the same curatorial attention that is normally reserved for older, more urbane and more elite artifacts."[91] But in giving the gas station that attention, Vieyra is less interested in making a place for gas stations in an expanded canon than in subtly upending accepted conventions of history and historical narratives, told, all too frequently at the time, strictly through stylistic innovation and progress. The gas station, he argued, was "rarely an architectural trendsetter." This, he implied, is one important reason, along with low cultural status, that historians and critics had largely ignored it. Indeed, Vieyra's very brief gas station bibliography consists of exactly two references: Henry-Russell Hitchcock's venerable *H.H. Richardson and His Times* (1936), which, as we saw in chapter 3, included a digression on roadside buildings in its conclusion, and, three decades later, the early writings of Venturi and Scott Brown as they searched for meaning in the parking lots and commercial strips.[92]

Unmentioned in the text, but included in Vieyra's notes, is another architectural history that insisted on the significance of not only the gas station, but also of a range of "auto-generated structures" that had not yet gotten their scholarly due. And it examines those buildings within the context of a broader subject that many historians still considered as intellectually peripheral as the spaces of the car: the architecture of the recent past in Southern California. In *L.A. in the Thirties, 1931–1941,* published in 1975 (the same year as the reprint edition Esther McCoy's

1960 volume, *Five California Architects*), David Gebhard and Harriette Von Breton examine the growth of "auto-oriented design" in the city's architectural and urban form from the 1920s to the 1940s.[93] They consider, in particular, the evolution of commercial strips and the development of drive-in commercial types such as restaurants, theaters, and banks, as well as the reconfiguration of larger retail institutions, including department stores and supermarkets, to accommodate cars through parking areas and garages, which became increasingly important in these decades. What is significant about *L.A. in the Thirties* is that it places these buildings alongside examples of modernist, moderne, and revivalist design, including the work of R. M. Schindler, Richard Neutra, Robert Derrah, Paul R. Williams, and Albert C. Martin Sr.

By flattening typological and stylistic hierarchies, Gebhard and Von Breton give the architecture of the automobile in this particular place and time the same consideration as work generally considered, in Fitch's terms, "more urbane and elite." This must have been especially effective in the exhibition on which the Gebhard/Von Breton book was based. On display at the University of California, Santa Barbara Art Galleries, where Gebhard was director, the show consisted mostly of large-format photographs (including aerial views) arranged to emphasize the curators' anti-hierarchy thesis into three main sections that explored "imagery and its uses" in the commercial, public, and residential spheres. According to one reviewer, this arrangement evoked "a palatable Zeitgeist with its catholic attention to 'high,' 'low,' and 'middle-brow' art" (Gebhard and Von Breton are the ones who used these terms).[94] That such *catholic* curation provoked commentary indicates yet again the novelty of the approach. The *L.A. Times* used the same word in its review, also calling the show "happily unconventional" in the way it extended the "normal limits" of architecture exhibitions. Obviously, the inclusion of roadside buildings in a broad spectrum of architecture was not yet a mainstream proposition, even if it had become more palatable, usually in direct proportion, it would seem, to the intensity of nostalgia it provoked. *L.A. in the Thirties,* for example, was "a Proustian experience" for viewers and readers of a certain age and this, reviewers implied, was its main appeal for the general public.[95] Slowly, however, with each new book, article, or exhibition, the study of the roadside gained an additional measure of specialist and generalist respect, with Gebhard's own subsequent work providing the model for an autopian architectural history at the intersection of the two. This occurred most obviously in the guides to California architecture that he coauthored with Robert Winter, then a young faculty member at Occidental College. While they recognized the need for a broad-reaching "general survey," research for their first guide, published in 1965, was occasioned by the "special circumstances" of the joint meeting in Los Angeles in the winter of 1964 of two learned societies with a keen interest in visual culture (the College Art Association and the Society of Architectural Historians). For this reason, Gebhard and Winter set out to give the guide "some quirks," deliberately including buildings that "went against the high taste of the time." In the 1977 edition of *A Guide to Architecture in Los Angeles and Southern California,* and clearly reflecting the revisionist impulses of *L.A. in the Thirties,* their contrariness of taste had continued to evolve, becoming, by their own admission, "a bit perverse." Their selection now included a full range of autopian architecture, from modernist shopping centers and motels (by Albert C. Martin and Richard Neutra, among others), to roadside stands deploying "programmatic imagery" of the building-as-sign variety theorized by Venturi and Scott Brown, whom, along with J. B. Jackson, they credit for having opened their eyes to "a new world of perception."[96]

Gebhard would further theorize "Programatic [sic]" architecture in his introduction to *California Crazy,* a 1980 picture book of vernacular roadside buildings whose title suggested a popular orientation that belied the erudition of the historian's text. In fact, there was no mismatch between the book's titular enthusiasm and Gebhard's essay, which demonstrated that it was possible to produce serious scholarship about a "non-serious" subject. Gebhard began by explaining the emergence of programmatic buildings in Southern California as a direct result of its cultural identity as "the land of the unique" (when compared to the rest of the country) and "Automobile-Land," which combined with a mild climate to produce an impressive number of larger-than-life hot dogs, donuts, coffeepots, and the like, for which Gebhard found ample evidence in built examples and patent drawings. But Gebhard also situated programmatic buildings in a tradition of ornamental architecture stretching back as far as ancient Rome (he quotes Pliny the Younger), and he draws a parallel between the programmatic edifices of prewar Southern California and historical efflorescences in sixteenth-century Rome, eighteenth-century England, and Enlightenment France, where the work of Claude-Nicholas Ledoux, Étienne-Louis Boullée, and Jean-Jacques Lequeu provided his pointed comparisons. From there, Gebhard moves to nineteenth-century New Jersey, noting that James Lafferty based his 1881 Lucy the Elephant (in Margate) on a French design of 1758, before arriving, finally, in twentieth-century Los Angeles and emphasizing again the car's role in promoting "a new wave of direct Programatic [sic] architecture." Though most of the essay is devoted to categorizing the diverse formal vocabulary of roadside specimens dating from "the heyday" years of the 1920s and 1930s, Gebhard also catalogued postwar examples. More significantly, he concluded the essay by reflecting on shifting attitudes of his own day, noting how the disdain of "America's upper middle class, professional planners, and the high art world" was transformed in the 1960s and 1970s, which he attributed to the combined influence of Dadaism, surrealism, and pop, until "a high arter and a good bourgeois will respond with equal ardor to those few remaining vestiges of our Programatic [sic] near-past."[97]

Ada Louise Huxtable anticipated Gebhard's sentiment and his roadside scholarship in a lengthy feature in the *New York Times Magazine* that offered an insightful critique of what could by then, in the late 1970s, be called the historical turn in autopian studies: "Some say it's junk, but more and more experts are finding aesthetic merit and cultural meaning in the vernacular environment." Her ostensible subject was a 1978 show at the Cooper-Hewitt National Design Museum, *Place Product Packaging,* that looked at the history of diners, gas stations, fast food restaurants, and museum villages as a way of exploring contemporary themed environments. But for Huxtable, this exhibition offered an opportunity to probe the larger significance of "Architecture for a Fast-Food Culture" as she catalogued new work in the field, and especially since she had reviewed *Signs of Life* in 1976. Huxtable began by situating this within the broader backward glance of the 1970s, what she called the "new nostalgia" for "the Brave Old World," and pointing out the lack of consensus that existed among critics who viewed "the artifacts of near-history" as either "the revelation of great truth or a cultural disaster."[98] Huxtable herself

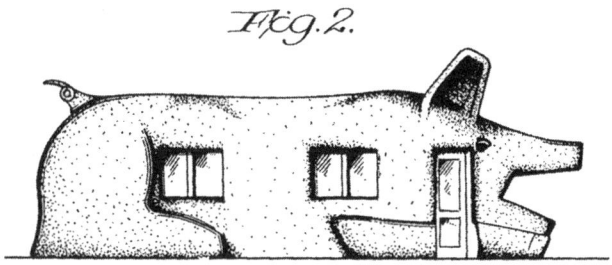
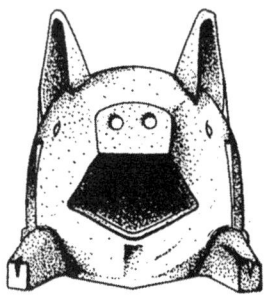

Figure 75. Warren Lee, "Design for a Refreshment Building [recumbent pig]," U.S. Patent No. 93,665, 1934.

was probably somewhere in the middle. She was an ardent preservationist, who regularly bemoaned the demolition of historic buildings in the name of so-called progress, especially when it resulted in mediocrity, as at New York's Pennsylvania Station. In "Pow! It's Good-By History, Hello Hamburger," for example, Huxtable skewered the replacement of a Greek Revival farmhouse with a Burger King in Madison, Wisconsin, in 1971.[99] But she was too attentive an architectural and cultural observer to fail to notice what else was happening on the roadside as the decade proceeded.

Importantly, Huxtable recognized the "increasing seriousness" of the new historical work as it moved beyond the "sentimental journey" phase into a coherent "movement" that deployed "scholarly analysis" based on "the techniques of conventional art history" in order to study "the iconography of these building types." To emphasize the seriousness of method and intention, Huxtable made a provocative comparison, one that echoed similar sentiments by Jackson and Banham: the study of roadside buildings was not unlike "the study of the stylistic development and facade changes of cinquecento churches." The new roadside histories, Huxtable implied in 1978's "Architecture for a Fast-Food Culture," were revealing that autopia had a formal language (and maybe even a canon) as recognizable and categorical as that of the High Renaissance, notwithstanding the obvious differences of material and detail—neon and Googie in place of travertine and classicism. For Huxtable, a critic always attuned to the larger import of architecture and its history, this was not an insular academic debate: "Today we are revising, and rewriting, contemporary art history, and in particular the history of the uses of art and taste. It is a little like a trick with mirrors, because we are also making history in the process."[100] In 1980, Huxtable revisited the shift in attitude toward the roadside to see how writing history had changed history in the intervening two years. On the *New York Times* editorial page she observed that "Americana Is Where You Find It," noting how "a move by younger scholars" to study "the commercial artifacts of a consumer culture" had produced a "heated debate" about what constituted historical notability. With books on gas stations and diners, and examples of both on the National Register, Huxtable concluded that the roadside was no longer the "unsung vernacular" that it once was. However successful the new inclusivity was in broadening the "American architectural heritage," it also offered serious challenges to preservation: "it would be ludicrous to freeze motels for posterity," Huxtable observed, "but not much sillier than embalming all of George Washington's overnight stops." The critical issue for Huxtable was the same one that the autopian analysts we encountered in chapter 4 had tried to sort out: what standards to use when those of Colonial Williamsburg no longer applied.[101]

Digging the Haunted Highway

The Society for Commercial Archeology (SCA) was already deeply engaged with these issues, as Huxtable had noted in her editorial. A few months before, Paul Goldberger, also writing in the *Times*, described the group as "a reputable society of academics devoted to the preservation of roadside landmarks."[102] Though one doubts that SCA members really cared if the newspaper of record validated their character and credentials, it probably didn't hurt their fledgling organization. SCA was the brainchild of Chester H. Liebs, historian, preservationist, and founding director (1975) of the historic preservation program at the University of Vermont, where he first began to study—and teach—the physical landscapes of the car. This was unlikely research in a state defined then, as now, by its farms and villages, but Liebs recognized that urban and exurban development threatened historic diners and drive-ins as much as it did historic barns and town greens. As Richard Longstreth has noted, Liebs was among the earliest scholars to argue in print for a concerted effort to document and preserve the recent past.[103] In 1976, Liebs complained of the persistent popular confusion about the chronological parameters of the "good old days" of the twentieth century, particularly as it concerned buildings and ephemera related to the car. He noted, for example, a general failure to distinguish the milieu of the Model T from that of the streamlined sedans of the Depression decade. This mattered, Liebs argued, because it muddied what constituted "historical value," allowing the built artifacts of commercial culture to be destroyed or altered at an alarming rate. By the year 2000, he speculated, the United States would have plenty of Victoriana, but "almost no remaining movie palaces, roadside diners, or exuberant bits of mimetic architecture."

Writing in *Possibilities* in 1976 (a quarterly journal he also edited), Liebs urged readers "[to] accept our aging century."[104] In 1978 he repeated this plea with greater detail and color photographs in *Historic Preservation,* a bimonthly magazine with a considerably larger, national circulation. Liebs celebrated isolated preservation triumphs—diners restored to their former luster, giant milk bottles spared the wrecking ball, gas stations declared city landmarks (even, he noted, as the energy crisis spurred their continued destruction)—and also modestly highlighted the promising activities of the newly formed Society for Commercial Archeology, of which he was currently president.[105]

The SCA's ambitions as an organization were straightforward: it sought to promote public awareness, distribute information, and encourage preservation of "the artifacts and structures, signs and symbols of the American commercial process."[106] In addition to annual meetings, with paper sessions and tours, the SCA published a newsletter and a journal. These featured reviews of books (*White Towers,* Banham's *Los Angeles*) and even movies notable for their use of "period Main Streets and early highway strips." *American Graffiti* was celebrated as the film that "started it all" by creating "a compelling visual landscape and a heavy dose of nostalgia."[107] The newsletter published reports on SCA activities and initiatives, "obituaries" for demolished buildings, and notices about research strategies and methodologies. The early issues of the newsletter also included discussions of "definitions and boundaries of commercial archeology." This was important to the SCA since, at the time of its incorporation in 1977, the society did not represent a distinct academic discipline or professional specialization, mainly because something called "commercial archeology" did not exist in institutionalized form. (It would be two more years before Chester Liebs taught what the SCA claimed was the first university course in commercial archeology when he offered "Architecture, Advertising, and the American Roadside" as part of the American Vernacular Summer Institute at Boston University.) The SCA's first members and directors were historians, geographers, anthropologists, architects, preservationists, and enthusiasts with an interest in the commercial landscape. There were even a few archeologists, one of whom took exception to the society's use of the term in an early newsletter, arguing that it obscured the SCA's goals more than it revealed them, since most people associated archeology with the excavation of antiquities, or at least digging up artifacts of any age below the surface of the ground. This was certainly *not* the kind of fieldwork in which SCA members typical engaged. At the end of its first decade, the society even considered changing its name because, as the board stated in a questionnaire circulated to the membership, "the word archeology confuses people," even those who enthusiastically supported the SCA's mission.[108] Ultimately, though, identifying themselves with archeology served a polemical purpose.

In 1971, Chester Liebs had cofounded the Society for *Industrial* Archeology to promote research into the heritage of manufacturing and technology in the United States. Early on, Liebs saw direct parallels between American industrial landscapes and what he later recalled as "another huge phylum of the built landscape—the commercial places, signs, and symbols along the American highway." Within a few years, Liebs was actively facilitating knowledge transfer from the "industrial" to the "commercial," now in the service of what an early SCA newsletter called "the heritage of the automobile and the highway." This research was rightly *archeological* in the context of "above ground archeology," a term coined in the early 1970s to identify an outgrowth of historical archeology in the service of material culture. According to historian Thomas J. Schlereth and anthropologist John L. Cotter, who helped articulate its theory and practice, above-ground archeology used many of the same analytical and interpretive techniques as the "below-ground" discipline, especially stratification, typology, iconography, seriation, and diffusion.[109] Liebs deployed each of these methods in the "out of production" theory of commercial archeology he contributed to a "forum on the assessment of American roadside architecture" sponsored by the Society of Architectural Historians in 1980, when David Gebhard was SAH president. For Liebs, "out of production" meant that the artifact (structure or sign) was obsolete due to materials, type, location, form, or any of the countless other ways in which the signs and structures of the commercial sphere were subject to relentlessly competitive social and economic pressures—including, he noted several times, the impact of the energy crisis on the car's spatial domains.[110] Using these criteria, once a structure or sign was *out of production,* it became significant regardless of its age, but this was not, for Liebs, an invitation to festishize (or preserve) every surviving instance of commercial ephemera. He understood that in an automotive age of mass consumption, value accrued to roadside artifacts not individually (whether at the scale of the sign or the building), but as components of a larger system of production and distribution. The process the object represented was more important than the object itself. For Liebs, analysis to establish value required detailed recording in the field and documentation in the archives—and both were a necessary prerequisite for roadside preservation. Since, he conceded, it was neither practical nor possible to preserve every roadside artifact, establishing *out of production* significance was a way of making informed preservation decisions. And these became increasingly urgent the longer the roadside artifact was out of production, since competitive forces all but assured its destruction, modification, or abandonment. In a reply to Liebs in the same SAH forum, Marc Treib, despite mild sarcasm, saw obvious parallels between classical and commercial archeology: "Certainly a classification system paralleling that of Minoan pottery could easily be created!" He even speculated on how a preserved commercial strip, frozen in time, might function once it was protected from the restless market forces that brought it into being.[111]

Archeology was also a touchstone for Denise Scott Brown when she reviewed Liebs's *Main Street to Miracle Mile* in the *New York Times.* Calling Liebs's book "probably the first general history of the strip," Scott Brown—echoing Huxtable's review of her own work in *Signs of Life* of 1976—noted its appearance at a time (1985) when the commercial landscape was still the subject of "moral and esthetic outrage" and considered "too mundane to merit serious scholarship." In fact, Liebs's now classic study should be seen as the culmination of the pioneering research and documentation of the 1970s, work that, as we've seen, tapped into the broader cultural nostalgia to insist upon the importance of the American roadside as architecture and urbanism. But *Main Street to Miracle Mile* was no mere compilation. Though Liebs acknowledged that his book grew out of the work of many figures already discussed in this chapter, and he stated explicitly that his goal was to offer "an overview of the field," Liebs also took pains to distinguish his project from "probably the best-known work" on the topic, *Learning from Las Vegas.* Liebs does this by laying bare the earlier book's polemical heart, explaining how Venturi, Scott

Brown, and Izenour studied the roadside not as an end in itself, or even as a way to understand the larger culture per se. Instead, he rightly argued, they used the roadside "as a metaphor" for a more inclusive architectural language, whether architects were designing buildings on or off the strip. However provocative it was as a design manifesto, *Learning from Las Vegas* was "never intended as a history of roadside building." By contrast, *Main Street to Miracle Mile* absolutely was. Importantly, the book is also a methods primer for approaching and interpreting the autopian landscape as "a cultural landscape that is quintessentially American," as Liebs stated with a nod to J. B. Jackson. Like Jackson (and many of the thinkers we encountered in the last chapter), Liebs explicitly states that the book is premised on "that most ubiquitous of twentieth-century vantage points, behind the windshield of a moving car." As with the highway *analystes* who preceded him, Liebs's mobilized POV is essential to his study, providing spatial, visual, and chronological context for his exploration of the "common but confusing" experience of driving the commercial strip. For Liebs that experience is, methodologically speaking, where the rubber meets the road in *Main Street to Miracle Mile,* given his assertion that he tested and checked all of the book's conclusions by collecting empirical data in the field, from "the greatest repository of evidence on the evolution of twentieth-century roadside commerce" during 20,000 miles of cross-country driving.[112]

Denise Scott Brown also found that fieldwork noteworthy with respect to Liebs's method. Prompted by his connection to the SCA, Scott Brown argued that Liebs "approaches the roadside as an archeologist," taking this as his starting point for *excavating* the auto showrooms, gas stations, supermarkets, miniature-golf courses, drive-in theaters, motels, and restaurants that lined U.S. roads and highways beginning in the second decade of the twentieth century. Liebs, Scott Brown contended, had to "dig" for artifacts and evidence because of the paucity of "interpretive texts." Though the artifacts were still lining U.S. 1, she argued, the written records existed mainly on the pages of *Progressive Grocer* and *National Petroleum News.* "Until the everyday environment becomes part of scholarly culture, the archeological methods will prevail." Of course, Liebs's book, along with the work just surveyed, was proof that such a culture was nascent, but Scott Brown was not alone in wishing for a few more historians in this growing college of *road* scholars. Though Thomas Schlereth detected a "populist movement in architectural history" by 1981, in his view, much of this work (and he included *White Towers*) was still archeological in its most basic form, dealing with the "tentative typology" and the "preliminary classification system" and offering "a descriptive study rather than an interpretive analysis." The roadside, he concluded, "still awaits its historian—a Boorstin, a Stewart, a Giedion" who could "integrate and interpret" in the broadest cultural context its disparate artifacts, be they architectural, aesthetic, or advertising.[113]

A few years earlier, Reyner Banham had made a similar declaration about the historian on the highway, though *his* is marked by deeper intellectual longing and a considerable dash of humor: "Being a historian to the marrow, I have wished that some Pevsner of the Interstates had written a multi-volume *The Motels of America,* giving dates and attributions and off-the-cuff critiques."[114] This was a riff he began years earlier in "The Missing Motel" (see chapter 4); now, the occasion was Banham's review of David Macaulay's *Motel of the Mysteries* (1979). At autopia's twilight, Macaulay's book, as viewed through Banham's critical lens, casts long shadows on its history, historiography and archeological import. In graphic form the book tells the tale of an epic excavation that takes place two millennia after the entirety of North America was buried under a mixture of pollution and junk mail toward the end of the twentieth century. Occurring without warning in 1985, this "cataclysmic coincidence," as Macaulay describes it, preserved the civilization, Pompeii-style, for discovery by future generations, who speculate wildly on the use and meaning of what instantly became our built and manufactured detritus, including the Gateway Arch, the supersonic jet, and the push-button telephone. With Piranesian precision, Macaulay's drawings vividly portray the territories of the automobile as illegible landscapes of perplexing commercial and infrastructural ruins. The vast network of curves and stripes that cover the extent of the continent, which readers recognize as interstate lanes and cloverleaves, clearly served as extraterrestrial landing strips. How else to explain their scale and complexity (see figures 36, 43, 55) and the extent to which the built landscape had been altered to accommodate them? The inscriptions mounted on giant poles that occur in regular clusters obviously demarcated ceremonial or processional routes. How else to make sense of their color and variety? It mattered little whether Macaulay was evoking the quotidian honky-tonk of U.S. 1 on the East Coast or the pulsating grandeur of U.S. 91 in Las Vegas, so familiar were these future "monument rows" in the 1970s (see color plates 7, 8, and 16). Most of the book concerns a Howard Carter–like figure digging at a site the archeologist identifies as a "vast funerary complex," though it is obvious a typical highway motel—its massive sign, parking lot, parked cars, standardized rooms, plastic ferns, and chipped Formica astonishingly intact.[115]

When *Motel of the Mysteries* appeared in 1979 it was something of a departure for Macaulay, a Rhode Island School of Design–trained architect and illustrator whose best-known books were playful but pedagogic, introducing young readers to the wonders of architecture and planning through "you were there" recreations of the design and construction of such historic monuments as Egyptian pyramids, Roman towns, and Gothic cathedrals.[116] Though his *Great Moments in Architecture* (1978) hinted at a more sardonic or, at least, less reverential approach to iconic buildings, *Motel of the Mysteries* is fully steeped in knowing ironies. It contains sly references to a range of 1970s cultural phenomena, high and low, pop and postmodern—from Erich von Däniken's bestselling book *Chariots of the Gods?* to the Metropolitan Museum of Art's blockbuster exhibition *Treasures of Tutankhamen*, from Venturi and Scott Brown's *Learning from Las Vegas* to Philip Johnson's AT&T Building—and Macaulay's humor is, by turns, gimlet-eyed and prepubescent. Indeed, with every turn of the page, the book becomes increasingly silly, and the potty jokes alone might have been enough to consign it to the realm of juvenile literature rather than architectural discourse had Reyner Banham not decided to review *Motel of the Mysteries* in a *New Society* column of June 1980, along with Warren Belasco's *Americans on the Road*.

While Banham finds Macaulay's book amusing, he is skeptical of the implicit snobbery of his premise. In Banham's reading, *Motel of the Mysteries* is meant to be funny not because of the archaeological misinterpretations, most of which are howlers, but because of the apparent absurdity of late twentieth-century roadside effluvia ever becoming historically significant. For Banham, this was problematic not only, as he notes, because of the early work of the Society for Commercial

Archeology, but because, as we have seen, he had been poking around American highways himself since the mid-1960s, and had found plenty of examples of the drive-in typologies that he had already posited as making a serious contribution to architecture and culture. And this helps explain Banham's frustration with the glib condescension and "European contempt for motel culture" on display in *Motel of the Mysteries* (Macaulay was a Brit raised in New Jersey). As we discussed in the last chapter, in 1965 Banham had speculated that fin-de-siècle hindsight might reveal the zeitgeist of American architecture in a Midwest motel.[117] Thus, for Banham in 1980, studying motels and diners, and the highways connecting them was, in the U.S. context, as reasonable and inevitable as studying the nineteenth-century remains of the industrial revolution in the UK. Banham grasped that to comprehend the American Autopia, the historian needed to excavate the roadside—sometimes literally, through oily fieldwork on blighted strips, but also methodologically, in an almost Foucauldian sense of an archeology that scraped away the surface of cultural codes to reveal their underlying, animating ideas.

To prove his point, Banham offered, *pace* Belasco, a brief overview of the social and typological evolution of the motel, from its auto-camp origins to what he called the "mature developed form" satirized in Macaulay's book, throwing in an exegesis on the gas station for good measure. To convey a sense of knowledge apprehended from his own behind-the-wheel research into "the whole Road-American culture," Banham refers not to generic types, but to actual buildings in particular places, along specific roads. His gas station is in Remsen Corner, Ohio, just off I-271; his motel is in Groom, Texas, directly *on* U.S. 66. By the time Banham was writing this essay, the construction of I-40 had already obliterated large stretches of Route 66, and while it would be a few more years before the Mother Road was officially decertified, from Banham's perspective it was already a phantom, shadowing the interstate as it headed west along much of the historic route. For Banham, "the haunted highway" was a useful conceit for exposing the persistence of the past in the present, on the road and in the roadside literature. But Banham also understood that while I-40 had paved over much of U.S. 66, the "highway of modern legend" would continue to loom large in cultural memory—so large, in fact, that in 1990, only five years after its decertification, Congress authorized a study on how best to commemorate Route 66's "national significance."[118] The same was true of autopia as a whole: the ghost that haunted the culture of nostalgia of the 1970s was not quieted in the ensuing decades, whether earlier car-centric buildings and landscapes were documented, demolished, or derelict. Even now, in the twenty-first century, the specter of autopia is haunting America.

The pioneering work surveyed in this chapter was the beginning of an ongoing autopian reckoning, a coming to terms with the car's impact on urban and architectural thought that *American Autopia* has continued. But in excavating the ideas and attitudes that fueled this discourse in the middle of the twentieth century, this book does not lay autopia's ghost to rest. In fact, in refusing to exorcise the specter, *American Autopia* is, itself, contributing to a contemporary autopian discourse. Though this book's project is resolutely historical, in revealing autopia's views, aims, and tendencies vis-à-vis the built environment, it is relevant and even vital in the present. Right now, while roadside enthusiasts are fetishizing a bygone autopia, seeing in its monuments and artifacts a more innocent automotive age, roadside theorists are imagining autopia anew, regarding electric and autonomous vehicles, and car sharing and ride hailing, as the fulfillment of a long-sought promise: the possibility of perfectibility in the territories of the automobile, where in the United States alone 250 million motorcars travel on 2.5 million paved miles. Before we remake our metropolitan landscapes once more in the car's image, we should take a good look in the rearview mirror. In the automobile utopia, we have been down this road before.

NOTES

INTRODUCTION

1. "Disneyland Autopia," *Road & Track,* September 1955, 32. Lester Nehamkin, "Roadsters in Tomorrowland," *Hot Rod*, October 1955, 62–63.

2. "Disneyland Progress Report," *Disneyland* (American Broadcast Company, aired February 9, 1955).

3. Ub Iwerks, *Mickey Mouse in The Barn Dance* (Disney Cartoons, 1929). Walt Disney, *Mickey Mouse in Traffic Troubles* (Columbia Pictures, 1930).

4. Chester H. Liebs, *Main Street to Miracle Mile* (1985; rpt. Baltimore, Md.: Johns Hopkins University Press, 1995). Richard Longstreth, *The Drive-In, the Supermarket, and the Transformation of Commercial Space in Los Angeles, 1914–1941* (Cambridge, Ma.: MIT Press, 1999).

5. "Building Expansion Noted: Phoenix Reports Construction," *Los Angeles Times,* 6 October 1929, 76. "Autopia Motor Park," tourist brochure, 1930s. "Highway Travelers, U.S. 80, 60, 89," advertisement, *Los Angeles Times*, 3 January 1933, 128. Stewart Sterling, "How to Pick a Motel," *Los Angeles Times*, 21 August 1949, 173. "Autopia Guest Lodge Leased for Ten Years," *The Arizona Republic*, 11 April, 1949, 7.

6. Art Ryon, "Walt Disney Always Does Things Right," *Los Angeles Times,* 17 June 1959, 51. Del Schrader, "Subs, Mountains Add Lure to Disneyland," *Los Angeles Times*, 12 July 1959, 15, 17.

7. "Signals That Think as Well as Blink," *Los Angeles Times,* 25 February 1960, 45. "Freeways at the Crossroads," *Los Angeles Times*, 5 April 1964, 258.

8. Art Seidenbaum, "Wanted: A Master Plan for Urban Action," *Los Angeles Times,* 4 March 1964, 55, 60. Art Seidenbaum, "Urban Planning in Southland Has Lots of Room to Grow," *Los Angeles Times,* 16 January 1966, 341.

9. Reyner Banham, "Roadscape with Rusting Nails," *The Listener* 80 (29 August 1968): 267–68.

10. Reyner Banham, *Los Angeles: The Architecture of Four Ecologies* (1971; rpt. London: Penguin Books, 1990), 21, 23, 35.

11. Banham, *Los Angeles,* 127–28.

12. Peter Plagens, "Los Angeles: The Ecology of Evil," *Artforum* (December 1972), 67–76.

13. Banham, *Los Angeles,* 213.

14. John Pastier, "Britisher Examines Four 'Ecologies' of Los Angeles Area," *Los Angeles Times,* 13 June 1971, 140, 156.

15. Reyner Banham, "What is the Main Drag of the American Fantasy?," *Los Angeles Times West Magazine,* 8 November 1970, 36, 39, 41.

16. Quoted in Stephanie Salomon and Steve Kroeter, "Still Learning from Denise Scott Brown," *Designers & Books,* 7 January 2014, www.designersandbooks.com. Reyner Banham, "Towards a Million-Volt Light and Sound Culture," *Architectural Review* 141 (May 1967): 331.

17. Banham, "What is the Main Drag?," 39, 41.

18. Banham, "What is the Main Drag?," 41.

19. Robert Venturi and Denise Scott Brown, "A Significance for A&P Parking Lots or Learning from Las Vegas," *Architectural Forum* 128 (March 1968): 36–42, 89, 91.

20. Venturi and Scott Brown, "A Significance for A&P Parking Lots," 36.

21. Martino Stierili, *Las Vegas in the Rearview Mirror* (Los Angeles: Getty Research Institute, 2013). Aron Vinegar and Michael J. Golec, eds., *Relearning from Las Vegas* (Minneapolis: University of Minnesota Press, 2009). Nigel Whiteley, *Reyner Banham: Historian of the Immediate Future* (Cambridge. Mass.: MIT Press, 2001).

1. THE CAR AND WHAT CAME OF IT

1. Public Roads Administration, *Highway Statistics Summary to 1945* (Washington, D.C.: GPO, 1947), 18.

2. Historic American Engineering Record, *Bronx River Parkway Reservation,* HAER No. NY-327 (Washington, D.C.: National Park Service, 2001).

3. Harry W. Perry, "The New Home of the Automobile Club of America," *Scientific American* 96 (27 April 1907): 349–50. "Automobile Club of America," *Brickbuilder* 16 (May 1907): plates 65–68.

4. David Hennen Morris quoted in "The Laying of the ACA Cornerstone," *The Automobile* 14 (29 March 1906): 571.

5. Ernest W. Burgess, "The Growth of the City," in Robert E. Park, Ernest W. Burgess, and Roderick D. McKenzie, *The City* (1925; rpt. Chicago: University of Chicago Press, 1967), 60.

6. "Pittsburgh Show Has Attendance of 8,500 on Opening Night," *The Automobile* 30 (22 January 2014): 278.

7. Gulf Refining Company advertisement, reprinted in Craig Thompson, *Since Spindletop: A Human Story of Gulf's First Half-Century* (Pittsburgh, Pa.: Gulf Oil Company, 1951), 62.

8. "J. H. Giesey Dies Houston, Texas, November 13," *Dallas Morning News,* 14 November 1938, 10.

9. Henry Van Brunt, "The Present State of Architecture," in Brunt, *Greek Lines and Other Architectural Essays* (Boston: Houghton, Mifflin, 1893), 221–22.

10. Mary Woods, "The First American Architectural Journals," *Journal of the Society of Architectural Historians* 48 (June 1989): 130–38. "The Automobile Carriage in Europe," *American Architect and Building News* 65 (15 July 1899): 18.

11. "A Long Road and Old," *Architectural Record* 24 (July 1908): 73. "Widening Fifth Avenue," *Architectural Record* 24 (September 1908): 244.

12. "Latin Inscriptions for Public Buildings," *American Architect and Building News* 92 (23 November 1907): 162. "The Structural Design of Buildings," *American Architect and Building News* 87 (25 February 1905): 56.

13. "Garage in Brooklyn," *Brickbuilder* 19 (January 1910): plate 6. "Garage and Studio in Marion," *Brickbuilder* 19 (August 1910): plate 110.

14. "The Brickbuilder's Annual Architectural Terra Cotta Competition: A Public Garage," *Brickbuilder* 21 (October 1912): 282.

15. "The Increasing Importance of Good Architecture in Farm Buildings, *American Architect* 107 (10 March 1915): 169.

16. F. A. Fairbrother, "Planning of Automobile Sales & Service Buildings, Part I," *Architectural Forum* 33 (August 1920): 39.

17. Wirt C. Rowland, "Architecture and the Automobile Industry," *Architectural Forum* 32 (June 1921): 199, 206, 204, 201.

18. "News from Various Sources," *American Architect* 117 (5 May 1920): 560. "Special Correspondence," *American Architect* 117 (26 May 1920): 658. "A New Building for the Motor Transport Industry," *American Architect* 119 (6 April 1921): 429.

19. A. D. Taylor, "Garage and Entrance Turns," *American Architect* 115 (21 May 1919): 699. "Data for the Planning of Public Garages," *Architectural Forum* 37 (November 1922): 62.

20. Charles George Ramsey and Harold Reeve Sleeper, *Architectural Graphic Standards* (1932; facsimile ed. New York: John Wiley & Sons, 1989), 199, 200–201.

21. Tyler Stewart Rogers, "Automobile and the Private Estate: Dimensions of Automobiles," *Architectural Forum* 32 (April 1920): 171–74.

22. Preston J. Bradshaw, "An Automobile Sales and Service Building," *Architectural Forum* 34 (February 1921): 65.

23. Alexander C. Guth, "The Automobile Service Station," *Architectural Forum* 45 (July 1926): 33–40, 48, 41–42.

24. Guth, "The Automobile Service Station," 33–40.

25. Mardges Bacon, *Le Corbusier in America* (Cambridge, Mass.: MIT Press, 2001), 18–19.

26. Michael A. Mikkelson, "A Word about the New Format," *Architectural Record* 63 (January 1928): 1–2.

27. Erich Mendelsohn, *Amerika* (1926; rpt. Mineola, NY: Dover Publications, 1993), xi.

28. Hyungmin Pai, *The Portfolio and the Diagram* (Cambridge. Mass.: MIT Press, 2002), 150–52. Susanne Lichtenstein, "Editing Architecture: Architectural Record and the Growth of Modern Architecture, 1928–1938" (PhD diss., Cornell University, 1990), 543–54.

29. Suzanne Strum, "Informational Architectures of the SSA and Knud Lönberg-Holm," *Nexus Network Journal* 14 (2012): 35–52. Paul Makovsky (research by Marc Dessauce), "The Invisible Architect of Invisible Architecture," *Metropolis,* June 2014, 102–18.

30. K. Lönberg-Holm, "The Gasoline Filling and Service Station," *Architectural Record* 67 (June 1930): 561–62.

31. Lönberg-Holm, "Gasoline Filling and Service Station," 563.

32. Lönberg-Holm, "Gasoline Filling and Service Station," 564, 577, 584.

33. Table 3.6, "Vehicles per Thousand People in the United States, 1900–2012," in Stacy C. Davis, Susan W. Diegel and Robert G. Boundy, *Transportation Energy Data Book:* (Oak Ridge, Tenn.: U.S. Department of Energy, July 2014).

34. Lönberg-Holm, "Gasoline Filling and Service Station," 582, 570–71, 578.

35. Lönberg-Holm, "Gasoline Filling and Service Station," 580.

36. Lönberg-Holm quoted in Andrew M. Shanken, "From the Gospel of Efficiency to Modernism," *Design Issues* 21 (Spring 2005): 39.

37. Lönberg-Holm, "Gasoline Filling and Service Station," 579, 570.

38. Liebs, *Main Street to Miracle Mile,* 99–100.

39. Lönberg-Holm, "Gasoline Filling and Service Station," 571.

40. Hannes Meyer to K. Lönberg Holm, 17 September 1929, author's translation. Hannes Meyer, "Building/Bauen" (1928) in *Programs and Manifestoes on 20th-Century Architecture,* ed. Ulrich Conrads, trans. Michael Bullock (Cambridge. Mass.: MIT Press, 1970), 120.

41. Myron W. Serby, "Stadium Planning and Design," *Architectural Record* 69 (February 1931): 162–63. Myron W. Serby, *The Stadium* (New York: American Institute of Steel, 1930), 10.

42. "Illustrated News: Camden Drive-In," *Architectural Record* 74 (August 1933): 146. Richard M. Hollingshead Jr., "Drive-In Theater," U.S. Patent No. 1909537 (Washington, D.C.: U.S. Patent and Trademark Office, 1933).

43. Mendelsohn's visit is mentioned in Anthony Alofsin, *Frank Lloyd Wright: Europe and Beyond* (Berkeley: University of California Press, 1999), 215n13. Wright, quoted in Mark Reinberger, "The Sugarloaf Mountain Project and Frank Lloyd Wright's Vision of a New World," *Journal of the Society of Architectural Historians* 43 (March 1984): 48.

44. Wright quoted in Reinberger, "The Sugarloaf Mountain Project," 48. Frank Lloyd Wright, *Modern Architecture* (1931; rpt. Princeton, N.J.: Princeton University Press, 2008), 109–11.

45. Lewis Mumford, *Technics and Civilization* (New York: Harcourt, Brace and Company, 1934), 236–37, 271–72. Knud Lönberg-Holm, "Planning the Retail Store," *Architectural Record* 69 (June 1931): 497.

46. Frederick Lewis Allen, *Only Yesterday* (1931; rpt. New York: John Wiley & Sons, 1997), 4–5, 126. Robert S. Lynd and Helen Merrell Lynd, *Middletown* (1929; rpt. New York: Harcourt, Brace & World, 1956), 253–54.

47. Lönberg-Holm, "Planning the Retail Store," 499, 514.

48. See Howard Whipple Green, "Retail Outlets per 1000 Families," *Architectural Record* 80 (August 1936): 85–90.

49. Frederick Kiesler, *Contemporary Art Applied to the Store and Its Display* (New York: Brentano's, 1930), 85–87.

50. Lönberg-Holm, "Planning the Retail Store," 514. Park and Shop appears on page 499, identified only by name and location.

51. Richard Longstreth, "The Neighborhood Shopping Center in Washington, D.C., 1930–1941," *Journal of the Society of Architectural Historians* 51 (March 1992): 14. See also Longstreth, *The Drive-in*, 33–76.

52. "Proposed Drive-In Market, Los Angeles," *Architectural Record* 65 (June 1929): 606.

53. "Neighborhood Shopping Centers," *Architectural Record* 71 (May 1932): 331–32. See also Thomas S. Hines, "Designing for the Motor Age: Richard Neutra and the Automobile," *Oppositions* 21 (Summer 1980): 46. Longstreth, *The Drive-in*, 63–68.

54. "Neighborhood Shopping Centers," 325–32.

55. "Building Types: Community Shopping Centers," *Architectural Record* 87 (June 1940): 100–101, 103, 104–6.

56. Clarence S. Stein and Catherine Bauer, "Store Buildings and Neighborhood Shopping Centers," reprinted with addenda from *Architectural Record* 77 (February 1934): 1–13.

57. Morris Ketchum, "Services for Sale," *Architectural Record* 90 (July 1941): 84–85, 88–89.

58. Roger W. Sherman, "The Ivory Tower and the Motor-Car," *Architectural Forum* 54 (February 1931): 224.

59. Public Roads Administration, *Highway Statistics Summary to 1945*, 18.

60. William Orr Ludlow, "Leisure Seen as a Stimulus to Business" in "How Can Architects Develop Business?," *Architectural Record* 73 (May 1933): 310.

61. S. J. Warberg, "Notes on Drafting and Design," *Architectural Record* 68 (July 1930): 71. Harvey Wiley Corbett, "Skyscrapers, Garages and Congestion," *Architectural Forum* 52 (June 1930): 825–26. Gilmore D. Clarke, "Transportation—An Expanding Field for Modern Building," *Architectural Record* 90 (October 1941): 43.

62. "Portfolio of Special Building Types: Roadside Diners for Motorists," *Architectural Record* 76 (July 1934): 56–57. W. F. R. Ballard, "Spacefield Village, A Princeton Thesis," *Architectural Record* 72 (November 1932): 333–35.

63. "Auto City Yields Motorized Market," *Architectural Record* 83 (April 1938): 68. Raymond Hood, "A City under a Single Roof," *The Nation's Business* 17 (November 1929): 18–20.

64. "Building Types Study: Recreation Structures, *Architectural Record* 89 (April 1941): 84–85. "Portfolio of Stores and Shops," *Architectural Record* 76 (December 1934): 454. "Automobile Shopping Centers," *Architectural Record* 76 (July 1934): 43.

65. "New Theater in Pineapple Land Designed for Autoists," *Architectural Record* 83 (April 1938): 53–54.

66. Figures cited in "Roadside Cabins for Tourists," *Architectural Record* 74 (December 1933): 457. John J. McCarthy and Robert Littell, "Three Hundred Thousand Shacks," *Harper's*, July 1933, 182.

67. "Roadside Cabins for Tourists," 458–59. "Portfolio of Special Building Types: Tourist Cabins," *Architectural Record* (February 1935): 95–97.

68. Douglas Haskell, "Architecture on Routes U.S. 40 & 66," *Architectural Record* 81 (May 1937): 19.

69. Wright quoted in Reinberger, "The Sugarloaf Mountain Project," 46. Wright, *Modern Architecture,* 109–11.

70. Lönberg-Holm, "Gasoline Service and Filling Station," 584, 563. Lönberg-Holm, "Planning the Retail Store," 497.

71. Henry Adams, *The Education of Henry Adams* (Boston and New York: Houghton & Mifflin Company, 1918), 380, 469–70.

72. "Automobility," *New York Times* 3 March 1922, 12; "Automobility," *New York Times*, 7 July 1931, 22.

73. Cotten Seiler, *Republic of Drivers* (Chicago: University of Chicago Press, 2008), 1–16.

74. Wright, *Modern Architecture,* 62.

75. Stiles O. Clements, "Los Angeles: New Store Provides for Motorized Patron," *Architectural Record* 84 (November 1938): 43. Richard Longstreth, *City Center to Regional Mall* (Cambridge, Mass.: MIT Press, 1997), 136–38.

76. "Mobility: A Controlling Factor in Design," *Architectural Record* 84 (August 1938): 67–68.

77. Louis M. Hacker, Rudolf Modley, and George R. Taylor, *The United States: A Graphic History* (New York: Modern Age Books, 1937), 81, 87.

78. Burgess, "Growth of the City," 58–60.

79. "Mobility," 68.

80. "Mobility," 69. The same image of the pretzel also appears in Sigfried Giedion, *Space, Time, and Architecture,* 5th edition (Cambridge, Mass.: Harvard University Press, 1969), 829.

81. National Resources Committee, *The Problems of a Changing Population* (Washington, D.C.: GPO, 1938), 117. Lawrence B. Anderson, John E. Burchard, and Frederick G. Fassett, "American Architecture: 1891–1941, Part II," *Architectural Record* 89 (February 1941): 35.

82. Anderson et al., "American Architecture, Part II," 37.

2. ROADSIDE METROPOLIS

1. Ulrich Keller, *The Highway as Habitat* (Santa Barbara, Calif.: University Art Museum, 1986), 9. Karl Raitz, "American Roads, Roadside America," *Geographical Review* 88 (July 1998): 368.

2. See Kathleen Hulser, "Visual Browsing," in *Suburban Discipline,* ed. Peter Lang (New York: Princeton Architectural Press, 1997), 8–19. Mitchell Schwarzer, *Zoomscape* (New York: Princeton Architectural Press, 2004), 70–117. Iain Borden, *Drive* (London: Reaktion Books, 2013), chapters 1–3.

3. Federal Highway Administration, "State Motor Vehicle Registrations, by Years, 1900–1995," Highway Statistics Summary to 1995, https://www.fhwa.dot.gov/ohim/summary95/mv200.pdf. Office of Public Roads and Rural Engineering, *Bulletin No. 390: Public Road Mileage and Revenues in the United States* (Washington, D.C.: GPO, 1914), 5.

4. Edgar Chambless, *Roadtown* (New York: Roadtown Press, 1910), 40, 46–47, 116, 37–38, 184.

5. Quoted in "A One-Line City Plan to Avoid Congestion," *New York Times,* 19 March 1933, sec. 8, 6.

6. Warren H, Manning, "If the State Is to Grow," *New York Times,* 20 November 1921, sec. 7, 4, 6. Manning quoted in "State and National Planning, *New York Times,* 21 November 1921, 14. J. Ogden Armour, "Good Roads, Past and Present," *American Architect* 117 (30 June 1920): 797.

7. Benton MacKaye, "An Appalachian Trail," *American Institute of Architects Journal* 9 (October 1921): 325–30.

8. Lewis Mumford, "The Fourth Migration," *The Survey,* 1 May 1925, 130–33.

9. Clyde L. King, "Foreword to *The Automobile,*" *Annals of the American Academy of Political Science* 116 (November 1924): vii. M. H. James, "The Automobile and Recreation," *Annals* 116 (November 1924): 33–34. William Joseph Showalter, "The Automobile and the Pioneer," *Annals* 116 (November 1924): 21.

10. Benton MacKaye, *The New Exploration* (1928; rpt. Urbana: University of Illinois Press, 1956), 54–55.

11. Benton MacKaye, "The Townless Highway," *New Republic,* 12 March 1930, 93–95. Benton

MacKaye and Lewis Mumford, "Townless Highways for the Motorist," *Harper's,* August 1931, 347–56.

12. New England Regional Planning Commission, *The Problem of the Roadside,* Publication No. 56 (Boston: National Resources Committee, 1939), frontispiece.

13. Karal Ann Marling, *The Colossus of Roads* (Minneapolis: University of Minnesota Press, 1984), 43.

14. Max Horkheimer and Theodor W. Adorno, *Dialectic of Enlightenment* (1987; ed. Gunzelin Schmid Noerr, trans. Edmund Jephcott, Stanford: Stanford University Press, 2002), 94–136, 183–84. See also Detlev Claussen, "Intellectual Transfer: Theodor W. Adorno's American Experience," *New German Critique* 97 (Winter 2006): 5–14.

15. James Agee, "The Great American Roadside," *Fortune,* September 1934, 53–56, 177.

16. Agee, "Great American Roadside," 53.

17. This was two years before they collaborated on *Let Us Now Praise Famous Men.* Judith Keller, "Evans and Agee: The Great American Roadside," *History of Photography* 16 (Summer 1992):170–71.

18. Agee, "Great American Roadside," 54, 58, 172.

19. Agee, "Great American Roadside," 61. Allred, *American Modernism and Depression Documentary* (New York: Oxford University Press, 2010), 119.

20. Agee, "Great American Roadside," 177.

21. Lewis Mumford, "Writers' Project," *New Republic,* 20 October 1937, 306–8.

22. Christine Bold, *The WPA Guides: Mapping America* (Jackson: University of Mississippi Press, 1999), xiii–xvi.

23. Federal Writers' Project, *Idaho* (Caldwell, Idaho: Caxton Printers, 1937), 78, 86, 160, 170, 206, 210, 246–47, 269.

24. Sterling Brown, "The Negro in Washington," in Federal Writers' Project, *Washington* (Washington, D.C.: GPO, 1937), v, 68–91, 150, 198–99, 513, 710.

25. Federal Writers' Project, *Idaho,* 196, 284.

26. Federal Writers' Project, *Washington,* 7, 112, 574–75, 773–86.

27. Frederick Gutheim, "America in Guide Books," *Saturday Review of Literature,* 14 June 1941, 3.

28. Federal Writers' Project, *Wyoming* (1941; rpt. New York: Oxford University Press, 1956), 4.

29. Alsberg quoted in Jerrold Hirsch, *Portrait of America: A Cultural History of the Federal Writers' Project* (Chapel Hill: University of North Carolina Press, 2003), 91. Katherine Kellock, "The WPA Writers," *American Scholar* 9 (Autumn 1940): 476.

30. Federal Writers' Project, *Washington,* 773, 776, 837.

31. Federal Writers' Project, *U.S. One: Maine to Florida* (New York: Modern Age Books, 1938), iii, xi–xv.

32. "Tooling Down This Side of America," *New York Times,* 20 March 1938, sec. 7, 5.

33. Quoted in Bold, *The WPA Guides,* 66.

34. Federal Writers' Project, *U.S. One,* xvii–xviii.

35. Kellock to Alsberg, Jacksonville, Florida, 20 January 1936 in *Field Reports,* Records of the Federal Writers' Project, National Archives Record Group 69.5.5, Washington, D.C. Kellock quoted in Hirsch, *Portrait of America,* 55–56; Bold, *The WPA Guides,* 68.

36. Ilya Ilf and Eugene Petrov, *Little Golden America,* trans. Charles Malamuth (New York: Farrar & Rinehart, 1937), 81.

37. They don't identify the location; the highway sign indicates NJ-40 east of Camden. Erika Wolf, ed., *Ilf and Petrov's American Road Trip* (New York: Princeton Architectural Press, 2007), 13.

38. Gutheim, "America in Guide Books," 3.

39. Kellock, "The WPA Writers," 474.

40. Federal Writers' Project, *U.S. One,* 124, 127–30.

41. Federal Writers' Project, *U.S. One,* 124, 127, 131.

42. "FSA Permanent Shooting Assignment: The Highway," reprinted in Keller, "Evans and Agee," 203.

43. Dorothea Lange, "New Mexico Desert, Highway No. 70," June 1938. Arthur Rothstein, "Highway U.S. 40 through Elko County, Nevada," March 1940. Arthur Rothstein, "Lincoln Highway approaching Paradise, Pennsylvania," December 1941. All in Library of Congress, Farm Security Administration–Office of War Information Photographic Collection.

44. "America: Millions of People Set out to See Their Country," *Life,* 27 June 1938, 24.

45. Frank Lloyd Wright, "*Broadacre City:* An Architect's Vision," *New York Times Magazine*, 20 March 1932, 8–9.

46. "America: It Is Big," *Life,* 27 June 1938, 41.

47. Frank Lloyd Wright, "Broadacre City," *Architectural Record* 77 (April 1935): 243–54.

48. Wright, "*Broadacre City:* An Architect's Vision," 8–9.

49. "America: It Is Big," 41.

50. John Gunther, *Inside U.S.A.* (1947; rpt. New York: New Press, 1997), 912. Arthur Schlesinger Jr., "Foreword to the 1997 Edition," *Inside U.S.A.,* xvii, xix.

51. Gunther, *Inside U.S.A.,* 910, 217, 597, 277, x–xiii, 72.

52. Gunther, *Inside U.S.A.,* 147, 339, 230, 43–45.

53. Gunther, *Inside U.S.A.,* 277.

54. George R. Stewart, *Names on the Land* (1945; rpt. New York: New York Review of Books, 2008), 4.

55. Stegner quoted in Donald M. Scott, *The Life and Truth of George R. Stewart* (Jefferson, N.C.: McFarland, 2012), 143–44.

56. George R. Stewart, *U.S. 40: Cross Section of the United States of America* (Boston: Houghton Mifflin, 1953), 9, 35, 3.

57. "Books Briefly Noted: *U.S. 40: Cross Section of the United States of America*," *New Yorker*, 28 March 1953, 132.

58. Hilaire Belloc, *The Old Road* (1903; rpt. London: Constable and Company, 1911), 3–4. Hilaire Belloc, *The Road* (London: T. Fisher Unwin, 1924), n.p.

59. See Jorge Otero-Pailos, "Eucharistic Architecture: Jean Labatut and the Search for Pure Sensation," in Otero-Pailos, *Architecture's Historical Turn* (Minneapolis: University of Minnesota Press, 2010), 25–63.

60. "Princeton Adds 'Listening Post,'" *New York Times*, 20 July 1941, D4.

61. Melville C. Branch Jr., "Too Little Planning Too Late," *Princeton Alumni Weekly*, 24 April 1942, 7–9.

62. Bureau of Urban Research, *Urban Planning and Public Opinion* (Princeton University, Publication Series No. 2, February 1942), 9–17.

63. Jean Labatut, "Introduction," in *Highways in Our National Life*, ed. Labatut and J. Wheaton Lane (Princeton, N.J.: Princeton University Press, 1950), v–vi.

64. Robert Moses, "Indian Trails, Roman Roads, and the Express Highways of Today," *New York Times Book Review*, 4 June 1950, 4. Stewart, *U.S. 40*, 311.

65. John O. Brew, "The Highway and the Anthropologist," in Labatut and Lane, *Highways in Our National Life*, 4–6, 9.

66. Frances E. Merrill, "The Highway and Social Problems," in Labatut and Lane, *Highways in Our National Life*, 135–43.

67. Carle C. Zimmerman, "The Highway from the Point of View of a Sociologist," in Labatut and Lane, *Highways in Our National Life*, 123–34.

68. Walter Firey, Charles P. Loomis, and J. Allan Beegle, "The Fusion of Urban and Rural," in Labatut and Lane, *Highways in Our National Life*, 154–63. Labatut, "Summation," in Labatut and Lane, *Highways in Our National Life*, 472–75.

69. Stewart, *U.S. 40*, 4–5, 134–35.

70. Stewart, *U.S. 40*, 4–5, 22–23.

71. Stewart, *U.S. 40*, 29, 78–79, 300, 23.

72. Firey et al., "The Fusion of Urban and Rural," 154–63.

73. Stewart, *U.S. 40*, 5, 298–300. J. B. Jackson, "Books," *Landscape* 3, no. 1 (Summer 1953): 29.

74. Jean Gottmann, "Revolution in Land Use," *Landscape* 8, no. 2 (Winter 1958–59): 15–21. Jean Gottmann, "Megalopolis," *Economic Geography* 33 (July 1957): 189–200.

75. "Megalopolis, U.S.A." *New York Times*, 25 January 1953, sec. 4, 9. "Study to Consider Seaboard as a City," *New York Times*, 14 January 1957, 34. "City Chain in East Forming a System," *New York Times*, 26 May 1958, 32. Jean Gottmann, *Megalopolis* (New York: Twentieth Century Fund, 1961), 16, 9, 770.

76. Gottmann, *Megalopolis*, 5, 385–92, 8, 17.

77. Gottmann, *Megalopolis,* 773, 12, 684, 390. Rem Koolhaas, *Delirious New York* (1978; rpt. New York: Monacelli Press, 1994), 10. Gottmann, *Megalopolis,* 15, 215, 772, 9.

78. Gottmann, *Megalopolis,* vii.

3. AUTOPIA AND ITS DISCONTENTS

1. Federal Highway Administration, "State Motor Vehicle Registrations, by Years, 1900–1995," Highway Statistics Summary to 1995, https://www.fhwa.dot.gov/ohim/summary95/mv200.pdf.

2. Morton and Lucia White, *The Intellectual versus the City* (Oxford, UK: Oxford University Press, 1962), 1. William H. Jordy, "Review of *The Intellectual versus the City,*" *Mississippi Valley Historical Review* 49 (March 1963): 683–85. Ogden Nash, "Song of the Open Road," *New Yorker,* 15 October 1932, 18.

3. Frederick Lewis Allen, *The Big Change* (New York: Harper & Brothers, 1952), 122–31.

4. Sinclair Lewis, *Main Street* (New York: Harcourt, Brace & Howe, 1920), n.p. F. Scott Fitzgerald, *The Great Gatsby* (New York: Charles Scribner's Sons, 1925), 26.

5. [Paul Peters], "Speaking of Pictures—Road Signs," *Life.* 27 June 1938, 4–6.

6. Margaret Bourke-White, Photographs 50699959 and 50693763, LIFE Picture Collection, Getty Images.

7. [Peters], "Speaking of Pictures," 5. "What to See in America," *Life* (27 June 1938), 32.

8. Daniel Bluestone, "Roadside Blight and the Reform of Commercial Architecture" in *Roadside America,* ed. Jan Jennings (Ames: Iowa State University Press, 1990), 170–84. Catherine Gudis, *Buyways* (New York: Routledge, 2004), 163–95.

9. Jesse Merle Bennett, *Roadsides* (Boston: Stratford Company, 1936), 162. New England Regional Planning Commission, *Problem of the Roadside,* 8.

10. David R. Levin, *Public Control of Highway Access and Roadside Development* (Washington, D.C.: GPO, January 1947), 5–6.

11. Levin, *Public Control of Highway Access,* 2–4.

12. Stuart Chase, "The Mad Hatter's Dirty Teacup," *Harper's,* April 1930, 581, 583.

13. Frederick Lewis Allen, "Crisis in the Suburbs: The Big Change in Suburbia, Part II," *Harper's,* July 1954, 47–53. Frederick Lewis Allen, "Crisis in the Suburbs: The Big Change in Suburbia, Part I," *Harper's,* June 1954, 23–28.

14. Bernard DeVoto, "The Easy Chair: Notes from a Wayside Inn," *Harper's,* June 1940, 445–48. W. H. Auden, "Introduction to *The American Scene,*" in *The Complete Works of W.H. Auden,* ed. Edward Mendelsohn (Princeton, N.J.: Princeton University Press, 2002), 282.

15. Bernard DeVoto, "The Easy Chair: Motel Town," *Harper's,* September 1953, 45–48.

16. DeVoto, "Motel Town," 45–48.

17. [John Kouwenhoven], "After Hours: American Landscape I," *Harper's,* January 1950, 101.

18. Bernard DeVoto, "The Easy Chair: Outdoor Metropolis," *Harper's,* October 1955, 12–21.

19. David Riesman and Eric Larrabee, "Autos in America," *Encounter,* May 1957, 35. Carl Feiss, "Highways and Land Use: Myths and Mysteries of the Master Plan [Z1741]," in Urban Land Institute, *The New Highways: Challenge to the Metropolitan Region* (Bloomfield: Connecticut General Life Insurance Company, 1958), 3. Lewis Mumford, "Skyway's the Limit" *New Yorker,* 11 November 1959, 186.

20. E. B. White, "Letter from the East," *New Yorker,* 24 December 1955, 60–64. J. B. Jackson, "Other-Directed Houses," *Landscape* 6 (Winter 1956–57), 29–30.

21. Herbert Brean, "Dead End for the U.S. Highway," *Life,* 30 May 1955, 104–6, 109–10, 112, 115–16, 118. Wilfred Owen, *Cities in the Motor Age* (New York: Viking Press, 1959), n.p.

22. Christopher Tunnard, "Scene," *Architectural Review* 108 (December 1950): 345–47.

23. Mira Engler uses this term in *Cut and Paste Urban Landscape: The Work of Gordon Cullen* (Abingdon and New York: Routledge, 2016), 114–15. See Gordon Cullen, "Townscape Casebook," *Architectural Review* 106 (December 1949): 363–74.

24. Tunnard, "Scene," 345–47.

25. "Case Study: Details," *Architectural Review* 108 (December 1950): 376.

26. Christopher Tunnard et al., "Case Study: City," *Architectural Review* 108 (December 1950): 361–62.

27. Henry-Russell Hitchcock, "Autumn 1950: The Way Things Are," *Architectural Review* 108 (December 1950): 389, 393. Henry-Russell Hitchcock, *The Architecture of H. H. Richardson and His Times* (1936; rev. Cambridge, Mass.: MIT Press, 1961), 302–3.

28. "Towards a New Environment," *Architectural Review* 108 (December 1950): 396, 387.

29. "Man Made America: Introduction," *Architectural Review* 108 (December 1950): 339–42. "Man Made America: Conclusion," *Architectural Review* 108 (December 1950): 414–16.

30. "Man Made America: Introduction," 339–42. "Man Made America: Conclusion," 414–16. Mies quoted in Philip C. Johnson, *Mies van der Rohe* (New York: Museum of Modern Art, 1947), 183.

31. "Poor Old U.S.," *Time,* 5 February 1951, 48. Douglas Haskell, "Architecture on U.S. 40 and 66," *Architectural Review* 81 (February 1937): 101–8.

32. Douglas Haskell, "A Reply to: Man Made America," *Architectural Forum* 94 (April 1951): 158–59. Douglas Haskell, "Can Roadtown Be Damned?," *Architectural Forum* 103 (December 1955): 166.

33. Douglas Haskell, "Architecture in America, Part I," *Architectural Forum* 103 (September 1955): 107–12.

34. Douglas Haskell, "Architecture in America, Part II," *Architectural Forum* 103 (October 1955): 120, 117. Mary Mix Foley, "The Debacle of Public Taste," *Architectural Forum* 106 (Feb-

ruary 1957): 1. See Janet Abu-Lughod and Mary Mix Foley, "Consumer Strategies" in Nelson N. Foote, et al., *Housing Choices and Housing Constraints* (New York: McGraw-Hill, 1960), 71–271.

35. Foley, "The Debacle of Public Taste," 142–43.

36. Foley, "The Debacle of Public Taste," 143–44.

37. Foley, "The Debacle of Public Taste," 144–45, 238, 240.

38. Foley, "The Debacle of Public Taste," 240, 242, 244, 246, 248.

39. Douglas Haskell, *Building, U.S.A.* (New York: McGraw-Hill, 1957), v. Foley's essay is reprinted as "The Public," 112–29.

40. "Forum Editors Reply," *Architectural Forum* 103 (September 1956): 113. Foley, "The Public," 124, 128.

41. [John K. Jessup], "American—the Beautiful?," *Life,* 3 June 1957, 34.

42. William H. Whyte, *The Organization Man* (1956; rpt. Garden City, N.Y.: Doubleday, 1957), 10, 347, 12, 331, 301, 337.

43. Whyte, *The Organization Man,* 372, 305.

44. Orville Prescott, "Books of the Times: *The Organization Man,*" *New York Times,* 14 December 1956, 27.

45. Robert Bruegmann, *Sprawl: A Compact History* (Chicago: University of Chicago Press, 2005), 119.

46. Paul Windels. "The Metropolitan Region at the Crossroads," in *American Planning and Civic Annual* (Washington, D.C.: American Planning and Civic Association, 1948), 61–66.

47. Catherine Bauer, "First Job: Control New-City Sprawl," *Architectural Forum* 105 (September 1956): 105–12.

48. Bauer, "First Job," 106–12.

49. "Highwaymen at Work," *Life,* 5 August 1957, 26.

50. William H. Whyte, "A Plan to Save Vanishing U.S. Countryside," *Life,* 17 August 1959, 88–90, 92, 94, 96, 99–100, 102.

51. See Felix Belair Jr., "President Sets Up Goals Commission," *New York Times,* 4 February 1960, 18.

52. William H. Whyte, "Urban Sprawl" in *The Exploding Metropolis,* ed. William H. Whyte (1958; rpt. Berkeley: University of California Press, 1993), 133–34.

53. President's Advisory Committee on a National Highway Program, *A 10-Year National Highway Program: Report to the President* (Washington, D.C.: GPO, 1955), 26.

54. Whyte, "Urban Sprawl," 115.

55. Whyte, "Introduction," in *Exploding Metropolis,* 9, 8. Francis Bello, "The City and the Car" in *Exploding Metropolis,* 37.

56. Charles Grutzner, "Rise of the Urban Region," *New York Times,* 27 January 1957, 1, 72.

57. Harrison E. Salisbury, "Cities in the Grip of Revolution," *New York Times Book Review,* 5 October 1958, 1, 20. Charles Poore, "Books of the Times," *New York Times,* 9 October 1958, 35.

58. Roland Barthes, "The New Citroën (1955)," in Barthes, *Mythologies* (1957; trans. Annette Lavers, New York: Noonday Press, 1972), 88. Flaminio Bertoni was stylist for the DS; André Lefèbvre was the engineer.

59. Alvin Toffler claimed that between 1950 and 1970, the United States completed 200 miles of paved roads every day. *Future Shock* (New York: Bantam Books, 1970), 76.

60. Riesman and Larrabee, "Autos in America," 34.

61. Lewis Mumford, "The Highway and the City," *Architectural Record* 123 (April 1958): 179–80. Mumford reprinted the essay in *The Highway and the City* (New York: Harcourt, Brace & World, 1963), 234–46, eliminating the headings and the illustrations.

62. Mumford, "The Highway and the City," 185. Mumford, *The Highway and the City,* 242–43.

63. Frank Lloyd Wright, "Town Hall Lecture, Ford Auditorium," Detroit, October 21 1957, reprinted in *Truth Against the World,* ed. Patrick J. Meehan (New York: Wiley, 1987), 144–45.

64. Wright, "Town Hall Lecture," 145.

65. Mumford, "The Highway and the City," 170.

66. Quoted in *To New Horizons,* dir. Jam Handy (Detroit: General Motors, 1940) and *Give Yourself the Green Light*, dir. Jam Handy (Detroit: General Motors, 1954).

67. Mumford, "The Highway and the City," 181.

68. Peter Blake, "The Ugly America," *Horizon,* May 1961, 4–19. Peter Blake, "The Suburbs Are a Mess," *Saturday Evening Post,* 5 October 1963, 14–16. Peter Blake, *God's Own Junkyard* (New York: Holt, Rinehart and Winston, 1964), 7–9, 14, 16.

69. Blake, *God's Own Junkyard,* 7–9, 14, 16. Peter Blake, *No Place Like Utopia* (New York: Alfred A. Knopf, 1993), 293.

70. Blake, *God's Own Junkyard,* 140, 141, 142.

71. Blake, *God's Own Junkyard,* 8–9, 142.

72. Blake, *God's Own Junkyard,* 32.

73. Robert Venturi, *Complexity and Contradiction in Architecture* (New York: MoMA, 1966), 102–3.

74. John Auwaeter, "The Big Duck National Register Nomination Form," 1997.

75. See Venturi and Scott Brown, "A Significance for A&P Parking Lots," 36–43, 91. Robert Venturi and Denise Scott Brown, "On Ducks and Decoration," *Architecture Canada* 45 (October 1968): 48–49.

76. Paul Ylvisaker, "The Villains Are Greed, Indifference—and You," *Life,* 24 December 1965, 92–93. Peter Blake, "Astride the Open Road," *Life,* 24 December 1965, 49. Blake, *God's Own Junkyard,* 7.

4. LEARNING FROM AUTOPIA

1. Bureau of the Census, U.S. Department of Commerce, "Population of Urbanized Areas: April 1, 1950," in *1950 Census of Population: Preliminary Counts,* Series PC-3, No. 9 (February 1, 1951), 1–2. Michael Ratcliffe, *U.S. Census Bureau: A Century of Delineating a Changing Landscape* (white paper), December 2016, 2–3.

2. Turpin C. Bannister, ed., *The Architect at Mid-Century: Evolution and Achievement* (New York: Reinhold Publishing, 1954), 4–6, 8–9, 175, 407. Francis Bellamy, ed. *The Architect at Mid-Century: Conversations across the Nation* (New York: Reinhold Publishing, 1954), 19.

3. Gordon quoted in Bellamy, *The Architect at Mid-Century: Conversations,* 19.

4. Wright, "*Broadacre City:* An Architect's Vision," 9. Wright, "Town Hall Lecture," 146.

5. Stuart Preston, "North of New York," *New York Times,* 11 August 1957, Sec. 2, 6. "Symbolic Setting: Fine New Building Meets Challenge of City Crisis," *Life*, 21 October 1957, 49. Richard H. Parke, "Housing Is Linked to Road Planning," *New York Times,* 10 September 1957, 35.

6. James Rouse, "The Highways and Urban Growth," in Urban Land Institute, *The New Highways, Technical Bulletin No. 31* (1957), 27–29. John Ely Burchard, "Caliban or Ariel? [Z1785]," in *The New Highways: Challenge to the Metropolitan Region,* 7–9.

7. "Excerpts: What People Said at Connecticut General's Symposium on Highways," *Architectural Forum* 107 (November 1957): 197. Lewis Mumford, "Address [Z1792]," in *The New Highways: Challenge to the Metropolitan Region,* 3–5.

8. Wilfred Owen, *The Metropolitan Transportation Problem* (Washington, D.C.: Brookings Institution, 1956), 8, 24–25, 31, 252–54.

9. Owen, *Cities in the Motor Age,* 3. Here, Owen summarized the papers and panels in a single narrative.

10. Haskell, "Architecture on Routes U.S. 40 & 66," 18–19, 22.

11. Haskell, "Can Roadtown Be Damned?," 166.

12. Haskell, "Architecture in America, Part II," 116–17.

13. Haskell, "Architecture in America, Part I," 111–12. Haskell, "Architecture in America, Part II," 120. Douglas Haskell, "Editorial," *Architectural Forum* 109 (August 1958): 1.

14. Haskell, "Architecture in America, Part I," 112, 107. Haskell, "Architecture in America, Part II," 121.

15. Douglas Haskell, "Googie Architecture," *House & Home* 1 (February 1952): 86–88. Douglas Haskell, "Architecture and Popular Taste," *Architectural Forum* 109 (August 1958): 105–6.

16. Haskell, "Architecture in America, Part II," 120, 117.

17. Haskell, "Architecture and Popular Taste," 109. Paul Rudolph, "Six Determinants of Architectural Form," *Architectural Record* 120 (October 1956): 188.

18. This address was published as Paul Rudolph, "To Enrich Our Architecture," *Journal of Architectural Education* 13 (Spring 1958): 9–10.

19. Rudolph, "Six Determinants," 190. Rudolph, "To Enrich Our Architecture," 10–11.

20. Rudolph, "To Enrich our Architecture," 10.

21. Rudolph quoted in John Wesley Cook, *Conversations with Architects* (New York Praeger, 1973), 117. Rudolph quoted in Peter Wolf, *Evolving City* (New York: American Federation of the Arts, 1974), 54, 60.

22. Victor Gruen, *The Heart of Our Cities* (New York: Simon and Schuster, 1964), 153–54.

23. Victor Gruen, "Cityscape and Landscape," *Arts & Architecture* 72 (September 1955): 18.

24. Gruen, "Cityscape and Landscape," 19, 36.

25. Victor Gruen and Larry Smith, *Shopping Towns USA* (New York: Reinhold Publishing, 1960), 17, 18, 22.

26. Gruen, "Cityscape and Landscape," 36.

27. Longstreth, *City Center to Regional Mall,* 238–46.

28. "Gruen and Krummeck, Milliron's (Los Angeles, Calif.)" [March 1949, Job #434], Julius Shulman Photography Archive, 1936–1997, Series IV, Getty Research Institute, Images 434–74. Banham, *Los Angeles,* 153. "Towards a New Environment," 396, 387.

29. "Modern Living: 20th Century Bazaar," *Life,* 30 August, 1954, 81–83. David Smiley, *Pedestrian Modern* (Minneapolis: University of Minnesota Press, 2013). M. Jeffrey Hardwick, *Mall Maker: Victor Gruen, Architect of an American Dream* (Philadelphia: University of Pennsylvania Press, 2003). Alex Wall, *Victor Gruen: From Urban Shop to New City* (Barcelona, Spain: Actar Publishing, 2005).

30. "The Splashiest Shopping Center in the U.S.," *Life,* 10 December 1956, 61.

31. "A Controlled Climate for Shopping," *Architectural Record* 120 (December 1956): 195. "Pleasure-Domes with Parking," *Time,* 15 October 1956, 98–99.

32. Victor Gruen, "How to Handle This Chaos of Congestion," *Architectural Forum* 105 (September 1956): 130–35.

33. "Central City, Fringetown, Roadtown," *Architectural Forum* 105 (September 1956): 114–29.

34. Gruen, "How to Handle This Chaos of Congestion," 131.

35. J. B. Jackson, "The Stranger's Path," *Landscape* 7, no. 1 (Autumn 1957): 15. J. B. Jackson, "The Imitation of Nature," *Landscape* 9, no. 1 (Autumn 1959), 9–10. J. B. Jackson, "Roads Belong in the Landscape," in Jackson, *A Sense of Place, a Sense of Time* (New Haven, Conn.: Yale University Press, 1994), 190.

36. Timothy Davis, "Looking Down the Road: J. B. Jackson and the American Highway Landscape" in *Everyday America: Cultural Landscape Studies after J. B. Jackson,* ed. Chris Wilson and Paul Groth (Berkeley: University of California Press, 2003), 71.

37. Grady Clay, "Main Street 1969," *Landscape* 7, no. 1 (Autumn 1957): 3–4. Roland Rainer, "Space and the Modern Highway," *Landscape* 2, no. 3 (Spring 1953): 7.

38. J. B. Jackson, "Metamorphosis," *Annals of the Association of American Geographers* 62 (June

1972): 155, 158. J. B. Jackson, "To Pity the Plumage and Forget the Dying Bird," *Landscape* 17, no. 1 (Autumn 1967), 1–4. J. B. Jackson, "Images of the City," *Landscape* 11, no. 1 (Autumn 1961), 3–4. Jackson, "The Stranger's Path," 12–13. J. B. Jackson, "Two Street Scenes," *Landscape* 3, no. 3 (Spring 1954), 4–5.

39. J. B. Jackson, "Auto Territoriality," *Landscape* 17 (Spring 1968), 1–2. J. B. Jackson, "The Social Landscape," in *Landscapes: Selected Writings of J. B. Jackson*, ed. Ervin H. Zube (Amherst: University of Massachusetts Press, 1970), 147, 149–51.

40. Jackson, "Other-Directed Houses," 30.

41. Herb Gans, "Urbanism and Suburbanism as Ways of Life: A Reevaluation of Definitions," in Gans, *People and Plans: Essays on Urban Problems and Solutions* (New York: Basic Books, 1968), 42.

42. [Kouwenhoven], "After Hours" 101.

43. Jackson, "Other-Directed Houses," 32–34.

44. Jackson, "Other-Directed Houses," 31, 34–35. Jackson, "The Social Landscape," 148–49, 152.

45. Jackson, "The Imitation of Nature," 12. Jackson, "Metamorphosis," 158.

46. On ACTION see "The American Council to Improve Our Neighborhoods," *American Journal of Public Health* 46 (November 1956): 1445–46.

47. Martin Meyerson and Jaqueline Tyrwhitt, *The Face of the Metropolis* (New York: Random House, 1963), 7–8, 32, 23.

48. Meyerson and Tyrwhitt, *The Face of the Metropolis*, 179–80, 8, 22–27.

49. Christopher Tunnard and Boris Pushkarev, *Man-Made America: Chaos or Control?* (New Haven, Conn.: Yale University Press, 1963), ix, 259.

50. Tunnard and Pushkarev, *Man-Made America*, 13–31, 36, 322–23.

51. Tunnard and Pushkarev, *Man-Made America*, 322, 326, ix.

52. Tunnard and Pushkarev, *Man-Made America*, 331–34, 324, 319, 320, 325–26.

53. Tunnard and Pushkarev, *Man-Made America*, 159, 263, 266.

54. Tunnard and Pushkarev, *Man-Made America*, 263, 266.

55. Lawrence Halprin, *Freeways* (New York: Reinhold Publishing, 1966), 5, 12, 17, 40.

56. Halprin, *Freeways*, 22–23, 17.

57. Halprin, *Freeways*, 68, 47, 86, 23, 27.

58. Halprin, *Freeways*, 158, 85–86, 17.

59. Halprin, *Freeways*, 37. Lawrence Halprin, *Cities*, rev. ed. (Cambridge. Mass.: MIT Press, 1972), 208–11.

60. Halprin, *Freeways*, 87–89.

61. Kevin Lynch, *The Image of the City* (Cambridge, Mass.: MIT Press, 1960), 41–43, 56.

62. Donald Appleyard, Kevin Lynch, and John Myer, *A View from the Road* (Cambridge, Mass.: MIT Press, 1964), 3–4, 12–14.

63. Appleyard et al., *A View from the Road,* 19, 20–21.

64. Appleyard et al., *A View from the Road,* 22–25, 27, 8–12. The authors also cite the notation system of architect Philip Thiel, who was influenced by Lynch. See Thiel, "A Sequence-Experience Notation," *Town Planning Review* 32 (April 1961): 33–52.

65. Appleyard et al., *A View from the Road,* 27, 35.

66. Lynch, *The Image of the City,* 56–57. Appleyard et al., *A View from the Road,* 37–39, 57.

67. Appleyard, et al., *A View from the Road,* 7, 63.

68. Appleyard et al., *A View from the Road,* 4, 13. See Jackson, "Auto Territoriality," reprinted in Jackson, *Landscape in Sight: Looking at America,* ed. Helen Lefkowitz Horowitz (New Haven, Conn.: Yale University Press, 1997), 353.

69. Loudon Wainwright, "Blight Blossoms on the American Highway," *Life,* 24 July 1970, 26–33. See also John Neary, "The Necessary Law Exists. Here Is Why It Does Not Work," *Life,* 24 July 1970, 34.

70. Walter McQuade, "Giving Them What They Want: The Venturi Influence," *Life,* 14 April 1972, 17.

71. Lawrence Alloway, "The Arts and Mass Media," *Architectural Design* 28 (February 1958), 34. See also Nigel Whitely, *Art and Pluralism: Lawrence Alloway's Cultural Criticism* (New York: Oxford University Press, 2012), chapters 16 and 22.

72. Lawrence Alloway, "City Notes," *Architectural Design* 29 (January 1959), 34–35. Reprinted in Alloway, *Imagining The Present: Context, Content, and the Role of the Critic,* ed. Richard Kalina (New York: Routledge, 2006), 65–70.

73. Alloway, "City Notes," 65–70.

74. Haskell, "Architecture and Popular Taste," 105–9.

75. Alloway, "City Notes," 69.

76. Lawrence Alloway, "Hi-Way Culture: Man at the Wheel," *Arts* 41 (February 1967), 30.

77. Calvin Tompkins, "Ed Ruscha's L.A.," *New Yorker,* 1 July 2013, 53.

78. Alloway, "Hi-Way Culture," 31, 30.

79. Tom Wolfe, "There Goes (VAROOM! VAROOM!) That Kandy Kolored (THPHHHHHH!) Tangerine-Flake Streamline Baby (RAHGHHHH!) around the Bend (BRUMMMMMMMMMMMM-MMMM . . .)," *Esquire,* November 1963, 114–18, 155, 158, 160, 162, 164, 166, 168. Tom Wolfe, "LAS VEGAS (What?) LAS VEGAS (Can't Hear You! Too Noisy) LAS VEGAS!!!!," *Esquire,* February 1964, 98, 100.

80. Tom Wolfe, "The New Life Out There: Electro-Graphic Architecture," *New York,* 9 December 1968, 47–50. Tom Wolfe, "I Drove around Los Angeles and Its [*sic*] Crazy! The Art World is Upside Down," *Los Angeles Times,* 1 December 1968, 18–22, 25, 27. The articles are nearly identical, though the *L.A. Times* included three additional footnotes about architects, including Robert Venturi, whose work resonated with Wolfe's argument.

81. Wolfe, "The New Life Out There," 47–50, and Wolfe, "I Drove around Los Angeles and Its [*sic*] Crazy!, 18–22, 25, 27.

82. Alloway, "Hi-Way Culture," 31–32.

83. Venturi and Scott Brown, "A Significance for A&P Parking Lots," 38–39.

84. Denise Scott Brown and Robert Venturi, "The Highway," in *The Highway: An Exhibition* (Philadelphia: Institute of Contemporary Art, University of Pennsylvania, 1970), 9–10, 12–13, 16.

85. Alloway, "Hi-Way Culture," 33.

86. Reyner Banham, "A Set of Actual Monuments," *Architectural Review* (April 1989), reprinted in *A Critic Writes: Essays by Reyner Banham* (Berkeley: University of California Press, 1996), 283.

87. Reyner Banham, "The Haunted Highway, *New Society* 52 (19 June 1980), 299.

88. Reyner Banham, *Theory and Design in the First Machine Age* (London: Architectural Press, 1960), 328–30.

89. Museum of Modern Art, "Press Release No. 50," 18 May 1965, 2. Museum of Modern Art Press Archives, www.moma.org.

90. Reyner Banham, "The Missing Motel," *The Listener* 74 (5 August 1965): 191–94. Reyner Banham, "The Missing Motel: Unrecognized American Architecture," *Landscape* 15 (Winter 1965–66): 4–6. Museum of Modern Art, "Press Release No. 50," 3. Drexler, quoted in Banham, "The Missing Motel" (1965), 192. Vincent Scully, *American Architecture and Urbanism* (New York: Praeger, 1969), 198.

91. Banham, "The Missing Motel" (1965),191–94.

92. Banham, *Los Angeles,* 112, 118–19, 123–24, 195.

93. Banham, *Los Angeles,*195, 111–12, 118–19, 123–24.

94. Charles Moore, "You Have to Pay for the Public Life," *Perspecta* 9/10 (1965): 58, 63–65, 95–97.

95. Charles Moore, "Plug It in, Rameses, and See if It Lights up. Because We Aren't Going to Keep It Unless It Works," *Perspecta* 11 (1967): 35–36, 40, 42.

96. Banham, "Roadscape with Rusting Nails," 267–68. Banham, *Los Angeles,* 139. Moore, "Plug It in, Rameses, 34–36.

97. Banham, *Los Angeles,* 213.

98. Banham, *Los Angeles,* 139.

5. THE TWILIGHT OF AUTOPIA

1. In 1934, Walter Dorwin Teague designed Texaco's streamlined station prototype and "banjo" sign. In 1964, Peter Müller-Munk redesigned the sign and produced a new station prototype without a retrofit for existing buildings. John Jakle and Keith Sculle, *The Gas Station in America* (Baltimore, Md.: Johns Hopkins University Press, 1994), 150–52.

2. Federal Highway Administration, "Highway Finance Data: Numbers of Registered Vehicles—Automobiles, Trucks, and Buses, 1970–2006" (2008), www.fhwa.dot.gov. Bureau of Transportation Statistics, U.S. Department of Transportation, "National Transportation Statistics: Public Road and Street Mileage in the United States by Type of Surface," https://www.bts.gov/topics/national-transportation-statistics. U.S. Environmental Protection Agency, *Report on Light-Duty Automotive Technology, Carbon Dioxide Emissions, and Fuel Economy Trends: 1975–2013* (December 2013).

3. "Going after the Oilmen," *Time,* 30 July 1973, 59. James P. Sterbas, "Gasoline Shortage Brings Prosperity to Many Name Brand Dealers," *New York Times,* 14 July 1973, 27.

4. Edward Cowan, "Nixon Sets Voluntary Curbs in Oil and Gas Shortage," *New York Times,* 11 May 1973, 23.

5. David Bird, "11 Amoco Stations Ration Gas Here," *New York Times,* 11 May 1973, 23. David Bird, "A Mobil Dealer's Sales Are Up 400% Despite Reports of Gasoline Shortage," *New York Times,* 18 May 1973, 78. David Bird, "Gasoline Scarcity: Is It a Myth?," *New York Times,* 30 May 1973, 32.

6. "The Arab Oil Threat," *New York Times,* 23 November 1973, 34.

7. Andrew Malcolm, "A Wyoming Gas Station on a Busy Summer Day," *New York Times,* 5 August 1973, 186. David Bird, "Drivers Unfazed by Gas Scarcity," *New York Times,* 21 May 1973, 13. "Panic at the Pump," *Time* 103, 14 January 1974, 15. Ben Franklin, "Curb on Driving under U.S. Study," *New York Times,* 15 December 1973, 70. Bird, "Gas Scarcity: Is It a Myth?," 32, and "Highways of Violence," *Time,* February 11, 1974, 28. "The Fuel Crisis Begins to Hurt," *Time,* 17 December 1973, 36.

8. "Stepping on the Gas to Meet a Threat," *Time,* 26 November 1973, 29.

9. Ernest Holsendolph, "Keeping McDonald's Out in Front," *New York Times,* 30 December 1973, 83. Douglas E. Kneeland, "Garish Strips Stir Hostility, Coast to Coast," *New York Times,* 28 November 1971, 1, 52.

10. Figures cited in "Rapid Rise of the Host with the Most," *Time,* 12 June 1972, 89–97. On the development of Holiday Inn see "The Nation's Innkeeper," chapter 9 in John A. Jakle and Keith A. Sculle, *The Motel in America* (Baltimore, Md.: Johns Hopkins University Press, 1996), 261–85.

11. Alexander R. Hammer, "Dow Stock Index Off by 28.67," *New York Times,* 20 November 1973, 58.

12. "The Rush to Stay Home," *Time,* 25 February 1974, 36. Marilyn Bender, "The Hospitality Crusade," *New York Times,* 26 August 1973, 133, 143.

13. Quoted in Ernest Holsendolph, "Cooler Economy," *New York Times,* 18 November 1973, 186.

14. David Nye, "The Energy Crisis of the 1970s as a Cultural Crisis," in *Living with America, 1946–1996,* ed. Rob Kroes and Cristina Giorcelli (Amsterdam: VU Press, 1997), 82–102.

15. Joseph Alsop, "What Can We Do about Our Fading Age of Fossil Fuels?," *Los Angeles Times,* 19 April 1973, C3.

16. Robert Wright, "A Dim Las Vegas Wonders What Its Odds Are in the Fuel Crisis," *New York Times,* 12 December 1973, 49, 94. "Strip Yields to Pressure: Lights Go Out in Las Vegas," *Los Angeles Times,* 16 November 1973, A3.

17. Andrew Malcolm, "Fuel Rationing Could Hobble That Work Horse of Suburbia," *New York Times,* 17 December 1973, 42.

18. Timothy G. Smith, "We'll Save Some Fuel—But Consider the Costs: A Way of Life Will Disappear," *Los Angeles Times,* 18 November 1973, G1.

19. "The Arab's New Oil Squeeze: Dimouts, Slowdowns, Chills," *Time,* 19 November 1973, 110.

20. John Hudson, "Density and Pattern in Suburban Fringes," *Annals of the Association of American Geographers* 63 (March 1973): 28.

21. Christopher W. Wells, *Car Country: An Environmental History* (Seattle: University of Washington Press, 2012). See also Thomas W. Hanchett, "U.S. Tax Policy and the Shopping-Center Boom of the 1950s and 1960s," *American Historical Review* 101 (October 1996): 1082–110.

22. "A Time of Learning to Live with Less," *Time,* 3 December 1973, 53. "The Arab's New Oil Squeeze," 110. Robin Reisig, "The Gasoline Shortage Is Giving the Travel Industry the Chills," *New York Times,* 2 December 1973, 645, 667.

23. Stefan Kanfer, "The (Possible) Blessings of Doing Without," *Time,* 12 December 1973), 60.

24. Ernest Dickinson, "Abandonment of Service Stations Accelerates," *New York Times,* 2 December 1973, section 8, 1, 6.

25. William D. Smith, "Gas Stations: A Way of Life is Changing," *New York Times,* 27 May 1973, section 3, 1.

26. Stewart Udall, "The Last Traffic Jam," *The Atlantic,* 1 October 1972, online edition.

27. William V. Shannon, "The Untrustworthy Highway Fund," *New York Times Magazine,* 15 October 1972, 31. "Highway Lobby Triumph," *New York Times,* 29 July 1973, 195.

28. Udall, "The Last Traffic Jam," n.p.

29. "The Painful Change to Thinking Small," *Time* 102, 31 December 1973, 20–21.

30. Edwin L. Dale Jr. "Auto-Suggestion: Time to End the Big Affair," *New York Times Magazine,* 10 June 1973, 13, 92–93.

31. Joint Congressional Committee quoted in Alsop, "What Can We Do about Our Fading Age of Fossil Fuels?," C3. Udall, "The Last Traffic Jam," n.p.

32. John Jerome, *The Death of the Automobile: The Fatal Effect of the Golden Era, 1955–1970* (New York: W. W. Norton & Company, 1972), 13, 103, 239.

33. James J. Flink, *America Adopts the Automobile, 1895–1910* (Cambridge, Mass.: MIT Press, 1970).

34. Charles Reich, *The Greening of America: How the Youth Revolution Is Trying to Make America Livable* (New York: Random House, 1970).

35. Elisabeth Kübler-Ross, *On Death and Dying* (New York: Macmillan, 1969).

36. James J. Flink, "Three Stages of American Automobile Consciousness," *American Quarterly* 24 (October 1972): 451–73.

37. James J. Flink, *The Car Culture* (Cambridge, Mass.: MIT Press, 1975), 191, 233.

38. Frederick Jackson Turner, "The Significance of the Frontier in American History," in Turner, *The Frontier in American History* (New York: Henry Holt and Company, 1921), 1–38.

39. George W. Pierson, "The M-Factor in American History," *American Quarterly* 14 (Summer 1962, part 2: supplement): 275, 278.

40. Flink, *The Car Culture,* 233.

41. James J. Flink, *The Automobile Age* (Cambridge, Mass.: MIT Press, 1988), 404, 377–78.

42. Fredric Jameson, "Postmodernism and Consumer Society," in *The Anti-Aesthetic,* ed. Hal Foster (Port Townsend, Wash.: Bay Press, 1983), 116. Charles Champlin, "A New Generation Looks Back in *Graffiti,*" *Los Angeles Times,* 29 July 1973, N1.

43. For an analysis of the cars in relation to the characters, see Jack DeWitt, "Cars and Culture: The Cars of *American Graffiti,*" *American Poetry Review,* September/October 2010, 47–50.

44. Stanley Kauffmann, "Films Worth Seeing: *American Graffiti,*" *New Republic,* 6 October 1973, 22. Stanley Kauffmann, "On Films: *American Graffiti,*" *New Republic,* 15 September 1973, 22, 33.

45. Fredric Jameson, "The Cultural Logic of Late Capitalism" (1984), reprinted in *Postmodernism, or, the Cultural Logic of Late Capitalism* (Durham, N.C.: Duke University Press, 1991), 19.

46. Jon Nordheimer, "Teenage Drivers Still Cruise, but Without that Old Fervor," *New York Times,* 7 April 1974, 47.

47. "Of Crisis and Confidence," *Time,* 25 February 1974, 11.

48. Roger Ebert, "America Graffiti," *Chicago Sun-Times,* 11 August 1973, www.rogerebert.com.

49. For an early definition of the drive-in, see Meyer Berger, "The Log of a Rolling Motorist," *New York Times,* 13 June 1937, section 10, 4. *1964 Drive-In Operators Handbook* quoted in Liebs, *Main Street to Miracle Mile,* 211.

50. Jerry Beigel, "Growing Up in Early 1960s," *Los Angeles Times,* 22 September 1972, D15.

51. "H. Dobbs, Began Famed Drive-in Eatery," *San Francisco Chronicle,* 18 August 1984, online editon.

52. Jean Baudrillard, "History: A Retro Scenario," in Baudrillard, *Simulacra and Simulation* (1981; trans. Sheila Faria Glaser, Ann Arbor: University of Michigan Press, 1994), 44.

53. Michael Karl Witzel, *The American Drive-In* (Osceola, Wisc.: MBI Publishing, 1994), 178–82. In 2002, high-rise luxury condominiums were built on the site.

54. "Meanwhile, Drive-In Restaurants Fade Away," *New York Times,* 8 August 1978, A12.

55. Mels in Sherman Oaks was originally Kerry's (Armet and Davis, 1953); Mels in Hollywood was originally Ben Frank's (Lane and Schlick, 1962). Alan Hess, *Googie Redux: Ultramodern Roadside Architecture* (San Francisco: Chronicle Books, 2004), 109, 113.

56. Leo Marx, *The Machine in the Garden* (New York: Oxford University Press, 1964), 5–7, 103–4.

57. Richard Longstreth, "When the Present Becomes the Past," in *Past Meets Future: Saving America's Historic Environments,* ed. Antoinette J. Lee (Washington, D.C.: Preservation Press, 1992), 249n2.

58. "Talk of the Town: Symbols," *New Yorker,* 15 March 1976, 28. Ada Louise Huxtable, "The Pop World of the Strip and the Sprawl," *New York Times,* 21 March 1976, section 2, 28. Venturi and Rauch (Robert Venturi, Steven Izenour, and Denise Scott Brown), *Signs of Life: Symbols in the American City* (New York: Aperture, Inc., in association with Smithsonian Institution, 1976), n.p.

59. Huxtable, "The Pop World of the Strip and the Sprawl," 28. Venturi and Rauch, *Signs of Life,* n.p.

60. John Margolies, *The End of the Road* (New York: Penguin Books, 1981), 13–15.

61. Telethon, "Roadside Mecca," *Progressive Architecture* 54 (November 1973): 124–29.

62. Margolies, *The End of the Road,* 14–15.

63. Vivien Raynor, "On the Roadsides Again," *New York Times,* 2 August 1981, online edition. Margolies, *The End of the Road,* 12.

64. Margolies, *The End of the Road,* 13. Andy Grundberg and Julia Scully, "U.S.A.: Pushing the Limits," *Modern Photography* (July 1976), 80.

65. Folke T. Kihlstedt, "Review," *Journal of the Society of Architectural Historians* 40 (December 1981): 339–40.

66. "Fast Food," *New Yorker,* 30 September 1972, 33.

67. William Versaci, "About *Perspecta* 15," *Perspecta* 15 (1975): 7.

68. Richard J. S. Gutman, "Diners: Overlooked Sophistication," *Perspecta* 15 (1975): 41–53.

69. Richard J. S. Gutman and Elliott Kaufman, *American Diner* (New York: Harper & Row, 1979). Gutman wrote the essay; Kaufman took the photographs.

70. Paul Hirshorn and Steven Izenour, *White Towers* (Cambridge, Mass.: MIT Press, 1979), v–vii.

71. Paul Hirshorn and Steven Izenour, "Learning from Hamburgers: The Architecture of White Towers," *Architecture Plus* 1 (June 1973): 46–55.

72. Robert Venturi, Denise Scott Brown, and Steven Izenour, *Learning from Las Vegas* (1972; rev. Cambridge, Mass.: MIT Press, 1977), 3.

73. Hirshorn and Izenour, *White Towers,* vi.

74. Hirshorn and Izenour, *White Towers,* v. Steven Izenour, lecture at SCI-Arc, 1 January 1977, digitized videotape, SCI-Arc Media Archive, http://sma.sciarc.edu.

75. Paul Hirshorn, "Preface," in Hirshorn and Izenour, *White Towers* (1979; rpt. Cambridge, Mass.: MIT Press, 2007), vi.

76. Public Law 102–575, National Historic Preservation Act of 1966, as amended through 1992, http://www.nps.gov/history/local-law/nhpa1966.htm. Barry Mackintosh, *The Historic Sites Survey and National Historic Landmarks Program* (Washington, D.C.: Department of the Interior, 1985), 72.

77. Brent Glass and Mary Alice Hinson, "Shell Service Station National Register Nomination Form," 1975. David Chase, "Modern Diner National Register Nomination Form," 1977. Hugh Henry, "Miss Bellows Falls National Register Nomination Form," 1982.

78. Hirshorn and Izenour, *White Towers* (1979), 50. Sally Zimmerman, "Landmark Designation Study Report for White Tower Restaurant, 25 Central Square Landmark," 10 May 1999, Cambridge Historical Commission, Cambridge's Local Landmarks, http://www2.cambridgema.gov.

79. Warren James Belasco, *Americans on the Road: From Autocamp to Motel, 1910–1945* (Cambridge, Mass.: MIT Press, 1979), vii–viii. Folke T. Kihlstedt, "Review of *Americans on the Road*," *Winterthur Portfolio* 17 (Summer/Autumn 1982): 169–70.

80. Jakle and Sculle, *The Gas Station in America,* 11–12. John A, Jakle and Keith A. Sculle, *Remembering Roadside America: Preserving the Recent Past as Landscape and Place* (Knoxville: University of Tennessee Press, 2011), 1–2.

81. Jakle and Sculley, *The Gas Station in America,* 20, 12.

82. John A. Jakle, "The American Gasoline Station, 1920–1970," *Journal of American Culture* 1, no. 3 (Fall 1978): 537.

83. Jakle, "The American Gasoline Station," 539.

84. Editorial mission from masthead, *Journal of American Culture* 1 (Fall 1978), n.p.

85. Jakle, "The American Gasoline Station," 539.

86. Herbert J. Gans, *Popular Culture and High Culture: An Analysis and Evaluation of Taste* (New York: Basic Books, 1974), vii.

87. "Thematic Sessions of the 31st Annual Meeting of the Society of Architectural Historians, San Antonio, Texas, 5–10 April 1978," *Journal of the Society of Architectural Historians* 37 (October 1978): 226.

88. James Marston Fitch, "Foreword," in Daniel Vieyra, *"Fill 'er Up": An Architectural History of America's Gas Stations* (New York: Macmillan Publishing, 1979), ix.

89. John Maass, "Where Architectural Historians Fear to Tread," *Journal of the Society of Architectural Historians* 28 (March 1969): 6. Editor's note in Robert C. Wheeler, "Frank Lloyd Wright Filling Station," *Journal of the Society of Architectural Historians* 19 (December 1960): 174–75.

90. Paul Goldberger, "Design Notebook: A Leisurely Look at Our Roadside Architecture," *New York Times,* 21 February 1980, C10.

91. Fitch, "Foreword," ix.

92. Vieyra, *Fill 'er Up,* xiii–xiv. Hitchcock, *The Architecture of H. H. Richardson*, 302–3. Venturi and Scott Brown, "A Significance for A&P Parking Lots," 36–43.

93. David Gebhard and Harriette Von Breton, *L.A. In the Thirties, 1931–1941* (Layton, Utah: Peregrine Smith Inc., 1975).

94. Thomas S. Hines, "Review of Esther McCoy, *Five California Architects,* David Gebhard and Harriette Von Breton, *L.A. in the Thirties,* and David Gebhard, *Schindler,*" *Journal of the Society of Architectural Historians* 35 (December 1976): 325.

95. John Pastier, "Funny, It Didn't Look Depressed," *Los Angeles Times,* 14 April 1975, section IV, 12. Robert Kirsch, "They Have Seen the Past and It Worked," *Los Angeles Times Book Review,* 3 August 1975, 3.

96. David Gebhard and Robert Winter, *A Guide to Architecture in Los Angeles and Southern California* (Santa Barbara, Calif.: Peregrine Smith, 1977), 5, 413, 710.

97. David Gebhard, "Introduction," in Jim Heimann and Rip Georges, *California Crazy: Roadside Vernacular Architecture* (San Francisco: Chronicle Books, 1980), 11–25.

98. Ada Louise Huxtable, "Architecture for a Fast-Food Culture," *New York Times Magazine,* 12 February 1978, 23.

99. Ada Louise Huxtable, "Pow! It's Good-By History, Hello Hamburger," *New York Times,* 21 March 1971, section 2, 23.

100. Huxtable, "Architecture for a Fast-Food Culture," 25, 32, 36.

101. Ada Louise Huxtable, "Editorial Notebook: Americana Is Where You Find It," *New York Times,* 1 August 1980, A22.

102. Goldberger, "Design Notebook," C10.

103. Longstreth, "When the Present Becomes the Past," 249n3.

104. Chester Liebs, "Accepting Our Aging Century," *Possibilities for Management of Vermont's Built Environment* 1, no. 3 (1976): 1.

105. Chester Liebs, "Remembering Our Not-So-Distant Past?," *Historic Preservation* 30 (January-March 1978): 30–35.

106. "Concerning SCA," *Society for Commercial Archeology News Journal* 1 (September 1978): 3.

107. "Reviews [*White Towers*]," *SCA News Journal* 1 (November 1979): 6. "Reviews [Banham's Los Angeles]," *SCA News Journal* 1 (September 1978): 4. "Recommended [*American Graffiti*]," *SCA News Journal* 1 (April 1979): 4.

108. "CA: Dialogue on an Emerging Field," *SCA News Journal* 1 (September 1978): 3. George F. Fielder, "An Archeologist on Archeology," *SCA News Journal* 1 (October 1980): 2. "Questionnaire," insert in *SCA News Journal* 2 (November 1985).

109. Chester Liebs, "The Meeting That Sparked the Birth of the SCA," *SCA Journal* (Spring 2017): 14. Peter H. Smith, "On Commercial Archeology," *SCA News Journal* 1 (September 1978): 3. On above-ground archeology see Thomas J. Schlereth, "The City as Artifact," *American Histor-*

ical Association Newsletter 14 (February 1977): 7–9, and John L. Cotter, "Above-Ground Archeology," *American Quarterly* 26 (August 1974): 266–80.

110. Chester Liebs, untitled essay in "The Assessment of American Roadside Architecture," *The Forum: Bulletin of the SAH Committee on Preservation* (June 1980): n.p.

111. Marc Treib, untitled essay in "The Assessment of American Roadside Architecture," *The Forum: Bulletin of the SAH Committee on Preservation* (June 1980): n.p.

112. Denise Scott Brown, "From Strip to Shining Strip," *New York Times Book Review,* 20 April 1986, 15. Liebs, *Main Street to Miracle Mile,* xiii–xiv, 237.

113. Scott Brown, "From Strip to Shining Strip," 15. Thomas Schlereth, "Review of *White Towers,*" *Winterthur Portfolio* 16 (Spring 1981): 121–23.

114. Banham, "The Haunted Highway," 297–99.

115. David Macaulay, *Motel of the Mysteries* (Boston: Houghton Mifflin, 1979), 10, 12.

116. David Macaulay, *Cathedral: The Story of Its Construction* (Boston: Houghton Mifflin, 1973). David Macaulay, *City: A Story of Roman Planning and Construction* (Boston: Houghton Mifflin, 1974).

117. Banham, "The Missing Motel" (1965), 194.

118. Banham, "The Haunted Highway," 298. "Final Chapter Is Written for Route 66," *New York Times,* 29 June 1985. "Route 66 Study Act of 1990," Public Law 101-400, 101st Congress, 28 September 1990.

INDEX

Italicized page numbers refer to illustrations, and CP followed by a number denotes plates in the color gallery following page 168.

Abu-Lughod, Janet, 146
Action for a Better Los Angeles Environment (ABLE), 4–5
Adams, Henry, 61–62, 162
Adams, Wilbur Henry, 56
Adorno, Theodor, 79–80
advertising: and architecture, 21, 27, 28, 35; in art, 33, 82, *CP3, CP4;* in scholarship, 188, 260, 312; ubiquity of, 92, 139, 148, 241. *See also* billboards; signage
Agee, James, 79–83, 89, 202, 296
air travel, 34, 63, 103, 105, 245. *See also* TWA Flight Center (New York)
Allen, Frederick Lewis, 48, 124, 130–31
Alloway, Lawrence: America, impressions of, 236–38; "The Arts and Mass Media," 236; and Banham, 249, 260; CinemaScope analogy, 237, 240; highway culture, 238–43, 246, 299; and Margolies, 288. *See also* "Hi-Way Culture" (Alloway)
Alsberg, Henry, 85, 87, 91
American Council to Improve Our Neighborhoods (ACTION), 207
American Diner (Gutman and Kaufman), 288–90, 294, 301. *See also* architecture, car-oriented; diners; fast food industry
"American Gasoline Station, 1920–1970, The" (Jakle), 298–99. *See also* architecture, car-oriented; gas station(s); service station(s)
American Graffiti (film), *264,* 278–82, 308

American Guide series, 84–104, 108, 120, 125; *Idaho: A Guide in Word and Picture*, 84–85; *U.S. One: From Maine to Florida*, 89–100, *90, 97, 98,* 120, 125; *Washington: City and Capital,* 85–86. See also tourism
American Historical Association (AHA), 275, 277
American Institute of Architects (AIA), 176–77, 246
American landscape, uniqueness of, 172–73, 182–83, 207, 314
Americans on the Road (Belasco), 295–97, 313
Amerika (Mendelsohn), 31–32
Anderson, Lawrence, 66–67
Appalachian Trail, 75
Appleyard, Donald, 225, 229, 234, 239
archeology, 307–14. See also *Motel of the Mysteries* (Macaulay); Society for Commercial Archeology (SCA)
architecture, car-oriented: in art, 284–85; building types, 15–61, 131–33, 140, 166–67, 198, 288–94, 298; critique of, 141, 147–50, 252–53, 287; design, 243–46, 289–90; as minor architecture, 25–30; modernism, 29–61, 140–41; oil crisis, effects of, 268–69; prefabrication, 41–42, 59, 289; preservation, 295; quantity of, 253–54; scholarship about, 55, 201, 252–56, 288–315; style, 141, 186, 290, 303–4. See also diners; drive in(s); gas station(s); motel(s); parking; service station(s)
"Architecture for a Fast-Food Culture" (Huxtable), 306
Arizona: Kingman, *58, 59, 60;* Seligman, *151;* Speedway Boulevard (Tucson), 235, *CP8*
Armet & Davis, 254, 255, 282

Armour, J. Ogden, 74–75
Auden, W. H., 131
auto camps, 15, *58,* 58–61, *59, 60,* 64, *65,* 296, 314. See also cabins, tourist; tourism
Automobile Club of America (ACA), 16–18, *17*
Automobile Objective, 44, 46–47
automobile(s): architectural impact, 18–25, 27, 42, 55, 57, 63, 78; consciousness, stages of, 276–77; in culture, 161–62, 177; death of, 277–78; democracy, rhetoric of, 62, 164–65; design, 26–27, 163–65, 250, 274, 307; districts, 17, 18, 21, 23; industry, 55–56, 163–65, 185, 268, 274, 275; sociological effects, 77, 80, 111, 272–73; ownership, 15, 20, 25–26, 36, 54, 72–73, 104, 106, 123, 175, 270–71, 285; problems of, 276–77; urban impact, 18, 54, 61, 62–63, 73–77, 109–10, 120, 152, 160–61, 175–82, 200–201, 273–74. See also architecture, car-oriented; urbanization
automobility: as American value, 101–4, 106–7; devotion to, 162, 165; effects of, 61–69, 154–55; end of, 278–79; institution, 79–83; scholarship on, 72, 109; social mobility, metaphor of, 111, 273; social order of, 203; urban, 223–25
Autopia, American, definition of, 2, 4
Autopia, Disneyland, 1–2, 4, 6, *CP1*
autopia, definition of, 3–4
auto territoriality. *See under* Jackson, J. B. (John Brinckerhoff)
auto-tourism. *See* tourism

Baeder, John, 284
Baker, Geoffrey, 200
Baltimore, Maryland: Baltimore Beltway, 158, *159;* Baltimore–Washington Parkway, 220;

344   INDEX

corridor, Baltimore to Washington, 128, 134, 208

Banham, Reyner, *xvi,* 5–11; and Autopian scholarship, 298, 300, 306; Loos translation, 149; *Los Angeles: The Architecture of Four Ecologies,* 5–8, *254,* 254–55, 257, 260–63, *261, 262,* 283, 308; Margolies, comparison, 287–88; Milliron's Department Store, interest in, 193; monuments of Autopia, 249–55, 306; Moore, comparison, 257, 260; *Motel of the Mysteries,* review of, 312–14; Wolfe, interest in, 246

Barris, George, 243

Barthes, Roland, 161–62

Baudrillard, Jean, 281

Bauer, Catherine, 53, 156–57, 158, 177

Bauhaus, 31, 37, 39, 42–43, 178, 293

Bay Area. *See under* California

Beard, Charles and Mary, 91, 93–94

Beegle, J. Allan, 117

Belasco, Warren James, 296–97, 313, 314

Bel Geddes, Norman, 164

Bello, Francis, 160

Belloc, Hilaire, 109

Belluschi, Pietro, 195

Bennett, J. M., 127

Bertoia, Harry, 195

Big Duck (Long Island, New York). *See under* programmatic architecture

Bill, Max, 217–18

billboards: anti-, 78, 127, 157, 163, 167, 191, 205, *211;* in art, 284; part of roadscape, 32, 67, 77, 104, 117, 139; significance of, 237–38, 250, 257–60, 287; size of, 116–17; ubiquity of, 92, 124, 128. *See also* advertising; signage

Birrell, Don, 256

Blake, Peter, 166–73, 242, 292

blight: environmental, 164, 274; lack of 235–36, 257–60, 273, 287, 314; result of abandonment, 272; roadside, 126–29, 133, 140, 181, 191–92, 205, 212. *See also* slums; ugliness

Bluestone, Daniel, 127

Boernge, Herman, 243, 247

Bold, Christine, 84

Boston, Massachusetts, 119, 129, 133, 183, 208, 295; Central Artery, 222, *233,* 234; Northeast Expressway, 230–31

Bourke-White, Margaret, 125–26; photographs by, *126, 127*

Brean, Herbert, 134–36

Brew, John, 110–11, 115

Broadacre City, 47, 60, 62, 103, 177. *See also* Wright, Frank Lloyd

Brown, Sterling, 86

Bruegmann, Robert, 155

Burchard, John, 66–67, 180, 181

Burgess, Ernest, 18, 64

cabins, tourist, 58–61, 79, 82, 98, 132, 141. *See also* auto camps; tourism

California: Bay Area, 115, 212, 218, 280; the Boardwalk (Marin County), 212, *213;* Carquinez Strait, *219;* Modesto, 278, 279; Ships Coffee Shop (Westwood), 255; Southern, 79, 106, 301–3. *See also* Banham, Reyner; Los Angeles, California; San Francisco, California

California Crazy (Gebhard), 303

capitalism, American, 79, 80, 184, 279, 287

"Car Country," 271, 274

cars. *See* automobile(s)

census. *See* U.S. Bureau of the Census

centertown, 197–98

Chambless, Edgar, 72–74, 75, 83
Chase, Stuart, 129–30
Chermayeff, Ivan, 287
Church, Thomas, 212
Cities in the Motor Age (Owen), 136
City Beautiful movement, 22, 127
cityscape, 190–97, 208, 210, 232; subcityscape, 190–91, 193, 195, 197, 207–79, 210; suburbscape, 190; technoscape, 190; transportationscape, 190. *See also* Gruen, Victor
Clark, Edward, 136, 182, 208; photograph by, *135*
Clarke, Gilmore, 37, 55, 96–97, 165
Clay, Grady, 200
Clay, General Lucius, 159. *See also* Committee on a National Highway Program
Clay Commission. *See* Committee on a National Highway Program
Clean Air Act, 266
Clements, Stiles O., 63
Cohen, Elaine Lustig, 167
commercial strip. *See* strip, commercial
Committee on a National Highway Program, 159–60
commuting, 7, 128, 197, 230, 273
Connecticut: Connecticut General (Bloomfield), 136, *179*, 179–80, 183, 208, 249, 300; —, urban symposium (1957), 136, 178–82, 195, 197, 199; Connecticut Post Center (Milford), 257, *258–59;* Connecticut Turnpike, 257; Merritt Parkway, 105, 128; New Haven, 128, 136–37, 188; New London, *139*. *See also* Temple Street Garage (New Haven, Connecticut)
consumerism: automotive, 131; culture of, 239, 249, 254, 267, 273; environmental impact, 235; expanding, 185, 276, 278–79, 307; habits, 48; of highways, 216; mass consumption, 79–80; popular taste, 145–48; psychology, 164–65; tourism, 84
Cooper, Muriel, 292, 293
Corbett, Harvey Wiley, 55
Corbusian, 141, 177. *See also* Le Corbusier
Cotter, John L., 309
Crawford, Ralston, 247
Cullen, Gordon, 137, 139–40, 167
Curry, John Steuart, 81–82; paintings by, *CP3, CP4*

D'Arcangelo, Allan, 239–40, 242, 246–48, 288; *U.S. Highway 1, No. 3, CP9*
Defense Highway Act (1956). *See* Interstate Highway System
Depression, Great: architectural profession during, 30, 290; consumerism during, 276; onset of, 73; roadside industry, 79; suburbanization, 130; vehicular sales, 54–58
design, data-driven, 30–38
Detroit, Michigan: automobile industry, 55–56, 163–65, 268, 274; modernism in, 250; Northland Shopping Center (near Detroit), 182, 193–94, *194,* 212; Woodward Avenue/MI-1, 39, 41
DeVoto, Bernard, 130–34, 242
Dickey, C. W., 57
diners, 140, 289–91, 295; Day and Night Diner (Palmer, Massachusetts), *290;* Miss Bellows Falls Diner (Bellows Falls, Vermont), 295; Modern Diner (Pawtucket, Rhode Island), 295. See also *American Diner* (Gutman and Kaufman); architecture, car-oriented; drive in(s); fast food industry; *White Towers* (Hirshorn and Izenour)

Disneyland (Anaheim, California), 1–2, 4, 6, 7, *CP1*; as public space, 255, 256
Disney World (Orlando, Florida), 269
District of Columbia. *See* Washington, D.C.
downtown: architects' interest in, 177, 190; congestion, 76, 195, 197; density, 63, 119; metropolis, part of, 208; pedestrian-oriented, 160, 263
Doxiadis, Constantinos, 207
Drexler, Arthur, 250–51, 253
drive in(s), 53–54, 132–33, 198, 210, 252, 302; economy, 274; markets, 51, 56; Mels Drive In (San Francisco, California), 264, 279–82, 339n55; movie theaters, 44, 140, 158, 201, *CP14*; preservation, 307, 311; restaurants, 201, 280, 282, 298; scholarship, 10, 255, 314. *See also American Graffiti* (film); architecture, car-oriented; fast food industry
drivers. *See* motorists
Dunn, Alan, cartoon by, *123, 163*

Earl, Harley, 164, 237, 250
"Easy Chair, The: Motel Town" (DeVoto), 131–33. *See also* motel(s)
Ebert, Roger, 279
Eisenhower administration: Commission on National Goals, 158; Defense Highway Act, 71; interstate program, 135, 159, 164, 178; urban renewal policies, 207. *See also* Interstate Highway System
El Camino Real, 20
Elisofon, Eliot, 186; photograph by, *187*
Emerson, Ralph Waldo, 180–81
End of the Road, The (Margolies), 285–59, 294, 295
energy crisis. *See* oil crisis (1973)

Erwitt, Elliott, 167
Evans, Walker, 82, 247
Exploding Metropolis (Whyte), 160–61

Face of the Metropolis (Myerson and Tyrwhitt), 207–8, 228
Fairbrother, Frederick, 23
Farm Security Administration (FSA), 82, 98–100, 167
fast food industry, 90–91, 180, 281, 291–95; Ernie's Hamburger Heaven (Missouri), 212, *213*; McDonald's, 244, 268–69, 284, 292, 299; White Tower, 288–89, 291–95, *294*. *See also American Diner* (Gutman and Kaufman); architecture, car-oriented; diners; *White Towers* (Hirshorn and Izenour)
Federal Aid Highway Act (1956), 156
Federal Aid Roads Act (1916), 75
Federal Writers' Project (FWP), 84–101, 125. See also *American Guide* series
Feininger, Andreas, 150, 185; photograph by, *151*
Feiss, Carl, 133–34
Fill'er Up: An Architectural History of America's Gas Stations (Vieyra), 299–301. *See also* architecture, car-oriented; gas station(s); service station(s)
Firey, Walter, 117
Fitch, James Marston, 300, 301, 302
Flink, James J., 275–78
Foley, Mary Mix, 145–52, 168, 186
Ford, Henry, 15, 271, 275; Ford Highland Park Plant (Michigan), 15, 276; Fordist, 15, 177; Ford Sales and Service Building (Highland Park, Michigan), 24, *25*
Fort Worth Plan, 190. *See also* Gruen, Victor

freeways: Disneyland ride, 4; elevated, 231; Embarcadero Freeway (San Francisco, California), 222–23, *227;* Freeway Park (Seattle, Washington), 220; *Freeways* (Halprin), 219–26, *221, 222, 226, 227;* Hollywood, 2; Las Vegas Strip, 7; point of view, driver, 216; as public space, 256, 260, 262; revolts, 273; Santa Ana, 2, 256; urban form, impact on, 4–6, 233–35, 281; urbanization, 185. *See also* highway(s); Interstate Highway System; MOTATION; parkways; turnpikes

Frey, Albert, 59, 296; photographs/drawings by, *58, 59, 60*

fringetown, 197–98

frontier, American, 106, 277–78. *See also* Turner, Frederick Jackson

Fuller, Buckminster, 37, 49, 250

Funaro, Bruno, 200

Gans, Herbert J., 124, 203, 270, 299

garages. *See under* parking

gasoline: importance of, 80; sale of, 15, 34; shortage, 130, 266–70, 286. *See also* oil crisis (1973); oil embargo

gas station(s): competition, 28–29; design, 34–38, *40, 92,* 297; first, 16; network, part of, 33–35; oil crisis, 272, *CP12;* scholarship, 298–301; standardization, 37–38, 39, 42; Union 76 gas station (Beverly Hills, California), 244–45, *245;* urbanism, 60–61. *See also* "American Gasoline Station, 1920–1970, The" (Jakle); architecture, car-oriented; *Fill'er Up: An Architectural History of America's Gas Stations* (Vieyra); service station(s)

Gebhard, David, 302–4, 309

General Motors (GM), 153, 161, 165, 273; Technical Center, 150, 208, 237, 249

Giedion, Sigfried, 64, 207, 312

Giesey, James H., 19–22

Glitter Gulch (Las Vegas). *See under* Las Vegas, Nevada

God's Own Junkyard (Blake), 166–73, *168, 169, 171. See also* blight; ugliness

Goff, Bruce, 250, 251

Goldberger, Paul, 300–301, 307

Goode, William, 177

Googie, 186, 212, 281–82, 290, 306; Johnie's Coffee Shop (Los Angeles, California), *254,* 254–55; Ships Coffee Shop (Westwood, California), 255

Gordon, Elizabeth, 177, 246

Gottmann, Jean, 118–21, 128, 134, 188, 200, 210

Graham, Anderson, Probst and White, 56–57

"Great American Roadside" (*Fortune*), 79, 80–83, 202

Greenbelt, Maryland, 93, 96, 170, *171. See also* suburb(s)

Greenberg, Clement, 236

Gropius, Walter, 31, 37, 50, 140, 250, 254

Gruen, Victor: cityscapes, 189–90, 197–99, 202, 208, 210–12; evaluation of autopia, 182; Milliron's Department Store, 141, *192, 193;* shopping centers and malls, 185. *See also* shopping centers; shopping malls

Grundberg, Andy, 288

Grutzner, Charles, 160–61

Gruzen, Barney, 56

Gudis, Catherine, 127

guidebooks, 84–108, 303; and *Life* magazine, 101, *102,* 103–4. *See also American Guide* series; *Guide to Architecture in Los Angeles and Southern California, A* (Gebhard and Winter); tourism

348 INDEX

Guide to Architecture in Los Angeles and Southern California, A (Gebhard and Winter), 303. *See also* guidebooks; tourism
Gunther, John, 104–8
Guth, Alexander C., 27–29, 33, 34–35
Gutheim, Frederick, 87, 93
Gutman, Richard, 288–90, 292, 295

Halprin, Anna, 221, 224
Halprin, Lawrence, 219–29, 234, 239
Haskell, Douglas: *Architectural Forum,* 194; *Architectural Review,* rebuke of, 144–46; architecture and popular taste, 238; on auto camps, 60–61; on autopia, 182–88; design concerns, 286; Gruen, comparison to, 190–91, 197, 199, 208; Jackson, comparison to, 202, 203, 243, 286; Margolies, influence for, 288; subject matter, 152; urban sprawl, 158
Heaton, Arthur B., 50–51
Heckscher, August, 121
Highway, The: An Exhibition (Institute of Contemporary Art, University of Pennsylvania), 247–48
Highway Beautification Act (1965), 171, 235
highway(s), 71–121; art, as work of, 228, 231, 235; commercial development along, 125–35; cross-sectional study of, 108, 110–18; culture, 82–83, 89, 115, 235–49; design of, 87–88, 216; as destination, 85–86, 108; early, 16, 72, 74; interchanges, 2, 15, 64, *65,* 165, 214, 247;—, cloverleaf, 88, 96, 132, 159, 222, 247; Highway Number 70 (U.S. 70; New Mexico); *99;* Lincoln Highway, 18, *70,* 81, *100,* 100, 238; luminosity, 204, 232–33; Mount Vernon Memorial Highway (MVMH), 86–88; ontological significance,

107–9, 111; paving, 87, 162; pre-interstate, 71–72, 119, 202; relation to town, 75–79; as symbol of America, 92; transcontinental, 113, 115, 117, 118, 238; visual art, impact on, 247–49. *See also* freeways; Interstate Highway System; parkways; turnpikes
Highway Trust Fund, 273
Highways in Our National Life (Labatut), 109–10, 112, 115, 117
Hirshorn, Paul, 288–89, 291–95
historic preservation. *See* preservation, historic
Hitchcock, Henry-Russell, 38, 140–42, 147, 193, 301
"Hi-Way Culture" (Alloway), 239–43, 246, 248
honky-tonks, 134, 185, 313; on northeast corridor, 125; vitality of, 145, 170, 186
Hopper, Edward, 247, 280
Horkheimer, Max, 79–80
housing: mass-produced, 184, 190; modernist, 50; public, 208; shortage, 26, 111; suburban, 130, 146, 167, 190, 198, 201; Wellesley Row Houses (outside Boston, Massachusetts), 208
Howard, Ebenezer, 156
human landscape, 203, 207, 234
Huxtable, Ada Louise, 284, 304–7, 310

IBM (International Business Machines), 154, 251
Ilf, Ilya, 91–92; photograph by, *92*
Illinois: Dan Ryan Expressway (Chicago), 222; Marshall Field (Evanston), *14, 57*
Image of the City, The (Lynch), 225, 228
Independent Group, 236
Indiana, Robert, 248

intermodal transportation, 181
Interstate Highway System, 71, 135, 156–61, 164–66, 178, 181; effect on businesses, 286; financing, 273; influence of car manufacturers, 165
Izenour, Steven, 8, 283, 288–89, 291–95, 311. See also *Learning from Las Vegas* (Venturi, Scott Brown, and Izenour); *White Towers* (Hirshorn and Izenour)

Jackson, J. B. (John Brinckerhoff): art and architecture of the strip, 219; auto territoriality, 201–2, 234; human landscape, 203, 207, 235; influence of, 303, 311; *Landscape,* 118–19, 200, 210, 251; odology, 89, 199–209; other-directed architecture, 202–6; social landscape, 202; on U.S. 1, 134, 210; drawing by, *204*
Jacobs, Jane, 158, 160, 263, 272
Jakle, John, 297–99
James, Henry, 131, 137, 144
Jameson, Fredric, 278–79
Jefferson, Thomas, 103, 115, 169–70
Jerome, John, 275
Jessup, John K., 152–53
Johnson, Charles, 291
Johnson, Lyndon, 171
Johnson, Philip, 38, 39, 143, 313
Jordy, William, 124

Kauffmann, Stanley, 279, 280
Kaufman, Elliott, 288–89, 339n69
Keats, John, 124, 152
Keller, Ulrich, 72
Kellock, Katherine, 87, 89, 91–93, 96, 101, 108
Ketchum, Morris, 53–54
Kiesler, Frederick, 49–50

Kihlstedt, Folke, 297
King, Clyde L., 77
King, John Lord, 212
Kocher, A. Lawrence, 30, 32, 59
Koolhaas, Rem, 121
Kouwenhoven, John, 203
Kristol, Irving, 133
Krummeck, Elsie, 141, 191–92; Milliron's Department Store (Los Angeles, California), 141–42, 191–93, *192, 193*

Labatut, Jean, 109–13
L.A. in the Thirties, 1931–1941 (Gebhard and Von Breton), 301–2, 303
landscape painting, 248–49
land use: East Coast, 119–20; influence of automobility, 76, 181; settlement patterns, 76–77, 112, 117; suburbanization, 130–31; transformation, 112, 200; urbanized, 134; zoning, 128–29. See also suburbanization; urbanization
Lange, Dorothea, 99, 247; photograph by, *99*
Lapidus, Morris, 167, 288
Larrabee, Eric, 133, 162, 164–65
Larson, C. Theodore, 38, 63–64
"Last Traffic Jam, The" (Udall), 272–73, 275
Las Vegas, Nevada: effect of oil crisis, 269–70, *CP16;* Glitter Gulch, 243, 270, *CP10;* the Strip, 7–11, 232, 243–45, 247, 260. See also *Learning from Las Vegas* (Venturi, Scott Brown, and Izenour); Izenour, Steven; Scott Brown, Denise; Venturi, Robert
Lautner, John, 186
Learning from Las Vegas (Venturi, Scott Brown, and Izenour), 8, 10; book design of, 292; importance of, 283; *Main Street to Miracle Mile,* difference from, 310–11;

preliminary work on, 248, 291; reference to, 313; and *Signs of Life* exhibit, 284. *See also* Izenour, Steven; Las Vegas, Nevada; Scott Brown, Denise; Venturi, Robert

Le Corbusier, 24, 31, 59, 156, 200, 254. *See also* Corbusian

Lee, Warren, "Design for a Refreshment Building," *305*

Levitt & Sons, 184

Levittown. *See under* motor suburbs

Lichtenstein, Susanne, 30, 32

Liebs, Chester, 3, 41, 307–11

localism, 28–29, 34

Lönberg-Holm, Knud, 31–52, 58, 61, 63, 64; diagrams/drawings by, *40, 45*

Longstreth, Richard, 3, 41, 51, 191, 283, 307

Loomis, Charles P., 117

Loos, Adolf, 149

Los Angeles, California, *xvi;* car-centrism, 225–26; dependence on highways, 106; Echo Park, *261;* expansion, 185; Hoot Owl Café, *148;* Johnie's Coffee Shop, *254, 254–55;* Milliron's Department Store, 141–42, 191–93, *192, 193;* motor age, city of, 130–31; programmatic architecture, 303–4; Sepulveda Boulevard, *262;* signage, 244–45, 260; Tail o' the Pup Hot Dog Stand, *CP5;* urban form, 157, 183; Wilshire Boulevard, 9, 63, 68, 254, 260–61. *See also* Banham, Reyner; California

Los Angeles: The Architecture of Four Ecologies (Banham). *See under* Banham, Reyner

Louisiana, Canal Street (New Orleans), *169;* comparison to Lawn at the University of Virginia, 169–70

Lucas, George, 278–81. *See also American Graffiti* (film)

Luce, Henry, 79, 101, 161

Ludlow, William Orr, 55

Lundy, Victor, 251

Lynch, Kevin, 225–26, 228–35, 239

Lyndon, Donlyn, 256, 257

Lynes, Russell, 152, 184

Maas, John, 300

Macaulay, David, 312–14

MacKaye, Benton, 75–76, 77–79, 83

Maine: in *U.S. One,* 88, 89, 90; vacationland, 133

Main Street, as concept: community center, 298; effect of oil crisis, 269; future of, 200; highway as, 152, 203; megalopolis as, 119; outmoded, 53; pop art, defined by, 142; replaced by commercial strip, 235; and roadtown, 183, 198; pedestrian orientation of, 10; in photography, 82; Venturi's misreading of Blake, 170. *See also Main Street to Miracle Mile* (Liebs)

Main Street to Miracle Mile (Liebs), 310–11

"Man Made America" (*Architectural Review*), 136–43, *138, 139,* 145, 193, 209

Man-Made America (Tunnard and Pushkarev), 209–19, *211, 213, 215, 217, 218, 219*

Manning, Warren H., 74–75

Margolies, John, 170, 285–89, 292, 295; photographs by, *CP5, CP6, CP14. See also End of the Road, The* (Margolies)

Martin, Albert C., 302, 303

Marx, Leo, 282

Maryland: College Park, *135,* 136, 182; Elkridge, *126;* Mondawmin (outside Baltimore), 195; U.S. 40 (in Funkstown), *116. See also* Baltimore, Maryland; Greenbelt, Maryland

Massachusetts. *See* Boston, Massachusetts
mass transit, 4, 272–73
McDonald's. *See under* fast food industry
McMurry, Robert, 152
megalopolis, 119–21, *120,* 128, 130, 188, 210. *See also* metropolis; urbanization
Mendelsohn, Erich, 31–32, 39, 46, 56
metropolis: early vision of, 72–79; motorized, 234; scale, 104, 176–77; zones, 208. *See also* megalopolis, urbanization
metropolitanization. *See* megalopolis
Meyerson, Martin, 207–8, 228
Michigan. *See* Detroit, Michigan; Ford, Henry
Midwest, 81, 82, 193
Mies van der Rohe, Ludwig, 39, 55, 143, 238, 250, 253
migration, 76–81, 106–7, 176, 277. *See also* nomadism
Mills, C. Wright, 152
mimetic architecture. *See* programmatic architecture
Minnesota: Minneapolis park system, 170; Nicolett Mall (Minneapolis) 219; Southdale Shopping Mall (near Minneapolis) 193, 195, *196,* 208
"Missing Motel, The" (Banham), 251, 254, 312. *See also* motel(s)
Model T (Tin Lizzie), 15, 275, 307. *See also* Ford, Henry
Modern Architecture, USA (MoMA exhibition), 250–53
modernism: and architecture, car-oriented, 39–47; architecture journals, cultivation by, 29–38; commercial, examples of, 56; Corbusian, 141; high-style architecture, relation to, 186–87; mainstream, 205; relevance of, 49; variety of, 250, 252–57, 293
mono-transportation, 161
monumentality, 5, 188, 206, 255–56
Moore, Charles, 255–60; Piazza d'Italia (New Orleans, Louisiana), 204–5. *See also* postmodernism
Moses, Robert, 110
MOTATION, 224–25; photographs/diagrams of, *226, 227*
Motel of the Mysteries (Macaulay), 312–14. *See also* archeology
motel(s): in art exhibition, 284; Autopia Auto Court (Phoenix, Arizona), 3–4; critique of, 131–33; corporatization of, 183, 269; culture, 314; in "The Great American Roadside," 82; Holiday Inn, 268, 269; Howard Johnson's, 166, 239; plans, 201, 284; preservation of, 307; scholarship of, 251–53; style, architectural, 140–41. *See also* architecture, car-oriented; auto camps; "Easy Chair, The: Motel Town" (DeVoto); "Missing Motel, The" (Banham)
motor camps. *See* auto camps
motorists: experience of, 116–17, 224, 229–33, *232,* 240–42, 261–63; motion, *230,* 237; national self-knowledge, 118; point of view, 98–101, 137, 212–18, 249, 311; urban stakeholder, 209
motor suburbs, 124; Levittown, 124, 153, 203; Park Forest, Illinois, 153–54; Radburn, New Jersey, 37, 75, 162, 194, 200
Mumford, Lewis: *American Guide* series, 84; anti-autopia, 162–66, 180–82, 185, 271; early car history, 48; mobility and migra-

tion, 76–79; parking, 86; urbanization, 134, 155
Myer, John R., 225, 229, 234, 239

Nairn, Ian, 167
Nash, Ogden, 124
National Resources Committee (NRC), 66
National Road, 115–16
Neutra, Richard, 51–52, 302, 303
New Deal, 66, 84, 99, 101. *See also* Works Progress Administration (WPA)
New England Regional Planning Commission, 78, 128
New Jersey: Admiral Wilson Boulevard (Camden), 167, *168*; —, drive-in theater, 44; Esso Refinery (Linden), *127;* IBM Garden State Office Building (Cranford), 251; landscape, parallel to Las Vegas, 244; Lucy the Elephant (Margate), 304; Pulaski Skyway (Jersey City), 94, *95,* 96, 105; roadscape of, 128; as roadtown, 74; Turnpike, 186, *187,* 230, 267; U.S. 1, 93–100. *See also* motor suburbs
New Typography, 31
New York: Bronx River Parkway, 16; East River Drive (FDR Drive), 228; Grand Central and Interboro Parkways, intersection of, 64; Hutchinson River Parkway, 37, 96, *97;* Long Island Motor Parkway, 16; Lower-Manhattan Expressway, 188; New York State Thruway, 267; Philadelphia, highway to, 133; superhighway, 96; Taconic State Parkway, 165; Union Turnpike, 64; U.S. 1, 94, 128, 135–36; Van Wyck Expressway, 252; Washington, D.C., highway to, 125. *See also* New York City

New York City: Automobile Club of America, *17;* auto row, 21; Ford Sales Building, 24; Rockefeller Center, 56, 194, 237; roadtown from, 74; skyscrapers, 243, 249; sprawl, 155; suburbs of, 130; Times Square, 121, 188; topographical architecture (Rudolph), 188; traffic congestion, 86; urban organization, 157. *See also* TWA Flight Center (New York)
Nixon administration, 266, 268, 276
nomadism, 106–7. *See also* migration
nostalgia: building types, 245; Disney, 1; end of automobility, 278–83, 286–88, 304, 308, 310, 315; roadside, 12; urban, 124, 207–8; zeitgeist, 301
Nye, David, 269–70

odology. *See under* Jackson, J. B. (John Brinckerhoff)
oil companies: big, 39, 267; Gulf Oil Refining Company, 19. *See also* Standard Oil
oil crisis (1973), 266–78, 282–83, 286, 296, 308, 309
oil embargo (1973–74), 3, 12, 267–68. *See also* oil crisis (1973)
Oklahoma: Conoco Glass House (Vinita), *217;* Will Rogers Turnpike, 217
Organization Man, The (Whyte), 153–54
other-directed architecture. *See under* Jackson, J. B. (John Brinckerhoff)
Oud, J. J. P., 31, 37, 50
Owen, Wilfred, 181–82

Packard, Vance, 152
Pai, Hyungmin, 30, 32
Park, Robert, 16

Park Forest, Illinois. *See under* motor suburbs
parking: availability, 17, 43, 49, 50, 53, 56–57, 86, 94, 109, 252, 257, 292, 302; challenges, 187–89; design, 27, 43–47, 52, 63, 67, 154, 187–88, 194–95, 201; garages, 20–21, 43, 55, 56, 57; Park and Shop (Washington, D.C.), *50,* 50–52; rooftop, *14,* 56, *57,* 192–93; stadium, *45;* surface, 195; underground, 220. *See also* architecture, car-oriented; Temple Street Garage (New Haven, Connecticut)
parkways, 116, 140, 214; Baltimore–Washington Parkway, 220; Bronx River Parkway (New York), 16; Grand Central and Interboro Parkways (New York), intersection of, 64; Long Island Motor Parkway (New York), 16; Merritt Parkway (Connecticut), 105, 128; Rock Creek and Potomac Parkway (Washington, D.C.), 86–87; Taconic State Parkway (New York), 165. *See also* freeways; highway(s); Interstate Highway System; turnpikes
Pastier, John, 7
Pennsylvania: Gulf station (Pittsburgh), *22;* Lankenau Hospital (Philadelphia), 208; Lincoln Highway (Paradise), *70;* Pennsylvania Turnpike, 132; Philadelphia, suburbs of, 130; Pittsburgh, East End, *3,* 18–22; superhighway to New York, 133; travel time, 63; White Tower buildings, 291–92
Peterson, Charles E., 300
Petrov, Yevgeny, 91–92
Pevsner, Nikolaus, 143, 312
Pierson, George, 277
Polevitzky, Igor, 56
Poore, Charles, 161
pop art and architecture, 236–49; monuments, autopian, 251–56; references to, 304, 313. *See also* D'Arcangelo, Allan; Googie; Ruscha, Ed; *Signs of Life: Symbols and the American City* (Venturi and Scott Brown)
postmodernism, 170, 204, 255, 278, 288, 293; reference to, 313. *See also* Moore, Charles; Scott Brown, Denise; Venturi, Robert
Prescott, Orville, 154
preservation, historic, 294–95, 306–30; National Historic Preservation Act (NHPA), 294, 297; National Register of Historic Places, 3, 170, 294–95, 297, 306
programmatic architecture: Big Duck (Long Island, New York), 170–71, *CP6;* disdain for, 147–50; folk architecture, 210; Lucy the Elephant (Margate, New Jersey), 304; repetition, 287; road stand, *CP5;* scholarship on, 303–4, *305;* service station, *CP15*
Puginian, 21, 148, 169
Pushkarev, Boris, 209–20, 228, 234–35. See also *Man-Made America* (Tunnard and Pushkarev)

racial segregation, 5, 85, 125, 260
Rainer, Roland, 200
Raisz, Erwin, 113; landform maps, *114*
Raitz, Karl, 72
Reagan, Ronald, 274
Regional Planning Association of America, 76, 162, 209
Riesman, David, 124, 133, 152, 162, 164
roads, as instrument of democracy, 111. *See also* freeways; highway(s); Interstate Highway System; parkways; turnpikes
roadtown, 72–79, 144–52, 183–84, 185, 197, 198
Roche, James, 273
Rogers, Tyler Stewart, 26–27, 36

Roosevelt, Franklin, 66, 84, 267
Roth, Ed, 243
Rothstein, Arthur, 99–100; photograph by, *100*
Rougier, Michael, 235
Rouse, James, 179–82, 207; Mondawmin (outside Baltimore), 195
Rowland, Wirt, 23–25
Rudolph, Paul, 187–89, 250–51; rendering of Temple Street Garage (New Haven, Connecticut), *174, 189*
Ruscha, Ed, 239–42, 248, 288, 293; photographs by, *241, 242*. See also *Thirtyfour Parking Lots in Los Angeles* (Ruscha); *Twentysix Gasoline Stations* (Ruscha)
Russell, T. Triplett, 56

Saarinen, Eero, 243, 251. See also TWA Flight Center (New York)
Salisbury, Harrison, 161
Salisbury, Mike, 244
San Francisco, California: Embarcadero Freeway, *222*, 222–23, *227*; freeway approach to, *221*; Ghiradelli Square, adaptive reuse of, 220; Los Angeles, compared to, 106, 222, 225, 238, 273, 280, 282
Saudi Arabia, 267
Sauer, Carl, 207
scatteration, 156, 180, 197. See also urban sprawl
Schader, Carl F., 3–4
Schlereth, Thomas J., 309, 312
Schlesinger, Arthur, Jr., 105
Scott Brown, Denise, 8–11, *CP2;* archeology, 310, 311; Big Duck, 170–71, 173; building-as-sign, 300, 303; early writings, 301; Gans's influence on, 203; *Learning from Las Vegas,* 291, 292–93, *CP2;* pop art, cultural importance of, 246–47; references to, 313; *The View from the Road,* influence of, 232. See also *Learning from Las Vegas* (Venturi, Scott Brown, and Izenour); "Significance for A&P Parking Lots, A" (Venturi and Scott Brown); *Signs of Life: Symbols and the American City* (Venturi and Scott Brown)
Sculle, Keith, 297–98
Scully, Julia, 288
Scully, Vincent, 252
Seidenbaum, Art, 5
Seidenberg, Roderick, 86
Seiler, Cotton, 62
Serby, Myron, 43
service station(s): building type, 27–29; closure, 272; design, 21–23, 38, 39–42, *40,* 56, 266; early, 19; Gulf station (Pittsburgh, Pennsylvania), *22;* Lindholm Service Station (Cloquet, Minnesota), 300; Shell Service Station (Winston-Salem, North Carolina), 295, *CP15.* See also architecture, car-oriented; gas station(s)
Shannon & Luchs, 50
Sherman, Roger, 54
shopping centers: in art, 163; building type, 50–54; community values, 185, 212; Connecticut Post Center (Milford), 257, *258–59;* department stores in, 183; design of, 56, 193–99; modernist, 303; Northland Shopping Center (near Detroit, Michigan), 182, 193–94, *194,* 212; Park and Shop (Washington, D.C.), 50–52; parking, 187; suburbia, symbolic of, 166; as town center, 200; and urban planning, 185, 191. See also Gruen, Victor; shopping malls

shopping malls, 179, 185; Mondawmin (outside Baltimore, Maryland), 195; Southdale Shopping Mall (near Minneapolis, Minnesota), 193, 195, *196,* 208. *See also* Gruen, Victor; shopping centers

Shore, Stephen, 284–85, 288

Shulman, Julius, 193; photographs by, *192, 193*

signage: architectural, 21–22, 28, 34, 41, 254, 281, 303; art, 33, 81–82, 247, 283–85, *CP3, CP4, CP9, CP13;* blight, 125–29, 132, *172, CP8;* business, 269, *CP11;* illuminated, 35, 57, 82, 221, 237, 252, 257; Las Vegas (Nevada), 7, *CP10, CP16;* neon, 31, 33, *33,* 35, 131, 132, 133, 134, 149, 157, 191, 204–5, 237, 243, 244–45, 252, 280–82, 284, 287, 291, 306; New London (Connecticut), *139;* oil crisis, 267, 270; prominence of, 116–17, 212, 243–45, 313; roadside, 6, 10, 67; significance of, 31–32, 80, 237–38, 257–60, 263, 283–85, 287, 297, 309–10; standardized, 15, 71, 87, 246; ubiquity of, 135, 139, 235–36, 241–42. *See also* advertising; billboards

"Significance for A&P Parking Lots, A" (Venturi and Scott Brown), 9–10, 170, 246–47

Signs of Life: Symbols and the American City (Venturi and Scott Brown), 283–85, 304, 310, *CP13*

Simmel, Georg, 155

Skidmore, Owings and Merrill, 140, 178, 238; Connecticut General Life Insurance Company Headquarters, *179*

slums, 110; documentation of, 117; result of urbanization, 117, 129–30, 133–35, 183, 190–91; roadside, 60, 153, 216, 272. *See also* blight; ugliness

Society for Commercial Archaeology (SCA), 307–14

Society for Industrial Archeology, 309

Society of Architectural Historians (SAH), 299, 303, 309–10; *Journal of (JSAH),* 288, 300

Southern California. *See under* California

Speedway Boulevard (Tucson, Arizona), 235, *CP8*

Spender, Stephen, 133

Standard Oil: Bayway Refinery (Elizabeth, New Jersey), 94; breakup of, 266; engineers, 36; facility (Bayonne, New Jersey) 33; photo documentation, 167, *168;* pumps, 16; SOHIO, 39; station design (Seattle, Washington), 19

Stegner, Wallace, 107–8

Stein, Clarence, 37, 53, 75, 76

Steinberg, Saul, 140

Stern, Martin Jr., 255

Stewart, George Rippey, 107–20, 134, 137, 216, 234, 312

Stoller, Ezra, *179,* 167, *253*

Strip, the (Las Vegas, Nevada). *See under* Las Vegas, Nevada

strip, commercial: architectural character of, 291; art, depicted in, *CP7, CP8, CP16;* "commercial formalism", 256–57; definition, 10; Depression-era, 55; driving along, 311; evolution of, 302; growth, 214; Las Vegas archetype, 247; Main Street, 235; preservation, 310; signage, 260

Strong, Gordon, *9,* 44, 46–47

Stryker, Roy, 98–99, 167

suburbanization, 119, 123–24, 130–32, 153–58, 228, 274. *See also* land use; suburb(s); urbanization

suburb(s): blight, 272; categorization of, 175–76; community, 185; gas station, 49,

272; postwar, 111; railroad, 18; shopping center, 166; suburbanites, 270–71; suburbscape, 190–91. See also fringetown; suburbanization

Teague, Walter Dorwin, 29, 335n1
Telethon, 286
Temple Street Garage (New Haven, Connecticut), *174*, 188–89, *189*, 250–51. See also Connecticut; Rudolph, Paul
Texas: Amarillo, *CP14*; Houston, *172*
Thirtyfour Parking Lots in Los Angeles (Ruscha), 240, 293. See also architecture, car-oriented; parking
tourism, 20, 46–47, 58–59, 84–107, 296, 303. See also cabins, tourist; guidebooks
townscape, 137–40, 167, 169–70. See also cityscape
traffic: circulation, 109–10, 119, 181; congestion, 54, 55, 71, 75, 78, 82, 163, 165, 185, 197, 273–74; New Jersey, 93, 96; study of, 38, 49, 52, 128, 140, 225; Washington, D.C., 86
travel guides. See guidebooks
Tripartite Unity (Bill), 217–18, *218*
Tugwell, Rexford, 99
Tunnard, Christopher, 136–40, 209–20, 228, 234; diagrams by, *138*. See also *Man-Made America* (Tunnard and Pushkarev)
Turner, Frederick Jackson, 277. See also frontier, American
turnpikes: Connecticut Turnpike, 257; New Jersey Turnpike, 186, *187*, 230, 267; Pennsylvania Turnpike, 132; Union Turnpike (Pennsylvania), 64; Will Rogers Turnpike (Oklahoma), 217. See also freeways; highway(s); Interstate Highway System; parkways

TWA Flight Center (New York), 251–52, *253*. See also air travel; New York City
Twentysix Gasoline Stations (Ruscha), 240, *241, 242*, 293. See also architecture, car-oriented; gas station(s); service station(s)
Tyrwhitt, Jaqueline, 207–8, 228

Udall, Steward, 272–73, 275
ugliness: architecture, 147–49, *148*; highway, 88, 125–29, 134, 216, 228; roadside, 166–69, 228, 287; rural, 153; signage, 28, 125–26, 205; streetscape, 235; study of, 118, 144–45; subcityscape, 190–91; urban fringe, *68*. See also blight; slums
urbanization; 175–83, 208, 222; decentralization, 48, 55, 67, 123, 175, 207–9, 220; explosive, 118–21; exurban, 180, 183; horizontality, 103, 119, 256; monotony, aesthetic, 137; rural metropolis, 74–75; scale of, 103–4; semi-, 111–12. See also cityscape; land use; suburbanization; urban planning; urban sprawl
urban planning, 181–82. See also Fort Worth Plan
urban renewal, 136, 156, 179, 207
urban sprawl: critiques, 77, 175–76, 180, 255, 274; effects, 155–61; Megalopolitan, 120; rurban, 157. See also scatteration
U.S. Bureau of the Census, 175–76, 177, 201
U.S. 40: Cross Section of the United States of America (Rippey), 107, *108*, 109, 110, 113, *114, 116*, 118

Van Brunt, Henry, 19, 300
Venturi, Robert, 8–11, *CP2*; Big Duck, 170–71, *173*; building-as-sign, 300, 303;

INDEX 357

Venturi, Robert (*continued*)
early writings, 301; Labutat's influence on, 109; *Learning from Las Vegas,* 291, 292–93, *CP2;* Moore employed by, 256; pop art, cultural importance of, 246–47; references to, 313; *The View from the Road,* influence of, 232. See also *Learning from Las Vegas* (Venturi, Scott Brown, and Izenour); "Significance for A&P Parking Lots, A" (Venturi and Scott Brown); *Signs of Life: Symbols and the American City* (Venturi and Scott Brown)

View from the Road, The (Appleyard, Lynch, and Myer), 225–34, *230, 232, 233*

Vieyra, Daniel, 299–301

Virginia, U.S. 1 (Gum Springs), *88*

Von Breton, Harriette, 302

Von Storch, Earl, 59

Washington, D.C.: Federal Triangle, 86; Howard Theatre, 85; Mount Vernon Memorial Highway (MVMH), 86–88; Park and Shop, *50,* 50–52; Rock Creek and Potomac Parkway, 86–87; U Street Corridor, 85

Washington, Seattle, 16, 19, 210, 220

Wayne, Kermit, 243

Weber, Kem, 55

Weiss, Steven, 282

Wells, Christopher, 271

West, American: depictions of, 99–101; highway in, 105–6; migration, 76, 81

White, E. B., 134

White, Morton and Lucia, 124

White Towers (Hirshorn and Izenour), 288–89, 291–94, *294,* 301, 308, 312. See also architecture, car-oriented; diners; fast food industry

Whittlesey, Julian, 59

Whyte, William H., 153–61, 165, 263, 270, 271

Wilde, Frazar, 178, 181

Wilshire Boulevard. See under Los Angeles, California

Windels, Paul, 155

Winter, Robert, 303

Wolcott, Marion Post, 94; photographs by, *95, 171*

Wolfe, Tom, 8, 243–48, 253–54, 283, 299

Wong, Gin, 244–45, 246. See also gas station(s)

Works Progress Administration (WPA), 84–101. See also New Deal

Wright, Frank Lloyd: car design, 163–64; critique of, 243; Gordon Strong Automobile Objective, 44–47, *46;* Lindholm Service Station (Cloquet, Minnesota), 300; modernism, origins of, 31; urbanism, 60–61, 62, 75, 103–4, 106, 124, 156, 177. See also Broadacre City

Wright, Henry, 55

YESCO, 243, 247

Ylvisaker, Paul, 171–72

Zeitvogel, Melvin, 244, 245–46; sign for Buick dealership (San Diego, California), *CP11*

Zimmerman, Carle, 111–12

Midcentury: Architecture, Landscape, Urbanism, and Design

American Autopia: An Intellectual History of the American Roadside at Midcentury
Gabrielle Esperdy

Indoor America: The Interior Landscape of Postwar Suburbia
Andrea Vesentini

Environmental Design: Architecture, Politics, and Science in Postwar America
Avigail Sachs

Detached America: Building Houses in Postwar Suburbia
James A. Jacobs